The Teaching Experience
An Introduction to Education
Through Literature

JACK C. WILLERS
History and Philos·phy of Education
Peabody College, Nashville, TN. 37203

Edited by

Elliott D. Landau
University of Utah

Sherrie L. Epstein
Psychological Services, Millbrae School District

Ann P. Stone
San Mateo Union High School District

Prentice-Hall, Inc., *Englewood Cliffs, New Jersey*

Library of Congress Cataloging in Publication Data

Main entry under title:

The Teaching Experience.

Includes bibliographies.
1. Teachers in literature.   2. Education—Addresses,
essays, lectures.   I. Landau, Elliott D.   II. Epstein,
Sherrie Landau.   III. Stone, Ann Platt.
LB1781.T4   371.1'02   75-37716
ISBN   0-13-892539-9

©1976 by Prentice-Hall, Inc., Englewood Cliffs, New Jersey

Printed in the United States of America

10   9   8   7   6   5   4   3   2   1

From "Mending Wall" from The Poetry
of Robert Frost edited by Edward Connery
Lathem. Copyright 1930, 1939, © 1969 by
Holt, Rinehart and Winston. Copyright ©
1958 by Lesley Frost Ballantine. Reprinted
by permission of Holt, Rinehart and Winston, Publishers.

Prentice-Hall International, Inc., London
Prentice-Hall of Australia Pty. Limited, Sydney
Prentice-Hall of Canada, Ltd., Toronto
Prentice-Hall of India Private Limited, New Delhi
Prentice-Hall of Japan, Inc., Tokyo
Prentice-Hall of Southeast Asia Pte. Ltd., Singapore

contents

Teaching the Exceptional Child   *189*

The School As Culture   *223*

The Power Structure in the School   *251*

introduction

Herb Thelen, in his book *Education and the Human Quest*[1] tells a story few professional educators will forget. It seems that a very complicated diesel locomotive just wouldn't start. After the Ph.D. types tried their hand at it, one of the blue collar men at the plant was asked to give it a whirl. He did. He pulled a little mallet from his pocket, circled the engine a few times, twisted a few knobs, and delivered two light taps on a whatsis. The engine roared into life. When asked for his bill, the old man said that $10,000 would be satisfactory. Asked for an itemization he replied: "Information about diesel engines — 50 cents. Tapping whatsis with tack hammer—50 cents. Knowing where to tap—$9,999.00."

For college instructors who have been teaching the introductory course to teaching and/or education and have wondered how to "turn the kids on," this book should have a special meaning. Knowing where to "tap" today's students is a crucial teaching problem. The relevancy of any "Introduction to Education" course is still a problem. Traditional texts in the field assiduously cover the facts and figures of the educational establishment. However, deciding to become a teacher is not only a matter of knowing starting salaries and the power of professional organizations—it is not just a matter of cognitive data; it is an emotional and intellectual commitment to a way of life.

In discussing child development in a previous book[2] we noted, "those who are teaching future teachers, counselors, psychologists, and nurses need to 'turn on' their students so that the learner wants to immerse himself in the field not only with a cognitive understanding of the field's concepts but with an affective commitment to the world of childhood." Similarly, we believe the world of teaching needs to be felt by prospective teachers. As good as many of the "Introduction to Education" texts are, their endless forays into facts, figures, tables of statistics, and court decisions cannot convert readers of the word into doers who feel impelled to make a difference in the world of childhood.

Allen Graubard[3] says, "More money doesn't make the schools more successful in important ways: the kids don't get less bored, the poor and minority youth don't find their life chances enhanced by new buildings with decorator colors and opaque projectors." While we may not totally agree with his "answer" to the problem, i.e., radical reform and the "free school" movement, we do feel that when teachers more fully share the feelings and experiences of youth, they will inevitably attempt to create, each in his own way, in his own classroom or learning center, a place for learning which will make school a more humane and totally instructive milieu.

We have opted for literature as a tool to help college students experience teachers, teaching, children, and communities. The art of the novel and the short story lies in the power to elicit emotion. Total involvement in the chal-

---

[1]Chicago: University of Chicago Press, 1972.
[2]*Child Development Through Literature* (Englewood Cliffs: Prentice-Hall, 1972), p. xiv.
[3]*Free the Children* (New York: Vintage Books, 1974).

lenges of teaching may come, if not from first-hand experience, from the perceptions of the literary artist. Indeed, personal experience alone, without the opportunity to reflect upon that experience, may be no more than a fleeting exercise in reading.

This text, an anthology with prolific annotation, is designed to help the future teacher involve himself and his emotions while at the same time keeping a certain distance from each tale. Dr. Michael Shiryon[4] has put it this way: "a story allows a person both the distance and the involvement at the same time. As reader or listener to a tale, one can see himself as an outsider, as an observer, and feel free to observe and weigh the issues and even make relatively objective judgments. He is not all involved in being defensive and desperately searching for rationalizations, as he may be when confronted with personal issues of his own."

As students discuss the variety of responses teachers make toward their students, colleagues, communities, schools, and selves, they will be at some "distance" from these literary events yet be involved through the psychological processes of projection and identification. Our experience with *Child Development Through Literature* has amply demonstrated that there will be profound emotional reactions to the vivid issues the literature provides.

The exchanges between authors and their editors sometimes result in ideas never conceived of by the writers. Such was the case in this book. It was Arthur Rittenburg, then our college text editor, who one day thought that a natural sequel to *Child Development Through Literature* would be a similar text vivifying the teaching experience itself. We acknowledge his genius though we also recognize that he sent us down a path untrodden—and we've loved every minute of it.

We are indebted to scores of teachers who have taught us. They are listed under our Acknowledgments. For intelligently typing this manuscript over and over again we have to thank Jan Garrett, student at the University of Utah. The many friends and relatives, husbands and wives who lived through the two years of labor deserve our gratitude. Again, the editors wish to thank Dr. Ladd Holt of the University of Utah for his contributions to the ways this book may be used.

acknowledgments

To the teachers we remember with respect, affection, and honor:

Elliott:
Mrs. Barnett (P.S. 86, The Bronx, New York City— Grade 2); Mrs. Bookbinder (P.S. 86, The Bronx, New York City—Grade 4); Mr. Sheridan (P.S.

[4]Department of Psychiatry, Kaiser Foundation Hospital, Oakland, California. In personal conference Dr. Shiryon has gone into some detail about what he calls "Literatherapy" (and what many students of education call "Bibliotherapy"). We quote freely and with permission from two of his papers—"Literatherapy-Theory and Application" (1973) and "Group Literatherapy-A Bibliotherapeutic Approach" (1970). Of course he was referring to Literatherapy as one means of having patients in an institution see their problems with some detachment as they discuss and respond to stories he reads to them.

86, The Bronx, New York City—Grade 8); Mr. Polakoff (The Bronx High School of Science, New York City—Biology); Mr. Nat Glicksman (The Bronx High School of Science, New York City—English); Dr. Herman Mantel (The Bronx High School of Science, New York City—Classics); Miss Goldstein (The Bronx High School of Science, New York City); Dr. Paul Schweitzer (The Bronx High School of Science, New York City—Philosophy); Dr. Eli Blume (The Bronx High School of Science, New York City—French); Dr. Howard Lane (New York University—Education); Dr. Beatrice Hurley (New York University—Education); Dr. Louis Raths (New York University—Education); Dr. Jan Veatch (New York University—Education); Fran Knight (New York University—Education); Dr. Nelson Adkins (New York University—English); Dr. Homer Watt (New York University—English); Dr. Lou Labrant (New York University—English); Dr. Margaret Schlauch (New York University—English); Dr. Earl Kelley (Wayne State—Education).

Sherrie:

Miss Howe (P.S. 86, The Bronx, New York City—Grade 3); Mrs. Sara Mandel (P.S. 86, The Bronx, New York City); Miss Meneeley (P.S. 86, The Bronx, New York City—Grade 7); Ms. Rose Bring (Walton High School, The Bronx, New York City—English); Mrs. Schlanger (Walton High School, The Bronx, New York City—Science); Dr. Leo Gurko (Hunter College, New York—Music); Gladys Mayo (Juilliard School, New York—Music); Dr. Irene Samuels (Hunter College, New York—English); Dr. Mary Rose Sheehan (Hunter College, New York—Psychology); Dr. Eugene Hartley (City College, New York—Social Psychology); Dr. Harold Abelson (City College, New York—Psychology); Mrs. Marjorie Wheeler (College of San Mateo—Education); Mrs. Caroline Kauffman (College of San Mateo—Education); Dr. Stephen Rausch (San Francisco State College—School Psychology); Dr. Patricia Hewitt (Scaramento State College—School Psychology); Dr. Harrison Gough (University of California at Berkeley—Psychology); Dr. Jack Fleming (University of California Extension—Psychology).

Ann:

Miss Former (Madison School, San Francisco—Grade 4); Mrs. Noreen McDonald (Roosevelt Jr. High, San Francisco—English); Mr. Al Giorgi (Roosevelt Jr. High—Algebra); Miss Edith Silberman (George Washington High, San Francisco—Chemistry); Mr. Vanderlaan (George Washington High, San Francisco—Geometry); Dr. Joseph Axelrod (San Francisco State College—English); Muriel Landers (San Francisco State College—Drama); Dr. Ed Cassidy (San Francisco State College—English); Dr. Carlos Lastrucci (San Francisco State College—Sociology); Dr. Fenton McKenna (San Francisco State College—Speech); Dr. Ed White (San Francisco State College—History); Dr. Clarence Miller (San Francisco State College—Drama); Dr. Margaret Lynch (San Francisco State College—Education); Dr. Richard Glyer (San Francisco State College—Speech); Helen Hatchett (San Francisco Adult Education); Dr. Michael Krasney (University of California at San Francisco—English); Dr. Michael Zimmerman (University of California at San Francisco—English); Ray and Zada Taft (Ray Taft Swim School—Water Safety Education).

to the instructor

The fictional pieces in this volume have been used successfully as the basis for weekly one-hour, seminar-type discussions. Other professors have used critical incidents in the stories as the focus for role-playing activities and creative fictional material. An inner group of students discusses selected incidents and an outer group surrounds them, listens to their discussion, and at appropriate times raises questions about the relevance and interpretation of content. In this way reaction is generated from two groups of students and from two vantage points—the inner group as it interprets the characters and events of the story, and the outer group as it perceives the same story and the responses of peers to the story.

Another way the selections may be used is to assign roles to students who then reinterpret selected incidents in the story under discussion. A group observes B group's interpretations and makes written suggestions; B observes A and does the same, and so on for all groups. The author's point of view as expressed through his characters and their behavior is thus subject to widespread pupil analysis. The selections also lend themselves to the subdivision of classes into six-six-six groups,[1] with either the Springboards for Inquiry or the students' personal responses as the basis for discussion. Where panel discussion techniques have been tried, each panel addressed itself to one or two of the springboard questions, thus bringing to the class the thinking of a group of students.

Another possibility is the use of different points of view. Students can be assigned to view characters, incidents, or solutions through the eyes of a teacher, a school psychologist, a parent, a principal, a social worker, or whatever view interests them. Discussions that present a variety of points of view bring out the complexity of student thinking.

A very effective way of organizing for discussion is merely to divide the class into open discussion groups that meet together for the semester, read each story and then decide for themselves what aspects of each story are worth discussing. A simple format can be given to the group in which they first look at what the story says and then ask "so what." In other words they first share the meaning the story has for them. When they agree upon a meaning they can see what relevance that meaning has for them as persons and potential educators.

---

[1]Six-six-six refers to six groups of six students for six minutes.

The Teacher

For years education was spoken of as the transmitter of culture. John Dewey and his disciples taught that each generation should define the world anew and that education should not transmit what has been; rather it should prepare students to create their present culture. This liberal progressivism shaped American education until Sputnik was launched, and Jerome Bruner, in his *Process of Education,* decided to " 'fashion' education in the image of scientific discovery, scholarly investigation, and theoretical understanding."[1] The late 1960s and early 70s brought us the revolution of the new breed of teacher, exemplified by the works of Dennison,[2] and culminated in 1970 with Charles Silberman's searing *Crisis in the Classroom.*[3] Critics in the early 70s had not yet disavowed the cult of personality of the teacher, but they began to focus on curriculum organization as they touted open schools,[4] free schools,[5] the individualization of instruction and deschooling society.[6]

The editors of this volume, without espousing any particular view, feel that the most perceptive literature on teaching has clearly reflected that what is crucial is the teacher and his person, not methodology or philosophy. Inevitably, the quality of the teacher's response to the humans with whom he interacts, and the quality of the "person" teaching are part of the persistent interest of educational innovators as they search for THE answer to the educational riddle—what is teaching?

In the days ahead, teachers will need to demonstrate that they are more than mere textbooks wired for sound. In one study teachers are being given the Edward's Personal Preference Test to determine what their personal needs are in 15 areas of human growth.[7] In this way, it may be possible to predict teacher success with minority groups before they take jobs with these groups. For purposes of this study, expertise in subject matter is not considered relevant. What a teacher "is" seems to be more important than what he knows.

[1]Jurgen Herbst, "The Anti-School—Some Reflections on Teaching," *Educational Theory* 18 (Winter, 1968):15.

[2]George Dennison, *The Lives of Children* (New York: Random House, 1969).

[3]Charles E. Silberman, *Crisis in the Classroom* (New York: Random House, 1969).

[4]Herbert Kohl, *The Open Classroom* (New York: Random House, 1970).

[5]Steve Bhaerman and Joel Denker, *No Particular Place to Go* (New York: Simon & Schuster, 1972). Sylvia Ashton-Warner, *Spearpoint—Teacher in America* (New York: Knopf, 1972). Jonathan Kozol, *Free Schools* (Boston: Houghton Mifflin, 1972).

[6]Ivan Illich, *Deschooling Society* (New York: Harper & Row, 1971). Everett Reimer, *School Is Dead* (New York: Doubleday, 1972). Allen Graubard, *Free the Children* (New York: Pantheon, 1973).

[7]Opal Patrick, graduate student at the University of Utah, is studying the personal preference needs of teachers who have been rated "great" or "super" by black, caucasian, Chicano, and oriental students.

In the Association for Supervision and Curriculum Development 1962 *Yearbook*, a definition of the adequate personality for teaching is sought. The basic premise of the volume is expressed in its first line, "whatever we do in teaching depends upon what we think people are like."[8] A reasonable corollary to this may well read, "whatever we do in teaching depends upon what we, the teachers, are like." Jersild maintains that the teacher's ability to understand and accept himself is a prerequisite to the task of helping children understand and accept themselves.[9] In studying the personal problems of teachers, Jersild identifies two areas of concern. The first involves the problem of meaning, the ancient search in which "through the ages, voices have again and again been raised, calling man home to himself, calling upon him once more to face the timeless question: "Who and what and why am I?"[10] The second area involves the problem of anxiety. On the surface some teachers seem to find their teaching lives rewarding, but "if the inner dimension of their personalities could be examined, many would show a large amount of tension appearing, say, in disproportionate resentment, competitiveness, discouragement, efforts to impress or placate, to play the game and to play it safe."[11] The teacher, more than other professionals, must look inward into himself in order to be able to interact in the "therapeutic milieu"[12] we define as the classroom.

Raths[13] and his associates have been studying values and the process of valuing as they, too, turn toward the problem of teachers continually clarifying their own values as they try to help children develop and assess theirs. As the meaning of the literary situations that follow form the basis of reflection, the reader, will, consciously or unconsciously, be undergoing a process of valuing. Any reader with a special interest in gaining insight into his own values would do well to consult the work of Raths and his associates.[14]

A student of education in the second half of the 20th century encounters many divergent and sometimes contradictory theories of what the teacher's role should be. No longer is there agreement that the teacher is first of all a "knower," a scholar. Many knowledgeable teachers have failed, and some superb teachers are far from intellectual. The role of the teacher has not been fixed immutably. The teacher has at various times been the authority figure whose word is law, the friendly, permissive leader who takes children

---

[8]ASCD, *Perceiving, Behaving, Becoming* (Washington, D.C.: ASCD, 1962).

[9]Arthur T. Jersild, *When Teachers Face Themselves* (New York: Bureau of Publications, Teachers College, Columbia University, 1955).

[10]Ibid., p. 5.

[11]Ibid., p. 6.

[12]Fritz Redl's term for the "turf" shared by students and teachers and any who work with children.

[13]Louis E. Raths, Merrill Harmin, and Sidney B. Simon, *Values and Teaching* (Columbus: Merrill, 1966).

[14]Louis E. Raths, Merrill Harmin, and Sidney B. Simon, *Teaching for Thinking* (Columbus: Merrill, 1967). Louis E. Raths, Merrill Harmin, and Sidney B. Simon, *Studying Teaching* (Englewood Cliffs, N.J.: Prentice-Hall, 1967). Louis E. Raths, Merrill Harmin, and Sidney B. Simon, *Teaching for Learning* (Englewood Cliffs, N.J.: Prentice-Hall, 1969). Louis E. Raths, Merrill Harmin, and Sidney B. Simon, *Meeting the Needs of Children* (Englewood Cliffs, N.J.: Prentice-Hall, 1972).

down primrose paths, and more recently the benevolent dictator who insists that children "have to do what they want to do." In the last year or so we have heard a great deal about the "competencies" approach to teaching with the dazzling notion of "performance-based objectives." Simply put, no researcher has any inside track. Somehow, despite footnotes, charts, graphs, and all the other paraphernalia of scholarship, it all boils down to the proposition that teaching is personal. Unique individuals who are real persons, who resemble no one else, and who cannot be precisely delineated by any "scientific" scale seem to be the best teachers. An architect refers to great buildings and cozy nooks he has designed as being "grabby." He defines a "grabby" piece of architecture as one that pulls you towards it— that motivates two people to turn to each other with simultaneous nods of approval and delight. So, what is a "grabby" teacher?

Perhaps Carl Rogers' term *the fully functioning personality* is the elusive devil we are seeking. Briefly, he says that the optimum human person, the "grabby" human who makes teaching personal, is "open to his experience." That is, he takes everything into his nervous system without being defensive. He is completely available to awareness. There is an absence of barriers in his sensitivity to the world around him. Rogers says, "to open one's self to what is going on *and* to discover in that present process whatever structure it appears to have—this to me is one of the qualities of the healthy life, the mature life. . . ."[15]

Earl Kelley refers not to "the fully functioning personality," but to the "fully functioning self."[16] Imagine a teacher who acts as if life in his classroom were a discovery, an adventure. Kelley would have the teacher be a person who thinks well of himself, thinks well of others, and believes in man's mutual need of one another. He believes that man is always in the process of becoming,[17] that the acceptance of change as a universal phenomenon brings about modifications of personality. He writes that since man will be treading new paths at all times, he must be able to acknowledge his mistakes. He concludes, "since life is ever-moving and ever-becoming, the fully functioning person is cast in a creative role. . . . He sees that creation is not something which occurred long ago and is finished, but that it is now going on and he is part of it. He sees the evil of the static personality because it seeks to stop the process of creation. . . . Life to him means discovering and adventure, flourishing because it is in tune with the universe."

Rogers and Kelley have each articulated psychologies which may be identified as growth and self-actualization propositions. Abraham Maslow,[18] writing in the same volume to which Kelley and Rogers con-

[15]Carl R. Rogers, "Toward Becoming a Fully Functioning Person," in *Perceiving, Behaving, Becoming*, ed. Arthur W. Combs (Washington, D.C.: ASCD, 1962), p. 26.

[16]Ibid., p. 9.

[17]The reply of a little girl to her teacher who was asked,"Who made you?" and replied, "I don't know, I'm not finished yet," seems to exemplify this concept of continual growth.

[18]Abraham H. Maslow, "Some Basic Propositions of a Growth and Self-Actualization Psychology," in *Perceiving, Behaving, Becoming*, ed. Arthur W. Combs (Washington, D.C.: ASCD, 1962).

tributed, lists thirty-eight propositions which are basic to self-psychology and especially important to the educator. In essence Maslow says that people have a core that is unique, observable, and growing and that without others' acceptance and love of this essential core, psychological health is impossible. When our basic needs for self-actualization and growth are not met, the result is general personality illness. Each of us must respect and recognize his own inner nature and must at one and the same time cultivate controls and spontaneity. A complete absence of frustrating situations is dangerous since a fully functioning individual must develop frustration-tolerance. Full growth towards self-actualization is rare and full of pain. Self-actualizing people minimize dichotomies. To such people work tends to be the same as play; vocations and vacations merge. Their lives are fused. Maslow writes, "self-actualization does not mean a transcendence of all human problems. Conflict, anxiety, frustration, sadness, hurt and guilt can all be found in healthy human beings. . . . To be untroubled when we should be troubled can be a sign of sickness."[19] Finally, Maslow tells us to grow up and not act as children and to recognize that self-actualized people (and this includes children) occasionally live out-of-time and out-of-the-world. He concludes by saying that the world is in itself interesting, beautiful, and fascinating.

The literature on the teacher's role is vast. Recent thought is less concerned with the impact of a teacher on the cognitive and more concerned with his role as a therapeutic agent. Purkey lists the following questions every teacher ought to ask himself:

Am I projecting an image that tells the student that I am here to build, rather than to destroy, him as a person?

Do I let the student know that I am aware of and interested in him as a unique person?

Do I convey my expectations and confidence that the student can accomplish work, can learn, and is competent?

By my behavior do I serve as a model of authenticity for the student?[20]

Thus, for Purkey, the teacher is one who consciously builds students' concept of self.

Lane and Beauchamp, both powerfully oriented toward the child development point of view, see the teacher primarily as an advocate or agent who sees to it that children get a fair deal.[21] Raths lists 12 functions of teaching, the first being that of "explaining, informing, showing how," the fifth being "clarifying attitudes, beliefs, problems," and the last, "participating in professional and civic life."[22] Melvin L. Silberman in an interesting

[19]Ibid., p. 45.

[20]William W. Purkey, *Self Concept and School Achievement* (Englewood Cliffs, N.J.: Prentice-Hall, 1970).

[21]Howard Lane and Mary Beauchamp, *Human Relations in Teaching* (New York: Prentice-Hall, 1955), p. 199. This volume is a "must-read."

[22]Louis E. Raths, "What Is a Good Teacher?" in *Childhood Education* 40, no. 9 (May 1964): 451.

experimental procedure noted four distinct attitudes which emerged as teachers were asked to describe their students. These were: attachment, concern, indifference, and rejection. The latter two, when the teacher "forgets the child is in the room" (indifference) or says, "I've given up," (rejection) are considered by Silberman as unworthy of professional behavior. When a teacher says, "you couldn't ask for a nicer boy. I would take him home" (attachment) or "if I could spend more time with him individually, he might grow, because he doesn't resist it, really" (concern), then he is playing a "proper" role, one in keeping with the injunctions of Rogers, Combs, Maslow, and Kelley.[23]

Marie Hughes and her associates lay the full burden of good teaching upon the verbal and nonverbal behavior of the teacher whose quality of response either facilitates or hinders student progress.[24] Ashley Montagu says, "the teacher's task is not an end in itself, but a means of communicating humanity, to join loving-kindness to learning. . . . It is personal influence which determines the size of a life in the quest for self, it is the teacher's personal influence that will count as much as and in a large number of cases more than anyone else's in helping the individual realize and fulfill himself."[25]

At about this point the reader is probably seriously asking himself what it is he will get into if he continues to pursue teaching as a career. It can fairly be said that the person has not yet been created who could fashion himself to both the classical and the perceptual model of teacher. Where are those who can devote their lives to a Helen Keller or to the Maori children as did Sylvia Warner?[26] How long did Kohl,[27] Kozol,[28] and the other critics stay with their classes? It seems appropriate to close with the story of the chicken and the pig walking down a country lane together. The chicken excitedly told the pig of his latest idea. "We'll prepare and franchise the best ham and eggs money can buy, and we'll make a fortune."

The pig thought it over and said, "It's easy for you to get enthused. For you it's just an occupation. For me it means total commitment."

[23]Melvin L. Silberman, "Teachers' Attitudes and Actions Toward Their Students," in *The Experience of Schooling*, ed. Melvin L. Silberman (New York: Holt, Rinehart & Winston, 1970), p. 84–91.

[24]"The Model of Good Teaching," in *Studying Teaching*, ed. James Raths, John R. Pancella, and James S. Van Ness (Englewood Cliffs, N.J.: Prentice-Hall, 1967).

[25]"Quest for Self," in *Individualization of Instruction: A Teaching Strategy*, ed. Virgil M. Howes (New York: Macmillan, 1970), p. 29.

[26]Sylvia Ashton-Warner, *Teacher* (New York: Bantam, 1971).

[27]Herbert Kohl, *Thirty-Six Children* (New York: Norton, 1968); pap. ed. (New York: New American Library, 1973).

[28]Jonathan Kozol, *Death at an Early Age* (Boston: Houghton Mifflin, 1967).

shall I teach?

For some people the choice of teaching, like that of medicine or the clergy, is the fulfillment of a childhood ambition based on a romanticized and idealized conception of the vocation. For others the mattress theory applies—having something to fall back on. Hopefully more people will consider the profession of teaching from realistic vantage points. In order to do this, there is data to be gathered about the work of the teacher and the quality of life teaching offers as well as data about ourselves that will help in deciding whether to make a career of education.

The decision to teach may be approached in a problem-solving way just as one might approach any important decision with far-reaching consequences. A problem-solving attitude requires that you follow an organized procedure.

First: Discuss the problem, Shall I Teach? Try it out with friends and family. Get their reactions to your ideas. Discuss it with people in the field. If you are deciding on a specialty, talk to teachers in the areas you are considering. Discuss job opportunities with advisers in the education office of your school.

Second: Generate possible solutions. This requires that you write down the pros and cons of teaching—think of the rewards and the drawbacks. Try to set down the pros and cons of the age group you are considering working with or the teaching specialty you may be thinking of. Your pro and con page might look like this:

	Pros	*Cons*
Practical Realities	1. Good working hours 2. Holidays and long summer vacation 3. Tenure 4. Sabbatical leave 5. Retirement benefits	1. Low salary for my education 2. Lots of paper work outside of school 3. Must interact with an overwhelming number of students 4. Not too much contact with other adults 5. Spend the day in the same room in the same building
Personal Traits	1. I like children 2. I have a lot of patience 3. I enjoy a challenge 4. I like being resourceful and spontaneous—I'm a "ham" underneath	1. I'm sensitive to criticism 2. I need to be physically active

6

Age Group and Subject Area	1. I would like to teach science in high school 2. I feel comfortable in a high school setting 3. You don't have to supervise high schoolers "at all times."	1. I would hate to teach science to kids who were completely disinterested or couldn't handle the concepts 2. Repetitiveness of teaching the same subject every year 3. High school kids are poorly behaved
Idealistic Values	1. Feeling of Accomplishment 2. Possible lasting quality of your influence 3. Social usefulness of teaching	1. Trying to meet needs of many students may be draining 2. Acceding to administrative details and demands may be demeaning

Third: Evaluate the ideas that you have generated in your second step. Look over the pros and cons you have listed and determine how much weight you can assign to each.

Fourth: Decide on the best solution. Considering your strengths you may decide yes you would do well to become a teacher of the learning disabled or no you are too judgmental to work with students' problems.

Fifth: Implement your solution—this may require that you change schools or register for specialized courses or seek more information about credentials in the field you have chosen.

If you decide to teach, you will find that the field of education offers the opportunity to change and grow. There are always new methods and materials. Many school districts offer in-service courses to present current materials and methodology. Staff development workshops designed to help teachers become more aware of themselves as they communicate and interact with others—students and colleagues—are becoming increasingly popular. Teachers need to evaluate themselves continually and be willing to change. As the teacher keeps his growing edge open to new ideas, he will prosper personally and professionally.

Gene Coghlan

Backward boy

"You didn't pass, Auber," Junior said. "You will be in the first grade again next year." It was the clap of doom.

When I smell spruce smoke I smell a great slice of my past; I smell Alaska and a little cluster of log buildings at the edge of a small lake sandwiched between the Wasilla Woods and the foothills of the Talkeetna Mountains. And I see only too painfully, too nostalgically clear, the first group of pupils I taught in Alaska—thirty-six motley, eager young faces representing eight grades.

And I see "Auber." The head of bushy black hair surmounted an enormous pair of limpid brown eyes. His small thin body clad in blue jeans and patched plaid shirt of threadbare cotton seemed scarcely adequate support for that great mass of hair and eyes.

It seems incredible after all these years that the pupil hardest to forget was the dumbest I ever taught. He couldn't even pronounce his own name on his first day at school.

"Say it again, please," I said. "I'm afraid I didn't hear it quite right."

"Auber," he said again. "Auber Dubois."

"He means *Albert*, teacher!" shrilly proclaimed a somewhat bigger boy who, I soon learned, was Auber's brother, Marcel, known to everybody as Junior.

I had gone north to teach—and with some half-formed hopes of finding a husband, although at the time I wasn't admitting the latter even to myself. I was the first teacher in the log school in Bulldozer, a

"Backward Boy" is reprinted by the kind permission of the author.

village that owed its existence to a stampede of World War II veterans in quest of a brave new world. Where there'd been only the scattered cabins of trappers, prospectors and fishermen, there had sprung into being a complete community.

There were a store and a post office—both in the same building—and Paulson's sawmill, a great open-sided shed with a flat roof and huge piles of lumber and slabs. There were the log church and the new log school. The school was off to one side in a clearing of its own on a flat woody bench overlooking a small oval-shaped lake.

My school was so new, in fact, that the freshly peeled spruce logs still gleamed whitely against the brown and yellow of the autumn birch leaves. My living quarters were to be in two rooms above the classroom. I had a wood-burning cookstove, a table and two chairs, a small built-in cupboard, a badly bruised davenport—and the lower half of an Army double-decker wooden bunk.

On the short opening day of school little is accomplished in the way of education. The teacher seats the pupils and tries to maintain order while she starts down the front row and up the next with necessary questions: What is your name? How old are you? What grade are you in?

Then discipline can be relaxed and the teacher—if she is conscientious—tries to work it out so that in spite of the age differences the entire classroom melts into one unit. I felt lucky in achieving just this kind of rapport on my first day at Bulldozer School. In fact, everything came off so incredibly well that when I announced early dismissal nobody wanted to leave.

One boy, a twelve-year-old native, told me that he wanted to stay but couldn't because he had to go and help his father "quarter-up" and pack out a moose they had killed that morning. I had never experienced anything like this! A warm feeling came over me, and I was at a loss what to say. So I asked the contentedly babbling faces about another odd thing I had noticed: "Don't any parents ever accompany beginners to school on the first day in Alaska?"

The clamor of answering voices rose to such a crescendo I had to signal for silence by waving my hand, palm forward, back and forth several times. At last I singled out a girl in blue jeans and blouse and said, "Would you please explain, miss?"

"Sure," she said quickly. "It's potato harvest and everybody's working."

"Your mothers too?" I asked.

"Of course, and we'd all have to pick spuds too if we went home now. That's why we want to stay in school."

All this time I was conscious of Auber's tremendous brown eyes glued to my face. He wasn't saying anything, but he certainly was taking it all in. His thick hair was unkempt and uncombed, long at the back and long at the temples where it tapered off to a point about midway down the ear.

"It is too nice a day to stay indoors," I announced. "We will go out and sit on the grassy bank and look across the lake at the beautiful scenery while we get better acquainted." This brought quite a gust of laughter, for they thought I must be joking.

Auber's brother spoke up, "We don't see nothing but scenery all our lives. This is the first school me and Auber ever been in and we like it. Our daddies built it and some of us bigger kids helped peel the logs." Junior was eight.

"How can this be your first school when some of you are in the eighth grade?" I asked.

"That's just the homesteader kids," Junior explained. "They all went to school 'outside.' Me an' Auber and some of the other kids never saw the inside of a real school. My mamma taught me. We don't even know what grade I'm in."

In the face of all the unprecedented enthusiasm for school I just couldn't coldly dismiss these children, not even after lunch—and all had brought lunches. I let them stay the full seven hours.

As it turned out, Junior was one of my brightest pupils. Auber was my slowest. A good teacher is supposed to be objective and impartial. I don't think many succeed. But Auber was the only pupil I ever openly favored, and he was the only teacher's pet I ever knew of who was gladly accepted as such by the other pupils—as though he were their pet too.

Auber, though small and thin, was tough as whang leather and active as a chickadee. Slow in scholastic things, he was quick in other ways. Right from the beginning, when there were bigger and stronger boys in the room, he took care of the huge stove—a converted 100-gallon gasoline drum. Only rarely did he need help to get a big log in far enough so he could close the stove door.

When I passed out the report cards on the last day of school in the spring, there were three "retainees"—educators' euphemism for "flunkers." I couldn't take my gaze from Auber, who had extracted his report card from the envelope and now held it opened before him. I knew he couldn't read "Failed," which I had written in longhand with a note for his parents that read: "I feel very badly about this. But it wouldn't be fair to the other first-graders if I passed Auber."

Auber looked toward Junior two rows away. When Junior finally glanced toward Auber and saw him holding the report card he said, "Teacher? May I speak to Auber?"

"Why, certainly, Junior. Didn't I say that you could all talk as long as you didn't yell?"

"But you didn't say we could leave our desks, and if I speak to Auber from here I will have to holler."

"You are right," I said. "You may leave your seat."

Now the other pupils were listening. By the time Junior reached Auber's desk it was dead quiet in the school.

"You didn't pass, Auber," Junior said. "You will be in the first grade again next year." It was the clap of doom.

For a moment Auber merely looked startled. He was even a slow learner of bad news. Then the great innocent eyes went shiny and the tiny triangle of face made a gallant effort to conceal heartbreak. The

dam broke and Auber's tears came in a deluge.

Junior Dubois placed his arm across Auber's shoulders as the sobs shook the little frame.

"You may move around and talk while I go upstairs and put some potatoes on to boil," I said. I had to fight to keep from bolting for the staircase against the west wall. The children were used to my quick trips to attend to my cooking and thought nothing of this one.

I burst into tears and flung myself on my cot with my face in my pillow. I couldn't shake Auber's stricken look and I wished I could just die. It took a good half hour to "put those potatoes on to boil."

The glow a teacher gets from watching a gifted student work can never compensate for the sadness when a "slow" child is denied promotion.

Albert Dubois became a project. I wanted to teach him so badly that I fear there were times when I was guilty of slackening off on the rest of the pupils. It just didn't seem possible that such a sensitive child, so kind and gentle and understanding, could really and truly be "dumb." I sought desperately for a chink in that delicate little psyche through which I might probe and inject some knowledge.

I also had to keep Auber two years in the fourth grade. By then he had learned some control; he also was able to read the word "Failed" without help from Junior. This time the brave little face won the battle of the tear ducts, and only the additional shininess in the big, tender brown eyes showed that the hurt was there. Auber exhibited a mild spurt his second year in the fourth grade. I couldn't have been more overjoyed if he had been my own son. *Now,* I hastily concluded, *my efforts are telling.* Soon *Auber's potentially fine brain will break its chains and he will catch up—maybe even pass the children he started to school with.* There were now only four of the latter, all in the sixth grade—an average group.

I redoubled my efforts. Auber had always been better than average at drawing, for he was a born observer. A teacher with eight grades, alas, has no time for an art class, no time for soap sculpture, no time for square dancing and no time for socializing. But here was one teacher who found time for one student's art. I know little of art myself, but I encouraged Auber to draw, draw, draw. His drawing never improved beyond the point his little spurt took it. The spurt also brought improvement in composition and enough improvement in other subjects to justify my passing Auber. But in looking back I am afraid I rationalized a little.

I was simply so gone on him that I could not bear again the terrific emotional punishment of denying him his promotion.

Nevertheless, at the end of seventh grade I had to break the boy's heart for the third time. If only he could have been a nasty pupil or a dumb brute of a child; but Auber, if anything, had become unbelievably good. He was my janitor, my fireman, my wood-packer-upper (upstairs to my living quarters) and my water boy. He had grown considerably, and the lower part of his face was now catching up with his eyes. His father kept that hair cut shorter, and Auber now occasionally used a comb.

When Auber began his second year in the seventh grade, Junior was starting his second year of high school at Wasilla, a bus run having been arranged by the Bulldozer community. Auber's sister, Grace, was in fifth grade while another sister, Marie, was in second. These other Dubois children were all above-average pupils.

One gray day in early November I sat correcting compositions at my desk in the poorly lighted classroom. The first one, written by a girl, read, "My mother was learning to drive the truck and she ran clean over the meat house daddy had just bilt." She never mentioned what daddy said. Then came the usual hodgepodge of dull or, at best, mediocre writing. The last composition, however, was a distinct surprise.

Auber had written it! His grammar and spelling were as discouraging as ever, which means he was at fourth-grade level or worse; but he wrote in a bold and legible hand.

Maybe I cry too easily; it just seems that everything of any importance that ever happened to Auber was tied to my tear ducts.

One cold day pa come faling along the trale. Me and Junior was diging in the snow for wood but it was all gone. Pas nose was wite and we new it was froze. Me and Junior sneked in the back dore wile pa fel in the front. Wen he stagered to the stoave and leand agen it Ma slammed the front dore shut that pa had left open and said HUG THAT STOAVE CLOSE YOU DRUNKERD. THE FIRES BEN OUT FOR HOURS [Auber used capitals for the quotation marks he never understood] Then pa slid to the flore and ma threw the comfiter over him. The girls were scaired and big eyed in the corner. We was all cold in bed that night but pa who slept the best. Pa sure can stand the cold.

Mrs. Stroup, whose husband trucked supplies to Bulldozer and hauled lumber to Anchorage, had once said to me, "Marcel Dubois tries hard in that simple way of his; but between you and me I think he could drink less and feed his family more." Then again, the father of one of my pupils, Jack Herkimer, had said, "Marcel is a trapper, and furs aren't worth anything. In the summer he is a salmon fisherman in Cook Inlet, and the salmon in Cook Inlet are nearly gone. They say Marcel drinks too much. I don't think he drinks a damn bit more than the rest of us; only they notice him more because they know he can't afford it. Anyway, that wife of his never lets him forget that she is educated, while he barely learned to read and write."

I was so pleased with Auber's graphic description of Marcel Dubois' drunken home-coming that I slipped the seventh-graders another composition assignment before the customary lapse of one week was up. I didn't dare praise Auber, although I wanted to in the worst way. I was so afraid a wrong move might throw Auber's creativity out of gear. Whereas I usually assigned the topic and made the pupils build their writing around it, this time I turned them loose to write about subjects of their own choosing.

Auber did it again. It wasn't much, only a short paragraph; still, if I could keep that little spark alive, maybe I could fan it into a full-blown flame.

Our home was quite. You could hear a snowflake drop. Then down

the stares fel my sister Marie. Ma she screamed and run to the bottom of the stares and said OH MY POOR BABY. Of course Marie was four then wich is a big baby any time. DON'T TUTCH HER pa yeled YOU WILL RUNE HER SPINE. Wile my fokes yeled at eatch other Marie she clumb the stares agen and fel right back down on purposs. She liked the atentson that mutch. She got a licken this time. It was a exiting day.

I saw Marcel Dubois in the store one day. I cornered him back in the little post office at the end of the dry-goods counter. "Marcel," I said, "Auber is beginning to write stories. Maybe you could quietly encourage him at home."

"Now, Lizbet," Marcel replied (he could never pronounce "Elizabeth"). "Please, I know Auber is slow. I know you try hard. He will soon be out of school. That is enough. I will teach him w'at I know—trapping, hunting, woodcutting; only I don't know about trapping because Auber say it is cruel. He lak the garden, but even so he say, 'The vegetable hurt too w'en you pull him, papa.'" Marcel looked at me with Auber's clear brown eyes. He had the same thick black hair. But where Auber was small and thin, his father was of medium height and heavy-set and strong. He had big hands and thick fingers. But he was known to be extremely generous and kindly—when he was sober, that is.

After we broke off our conversation and were standing in line for our mail at the general-delivery counter, Marcel said, "Auber will be sixteen in February. Then he can leave shool."

It made me mad. I snapped,

"You dumb old Frenchie; you just let Auber finish out the year. If you break that boy's heart, I will——" I didn't know what to say next. Marcel flashed his strong white teeth in a big grin and said, "Boy! Is me tough!"

Auber's creativity continued on a somewhat lighter note.

One day wen I come home from school Mrs. Fogerty stood behind ma who sat in a chare with her hare all flatened down and her head all nobby bumps. The house smelled awfle. YOU NEEDN'T TURN UP YOUR NOSE Mrs. Fogerty said YOUR MOTHER IS GETTING A PURMINNINT. The next day ma looked the prittiest we ever seen her. Her hare was fluffy and curley and brown. She looked a lot in the mear that day and she sang a lot. When pa come home with a load of wood in the truk he come in the house and said OH WHAT A BEUTY I GOT FOR A BRIDE. Ma blushed and us kids all laughed and claped our hands. She said to pa OH YOU DONT MEAN IT.

Truly I was riding on a cloud. All my years of trying to help an unfortunate pupil were at last bearing fruit. I continually had to force myself to remember that there were other pupils in my room too. With fingers crossed I read Auber's latest. It must have represented a Herculean effort on his part. It was written in two paragraphs!

My father had no job one fall and all him and ma chewd the rag about was how broke we was. The moose meat was gone and Frosty our dog was thin. He was a big husky and could pul three of us at one time on the sled.

Christmas morning wen we got up there was presants for all of us kids. I got a air rifle and Junior he got shoe packs and the girls got dolls. But we had only a rabit for dinner for us all and some boiled potatose. Then Junior he said WARE IS FROSTY. We couldnt find him and the girls and Junior cride. I felt bad to but I didnt want them to see me cry so I went and cride outside by Frostys house. Wen I herd dogs barking I looked up and saw Clem Baily go by with his dog team on the road to town and there was Frosty in the lead. I new Clem wauld not steal a dog so I new pa had sold dear Frosty to by us kids Cristmas preasants.

One night I lay awake wondering whether it was fair to withhold praise from a student who had never known anything but heartbreak and failure. I decided I would simply have to risk breaking the spell, come what may, and tell Auber that his compositions were the best in the school. In order to accomplish my purpose I kept him in at recess the following day.

"What did I do wrong, teacher?" he said before I could speak. A pupil was seldom kept in at recess unless it was for punishment or sickness.

"Why, Auber," I said, "you didn't do anything wrong. I kept you in simply to tell you that your compositions are the most interesting of all those in the whole school, including the eighth grade."

Auber's mouth opened in surprise, and his face became suffused with the deepest blush I had ever seen. I could actually see it start at the neckline and creep up in a crimson wave until it disappeared into his hairline. His soft eyes glistened, then dimmed behind the tears.

"Oh, teacher," he said in a near-whisper. "Oh, thank you." No other pupil would have thought to say thank you. So again I had to make a quick excuse to dash upstairs before my own tears could show.

February came and with it Auber's sixteenth birthday. I was relieved when I saw that his parents weren't going to take him out of school simply because he had reached the legal age beyond which he need not attend. I now dared hope I might guide him through the eighth grade. An eighth-grade diploma isn't much today, but it would probably be an unforgettable milestone in Auber's life—if he made it.

A flu epidemic hit the Wasilla Woods, and at one time I was on the verge of closing the school because absences had nearly reached the halfway mark. Auber and his sisters missed one Friday. Upon their return to school on Monday, Auber was extremely melancholy. *Well, I told myself, he'll snap back; this is probably the reaction from the soaring spirits he was in after I praised his work.* Nevertheless, Auber dutifully wrote his composition along with the others that day. I read his somber story after school.

Snow was faling and it was dark in our house even if it still was day time. Angela my baby sister was very sick. Pa had drove to Wasilla in the truk to call the docter in Palmer but the docter said to bring Angela to the hospittle. He wouldnt come to our house.

Angela was in her little birch crib in the corner. Her face was wite and she was to sick to talk. She only laid there and folowed us with her eyes. Ma held her hand and wispered to Pa

IT IS SO COLD. Then ma cride and Angelas face was witer then ever and she closed her eyes. Then pa said YOUR LITTLE SISTER IS GONE KIDS. We all cride then. The ground was froze and pa had to get Mr. Fogerty and Clem Baily to help dig the grave. They baried Angela under the big birch by the spring ware she use to play.

Upon inquiry at the store that evening I learned that what Auber had so straightforwardly written had been indeed truth. And it was also true that a doctor from nearby Palmer twenty-six miles away had refused to drive out to the Dubois home. This inhuman monster, according to Marcel Dubois' account, had said over the telephone, "Bring the kid into the hospital, buster; I can't drive way out yunder for a li'l ol' case of sniffles." Yet Marcel had patiently described his little daughter's condition. Marcel Dubois was also said to have sworn that someday he would drive to Palmer and choke the doctor to death right in the middle of the village square.

The sun had burned through the snow on the south slopes of the foothills, and the brown spots were growing into islands amid the diminishing white. The magpies had disappeared—a sure sign of spring; and the huge black-brown moose were edging back toward their summer feeding range in the willow-covered benches beyond the foothills and below the mountains.

Auber was aware of none of these harbingers of spring. While the other children, including his sisters, tumbled out to play at recess and noon, Auber refused to leave his desk.

"Auber," I said softly as he sat

there in the room now so bright with the sun streaming in the windows, "maybe if you could talk about Angela to me you would feel better afterward. We cannot bring your little sister back. She wouldn't want you to feel so sad, I'm sure."

Auber's sudden response was actually more than I had expected. It just poured out of him, everything about Angela, from the time she was born until she had died. He ended up quoting his mother upon hearing his father's threats to kill the doctor. " 'You mustn't, Marcel, you mustn't; he will pay for his sins like all of us on Judgment Day.' "

After breaking down and telling me all there was to tell, Auber began loosening up again. He wrote one composition which touched on Angela only briefly and indirectly. After that he mentioned his little sister just once.

Everybody spoke low for a long time after my little sister died. My other sisters couldn't got to school that day becaus they couldnt stop crying. Ma cooked and swep and sowed without a word. Pa sawed wood all day but he faced away from Angelas grave. Junior took me a side and said IF YOU TELL ANYBODY YOU SEEN ME CRYING I WILL BLACK YOUR EYES SAVVY. Of coarse I swore I wouldnt but I said WHAT WILL YOU DO IF YOU HAPPIN TO THINK ABOUT OUR DEAD SISTER WEN YOU ARE IN WASILLA SCHOOL? Junior tride to hold back the tears but couldnt so he gave me a wolp on the cheekbone and my eye swoll up and turn black and pa gave him a licken right after.

Some of Auber's pieces were old

happenings, some very recent. After reading one of them I began to wonder if maybe he wasn't making up some of the anecdotes he described. For this time Auber had written:

One day pa let Junior go with him into a pool hall at Palmer. The men playing pool soon found themselves a ball short. NO WONDER the ball was in Juniors mouth. Junior could mouth a bigger rock or egg then me but this here pool ball stumped him. Revern Ervin was drug in and he said IS YOUR HOUSE IN ORDER MY SON. Pa said the pool ball didnt hear a word. Wen Mr. Fabyan poured caster oil in an empty sardeen can and put it close Junior made a awfle face and the ball shot out of his mouth and he threw up. He was mitey tame after that.

Marcel Dubois and his wife, Catharine, called on me in my home above the school one spring evening when the sun's low rays were red behind the birches by the lake. Mrs. Dubois, in common with so many women who had married men of lower station, had gradually come to assume a martyr's air. While I made coffee in the percolator, she said that they had come to discuss Auber. "We want to thank you, Elizabeth, for being so patient with Auber. He just adores you, you know. Sometimes it makes me feel jealous, but I know I shouldn't. Let's just say I'm a mother and Auber is my boy."

"That's all right, Catharine," I replied. "Auber needs all of the help he can get from all of us. Lately he is showing signs of becoming an author, and I want to encourage him all I can." Of course, I didn't actually mean there was any chance of Auber's becoming another Mark Twain or a John Steinbeck.

"Author?" exclaimed Catharine Dubois. "Oh, wouldn't that be something! Auber a famous writer."

"Now, mamma," said Marcel. "Please. A farmer, yes, or a carpenter maybe, but Auber can never be a writer. Lizbet just say that to make us feel good."

But I doubt that his wife heard what he said. During most of the visit, she sat there in my old rocker with a faraway, dreamlike expression.

The term was nearing its end. I had become tired of the long Alaskan winters, and since it was obvious that I would never find a husband, I had decided to leave Alaska. I would get a teaching job in California or Florida. But before leaving I would promote Auber to the eighth grade.

Auber began acting uneasy, fidgety; he wouldn't look me in the eye. This was certainly a puzzler. Upon reading his next composition I suspected what was ailing him and I felt sick to my stomach.

Our ranch lies out in the beautiful woods ajacent to the flowery right side of the pitcheresk highway leading west from Wasilla, passing through Bulldozer, and trailing to an end in gorjes Goose Creek Canyon. Our home is a sturdy log structure with quaint dormer windows which overlook the snowy caps of the incomprabel Chucach Mountains. Queenly birches and stately spruce trees form a heavenly hailo around the flower strewn clearing surrounding our modist home. Our life is a marvlously kalidoscoopic bowl of fun and we live every inch of it to the uttermost hilt. We children play in the sparkling waters of our haply gurgling creek among the brilant-hued rainbow trouts and the shy ferns fringing the silvan banks. The panaramik clouds of spun gold an. . . .

It was ghastly. Auber watched me read and he hung his head in shame. I got him alone as soon as I could and I said, "Auber, don't feel bad. I know your mother told you to say all these things."

His voice came low and I had to strain to hear it. "I tried hard and I memorized it all. I didn't get the words all right, did I, teacher?"

"No," I replied. "You spelled a few wrong, Auber. But I am glad. I don't want you ever ever to let anybody tell you what to write in composition class." I gave Auber a note to give to his mother.

Catharine: You're not helping Auber this way. You are destroying what it has taken us all year to develop— Auber's sense of achievement, his hard-earned feeling of creative pride. Surely you understand.

But Auber continued to avoid my gaze and he seemed to back deeper into his shell. Finally I gave him a note with instructions for his father.

Marcel: Please stop your wife from doing Auber's writing for him. She isn't fooling me and she is harming Auber. Auber is a far better writer than his mother!

I derived a certain smug satisfaction from Auber's next-to-last contribution. It wasn't long, but I thought it was meaty.

The girls was down by the crick ware the trout was sponning. Me and Junior had a porkapine up a tree by the garden stump row. We herd ma and pa geting mader and ma was yeling loud. Sudinly she screemed so loud me and Junior got scaired and run to the house. Pa set on the old rocker holding ma across his lap and spanking her. Wen he saw us he said MAMA BET SHE WAS STRONGER THEN ME. Wen he laugfhed ma cride. Wen we got back the porkapine was gone.

The flurry of reports that must always mark the tag end of school term enveloped me so deeply that I was scarcely able to correct all of the papers in time for my final reports. Among the stack of test papers were the last theme assignments for the seventh grade which I had neglected to gather the day before. I plunged into the pile. Auber's contribution ground my frenzied tempo to a halt.

One day we all went to Ankerage with Mr. Fogerty in his stachen wagin. Wen we got back home our cow was in the house and the dore was open. Pa swore and yeled WHO LEFT THE COW IN THE HOUSE AND THE DORE OPEN? Nobody oaned up of coarse and pa grabed the rope to leed the cow out but she was to fat becawse she had eat all our potatose in the sack by the backdore. SENSE SHE IS HERE I MIGHT AS WELL MILK HER pa said. Ma got mad and cride agen. The cow slep in the house that night and pa led her out the next day. He said I DON'T SEE WY YOU BALL ALL THE TIME BECAWSE I DO THIS SAME THING EVER DAY IN THE BARN. Ma seems to cry mighty easy sense Angela died.

I left Alaska four years ago. Auber has written me many letters since then. He said——But let him tell it.

Dear Teacher: I started eigthe

grade and went only one munth. One day Mister Lane said BOY DON'T YOU KNOW ANYTHING? He had asked me wy I dident know any parts of speech and the other kids said AUBER DONT HAVE TO KNOW. Then Mister Lane got mad and yeled. WY DONT AUBER HAVE TO KNOW? HE GOSE TO THIS HERE SCOOL TO DONT HE? Then the other kids got scaired and I dident know what to say. Wen I got home I told pa I wanted to lieve the scool and he said AUBER I DONT LIKE YOUR NEW TEACHER TO. YOU LIEV THE SCOOL AND I WILL TEACH YOU HOW TO BE A GOOD GARDENEER. Mama got mad and went and seen Mister Lane and wen she come home said HOOOMPFF WHAT A FAT DUMMY. I FEEL LIKE TAKEING THE GIRLS OUT OF SCOOL TO. Of coarse she dident.

A year ago Auber wrote again.

Dear Teacher. Mr Girsmill is giving me a chanse to work for him at the GOVERMANT EXPEARMINT FARM. He said if I aint lazey as some hes had that I can maybee work steddy. I rote to him for a job and wen he red my leter he drove out to our house and said to pa BY GOD NOW MARCEL I NEVVER KNEW AUBER COULD WRITE. HE IS JUST THE MAN I NEED TO HELP ME RUN THAT DANGED FARM. Then he winked at pa but I saw him. I knew he was teesing me but I was so glad to get my first job that I dident care. And just think I make TWO DOLARS a hour. Ma and pa say put your money in the bank Auber and I tell them I will do that after the girls got deesant close and are famly dont owe a penny to nobody. If it wasnt for you teacher I couldent have wrote a leter to Mr. Girsmill and got a job. I am to bashfle to ask face to face.

Auber's letters have become few-er. But even so I still can't read one but what I see those great brown eyes and that stack of hair—and of course I end up crying.

discussion

Teachers hold strong impressions of the first class they ever taught. As memories of the entire class fade, the one or two children who were the hardest to teach often remain indelibly imprinted in the mind's eye. This may seem curious as one would expect memory to cherish the outstanding or gifted child. It must be that teachers feel a personal challenge to reach the child who seems unreachable. The uphill struggle to be successful under almost impossible odds makes the few glimmerings of painfully slow success particularly pleasurable and unforgettable. This special investment of time on the teacher's part creates a bond between teacher and student which in turn enhances the learning process.

Auber is a particularly appealing child. Even the other children approve when the teacher shows special interest in him. Although Auber has academic problems, he is able to shoulder his own weight doing chores and participating on the playground, making him a totally acceptable peer group member.

Elizabeth has internalized the principles that good teachers are "objective" and "impartial," and she is aware of some guilt for singling out Auber for special favor. Elizabeth labors under many tyrannies of "oughts" and "shoulds" about teaching. In Auber's case she thinks his traits of sensitivity and kindness and his keen ability to observe (as demonstrated in his drawings) are evidence that he can learn academic material readily if only she can find the key that will unlock his learning potential.

Today's teachers are more sophisticated about distinguishing between cognitive ability and intuitive and creative or social abilities. Despite their sophistication, however, teachers do not agree as to which abilities are to be developed inside the classroom. Many teachers would create a special curriculum for a boy like Auber thinking that traditional academic requirements would not be practical or appropriate goals for him. Woodworking or other manual skills might be substituted for the three Rs. The creative writing Elizabeth assigned would probably be the first subject excluded from Auber's special curriculum. Surprisingly, however, creative writing is Elizabeth's most vital link with Auber. It provides him with great satisfaction and an emotional outlet. In his own way he is creative and uses words well to express feeling with honesty and vitality. Elizabeth was wise to accept Auber's writing without undue criticism of his spelling and grammar. Her encouragement in this area was more important than perfecting his technical skills in writing. Elizabeth was truly a successful teacher with Auber for she reached the most difficult goal in teaching—helping her student to have a feeling of self-worth and dignity.

springboards for inquiry

1. How would you feel about teaching a student like Auber? Does this story challenge or discourage you?
2. What do you think of teachers working with the same students over a period of several years? What are the advantages and disadvantages?
3. Would you have retained Auber at any grade level as Elizabeth did? Why?
4. What are the advantages and disadvantages of teaching children with a wide age range in the same room?

Virginia Chase Perkins

The end of the week

Audrey Curtis stood in the safety zone with Freddie Kaufman, waiting for the streetcar that would take them to P.S. 31 for the preliminaries of the All-City Spelling Bee.

She was thirty—smart, trim, and attractive with even features, nice legs, and a well proportioned body. She looked completely normal, and she was.

She was efficient, too. Miss Forbes considered her the best teacher in the building. She was always holding her up—subtly, she believed—as an example to the others, commending her promptness and accuracy, her competence during fire drills, even her handwriting, neat and uniform and legible. "If I had half a dozen like you, Audrey," she often said in private, "I could run a model school." You had to be efficient when you were doing two jobs, Audrey Curtis always answered.

She sank back in her seat. It was the end. "It's the e-o-u-s ones I'm scared of," he had told her. "If I get one of them, I'm gone for sure."

Audrey Curtis had been married eight years. For the first three of these, her husband, Hank, now a salesman, had been in college. It had been fun to work then, fun at night to help Hank with his studies, to type his papers for him—write them sometimes—fun even to put up with the things they had to, living in a trailer. The long walk, carrying groceries and water. The lines in the community bathroom. The "alternatives" they used at night. But during the past five years, since Hank had been working, that fun had paled.

Every year regularly in September, he had assured her that that year would be her last. He was getting ahead, he told her. By summer he would be on his feet, and they wouldn't need her pay. But Hank was as optimistic as he was easygoing, and her last year never came.

She loved Hank, but she could see his faults, especially in April. No one else could. Every time she took him to school the girls made a tremendous fuss over him—even the older teachers. "How is that charming husband of yours?" Alyce Estabrooke and Caroline Treat kept asking. "You don't know how lucky you are to have him," Marjorie Fields said again and again. Only Phyllis ever said he was lucky to have her.

He never said it. He just took for granted that she would get him up and off in the morning, that she would see that the bills were paid, that she would write his letters for him as well as the reports his bosses praised. He took for granted, too, that most of their savings came from things she did without. He ate his lunch at the most expensive places—she carried hers; he had his clothes tailor-made—she made her own. He had to spend money, he said, to maintain his status. In his opinion, teachers had no status to maintain.

She didn't mind carrying the responsibility. She didn't mind doing without. What she minded was having him depend upon her efficiency and yet at the same time resent it. Whenever she tried to talk business to him he complained—jokingly, he always said afterward—about her being a schoolteacher. It was something he was forever bringing up before their friends. (He took for granted, too, that their friends should be from among his, not her, associates.) One of his pet jokes was that she wouldn't even let him speak unless he first raised his hand.

After eight years she should have been used to it. And she was—except in the spring. At other times when things piled up—the papers, the meetings, the housework—she could tell herself that it was almost over. That this year would be her last. That in just a few months she would have time to wash and iron

and sew. Time to have a garden with neat little rows of radishes and lettuce. Time to take trips with Hank, reading in the car while he made his calls. Of course it wouldn't be like having a baby to take care of: she had learned a long time ago that she could never have that. Still the prospect seemed wonderful. But when spring came the story always changed. Somehow there was never quite enough money ahead. "Just one more year, honey," Hank would say. "This next will positively be your last." He would be saying it again any day now. "Just one more year. That's all."

"A-c-c-o-m-m-o-d-a-t-e," Freddie whispered. "G-u-a-r-a-n-t-e-e."

She looked down at his strained, tight face. Freddie had worries, too. "How are you feeling?" she asked.

"All right, I guess." He was a thin, unappealing child with yellowish skin and dark eyes, one of which turned in a little. There was always a faint sour smell about him. "I'm pretty sure of the words on the list," he told her. "It's them others I'm worried about. The ones they spring."

She smiled at him, ashamed that she could not warm. "You'll do fine, Freddie. I know you will." She did not say "You'll win," for he wouldn't, of course, having an I.Q. of less than 100. She had been surprised when he asked her to coach him, for he had never shown any interest in spelling, much less skill. She had been hesitant, too, for it meant staying after school night after night. Hank liked everything done when he got home: the house picked up, dinner going, and a drink ready for him. It made him uncomfortable to see her work.

"Why do you want to try out, Freddie?" she had asked, hoping that, faced with giving a reason, he would decide he didn't want to, after all.

At first he hadn't answered. He had only dropped his eyes.

"Why, Freddie?" she repeated.

When the answer came, it was in a whisper. "So somebody will look at me," he said.

It always shook her to hear children speak, as they so often did, the naked truth.

"Of course I'll help you," she told him quickly. And she had helped him night after night—she didn't know how to do anything halfway—until, to her amazement, he had won the school contest. Of course only five had tried out; all the others were too wrapped up in television.

Both she and Miss Forbes were a little embarrassed about sending him to the district bee. "You're one of the few who understand how everything reflects on me, Audrey," Miss Forbes had said. But there was nothing else to do, and so she had gone on training him: if he was going to be there, even only so someone would look at him, he ought to do as well as he could, she had thought. Well, in a couple of hours it would all be over.

"Them u-o-u-s ones," Freddie went on, not whispering now, but speaking hoarsely. "If I get one of them, I'm gone for sure."

"Don't think of them now," she said.

A line of trucks went noisily by. For a moment his tension relaxed.

"You know that guy that won last year," he began when they had passed.

She didn't, but she nodded just the same.

"Well, somebody wanted his autograph. It was in the paper. I seen it."

"That was nice," she said. Could it be that Freddie dreamed of winning? He had never said so, never even hinted it before. Ought she to have said something earlier? *All you must expect, Freddie, is to do your best.* Ought she to say it now? That was one of the hardest things about teaching, knowing how far to encourage. Knowing when to say, "You can do it," and when to say, "Try something else." Most of all, what to say when there seemed to be nothing else to try.

"A-d-v-a-n-t-a-g-e-o-u-s," Freddie whispered.

She started to think about the party, glad in a way that she couldn't be there. "When are you going to be leaving us, too, Audrey?" someone would have been sure to ask. Years ago she had been foolish enough to tell them that the next year was her last. That was before Phyllis even came. And now Phyllis was leaving . . .

"Sometimes it's u-o-u-s," Freddie was saying, "and sometimes it's e-o-u-s, and sometimes it's just o-u-s."

She looked at him again, and once more felt the wave of guilt. "Do you have anything for luck, Freddie?" she asked.

He shook his head stiffly.

She opened her purse and took out a dime. "This ought to be good," she said. "It's a new one."

As he took it, his hand touching hers felt damp and cold.

"Thanks," he said. "I'll give it back afterwards," he added as the streetcar came in sight.

. . .

Audrey Curtis sat in the fourth row of the auditorium at P.S. 31. She didn't like sitting there. She would have preferred a seat in the shadow of the balcony where she could let her attention wander, but she remembered Freddie's reason. He would have few enough to look at him, at best. Though it was almost time to begin, only a scattering was present: a few mothers; some older children, probably past winners, looking knowing and superior; some young ones, probably aspirants, looking awed; and a dozen teachers who had come, no doubt, with as little enthusiasm as she had.

In the front row were the twelve contestants, nine of them girls—all of them larger and probably older than Freddie. He sat stiffly while they whispered around him. On the platform twelve chairs formed a semicircle. In the orchestra two more were placed for the judges, who stood now under the clock, talking to Miss McNeil, principal of 31, and Mr. Thompson, the district principal, who, compared to Lester Burke, was gauche and graceless. Miss Holenbeck wasn't with them. She seldom missed such an occasion, and when she did it always seemed a little flat somehow. A little ordinary.

A teacher came down the aisle, holding the numbers for the children to draw. Audrey Curtis hoped Freddie would get a high one. She wanted him to stand on the platform as long as he could.

He drew 5 and held it up for her to see. She nodded, trying to look enthusiastic.

Barbara Gould from 21 came up the aisle and stopped at the end of her row, assuming a posture of exhaustion.

"How are you standing it?" she asked.

Audrey gave an appropriate grimace. "Oh, I guess I'll last out the year," she answered.

Barbara Gould's face changed.

So did her voice. "You married girls," she said. "You should complain."

Audrey tried to laugh. She was used to such gibes. All married girls were. There was a lot single girls didn't know about marriage.

"Why you stick around at all is a mystery to me."

Audrey winced inside. "Oh, people are funny," she answered coolly.

"They sure are," Barbara Gould said with feeling, and started up her aisle.

The judges took their seats. The children filed to the stage, Mr. Thompson following. Unlike Lester Burke, he had no jokes, no small talk. He was all business, and that was the reason, people agreed, that he would never really get ahead. He stated the rules and began briskly.

"First word. Absence."

Number 1 spoke glibly. "Absence. A-b-s-e-n-c-e. Absence."

"Dissimilar."

Number 2 wet her lips and swallowed. "Dissimilar. D-i-s-s-i-m-i-l-a-r. Dissimilar."

"Hindrance."

"Hindrance. H-i-n-d-r—" Number 3 stopped and started over. "H-i-n-d-r-a-n-c-e. Hindrance."

"Intercede."

"Intercede. I-n-t-e-r-c-e-d-e. Intercede."

Freddie was next.

Her eyes moved on to Freddie. He didn't seem nervous any longer. He stood there straight and ready. She was the nervous one now, she thought.

"Calendar."

"Calendar. C-a-l-e-n-d-a-r. Calendar."

He spelled it calmly, enunciating each letter as she had taught him to do.

Relieved, her mind went back to Barbara Gould again. *Why you stick*

around at all is a mystery to me. . . .
If only she didn't have to. If only she could stay at home and cook and sew and wash. Stay at home where it was quiet all day, never having to deal with children who slouched, who daydreamed. Children who showed off, who copied. Children who had to be reminded. *Hats off. Hats off in the hall.* Children who had to be prodded . . .

Freddie's eye caught hers. She smiled at him, showing a confidence she didn't feel. Mr. Thompson was still on the list. Children almost never fell on the list, unless they were nervous. "I have faith in any child you train, Audrey," Miss Forbes often said. Yet there was a place where training stopped.

Mr. Thompson went three times down the line. No one fell. Then he drew a new list from his pocket. The line grew tense. Throats tightened. Fingers twisted.

"Assonance."

Number 1 spelled cautiously now, feeling her way. "Assonance. A-s-s-o-n-a-n-c-e. Assonance."

"Guarantee."

Number 2 hesitated, then spelled desperately, her eyes on the judge. "Guarantee. G-u-a-r-a-n-t-e-e. Guarantee."

"Accommodate."

Number 3, visibly nervous, rushed into it. "A-c-c-o-m-o—"

There was a murmur of sympathy from the audience, and she fled into the wings. Audrey Curtis joined the murmur, yet felt at the same time a secret relief. Freddie couldn't be the first one down anyway. That was something.

"Accommodate," Mr. Thompson repeated, his voice completely matter-of-fact.

Number 4 was ready. "Accommodate. A-c-c-o-m-m-o-d-a-t-e. Accommodate."

There was another murmur, this time of approval. Audrey did not join in. All her attention was on Freddie. He was waiting, straight and steady, not flinching like the others as his turn neared. If only he could spell one word, she thought—just one—beyond the list.

"Hemisphere."

"Hemisphere. H-e-m-i-s-p-h-e-r-e. Hemisphere." He spelled it easily, almost scornfully.

She relaxed. He had spelled it. He had stood up when one had fallen. Miss Forbes would be satisfied.

Her mind turned to Barbara Gould again. *You should complain.* Tonight perhaps Hank would tell her. He would come into the kitchen while she was trying to get dinner, come in with the usual bounce and kiss her. It always annoyed her to have him kiss her in the kitchen, for she had everything timed there, every move synchronized. "Listen, honey," he would say. "Just one more year. Isn't that swell?" Just one more year. Just one more year of children who chewed gum, who catcalled. Children who threw spit balls. Children who were forever wanting the pass . . .

Mr. Thompson was at the head of the line again. If he felt any surprise, he did not show it.

"Effectual."

Number 1 hesitated, asked the definition, then hesitated again. "Effectual. A-f—" she finally began.

There was an audible gasp from the line.

"Careful," Mr. Thompson said. "We want fair play."

Number 1 began all over. "Effectual. E-f-e-c-t—"

The judges shook their heads, simultaneously. The murmur came. And again Audrey Curtis felt the guilty, secret relief. "Anyway," she could say, "two fell ahead of him."

"Effectual," Number 2 said briskly. "E-f-f-e-c-t-u-a-l. Effectual."

There was a patter of applause. Number 3, red-eyed, came out of the wings and took a seat near her teacher.

One more and it would be his turn again.

"Dissertation."

Number 4 spelled in a whisper. The judges leaned forward.

Her eyes were still on Freddie. He was looking eager, really stimulated, she thought. Then, as his turn came, she saw him step forward a little, waiting.

"Courteous."

She sank back in her seat. It was the end. "It's the e-o-u-s ones I'm scared of," he had told her. "If I get one of them, I'm gone for sure."

"Courteous. C-o-u-r-t—" He hesitated. Yet he didn't seem rattled.

Think, Freddie. Think.

The auditorium was very quiet. If he gets this word, just this one, she thought. . . . Her mind whispered the letters to him. "E-o-u-s, Freddie. E-o-u-s." Whispered them frantically.

But he didn't need any help. His eyes swept over the audience, saw every watching face. Then with a look of satisfaction—almost exultation—he finished, repeated the word, and stepped back into his place.

. . .

Audrey Curtis lay on the davenport. Only the bridge lamp was on. It showed a room orderly for not having been touched all day, with dark green walls and white woodwork. (She had painted both herself.) The room was furnished with a television set, faced by two chairs:

a large red leather one with a matching footstool, and a smaller one, slip-covered in figured green. Beside each was an end table. One table held a pile of magazines, topped by *Time,* because of the red on its cover, and an ash tray—always emptied the last thing at night. The other held a sewing basket, heaped high. On the floor was a braided rug that she had made and intended to enlarge some day, and on the window sills were potted plants, all thriving. The only picture was a modernistic one that hung above the davenport. It had been given to them as a wedding present. Hank liked to hang it upside down on the sly and then very soberly ask guests what they thought of it.

She had been lying there for two hours already. Hank bowled on Friday evenings, and she had no dinner to get. Occasionally she asked some girls over—usually Phyllis and Roberta and Marjorie—to play bridge or canasta or watch television; but tonight she was completely disorganized, and was glad that she hadn't asked anyone in. Hank didn't care much for Roberta. She was too self-sufficient, he said. Marjorie, on the other hand, he found too deferential. Phyllis suited him exactly. He liked her stories, especially the one about Be Kind to Animals Week, when, acting upon the suggestion of some one downtown, she had taken her entire room out, trying to find a horse to be kind to.

She had come home, undressed, hanging and folding her clothes automatically, put on her robe, and gone into the kitchen: a shining kitchen, all white except for the red oilcloth ruffles that edged the shelves and the canisters that lined them. There she got herself a glass of milk, drank it, then, disregarding the breakfast dishes, lay down on the davenport, where she had been ever since.

Every teacher had a thrill when she saw a child do what he believed he couldn't, yet what she herself had known he could do all the time. But, sitting there in the auditorium of P.S. 31, she had seen a child do not only what she and Miss Forbes had believed he never could do, but far beyond what his I.Q. allowed. She was still lightheaded from it.

He hadn't won, of course. But he had placed third. Freddie Kaufman—the yellowish boy with the turned-in eye and the faint sour smell, the boy other children avoided—had stood up with a dignity no one could possibly have suspected and had spelled word after word while nine others, the champions of their schools, had fallen.

She had sat, first wondering how long his luck would hold, then hardly believing, then gradually confident. When it was over, she had rushed up to the platform and congratulated him, trying not to show her amazement. Then she had gone into the office to call Miss Forbes, who, dumbfounded, had said, "You deserve all the credit, Audrey." But she didn't deserve it, of course. And that wasn't the point at all, though she hadn't taken time to explain it then.

In the auditorium again, she had sat in the back row, watching. Congratulations over, Mr. Thompson and the judges had moved into the wings. The contestants stood in a noisy group, their voices high and mixed. Around the edges, saying little, were those who had failed early, and in the center among the win-

ners was Freddie, not ignored any longer, but accepted, deferred to.

Barbara Gould came up the aisle. "Too bad your boy didn't win," she said.

"Thanks," she had answered. But if he had won, she couldn't possibly have been more elated.

Finally he came, and they started out together. He didn't thank her, as she had thought he would. Not even after Miss McNeil stopped them on the stairs and said, "So Mrs. Curtis is your teacher. I might have known." He just walked on, a little ahead. But when they got into the Safety Zone he took the dime she had given him out of his pocket and handed it to her.

"Keep it," she said.

"Can I spend it?" he asked.

"Of course," she told him. But she felt a little hurt.

"For anything I please?"

"For anything you please."

He turned his head and looked at the traffic. "Then I'll pay your streetcar fare," he said. No thanks could have equalled that.

Sitting side by side on the streetcar, she had been aware of a new relationship between them. There was a teacher-child relationship that she had often thought about. It was a simple relationship. Unhampered by love, it was simpler than any parent-child relationship could be. If it was narrower, it could be straighter, more even, more honest, more companionable. Sitting there with Freddie, though they hardly talked at all, she had felt it at its best.

They had got off together at the school. Just as she was about to say good night, she remembered something.

"Freddie," she said, opening her purse and taking out a piece of pa-

per. "I'd like to have your autograph."
"Gee, Mrs. Curtis!" he said, and
wrote it, grinning. Then he waved
and started off.

She had started off, too, in another direction, knowing that she could
never be quite the same teacher
again.

discussion

Audrey Curtis receives a great deal of positive reinforcement from her
principal. Miss Forbes sees Audrey as a teacher who is competent and de-
pendable; even her handwriting is exemplary. On a personal level Audrey
has something in common with her pupil, Freddie. She too craves attention
and praise. The important person in her life is her husband, and each year
she anticipates leaving the teaching profession to do what she considers her
most rewarding occupation, keeping house for him. She views the difficulties of teaching realistically. Curbing the cat-calling, reprimanding the
gum-chewers, denying those who always want to "leave the room" are
unrewarding tasks which she would like to leave behind.

Audrey Curtis' experience with Freddie is enlightening and opens a new
experience for her. She has helped other children before, but she has never had as intense a personal experience with a child. Good teachers often
work hard to accomplish their goals with a class, but they infrequently have
the experience of bringing an individual child to a level of accomplishment
which is far beyond their expectation for that child. In fact, for Audrey
Curtis one of the most difficult aspects of teaching was knowing how far to
encourage individual students. It is not always easy to know which child can
do more if he tries or which student is working at his highest level of
achievement. Oddly enough, Freddie was one of those students she felt
rather certain about. She clearly saw him as a boy with an I.Q. of less than
100 and therefore limited. She did not count on the subtle ingredients of
success—self-confidence, a supportive adult, an overwhelming need to be
recognized, and tenacity. Audrey learned as much from Freddie as he
learned from her. In fact her experience with him probably marked the
turning point in her career. It seems that Audrey Curtis will be more realistic in the future and will more fully enjoy the rewards of teaching rather
than sustaining an illusion that greater satisfaction is awaiting her elsewhere.

springboards for inquiry

1. How do you explain Freddie's amazing performance in the spelling bee?
2. Explain your position as to whether teachers should be asked to work after
school to coach a student as Mrs. Curtis did?
3. Do you believe, as the writers of *Pygmalion in the Classroom*[1] do, that a teacher's
expectation for a child will affect his level of performance?

[1] Robert Rosenthal and Lenore Jacobson, *Pygmalion in the Classroom* (New York: Holt, Rinehart and Winston, 1968).

teaching styles

The teacher creates environments for learning by the methods that he uses. It has been said that the teacher is the architect of the environment. Given the same topic, teachers will "do" different things to the class and with the class because of their differing teaching styles. In their book *Models of Teaching* Joyce and Weil begin with an exercise designed to have the reader observe the methods and styles of teaching used by three social studies teachers in three separate classes of a large metropolitan high school.[1] All three teachers are working with 16 year olds. Their common assignment is to engage the students in a study of civil rights for black citizens in the United States.

The first teacher uses a pamphlet called *Voting Rights in Mississippi*, a federal report detailing attempts to negate black voting rights in Mississippi. The pamphlet arouses the students' sense of injustice, and the classroom discord which results pleases the teacher, because he is interested in encouraging the students to explore together their reactions to the subject at hand. As the teacher says, "the group interaction is the thing."[2]

In the second classroom the students are using what is known as the case study approach to the same topic. They are given 12 cases regarding the problem of black voting rights, and each case is composed of original documents, such as statutes and constitutional provisions and amendments. The students work in groups, study the cases, and then report and discuss their findings with the entire class. The students are studying history by behaving as historians, and the teacher believes that this method is more conducive to learning than is individual confrontation with materials.

One group uses group inquiry; the second uses historical methodology. A third method used is the traditional teacher lecture followed by student questions. Each method represents a different style of teaching, and each may be as effective as the other. Joyce and Weil find it an error to give one particular method any more credence than another.

> We find it desirable to begin by challenging the idea that there is any such thing as a perfect model and by deprecating the idea that we should limit our personal search for a model of teaching to any single one, however attractive it may seem.[3]

The teaching style that a teacher adopts in a classroom is usually generated by his view about human potentials and limitations. Personal persuasions infuse the works of different educators with their essential significance. Examples include Neill's emphasis of the uniqueness of individual children,[4] Torrance's belief in the world as cooperative and ever-

[1]Bruce Joyce and Marsha Weil, *Models of Teaching* (Englewood Cliffs, N.J.: Prentice-Hall, 1972).

[2]Ibid., p. 2.

[3]Ibid., p.3.

[4]A. S. Neill, *Summerhill* (New York: Hart Publishing, 1960).

changing,[5] and Skinner's orientation toward the significance of environ-ment and conditioning.[6] Whatever theorist the teacher finds himself at-tracted to, his theory inadvertently will have an impact upon his orientation in the classroom. In other words, if a teacher believes basically in the induc-tive teaching model, for example, as espoused by Hilda Taba, then he probably will find himself designing classroom instruction according to the concept of information processing, a concept implied in the inductive teaching model.[7]

The following material presents examples of methodology and stems primarily from the models discussed in the Joyce, Weil volume. We shall identify a few[8] of the more prominent and easily observable models:

1. *Inductive Teaching Model*—Major theorist: Hilda Taba. Taba devel-oped the inductive teaching model in order to stimulate children to think inductively. She presented material to her students in such a way that they gained the groundwork necessary for continued progress. The students first learned tasks; they then began to develop the ability to form concepts and interpret data, and they finally learned to generalize and apply princi-ples. In her book, *Teachers Handbook for Elementary Social Studies*,[9] Taba carefully outlines three principles of the inductive teaching method. 1. The inductive method encourages teachers to ask questions constantly, thereby stimulating students to develop concepts and venture opinions. The teacher might ask, "What did you see?," "What did you hear?," "What belongs together?," "How would you term these groups?" By eliciting re-sponses which list, group, label or categorize, the teacher helps children to concretize their concepts. 2. Questions which stimulate interpretation of data might resemble the following, "What did you notice?," "Why did this happen?," "What does this mean?," "What would you conclude?." 3. Final-ly, in the application of principle idea, the following could be used as mod-els for eliciting responses, "What would happen if . . . ?," "Why do you think this would happen?" or "What would it take for such-and-such to be generally true or probably true?."

2. *The Non-Directive Teaching Model*—Major theorist: Carl Rogers. One of the tenets of Rogerian psychology—that individuals are able to direct their own lives constructively and should be respected for and encouraged in their attempts to overcome personal difficulties[10]—has been adopted by many teachers as a basic methodology. Use of this teaching method results in little external structure, because the assumption is that the purposes and structure for learning should flow from students.

---

[5]Paul Torrance, *Guiding Creative Talent* (Englewood Cliffs, N.J.: Prentice-Hall, 1962).

[6]B. F. Skinner, *The Technology of Teaching* (New York: Appleton-Century-Crofts, 1968).

[7]See Hilda Taba, *Curriculum Development: Theory and Practice* (New York: Harcourt Brace Jovanovich, 1962).

[8]On pp. 11–13 the authors identify 16 models of teaching, the major theorists, their orien-tations, and the goals which are applicable.

[9]Hilda Taba, *Teachers Handbook for Elementary Social Studies* (Reading, Mass.: Addison-Wes-ley, 1967).

[10]Carl R. Rogers, *Client-Centered Therapy* (Boston: Houghton Mifflin, 1951).

3. *Operant Conditioning Model*—Major theorist: B. F. Skinner. The general orientation here is behavior modification; the theory would be operant conditioning. The theoretical background refers to the process of increasing the probability of occurrence of existing or new behavior in an individual by means of reinforcement. The most extensive application of operant conditioning to learning is the use of programmed instruction. Indeed there is often very little verbal response from the instructor except to reinforce the students positively. Reinforcement generally comes in the form of teacher approval; the student is thereby made aware that he has performed well and is stimulated to seek again this approval that he has performed well. Often grades are the only reinforcement needed. The objective of this method is to systematically disclose and teach the facts of a particular subject.

Generally teachers will find themselves—either in their pre-service or in their in-service work—consciously impressed with one or another methodology that will direct their teaching style. It should be noted, however, that choosing or adopting a particular methodology—however significant this may be—is only part of the problem of teaching. A teacher's unconscious reaction to events in the classroom, personal contact with students, even mannerisms, are all integral parts of the teaching process. Personal orientation will affect not only the adoption of a methodology but, to a significant extent, the entire relationship between teacher and student.

Max Steele

The cat and the coffee drinkers

"I'm not pleased with the way you're drinking coffee. . . . Coffee is a beverage to be enjoyed for its flavor. It is not a food to be enriched with milk and sugar. Only certain types of people try to gain nourishment from it. In general, they are the ones, I suspect, who show their emotions in public."

I sometimes wonder if the generation of mothers who from 1910 to 1940 sent their five-year-olds to the kindergarten of Miss Effie Barr had much of an idea what their children were learning in her one-room

"The Cat and the Coffee Drinkers" (pp. 1-15) from Where She Brushed Her Hair *by Max Steele. Copyright © 1963 by Henry Maxwell Steele. Originally appeared in* The New Yorker *and reprinted by permission of Harper & Row, Publishers, Inc.*

schoolhouse. Even though in 1930 the Southern town in which she lived was no longer small, and even though she was already in her seventies, Miss Effie knew all of the children in her school a year, and often longer, before they appeared before her for lessons. My mother, properly gloved and chapeaued, began taking me to call on her when I was four.

Her house was a good place to visit. It was large and gray, and was set well back from the same street that I lived on. It was the last "white" house before the Negro part of town, and the first Negro houses had been, up until the depression, part of the Barr properties. There were mossy brick steps leading from a hitching post up to a gravel walk that curved between overgrown boxwoods to a low porch with twelve slender columns. There, in the summer, in the shade of water oaks, Miss Effie, dressed in black, would be sitting, knitting or embroidering, while her big gray cat sat at, and sometimes on, her feet. Slow, uncertain music would be coming through open windows from the music room, where her older sister, Miss Hattie, gave piano lessons.

Miss Effie never seemed to watch a child on such visits, or offer him anything like cookies or lemonade, or say anything to endear herself to a youngster. Instead, she would talk lady talk with the mother and, hardly pausing, say to the child, "You can pull up the wild onions on the lawn if you've nothing better to do." There was no suggestion in her voice that it was a game or that there would be a reward. She simply stated what could be done if one took a notion. Usually a child did.

There was no nonsense about Miss Effie. One morning in late September, my mother and I were standing with eleven other mothers and children on the porch. Miss Effie looked everyone over carefully from where she stood with one hand on the screen door. She checked a list in the other hand against the young faces on the porch, to be sure that these were the children she had chosen from the

forty or more who had visited her in the summer. Apparently satisfied, or at least reconciled to another year of supplementing her income (for no Southern lady of her generation "worked"), she opened the door wide and said, in her indifferent tone, "Children inside." When one mother tried to lead her reluctant son into the dark parlor, Miss Effie said, "Mothers outside."

When the children were all inside and the mothers outside, Miss Effie latched the screen, thanked the mothers for bringing the children, and reminded them that classes began at eight-thirty and ended at noon. The tuition, two dollars a week, would be acceptable each Friday, and each child, as part of his training should be given the responsibility of delivering the money in an envelope bearing the parent's signature. She thanked the mothers again in such a way that there was nothing for them to do except wander together in a group down the gravel walk.

Miss Effie then turned to us, who were standing somewhat closer together than was necessary, in the center of the dark parlor, and said, "Since this is your first day, I want to show you everything. Then you won't be wondering about things while you should be listening."

She made us look at the Oriental carpet, the grandfather's clock, the bookcases of leatherbound volumes, the shelves on which were collections of rocks, shells, birds' nests, and petrified wood. She offered to let us touch, just this once, any of these things.

She would not let us into the music room, which was then empty, but indicated through the doorway the imported grand piano, the red plush seat where Miss Hattie sat during lessons, the music racks, the ferns, and the window seats, which she said were full of sheet music. "You're never to go in there," she said. "I don't go in there myself."

Next, she showed us the dining room, the den, and the hallway, and at the foot of the stairs she said, "We're going upstairs, and then you'll never go up there again." Barbara Ware, one of three girls in our class, began to whimper. "Don't worry," Miss Effie said, "you'll come back down. But there'll be no reason to go up again. I want you to see everything, so you won't have to ask personal questions, which would certainly be the height of impoliteness, wouldn't it? I mean, if you started wanting to know, without my telling you, where I sleep and which window is Miss Hattie's, I'd think you were rude, wouldn't I? I'll show you everything, so you won't be tempted to ask personal questions."

We went upstairs, and she showed us her room and where she kept her shoes (in the steps leading up to the side of her fourposter bed), where she hung her clothes (in two large armoires) and kept her hatbox (in a teakwood sea chest). The cat, she said, slept on the sea chest if he happened to be home at night.

She then knocked on the door of Miss Hattie's room and asked her sister, who was inside, if we might look in. Miss Hattie agreed to a short visit. After that, Miss Effie showed us the upstairs bathroom and explained that the bathtub faucet dripped all night and that was why a towel was kept under it.

Downstairs again, Miss Effie let us see the "new" kitchen, which was built in 1900, and the back porch, which had been screened in only four years before, and which had a small door through which the cat could come and go as he liked. We were as fascinated by everything as we would have been if we had never seen a house before.

"Now, out the back door. All of you." She made us all stand on the ground, off the steps, while she lowered herself, step by step, with the aid of a cane that she kept on a nail by the door. "Now you've seen my house and you won't see it again. Unless I give your mothers fruitcake and coffee at Christmas. And I don't think I will. Not this year. Do you ever get tired of fruitcake and coffee at Christmas?"

We said we did, since it was clear that she did.

"Over there is the barn, and we'll see it some other time, and that is the greenhouse, and we'll be seeing it often. And here is the classroom, where we'll be." She pointed with her cane to a square brick building that before the Civil War had been the kitchen. The door was open.

She shepherded us along a brick walk with her cane, not allowing any of us near enough to her to topple her over. At the door, she said, "Go on in."

We crowded in, and when we were all through the door she summoned us back out. "Now, which of you are boys?" The nine boys raised their hands, following her lead. "And which girls?" The three girls had already separated themselves from the boys, and nodded together. "All right, then, young gentlemen," she said, regarding us, "let's let the young ladies enter first. Or I may think you're all young ladies."

The girls, looking timid and pleased, entered. We started in after them.

"Wait just a minute, young gentlemen," she said. "Haven't you forgotten something?" We looked about for another girl.

"Me!" she announced. "You've forgotten me!" She passed through our huddle, separating us with her stick, and marched into the kitchen.

Inside, as well as out, the kitchen was mainly of brick. The walls and floor were brick, and the hearth and the huge chimney, except for a closet-cupboard on each side of it, were brick. The ceiling, however, was of beams and broad boards, and the windows were of wavy glass in casements that opened out like shutters. There were three large wooden tables, and at each table four chairs.

Again she had to show us everything. The fireplace would be used in only the coldest weather, she said. At other times, an iron stove at one side of the room would be used. A captain's chair, between the fireplace and the stove, was her own and not to be touched by us. A sewing table, overflowing with yarn and knitting needles, was for her own use, and not for ours. One cupboard, the one near her, held dishes. She opened its door. She would let us see in the other cupboard later. The tables and chairs and, at the far end of the room, some pegs for coats were all ours, to do with as we pleased. It was, she explained, our schoolroom, and therefore, since we were young ladies and gentlemen, she was sure we would keep it clean.

As a matter of fact, she saw no reason why we should not begin with the first lesson: Sweeping and Dusting. She opened the other cupboard and showed us a mop, a bucket, some rags and brushes, and three brooms. We were not divided into teams; we were not given certain areas to see who could sweep his area cleanest; we were simply told that young ladies should naturally be able to sweep and that young gentlemen at some times in their lives would certainly be expected to sweep a room clean.

The instruction was simple: "You get a good grip on the handle and set to." She handed out the three brooms and started us boys sweeping from the fireplace toward the front door. She made simple corrections: "You'll raise a dust, flirting the broom upward. Keep it near the floor." "Hold lower on the handle. You'll get more dirt." "Don't bend over. You'll be tired before the floor is clean."

When we swept, Miss Effie made a big red enamel coffeepot of coffee on a small alcohol stove. Since the room had not been swept, she admitted, all summer, there was a respectable pile of brick dust, sand, and sweepings near the door by the time she said, "We'll have lunch now." It was already ten o'clock. "After lunch, I'll teach you how to take up trash and to dust. Everyone needs to know that."

"Lunch," it happened, was half a mug of coffee each. One spoon of sugar, she said, was sufficient if we felt it necessary to use sugar at all (she didn't); there was milk for those who could not or would not (she spoke as though using milk were a defect of character) take their coffee black. I daresay not any of us had ever had coffee before, and Robert Barnes said he hadn't. "Good!" Miss Effie said. "So you have learned something today."

Miriam Wells, however, said, on reflection, that her parents wouldn't approve of her drinking coffee. "Very well," Miss Effie said. "Don't drink it. And the next time I offer you any, if I ever do, simply say 'No, thank you, Ma'am.'" (The next day, Miriam Wells was drinking it along with the rest of us.) "Let's get this clear right this minute—your parents don't need to know what you do when you're under my instruction."

Her firm words gave us a warm feeling, and from that moment on the schoolroom became a special, safe, and rather secret place.

That day, we learned, further, how to rinse out mugs and place them in a pan to be boiled later, how to take up trash, and how to dust. At noon, we were taught the right way to put on our sweaters or coats, how to approach, one at a time, our teacher (or any lady we should happen to be visiting) and say "Thank you" (for the coffee or whatever we had been served), and how to say goodbye and turn and leave the room without running or laughing. It wasn't as easy as you may think.

The next morning, Robert Barnes was waiting on his steps when I walked by his house. Since he and I lived nearer to the Barrs' than any of the other children, we were the first to arrive at the schoolhouse.

Miss Effie sat in her captain's chair brushing the cat, which lay on a tall stool in front of her. We en-tered without speaking. Without looking up, Miss Effie said, "Now, young gentlemen, let's try that again—outside. Take off your caps before you step through the door, and say 'Good morning, Ma'am' as you come through the door. Smile if you feel like it. Don't if you don't." She herself did not smile as we went out and re-entered in the manner she suggested. However, this time she looked directly at us when she returned our "Good mornings." Later, each child who entered the room in what she felt to be a rude way was sent out to try again.

Strangely enough, she did not smile at anyone, and looking back I see now that part of her efficiency was that she treated each child as an adult and each lesson as though it were a serious task. Even though there were occasional crying scenes or temper tantrums among us, she herself never lost her firm, rational approach. Sitting in her captain's chair, dressed in black from neck to toe, except for a cameo, small gold loop earrings, and a gold opal ring on her right hand, she was usually as solemn and considerate as a judge on his bench. It is strange that I can remember her calm expression and the dignity of her bearing, but not one feature of her angular face.

That morning, Miss Effie waited until all of us were properly in before addressing us as a class. "This is Mr. Thomas," she said of the cat on the stool. "He's a no-good cat and he doesn't like children, so leave him alone. I'd have nothing to do with him myself except that he happens to belong to me because his mother and grandmother belonged to me. They were no good, either.

But since he does belong to me and since he is here, we may as well talk about cats."

She showed us how to brush a cat, how he liked to be rubbed under his neck, how he didn't like his ears or whiskers touched, how his ears turned to pick up sounds, how he stretched and shut his paw pads when he was tickled on the stomach or feet, and how he twitched his tail when annoyed. "Mr. Thomas is a fighter," she said, and let us look at the scars from a dozen or more fights, "and he's getting too old to fight, but he hasn't got sense enough to know that."

She looked at us where we stood in more or less a large circle around her. "Now, let's see, I don't know your names. I know your mothers, but not your names." She would, she said, indicate us one at a time and we were to give our names in clear, loud voices while looking her right in the eye. Then we were to choose a chair at one of the three tables. "I hate the way most people become shy when they say their names. Be proud of it and speak up."

When the young ladies had finished giving their names, she said they did admirably well; they chose to sit at the same table. One or two boys shouted their names in a silly fashion and had to repeat. One or two looked away, to decide on a chair or to watch the cat, they claimed, and so had to repeat. I did not speak loud enough and had to say my name three times. One lad refused to say his name a second time, and that day and the next she called him Mr. No-Name. The third day afterward, he did not appear, nor the fourth nor fifth, and the next week a new boy from the waiting list gave his name in a perfect fashion and took Mr. No-Name's place.

We learned about cats and names the second day, then. The following day, Barbara Ware and Robert Barnes distinguished themselves by claiming to like their coffee black with no sugar, just the way Miss Effie was convinced it should be drunk.

At the end of the second week, we reviewed what we had learned by sweeping and dusting the room again. And each day we practiced coming in and leaving properly and saying our name in a way that sounded as though we were proud of it and of ourselves—which by then we were.

The third week, putting down the cat brush and shooing Mr. Thomas off the stool, Miss Effie said that she, too, was proud of the way we identified ourselves with eyes level and unblinking. "But now," she said, "I want to teach you to give a name that is not your own. Without any shiftiness."

She sat with both thin hands clasping the arms of her chair and gave a short lecture. Not everyone, she said, was entitled to know your name. Some people of a certain sort would ask when it was none of their business. It would be unnecessarily rude to tell them so. But we could simply tell such people a name that had nothing whatever to do with our own. She did not mention kidnapings, but talked rather about ruthless salesmen, strangers on buses and trains, and tramps and beggars wandering through the neighborhood.

For the purpose of practice, all of the young ladies would learn to give, in a courteous, convincing manner, the name "Polly Livingstone." The boys would be, when asked, "William Johnson" (a name I can still give with much more conviction than my own). That day and the next, each of us gave his real name before the coffee break, and after coffee his false name. We liked the exercises wherein we went up to her, shook her hand if she offered it, and gave our false names, confronting, without staring, her solemn gaze with ours. If we smiled, or twisted, we had to stand by the fireplace until we could display more poise.

At the end of the first month, Miss Effie said that she was fairly well pleased with our progress. "I have taught you, thus far, mainly about rooms. Most people spend most of their lives in rooms, and now you know about them." She mentioned some of the things we had learned. "What else have we learned about rooms?" she then asked, letting Mr. Thomas out the window onto the sunny ledge where he liked to sit.

"How to drink coffee," Miriam Wells said, rather proudly.

"No," Miss Effie said, "that has to do with another series, which includes how to accept things and how to get rid of things you don't want— fat meat, bones, seeds, pits, peelings, and [she added under her breath] parents." She paused for a moment and looked pleased, as though she might wink or smile, but her angular face did not change its expression very much. "No. Besides, I'm not pleased with the way you're drinking coffee." She then said for the first time a speech that she repeated so often that by the end of the year we sometimes shout-

ed it in our play on the way home. "Coffee is a beverage to be enjoyed for its flavor. It is not a food to be enriched with milk and sugar. Only certain types of people try to gain nourishment from it. In general, they are the ones, I suspect, who show their emotions in public." (We had, I'm sure, no idea what the speech meant.) She expected all of us by June, possibly by Christmas, to be drinking it black. "Is there anything else we need to know about rooms?" she asked.

"How to build them," Phillip Pike said.

"That," Miss Effie said, "you can't learn from me. Unfortunately. I wish I knew." She looked thoughtfully out the window to the ledge on which Mr. Thomas was grooming himself. "Windows!" she said. "How to clean windows."

Again the cupboard was opened, and by noon the next day we knew how to clean windows, inside and out, and how to adjust all the shades in a room to the same level.

When it turned cold in November, cold enough for the stove but not the fireplace, we settled down to the real work that gave Miss Effie's kindergarten its reputation. Reading. Miss Effie liked to read, and it was well known in the town and especially among the public-school teachers that the two or three hundred children she had taught had grown up reading everything they could find. She assured us that even though we were only five years old, we would be reading better than the third-grade schoolchildren by the end of the year.

Each morning, the stove was already hot when we arrived. She would brush Thomas awhile, and then, when we were all in our places and warm, she would hand out our reading books, which we opened every day to the first page and laid flat before us on the tables. While we looked at the first page, she began heating the big red enamel pot of coffee, and also, because we now needed nourishment to keep warm, a black iron pot of oatmeal. Then Miss Effie would sit down, allow Thomas to jump into her lap, and begin reading, always from the first page, in an excited tone. She would read to the point exactly where we had finished the day before, so that from necessity she read faster each day, while we turned our pages, which we knew by heart, when we saw her ready to turn hers.

Then, one after another, we went up to her and sat on Mr. Thomas's stool by the stove and read aloud to her while those at the tables either listened or read or played with architectural blocks. The child on the stool was rewarded at the end of each sentence with two spoonfuls of oatmeal if he read well, one if not so well. Since we each read twice, once before coffee and once after, we did not really get hungry before we left the school at noon. Of course, those who read fast and well ate more oatmeal than the others.

In addition to the reading lessons, which were the most important part of the day, we learned to take money and shopping lists to Mr. Zenacher's grocery store, to pay for groceries, and to bring them back with the change. Usually two or three of us went together to the store, which was in the next block. At the same time, three or four others might be learning to paint flowerpots or to catch frying-size chickens in the chicken yard back of the barn.

On sunny days that winter, we would all go out to the greenhouse for an hour and learn to reset ferns and to start bulbs on wet beds of rock. In March, we learned how to rake Miss Effie's tennis court, to fill in any holes with powdery sand, and to line up and tie strings properly so that later a Negro yardman could mark the lines on the court with lime. The tennis court was for rent to high-school girls and boys in the afternoons during the spring and summer.

By Easter time, we were all proficient sweepers, dusters, shoppers, bulb-setters, readers, and black-coffee drinkers. Miss Effie herself, now that spring was in the air, hated to sit all morning by the stove, where we'd been all winter. Usually, after an hour or so of reading, all aloud and at once, we would follow her into the yard and prune the "first-breath-of-spring," the jessamine, the yellow bells, and the peach and pear trees. We kept the branches we cut off and we stuck them in buckets of water in the greenhouse. Miss Effie printed a sign that said "Flowers for Sale," and we helped her tie it to a tree near the sidewalk. In addition to the flowering branches that we had forced, she sold ferns and the jonquils that we had set and that were now in bud.

All in all, spring was a busy time. And I remember only one other thing we learned. One warm May morning, we arrived to find Mr. Thomas, badly torn about the ears, his eyes shut, his breathing noisy, on a folded piece of carpet near the open door of the schoolhouse. We wanted to pet him and talk to him, but Miss Effie, regarding him constantly, said no, that he had obviously been not only a bad cat but a foolish one. She believed he had been hit by a car while running from some dogs, and that that was how the dogs got to him. (She and Miss Hattie had heard the fight during the night.) At any rate, he had managed to crawl under the steps, where the dogs couldn't get to him any more. At dawn she had come down and thrown hot water on the dogs and rescued him.

As soon as a Negro boy from her cousin's office arrived (her cousin was a doctor), she was going to teach us how to put a cat to sleep, she said.

We pointed out that he already seemed to be asleep.

"But," she explained, not taking her eyes from the cat, "we are going to put him to sleep so that he won't wake up."

"You're going to kill him?" Robert Barnes said.

"You could say that."

We were all greatly disturbed when we understood that this was the last we would see of Mr. Thomas. But Miss Effie had no sympathy, apparently, for the cat or for us. "He is suffering, and even if he is a no-good cat, he shouldn't suffer." When Barbara Ware began to whimper, Miss Effie said, "Animals are not people." Her tone was severe enough to stop Barbara from crying.

After the Negro boy had arrived with the package and left, Miss Effie stopped her reading, and, going to one of the cupboards, she got out a canvas bag with a drawstring top. "Now, if you young ladies will follow us, I'll ask the young gentlemen to bring Mr. Thomas."

We all rushed to be the ones to lift the piece of carpet and bear Mr. Thomas after her, through her garden, to the tool shed.

"Just wrap the carpet around him. Tight. Head and all," she instructed when we reached the tool shed.

After we had him wrapped securely, Miss Effie opened the package and read the label: "Chloroform." She explained to us the properties of the chemical while we rolled the cat tighter and stuck him, tail first, into the canvas bag. Miss Effie asked us to stand back and hold our breath. She then soaked a large rag with the liquid and poured the rest directly onto the cat's head and on the carpet. She poked the rag into the rolled carpet so that it hid Mr. Thomas completely. She then drew the drawstring tight and slung the cat, bag and all, into the tool shed. She shut the door and firmly latched it. "That'll cut out the air," she said.

Back in the schoolhouse, we tried to listen as she read, without her usual excited tone, but we were all thinking about Mr. Thomas in the tool shed.

"Well," she finally said, "if you will excuse me a moment, I'll go see if my cat is dead."

We watched from the windows as she walked with her cane through the garden to the tool shed. We could see her open the door and bend over the sack for a long time. At last, she straightened up and locked the door again. She came back with the same unhalting gait and stood for a moment in the sun before the open door of the schoolhouse.

"When I dismiss you, you're to go straight home. And if they want to know why you're home early"—she stopped and studied the ground as though she had lost there her cameo or her words—"tell them the only thing Miss Effie had to teach you today was how to kill a cat."

Without waiting for us to leave, she walked in her usual dignified fashion down the brick walk and up the back steps and into her house, shutting the kitchen door firmly behind her. I know that that was not the last day of school, for I remember helping to spread tablecloths over the reading tables, and I remember helping to serve teacakes to the mothers who came the last day and stood on the tennis court near a table where Miss Hattie was serving coffee. But the final, definite picture I have of Miss Effie is that of her coming through the garden from the tool shed and standing in the doorway a moment to say that she had nothing more to teach us.

discussion

Miss Effie is an unforgettable teacher. She is old and odd, but she possesses two important qualities. She teaches what is relevant, and she teaches with instinctive insight into how children learn best. In addition Miss Effie's communications to her pupils are simple and direct. Miss Effie treats children with the same respect she treats adults.

She understands the natural curiosity of children, and on the first day of school she wisely takes them through her large and mysterious house. No question could have been left in their minds after the thorough examination and explanation she offers. Miss Effie permits the children full reign to examine, peer, and touch. Every detail of her personal existence that might interest a child—from where she keeps her shoes to where she takes a bath—Miss Effie answers and explains. Since the children have no mysteries left to explore, Miss Effie then expects them to be able to learn without the distraction of wondering about their teacher.

Miss Effie gives directions in simple terms. She is sure to give one direction at a time, never overloading the young child. No task, from sweeping and dusting to saying thank you and goodbye, is too simple to learn. We do not condone Miss Effie's separation of the sexes nor her teaching the children to give false names unflinchingly, although the latter certainly adds humor to the story and suggests that all teachers have some pet lessons they deem essential. Miss Effie is remarkably consistent about reviewing past learnings to be sure they are not forgotten.

Without an inkling of B.F. Skinner and operant conditioning, she teaches her children as a disciple of Skinner might. In cold November she surrounds the hungry children with the warm and tantalizing smells of porridge and coffee. She immediately reinforces good reading of each sentence with two spoonfuls of oatmeal instead of one. Those who read fast and well eat a satisfying amount of oatmeal each morning. Arithmetic is learned by shopping and keeping store, both very practical and enjoyable ways to learn.

We may not wish to have Miss Effie reincarnate in our primary classroom today, but teachers today might do well to emulate some aspects of her teaching style.

springboards for inquiry

1. Which aspects of Miss Effie's teaching did you admire and which did you detest?
2. Detail those qualities of a young child you would most like to nurture in the classroom.
3. Research the effects of preschool education.[1]
4. Did Miss Effie believe in play as part of the curriculum? Discuss your views on the relevance of play in the preschool curriculum.[2]

James A. Michener

Who is Virgil T. Fry?

"May I ask you a question?" she said.
"Of course."
"Maybe you won't like it," she replied, hesitating a moment.
I laughed. "Certainly I will. What is it?"
"Why don't you teach the way Mr. Fry did?"

I have never known a man more fascinating than Mr. Virgil T. Fry. His fascination grows daily because I have never met him.

Mr. Fry, you see, was my predecessor in a small Indiana high school. He was a teacher of the social studies, and he was fired for incompetency. I was brought in to take his place.

Dr. Kelwell, the superintendent of schools in Akara, first told me about Virgil T. Fry. "Fry," he said, "was a most impossible man to work with. I hope you will not be like him."

"What was his trouble?" I asked.

"Never anything in on time. Very hard man to work with. Never took

Reprinted by permission from The Clearing House, *October 1941.*

advice," was the reply. Dr. Kelwell paused and leaned back in his chair. He shook his head violently: "Very poor professional spirit." He nodded as if to agree with himself, then repeated, "I hope you won't be like him."

The principal, Mr. Hasbolt, was considerably more blunt.

"You have a great chance here," he said. "Mr. Fry, your predecessor, was a very poor teacher. He antagonized everyone. Constant source of friction. I don't recall when we ever had a teacher here who created more dissension among our faculty. Not only his own department either. Everyone in this building hated that man, I really do believe. I certainly hope you won't make the same mistakes." He wrung my hand vigorously as if to welcome me as a

[1]See J. S. Bissell, "The Cognitive Effects of Preschool Programs for Disadvantaged Children" (Washington, D.C.: National Institute of Child Health and Human Development, 1971). See also G. A. Bogatz and S. Ball, *The Second Year of Sesame Street: A Continuing Evaluation,* vols. 1 and 2 (Princeton: Educational Testing Service, 1971).

[2]A helpful article to respond to this question is Millie Almy, "Spontaneous Play: An Avenue for Intellectual Development," *Child Study* 28, 2 (1966):2–15.

real relief from a most pressing and unpleasant problem.

The head of the social-studies department in which I worked was more like Dr. Kelwell than like Mr. Hasbolt. He merely hinted at Mr. Fry's discrepancies. "Very inadequate scholar. Very unsound. Apt to go off half-cocked," he mused. "In what way?" I asked. "Oh—lots of ways. You know. Crack-pot ideas. Poor tact in expressing them. You have a real opportunity here to do a good job. I certainly hope you won't make Fry's mistakes."

But if the head of my department was indirect, the head of the English department wasn't. "That man!" she sniffed. "He really was a terrible person. I'm not an old maid, and I'm not prudish, but Virgil T. Fry was a most intolerable person. He not only thought he could teach social studies and made a mess of it, but he also tried to tell me how to teach English. In fact, he tried to tell everyone how to do everything."

Miss Kennedy was neither an old maid nor prudish, and she was correct when she intimated that the rest of the staff felt as she did. Mr. Fry had insulted the music department, the science department, and above all the physical-education department.

Tiff Small was head of athletics. He was a fine man with whom I subsequently played a great deal of golf and some tennis. He wouldn't discuss Fry. "That pansy!" and he would sniff his big nose into a wrinkle. "Pretty poor stuff."

Mr. Virgil T. Fry's landlady ultimately became my landlady, too, and she bore out everything the faculty had said about her former boarder: "Never cleaned his room

up. Smoked cigarettes and dropped the ashes. I hope you don't smoke. You don't? Well, I'm certainly glad. But this Mr. Fry, my, he was a hard man to keep house for, I even pity the poor girl that got him."

Remembering Tiff Small's insinuation, I asked my landlady if Fry ever went with girls. "Him? He courted like it was his sole occupation. Finally married a girl from Akara. She was a typist downtown. Had been to the University of Chicago. Very stuck-up girl, but not any better than she had to be, if you want my opinion. Quite a girl, and quite good enough for him."

As the year went on I learned more about Fry. He must have been a most objectionable person, indeed, for the opinion concerning him was unanimous. In a way I was glad, for I profited from his previous sins. Everyone was glad to welcome me into the school system and into the town, for, to put it baldly, I was a most happy relief from Virgil T. Fry.

Apart from his personality he was also a pretty poor teacher. I found one of his roll books once and just for fun distributed his grades along the normal curve. What a mess they were! He had 18% A's where he should have had no more than 8%! His B's were the same. And when I reached the F's, he was following no system at all. One person with a total score of 183 was flunked. The next, with a total score of 179 had received a C! And in the back of his desk I found 247 term papers he had never even opened! I laughed and congratulated myself on being at least more honest than my predecessor, even if I excelled him in no other way.

I was in this frame of mind when

Doris Kelly, the sixteen-year-old daughter of a local doctor, came into my room one evening after school. "May I ask you a question?" she said.

"Of course."

"Maybe you won't like it," she replied, hesitating a moment.

I laughed. "Certainly I will. What is it?"

"Why don't you teach the way Mr. Fry did?"

I was taken aback. "How did he teach?" I asked.

"Oh," was the answer, "he made everything so interesting!"

I swallowed and asked her to elaborate.

"Well, Mr. Fry always taught as if everything he talked about was of utmost importance. You got to love America when you got through a course with Mr. Fry. He always had a joke. He wasn't afraid to skip chapters now and then.

"He could certainly teach you how to write a sentence and a term paper. Much better than the English teachers, only they didn't like it very much. And did you *read books* when Mr. Fry taught you! Ten, maybe, a year, and all in the very kinds of things you liked best. Hitler, strikes, the Constitution, and all about crime. Just anything you wanted to read.

"And class was always so interesting. Not boring." She stopped and looked at me across the desk with a bit of Irish defiance in her eye.

She was a somewhat mature girl and I concluded that she had had a crush on this remarkable Mr. Virgil T. Fry. "Did all the pupils feel that way?" I asked her.

"I know what you're thinking," she said, smiling. "But you're wrong. Everyone liked him. Almost every one of them did. And the reason I came in to see you this evening is that none of us like the way you teach. It's all so very dull!"

I blushed. Everyone had been telling me what a fine job I was doing. I stammered a bit, "Well, Mr. Fry and I teach two different ways."

"Oh, no," she insisted. "It's not that. Mr. Fry really taught. He taught us something every day. I'll bet you ask all the pupils they'll all say the same thing. He was about the only real teacher we had."

I became somewhat provoked and said a very stupid thing. "Then why was he fired?" No answer.

"You did know he was fired, didn't you?"

Doris nodded.

"Why?" I repeated.

Doris laughed. "Jealousy," she said.

I was alarmed. I wondered if the pupils really did dislike my teaching as much as Doris had implied. The next day in a class of which Doris was not a member I tried an experiment.

"Well," I said, "we've now reached the end of the first unit. I wonder if it wouldn't be a good idea to go back to a discussion of the big ideas of this unit?" I paused.

Not much response, so I added: "The way Mr. Fry used to do? Remember?"

Immediately all the pupils sat up and started to pay attention. Most of them smiled. Two of the girls giggled and some of the boys squirmed. They obviously wanted to accept my suggestion. "Tom," I asked, "will you take over?" for I had no idea what Mr. Fry's method was.

Tom nodded vigorously and came to the front of the room.

"All right," he rasped, "who will dare?"

"I will," said a girl. "I believe that Columbus came to the New World more for religious reasons than for commercial reasons."

"Oh!" groaned a group of pupils, snapping their fingers for attention. Tom called on one.

"I think that's very stupid reasoning, Lucille. Spain was only using religion as a mask for imperialism."

Lucille turned in her seat and shot back, "You wouldn't think so if you knew anything about Philip the Second."

And the debate continued until Tom issued his next dare. A pupil accepted and defiantly announced: "I think all that section about Spain's being so poor at colonizing is the malarkey. Everything south of Texas except Brazil is now Spanish. That looks pretty good to me."

I winced at the word "malarkey" and the pupils winced at the idea. The tigers of Anglo-Saxony rose to the defense of the text and the challenging pupil did his best to stand them off.

A few nights later I drove some other pupils to a basketball game in a nearby city. One of the boys observed, as we were coming home: "Class has been much better lately. I sort of like history now."

"How do you mean, better?" I asked.

"Oh, more the way Mr. Fry used to teach."

"Was Mr. Fry such a good teacher?" I asked.

"Oh, boy!" chortled the crowd, all at once. And one continued, "Was he? Boy, he could really teach you. I learned more from him than my big

brother did at the university, in the same course. That's a fact! I had to read more, too, but I certainly liked it."

"I always thought he was rather—well, sissy?" I observed.

"Fry? Oh, no!" the boys replied. "It's true he didn't like the athletic department and used to make some pretty mean cracks about athletes, but we all liked it a lot. No, Mr. Fry was a very good tennis player and could swim like a fish."

The question of reading bothered me. I had always aspired to have my pupils read a great deal, and here they were all telling me that last year they had read and this year they hadn't. I went to see Miss Fisher, the librarian, about it.

"No," she said, "the books aren't going out the way they did last year."

"Could it be that maybe Mr. Fry knew how to use the library better?" I asked.

"Oh, no!" was the laughing reply. "You're twice the teacher Mr. Fry was. All the staff thinks so. He was a terrible person around a library!"

This depressed me, and I sought for an answer outside the school. I went around that night to visit Dr. Kelley, Doris' father.

"The fact is," he said, "you're in a tough spot. Virgil T. Fry was a truly great teacher. You're filling the shoes of a master. I hear the children talking at table and about the house. Fry seems to have been the only teacher who ever really got under their skins and taught them anything."

He paused, then added. "As a matter of fact, the pupils find your teaching rather empty, but I'm glad to say they think it's been picking up recently." He knocked out his pipe and smiled at me.

"Then why was Fry fired?" I asked.

"Difference of opinion, I guess," the doctor replied. "Fry thought education consisted of stirring up and creating. He made himself very unpopular. You see, education is really a complete social venture. I see that from being on the school board. Fry was excellent with pupils but he made a terrible mess of his adult relationships."

"You're also a father," I said. "Don't you think your daughter deserves to have good teachers?"

He lit his pipe again. "Of course, if you want the truth, I'd rather have Doris study under Fry than under you. In the long run she'd learn more." He smiled wryly.

"At the same time, what she learns from you may be better for her in the long run than what she would have learned from Fry."

"May I ask you one question, Doctor?" I inquired. He assented. "Did you concur in Fry's dismissal?"

Dr. Kelly looked at me a long time and drew on his pipe. Then he laughed quietly. "I cut board meeting that night. I knew ahead of time that the problem was scheduled to come up."

"I think I would always cut board meeting," he answered. "Fry was a disruptive force. He was also a very great teacher. I think the two aspects balanced precisely. I would neither hire him nor fire him. I wouldn't fight to keep him in a school and I wouldn't raise a finger to get him out of one." I frowned.

He continued: "The fine aspect of the whole thing is that you, a beginning teacher, don't have to be all Fry or all yourself. You can be both a great teacher and a fine, social individual. It's possible."

Dr. Kelley laughed again as he showed me to the door. "Don't worry about it. And you may be interested to know that your superintendent, Dr. Kelwell, feels just as I do about the whole problem. He stood out till the last minute to keep Fry. Very reluctant to have him go."

I went home badly confused.

As I said before, I have never known a man so fascinating as Mr. Virgil T. Fry. Not a member of his faculty has a good word to say for him and not a pupil in any of his classes has an unkind word to say against him.

discussion

The views about Virgil T. Fry were as many and varied as the people who judged him. Like most strong characters he was either loved or hated. The lineup on Fry seemed to split between his colleagues and his students. His practices made a mockery of the standards other teachers held for the students. He played havoc with the grading system and ignored the term papers he assigned.

The students' views of Fry come as a delightful surprise toward the middle of the story. He stimulated his students to seek knowledge, to think, and to make judgments. He did not consider himself the center of attention in the classroom but encouraged interaction among the students. His style was unique. Because his ideas were not compartmentalized and were therefore unable to fit neatly into the traditional methodology of the social sciences, he impinged on the functioning of every department from physical education to English and science. We can speculate on why he harassed the librarian. As indifferent as he was to the standards of other adults, he probably flaunted her rules and regulations with abandon.

There are not many Virgil T. Frys around, and it is a question that honest educators will have difficulty in answering—can a school system afford to fire an individualist like Virgil T. Fry if most students think he is a good teacher? To what extent should students' opinions influence a school board to hire a teacher whom his colleagues cannot tolerate?

springboards for inquiry

1. How may we account for the disparity of opinion about Virgil T. Fry that existed among the students, the faculty, and administrators of that high school?

2. What traits may Virgil T. Fry have possessed to have given him the charisma that the story implied? Have you ever had a teacher who possessed similar qualities? Describe him.

3. Fry thought "education consisted of stirring up and creating." Compare his notion of education with Alfred N. Whitehead (*The Aims of Education*), John Dewey (any of his volumes), and any modern critic such as Holt, Kozol, Tillich, or Graubard.[1]

4. Would you have voted to fire Virgil T. Fry? Give reasons for your decision.

[1]Refer to any of their works cited in this volume.

the teacher as model

If you tiptoe quietly and stand just outside the door of your little girl's room you will hear her scolding, cajoling, ordering, or teaching just as her teacher did that day. We have never heard of little boys "playing school," but most girls will take their teachers (especially if they are females) as models for the games they play at home. Since play is the child's work, when they model their schoolteachers, they are selecting behaviors which they either admire or fear, and their play is a childish attempt to put their classroom experience together. In a very real sense, modeling the role of teacher is trying out the role in what may be accurately termed a precocious vocational aptitude or selection procedure. At the University of Utah, all elementary education students (98 percent female) write a brief biographical account of their lives up to the point of applying for admission to the program. When the facade of appropriate reasons for wanting to teach is penetrated we frequently read, "I've wanted to teach ever since I was a little girl playing school."

The teacher represents an adult authority figure who is often emulated, sometimes even worshipped. After visiting a child's teacher, one parent was shocked to discover that what he thought were self-generated mannerisms newly developed by his little boy were, in fact, gestures and speech patterns of the boy's teacher. We have known sixth grade girls to imitate the color combinations, lipstick, and nail polish worn by a favorite teacher. In early adolescence hero-worship is good—especially when the hero is a real person, a real teacher who has learned not to get his kicks from adolescent adoration. A teacher whose life is full and satisfying knows he provides a model. He understands the importance of projecting a mature adult image. He does not try to emulate the youth culture with the misguided notion that such action will help him relate to youth. When youths search for models, they do not want to relate to adolescents. They have no lack of adolescents to relate to among their peers. Imagine the shock of those earnestly searching for their becoming identities upon finding that, in fact, some of their teachers are madly scrambling to emulate those they teach. Youth should find in their teachers persons whose behavior beckons to be modeled.

Jay Neugeboren

Luther

Luther arrived at Booker T. Washington Junior High School (Columbus Avenue and 107th Street, Manhattan) in September of 1955, six months before I did. I met him at the end of February, the third week I taught there, when one of the assistant principals asked me to cover the cafeteria during fifth period for a teacher who had to be at a conference. "Good luck with the animals," I remember him saying.

I was on my guard when I entered the cafeteria; perhaps even a trifle scared. The stories I had been hearing in the teachers' lounge had prepared me to expect anything. During the winter months the students were not allowed to leave the lunchroom and the results of keeping them penned in—the fights, the food throwing, the high-pitched incessant chattering in Spanish, the way the Negro and Puerto Rican boys and girls chased each other around the tables—such things did, I had to admit, give the room a zoo-like quality.

The day I was assigned, however, was a Catholic holy day and many of the students were absent. Those who remained filled a little less than half of the large room and though they were noisy it was relatively easy

Reprinted with the permission of Farrar, Straus & Giroux, Inc. from Corky's Brother *by Jay Neugeboren, copyright © 1966, 1969 by Jay Neugeboren.*

"Christ, man," he said, stepping down from my desk and moving to the blackboard. He picked up a piece of chalk and wrote his name, printing it in capital letters. "How come you so tight? Why don't you loosen up? I ain't gonna do nothing. I just want to know about my composition. That's all."

to keep them in order. Luther sat at a table by himself, near the exit to the food line. Occasionally, I noticed, a few boys would come and sit next to him. The third time I patrolled his area, however, his table was empty and he stopped me.

"Hey, man," he said, poking me in the arm to get my attention, "you new here?"

He had a stack of about ten cookies in his other hand and he put one into his mouth as he waited for an answer. When I told him that I was not new, he nodded and looked at me. "You have any trouble yet?"

"No," I said, as sternly as possible. Despite my feelings of sympathy for the students, I knew that if I ever hoped to get anywhere with them I had to appear tough and confident. "No," I repeated, almost, I recall, as if I were challenging him, "I haven't."

Luther cocked his head to one side then and smiled slowly. "You will," he said, and went back to his cookies.

In the teachers' lounge, the first time I told the story, somebody asked if the boy who had stopped me was a little Negro kid, very black, with a slight hunchback. I said he was. The teachers laughed. "That's Luther," one of them said.

"He's batty," said another. "Just leave him be."

I repeated the story endlessly. It was the first anecdote of my teaching experience that excited admiration and some sort of reaction from those I told it to, and this was important to me then. I had no more direct encounters with Luther that term, though I did see him in the halls, between classes. I always smiled at him and he would smile back—or at least I thought he did. I could never be sure. This bothered me, especially the first time it happened. Through my retelling of the story, I realized, he had become so real to me, so much a part of my life that I think I took it for granted that our encounter had assumed equal significance in his life. The possibility that he had not even repeated the story to a single one of his friends disturbed me.

Once or twice during the term I spotted him wandering around the halls while classes were in session, slouching down a corridor, his body pressed against the tile walls. When I asked the other teachers if he was known for cutting classes, they told me again to just leave him be—that the guidance counselor had suggested the teachers let him do what he wanted to. He was harmless, they said, *if* you left him alone. Those teachers who had him in their classes agreed with the guidance counselor. Left alone, he didn't annoy them. When he wanted to, he worked feverishly—and did competent work; but when he didn't want to work he would either sit and stare or just get up, walk out of the room, and wander around the building. He was, they concluded, a mental case.

I returned to Booker T. Washington Junior High School the following September, and Luther turned up in one of my English classes. He had changed. He was no longer small, having grown a good five inches over the summer, and he was no longer quiet. When classwork bored him now, he would stand up and, instead of leaving the room, would begin telling stories. Just like that. He had his favorite topics, too—his cousin Henry who had epilepsy, Willie Mays, what was on sale at the supermarket, the football team he played on, the stories in the latest *Blackhawk* comic book. When he ran out of stories, he would pull *The National Enquirer* out of his back pocket and begin reading from it, always starting with an item in the "Personals" columns that had caught his eye. I never knew what to do. When I would yell at him to sit down and be quiet, he would wave his hand at me impatiently and continue. Moreover, no expression on his face, nothing he ever said, indicated that he thought he was doing anything wrong. An hour after disrupting a class, if I would see him in the corridor, he would give me a big smile and a hello. After a while, of course, I gave up even trying to interrupt him. I listened with the other students—laughing, fascinated, amazed.

I tried to remember some of his stories, but when I retold them they never seemed interesting, and so I purposely gave Luther's class a lot of composition work, trying to make the topics as imaginative as possible—with the hope, of course, that he would use one of them to let loose. But all the topics, he declared, were "stupid" and he refused to write on any of them. Then, when I least expected it, when I assigned the class a "How to—" composition, he handed one in. It was typewritten on a piece of lined notebook paper, single-spaced, beginning at the very top of the page and ending just at the first ruled line. It was titled "How To Steal Some Fruits."

How To Steal Some Fruits, by Luther Go to a fruit store and when the fruitman isn't looking take some fruits. Then run. When the fruitman yells "Hey you stop taking those fruits" run harder. That is how to steal some fruits.

The next day he sat quietly in class. When I looked at him, he looked down at his desk. When I called on him to answer a question, he shrugged and looked away. At three o'clock, however, no more than five seconds after I had returned from escorting my official class downstairs, he bounded into my room, full of life, and propped himself up on the edge of my desk.

"Hey, man," he said. "How'd you like my composition? It was deep, wasn't it?"

"Deep?"

"Deep, swift, *cool*—you know."

"I liked it fine," I said, laughing.

"Ah, don't put me on, man—how *was* it?"

"I liked it," I repeated, my hands clasped in front of me on the desk. "I mean it."

His face lit up. "You mean it? I worked hard on it, Mr. Carter. I swear to God I did." It was the first time, I remember, that he had ever addressed me by my name. He stopped and wiped his mouth. "How'd you like the typing? Pretty good, huh?"

"It was fine."

"Christ, man," he said, stepping down from my desk and moving to the blackboard. He picked up a piece of chalk and wrote his name, printing it in capital letters. "How come you so tight? Why don't you loosen up? I ain't gonna do nothing. I just want to know about my composition. That's all."

I felt I could reach him, talk to him. I wanted to—had wanted to for some time, I realized—but he was right. I was tight, uncomfortable, embarrassed. "Where'd you get a typewriter?" I offered.

He smiled. "Where I get fruits," he replied, then laughed and clapped his hands. I must have appeared shocked, for before I could say anything he was shaking his head back and forth. "Oh man," he said. "You are really deep. I swear. You really are." He climbed onto my desk again. "You mind talking?"

"No," I said.

"Good. Let me ask you something—you married?"

"No," I said. "Do you think I should be married?"

"It beats stealing fruits," he said, and laughed again. His laugh was loud and harsh and at first it annoyed me, but then his body began rocking back and forth as if his comment had set off a chain of jokes that he was telling himself silently, and before I knew it I was laughing with him.

"I really liked the composition," I said. "In fact, I hope you don't mind, but I've already read it to some of the other teachers."

"No shit."

"They thought it was superb."

"It's superb," he said, shaking his head in agreement. "Oh, it's superb, man," he said, getting up again and walking away. His arms and legs moved in different directions and he seemed so loose that when he turned his back to me and I noticed the way his dirty flannel shirt was stretched tightly over his misshapen back, I was surprised—as if I'd noticed it for the first time. He walked around the room, muttering to himself, tapping on desks with his fingertips, and then he headed for the door. "I'm superb," he said. "So I be rolling on my superb way home—"

"Stay," I said.

He threw his arms apart. "You win!" he declared. "I'll stay." He came back to my desk, looked at me directly, then rolled his eyes and smiled. "People been telling stories to you about me?"

"No."

"None?" he questioned, coming closer.

"All right," I said. "Some—"

"That's all right," he said, shrugging it off. He played with the binding of a book that was on my desk. Then he reached across and took my grade book. I snatched it away from him and he laughed again. "Oh, man," he exclaimed. "I am just so restless!—You know what I mean?"

He didn't wait for an answer but started around the room again. The pockets of his pants were stuffed and bulging, the cuffs frayed. The corner of a red and white workman's handkerchief hung out of a back pocket. He stopped in the back of the room, gazed into the glass bookcase, and then turned to me and leaned back. "You said to stay— what you got to say?"

The question was in my mind, and impulsively I asked it: "Just curious—do you remember me from last year?"

"Sure," he said, and turned his back to me again. He looked in the bookcase, whirled around, and walked to the side of the room, opening a window. He leaned out and just as I was about to say something to him about it, he closed it and came back to the front of the room. "Man," he exclaimed, sitting on my desk again. "Were you ever scared that day! If I'd set off a cherry bomb, you'd have gone through the fan." He put his face closer to mine. "Man, you were scared green!"

"Was I scared of you, Luther?" I asked, looking straight into his eyes.

"Me? Nah. Nothing to be scared of." He hopped off the desk and wiped his name off the blackboard with the palm of his hand; then he started laughing to himself. He looked at me, over his shoulder. "Bet I know what you're thinking now," he said.

"Go ahead—"

"You're thinking you'd like to *help* a boy like me. Right? You're getting this big speech ready in your head about—"

"No," I interrupted. "I wasn't."

He eyed me suspiciously. "You sure?"

"I'm sure."

"Not even with compositions? Oh, man, if you'd help me with compositions, before we'd be through with me, I'd be typing like a whiz." He banged on a desk with his palms, and then his fingers danced furiously on the wood as he made clicking noises inside his mouth. "Ding!" he said, swinging the carriage across. "Ain't it fun to type!"

"Okay," I said. "Okay. Maybe I was thinking that I would like to help you."

"I knew it, man," he said to himself. "I just knew it."

"You have a good mind, Luther—much better than you let on."

"I do, I do," he muttered, chuckling. I stood up and went to the closet to get my coat. "Okay. What do I get if I work for you?" he asked.

I shrugged. "Nothing, maybe. I can't promise anything."

"I *like* that, man," he said.

"Could you call me Mr. Carter?" I asked somewhat irritably. "I don't call you, 'Hey, you'—"

"Okay, Mr. Carter," he said. He took my coat sleeve. "Let me help you on with your coat, Mr. Carter."

We walked out of the room and I locked the door. "You ain't a *real* social worker like the others," he commented as we started down the stairs. He held the door open for me. "I do like that."

I nodded.

"Playing it close to the vest again, huh? Tight-mouthed."

"Just thinking," I said.

When we were outside, he asked me what he had to do.

"For what?" I asked.

"To get you to help me to be somebody, to educate myself—all that stuff."

"Do what you want to do," I said. "Though you might start by doing your homework. Then we'll see—"

"I know," he said, cocking his head to one side again. "If I play ball with you, you'll play ball with me. Right? Okay, okay. I know."

Then he was gone, running down the street, his arms spread wide as if he were an airplane, a loud siren-like noise rising and falling from him as he disappeared from view.

The next few months were without doubt the most satisfying to me of any during the eight years I've been a teacher. Luther worked like a fiend. He was bright, learned quickly, and was not really that far behind. He did his homework, he paid attention in class, he studied for tests, and he read books. That was most important. On every book he read I asked him to write a book report: setting, plot, theme, characters, his opinion of the book—and once a week, on Thursday afternoons, we would get together in my room for a discussion. During the remainder of the term he must have gone through at least forty to fifty books. Most of them had to do with sports, airplanes, and insects. For some reason he loved books about insects. All the reports came to me typed, and on some he drew pictures—"illustrations" he called them, which, he claimed, would be a help to me in case I had not read the book.

When we would finish talking about books, I would help him with his other subjects, and his improvement was spectacular. I looked forward to my sessions with him, to his reports, to just seeing him—yet from day to day, from moment to moment, I always expected him to bolt from me, and this pleased me. Every time he came to me for a talk I was truly surprised.

When the term ended, he asked if I would continue to help him. I said I would. He was not programmed for any of my English classes during the spring term, but we kept up with our weekly discussions. As the weather improved, however, he read less and less; I didn't want him to feel that he *had* to come see me every Thursday, and so, about a week before the opening of the baseball season, I told him I thought he had reached the point where he could go it alone. "When you feel like talking, just come knocking," I said. "We don't need a schedule." He seemed relieved, I thought, and I was proud that I had had the sense to release him from any obligation he might have felt.

Then, suddenly, I didn't see him anywhere for three weeks. I asked his homeroom teacher about him and she said she hadn't seen him either; she had sent him a few postcards but had received no reply. That very night—it was almost as if he had been there listening, I thought—he telephoned me at home.

"Is this Mr. Carter? This is Luther here."

"Hi, Luther," I said.

"I looked you up in the telephone book. You mind me calling you at home?"

"No, no. I don't mind."

"Okay," he said, breathing hard. "I just wanted to let you know not to worry about me because I'm not in school. Okay?"

"Sure," I said. "Sure."

"I had some things to take care of—you know?"

"Sure," I said.

"Man, you *know* you're itching to ask me *what?*" He laughed. "You are deep. I'll be back Monday."

That was all. On Monday, as he'd promised, he returned to school and came to visit me in my room at three o'clock. We talked for a while about the way the pennant race was going, and then he said, "Okay, let's cut the jazz, man. I got something to say to you." He seemed very intense about it and I told him that I was listening carefully. He pointed a finger at me. "Now, we stopped our sessions, right?"

"Right," I said.

"And the day after we stopped, I began to play the hook for three straight weeks, right?"

"Right."

"Okay. Now you can tell me it ain't so, but I'll bet you'll be thinking it was your fault. It ain't. If you want the truth, I ain't done a stick of work all term for *any* teacher—so don't go thinking that I stopped being a good student cause we stopped our meetings." He let out a long breath.

"I'm glad you told me," I said.

"Shit, man," he said, getting up and going to the door. "Don't *say* anything, huh? Why you got to *say* something all the time?" He came toward me. "*Why?*" He was almost screaming and I slid my chair back from the desk. He shook his head frantically. "Why, man?" he said. He reached into his side pocket and I started to stand up. Abruptly, he broke into laughter. "Oh man, you are deep! You are just so deep!" He clapped his hands and laughed at me some more. "Ra-ta-tat-tat!" he said as he banged on a desk. "You're real sweet, man! Just so sweet! Ra-ta-tat-tat! Comin' down the street!" He sat down in one of the seats. "But don't you worry none. I got seven liberry cards now and books growing out the ceiling. I got a liberry card for Luther King and one for Luther Queen and one for Luther Prince and one for Luther Jones and one for Luther Smith and one for Luther Mays and one for

Luther B. Carter." He banged on the top of the desk with his fist, then drummed with his fingers again. "But don't you worry none—ra-ta-tat-tat—just don't you worry—"

"I'm not," I said.

"That's all," he said, and dashed out of the room.

He attended classes regularly for about two weeks and then disappeared again for a week. He returned for a few days, stayed away, returned. The pattern continued. In the halls when we saw each other he would always smile and ask if I was worrying and I would tell him I wasn't. Once or twice, when he was absent, he telephoned me at home and asked me what was new at school. He got a big charge out of this. Then another time, I remember, he came riding through the schoolyard on a bicycle during sixth period, when I was on patrol. "Don't report me, man!" he yelled, and rode right back out, waving and shouting something in Spanish that made everybody laugh.

Near the end of May, the assistant principal in charge of the eighth grade called me into his office. He knew I was friendly with Luther, he said, and he thought that I might talk to the boy. For the past six or seven months, he told me, Luther had been in and out of juvenile court. "Petty thefts," the assistant principal explained. I wasn't surprised; Luther had hinted at this many times. I'd never pressed him about it, however, not wanting to destroy our relationship by lecturing him. The assistant principal said he didn't care whether I said anything to Luther or not. In fact, he added, he would have been just as happy to get rid of him—but before he was shipped off to a 600 school or put away somewhere else, he wanted to give me an opportunity to do what I could. More for me, he said, than for Luther.

About a week after this, on a Friday, Luther telephoned me.

"How've you been?" I asked.

"Superb, man," he said. "Hey, listen—we ain't been seeing much of each other lately, have we?"

"No—"

"No. Okay. Listen—I got two tickets to see the Giants play tomorrow. You want to come?" I didn't answer immediately. "Come on—yes or no—tickets are going fast—"

"I'd like to," I said. "Yes. Only—only I was wondering where you got the money for the tickets." I breathed out, glad I had said it.

Luther just laughed. "Oh man, you're not gonna be like that, are you? You been listening to too many stories again. That judge from the court must of been gassing with you. Tell you what—you come to the game and I'll tell you where I got the tickets. A deal?"

"A deal."

"Meet you in front of the school at eleven o'clock—I like to get there early to see Willie go through batting practice. Batting practice—that's more fun than the game sometimes. You know!"

He was waiting for me when I got there a few minutes before eleven the following day. "Let's go," he said, flourishing the tickets. "But don't ask me now, man—let's enjoy the game first. Okay?"

I did enjoy the game. The Giants were playing the Cardinals and to Luther's delight Willie Mays had one of his better days, going three-for-four at bat, and making several brilliant plays in the field. For most of the game I was truly relaxed.

Along about the eighth inning, however, I began to think about the question again—to wonder when would be the best time to ask it. Luther, it seemed, had forgotten all about it. The Giants were winning 5–2.

"Oh man," he said. "If only that Musial don't do something, we're home free. Look at Willie!" he exclaimed. "Ain't he the greatest that ever lived. He is just so graceful! You know? How you like to see a team of Willie Mayses out there? Wow!" Wes Westrum, the Giant catcher, grounded out, short to first, and the eighth inning was over. "One to go, one to go," Luther said. Then he jabbed me in the arm with his finger. "Hey, listen—I been thinking. Instead of an All-Star game every year between the leagues, what they ought to do one year is have the white guys against our guys. What you think?"

I shrugged. "I don't know," I said.

"Sure," he said. "Listen—we got Willie in center. Then we put Aaron in right and Doby in left. He's got the raw power. Some outfield, huh? Then we got Campy catching and Newcombe pitching. You can't beat that. That Newcombe—he's a mean son-of-a-bitch, but he throws. Okay. I been thinking about this a long time—" He used his fingers to enumerate. He was excited, happy. "At first base we put Luke Easter, at second Junior Gilliam, at short Ernie Banks, and at third base we bring in old Jackie Robinson, just to give the team a little class—you know what I mean? Man, what a line-up! Who could you match it with?"

When I said I didn't know, Luther eyed me suspiciously. "C'mon—Musial, Mantle, Williams,

Spahn—you name 'em and I'll match 'em man for man, your guys against ours." He stopped and cheered as a Cardinal popped out to Whitey Lockman at first. "What's the matter—don't you like the idea? Ha! Face it, man, we'd wipe up the field with you. Swish! Swish!" He laughed and slapped me on the knee. "Hey, I know what's bugging you, I bet—" He leaned toward me, cupping his hand over his mouth, and whispered in my ear. "Tell the truth now, would you have ever offered to help me if I wasn't colored?"

"Would I—?" I stopped. "Sure," I said. "Of course I would. Of course—"

Luther smiled, triumphantly, dubiously.

"Look," I said. "As long as we're asking questions, let me ask you something."

"About the tickets, right?"

"No," I said. "Forget the tickets. No long lectures, either. Just a question. Just one: how come you steal?"

"Oh man," he said, laughing. "That's an easy one! Because I'm not getting what I want and when you don't get what you want, man, you got to take. Don't you know that?"

I stared at him, not sure I had heard right. He winked at me. "Enjoy the ball game, man! Say hey, Willie!" he shouted as Mays caught a fly ball, bread-basket style, for the second out. "Ain't he the sweetest!"

A minute later the game was over and the players were racing across the field toward the clubhouse in center field, trying to escape the fans who scrambled after them. "They won't get Willie," Luther said. "He's too swift, too swift."

When we were outside, I thanked

Luther and told him how much I'd enjoyed the game. "How about a Coke or something?" I offered.

"Nah," he said. "I got things to do." He extended his hand quickly and I shook it, the first time we had ever done that. "Okay. You go get spiffed up and get a wife. Time you were married." He tossed his head back and laughed. "Ain't you married yet? No, no. *Smile,* man—how you gonna get a wife, never smiling." He started away, through the crowd. "Stay loose," he called back. "Don't steal no fruits."

I never questioned him again about stealing, but even if I'd wanted to, I wouldn't have had much opportunity. He didn't come to see me very often the rest of that year. When he returned to school in September of 1958 for his last year of junior high school, he had grown again. But not up. He never did go higher than the five-five or five-six he had reached by that time. He had taken up weightlifting over the summer, however, and his chest, his neck, his arms—they had all broadened incredibly. Instead of the dirty cotton and flannel shirts he had worn the two previous years, he now walked through the halls in laundry-white T-shirts, the sleeves rolled up to the shoulder, his powerful muscles exposed. There were always a half-dozen Negro boys following him around and they all dressed the way he did—white T-shirts, black chino pants, leather wrist straps, and—hanging from their necks on pieces of string— miniature black skulls.

The guidance counselor for the ninth grade came to me one day early in the term and asked me if I could give him any evidence against Luther. He claimed that Luther and his gang were going around the school, beating and torturing those students who refused to "loan" them money. All of the students, he said, were afraid to name Luther. "The kid's a born sadist," he added. I told him I didn't know anything.

The term progressed and the stories and rumors increased. I was told that the police in Luther's neighborhood were convinced that he and his gang were responsible for a series of muggings. I tried not to believe it, but Luther all but gave me conclusive proof one afternoon right before Christmas. He came into my room at three o'clock, alone, and said he had something for me. He said he trusted me not to tell anybody about it or show it to anyone. I said I wouldn't.

"Okay, man—here it is—" His eyes leapt around the room, frenzied, delirious. He took a little card from his wallet. "You might need this sometime—but don't ask me no questions. Ha! And don't you worry none. I'm doing okay. Expanding all the time. Don't you worry." I took the card from him. "See you now, Mr. Carter. See you, see you."

He left and I looked at the card. Across the top was printed THE BLACK AVENGERS, and below it was written: "Don't touch this white man. He's okay." It was signed by Luther and under his name he had drawn a skull and crossbones. I put the card in my wallet.

In January, to no one's great surprise, Luther was sent away to reform school in upstate New York. I was never exactly clear about the precise event that had led to it—the policeman assigned to our school said it had to do with brutally beating an old man; Luther's friends said it had to do with getting caught in a gang war. They claimed the fight was clean but that the cops had framed Luther. There was nothing in the papers. Luther had not contacted me, and I did not find out about it all until he'd already been shipped off.

I received a postcard from him that summer. It was brief.

> I hate it here. I can't say anymore or they'll beat shit out of me. I hate it. I'm reading some. I'll visit you when I get out and we'll have a session.

I answered the card with a letter. I told him I was sorry about where he was and that I'd be glad to talk to him whenever he wanted. I gave him some news of the school and included some current baseball clippings. I asked him if there was anything he needed and if there was anybody in his family he wanted me to get in touch with. I told him that in return for the time he'd taken me to the baseball game I had ordered a subscription to *Sport* magazine for him.

He replied with another postcard.

> Visiting day this summer is August 21. I'd like for you to come.

When I arrived, he seemed glad to see me, but I remember that he was more polite than he had ever been before—and more subdued. I wondered, at the time, if they were giving him tranquillizers. I was only allowed an hour with him and we spent most of that time just walking around the grounds—the school was a work-farm reformatory—not saying anything.

The visit, I could tell, was a disappointment to him. I don't know what he expected of me, but whatever it was, I didn't provide it. I wrote him a letter when I got home, telling him I had enjoyed seeing him and that I'd be glad to come again if he wanted me to. He didn't answer it, and I heard no more from him for a year and a half.

Then one day in the spring of 1961—just about the time of the Bay of Pigs invasion of Cuba, I remember—he popped into my room at school. He looked horrible. His face was unshaven, his clothes were filthy and ragged, his eyes were glazed. Underneath his clothes, his body had become flabby and he bent over noticeably when he walked. At first I didn't recognize him.

When I did, I was so glad to see him I didn't know what to do. "Luther—for crying out loud!" I said, standing up and shaking his hand. "How the hell are you?"

He smiled at me. "I'm superb, man—can't you tell from looking at me?" He laughed then, and I laughed with him.

"You've gotten older," I said.

"Past sixteen," he said. "That means I don't got to go to school no more—"

He waited, but I didn't offer an opinion. "How about going down with me and having a cup of coffee? I'm finished here for the day—just getting through with midterms."

"Nah," he said, looking down and playing with his hands. "I gotta meet somebody. I'm late already. But I was in the neighborhood, so I thought I'd come let you know I was still alive." He came to my desk and looked down. He shook his head as if something were wrong.

"What's the matter?" I asked.

"Don't see no wedding ring on your finger yet." He looked straight into my face. "Hey, man—you ain't a fag, are you?"

"No," I said, laughing. "Not that I know of—"

He laughed, his mouth opening wide. "Okay. That's all the gas for today. I'll see you, man."

During the next few months he visited me several times. Sometimes he looked good, sometimes bad—but I never could find out what he was doing with his days. He never gave a straight answer to my questions. More and more, I felt that he was asking me for some kind of help, but when I would touch on anything personal or even hint that I wanted to do something for him, with him, he would become defensive.

I didn't see him over the summer, but the following fall he came by periodically. He seemed to be getting a hold on himself and sometimes he would talk about going to night school. Nothing came of the talk, though. In November he was arrested and sent to Riker's Island—to P.S. 616, the combination prison-school for boys between the ages of sixteen and twenty. His sentence was for eighteen months and during the first three months I visited him twice. Both times all he wanted to do was talk about the English class we had had and the stories and compositions he had made up. He said he was trying to remember some of them for the English teacher he had there, but couldn't do it all the time. He seemed to be in terrible shape, and I didn't have much hope for him.

So I was surprised when I began getting postcards from him again.

"I am studying hard," the first one said. "There is a Negro who comes here to help me. I like him. I will be a new man when I come out. Yours sincerely, Luther." It was neatly and carefully written. The ones that followed were the same and they came at regular intervals of about five weeks. He told me about books he was reading, most of them having to do with Negro history, and about how he was changing. "Improving" was the word he used most.

I answered his cards as best I could and offered to come see him again, but he never took up any of my offers. When his eighteen months were up, I expected a visit from him. He never came. Sometimes I wondered what had become of him, but after the first few months passed and I didn't hear from him, I thought about him less and less. A year passed—two since we had last seen each other at Riker's Island—and then we met again.

I spotted him first. It was a beautiful summer night and I had gone up to Lewisohn Stadium for a concert. It had been good, I was relaxed and happy as I walked out of the stadium. Luther was standing at the corner of Amsterdam Avenue and 138th Street. He was wearing a dark blue suit, a white shirt, and tie. He was clean-shaven, his hair was cut short, and he looked healthy and bright. He was stopping people and trying to sell them newspapers.

"How are you, Mr. Carter?" he asked when I walked up to him. His eyes were clear and he seemed very happy to see me. "Interested in buying a newspaper to help the colored people? Only a dime—"

"No, thanks," I said. The paper he was selling, as I'd expected, was

Muhammad Speaks, the newspaper of the Black Muslims. "You look fine," I added.

"Thanks. Excuse me a second." He turned and sold a copy to somebody. People snubbed him but this didn't stop him from smiling or trying. I waited. When the crowd had gone, he asked me where I was going. "Home," I said. "Cup of coffee first?"

"No, thanks," he said. "Thanks, but no thanks."

"When did all this start?" I asked, motioning to the newspapers.

"At Riker's Island," he said. He put up a hand, as if to stop my thoughts from becoming words. "I know what you're thinking, what you hear on TV and read in the newspapers about us—but don't believe everything. We're essentially a religious organization, as you may or may not know."

"I know," I said.

"And it's meant a lot to me—I couldn't have made it without their help. They—they taught me to *believe* in myself." His eyes glowed as he twisted his body toward me. "Can you understand that?" It seemed very important to him that I believe him. "*Can* you?" He relaxed momentarily and shrugged. "I don't believe everything they teach, of course, but I follow their precepts: I don't smoke, I don't drink, I don't curse, I don't go out with women who aren't Muslims—I feel good *inside,* Mr. Carter. Things are straightening themselves out." He paused. "It hasn't been easy."

"I know," I said, and smiled.

He nodded, embarrassed, I thought. "I'm going back to school also—"

"I'm glad."

"Even my body feels good! I'm lifting weights again," he said. Then he laughed and the sound tore through the warm night. His eyes were flashing with delight. "Oh man—some day I'll be the head of a whole damned army! Me and my old hunchback." He laughed again, pleased with himself. His laughter subsided and he patted me on the shoulder. "Oh man, you are still so deep, so deep. Don't worry none, Mr. Carter. I don't go around advocating no violence." He chuckled. "I've got to go," he said, extending a hand. "It's been good seeing you again. Sure you don't want to buy a copy?"

"I'm sure," I said, shaking his hand. "Good luck to you, Luther. I'm glad to see you the way you are now—"

"Thanks." We looked at each other for a minute and he smiled warmly at me. Then I started toward the subway station. When I'd crossed the street, he called to me.

"Hey—Mr. Carter—"

I turned.

"Let me ask you something—do you still have that card I gave you?" He howled at this remark. "Oh man, I'd save that card if I were you! I'd do that. You never know when you might need it. You never know—"

I started back across the street, toward him. He tossed his head back and roared with laughter. "You never know, you never know," he repeated, and hurried away from me, laughing wildly. I stared at him until he disappeared in the darkness. Then I just stood there, dazed, unable to move—I don't know for how long. Finally I made myself turn around, and as I walked slowly toward the lights of Broad-way all I could feel was the presence of his muscular body, powerful, gleaming, waiting under his white shirt, his clean suit.

discussion

This poignant story illustrates the relationship between a dedicated middle class white teacher and a black child from the Harlem ghetto. The terrible paradox is that Mr. Carter is the child to the premature man of Luther. Luther is a turned-on radar set, and Mr. Carter desperately tries to remain real while attempting to emit the right sounds to be picked up by Luther's sophisticated scope. When the vibrations are right, as during the few months that Luther and Mr. Carter worked together successfully and uninterruptedly, Carter—the child-man, in this relationship—is ecstatic. For the ghetto man-child, Luther, it is a peaceful interlude in his war with himself and society.

Despite Mr. Carter's efforts, only momentarily can these two people touch in trust. When Luther shrinks back from Mr. Carter, he does so in a paroxysm of guilt, hurt, and perverted joy. His feelings tumble incoherently, and he becomes "unglued" emotionally—which explains some of his sprees, his copping out. Luther is not a "mental case" in that he does not have a diagnosed mental illness. However, he is an emotionally disturbed young man who has difficulty in controlling his impulsive acting out behavior. Whether we use the terminology of Freud or Erickson, transactional analysis, or social learning theory to label the disturbance, Luther represents the unpredictable, confused, sometimes violent casualty of the ghetto.

Luther's hunchback adds salt to his wounds. His view of himself adds up to zero and his deformity adds a red-flagged minus to that. He has nothing to lose. There is no evidence that he has learned a value system within the context of a family. His morality is learned in the harsh Harlem street. He says:

> I'm not getting what I want and when you don't get what you want, man, you got to take.

Throughout the story we are aware of Luther's search for a place or a way to lull the raging conflict that engulfs him. He experiments with different highs and even a few months of being "straight." He seems always to be over- or understimulated. There is no in-between for him. Life moves swiftly for Luther. With no ties and no previous learning to point the way to plan and consider alternatives and their consequences, he moves frantically from one action to another.

A well intentioned teacher like Mr. Carter cannot heal Luther's long standing emotional disturbance. Luther identifies so closely with his racial culture, that only a black teacher could have provided Luther with a helpful model at this point in time, i.e., during the civil rights movement. Even then, Luther's problems are so overwhelming that no teacher could have been totally successful in providing support and guidance. Luther is an extreme example of wounded minority students.

The sequences at the ballgame reveal a different Luther. He revels in the idea that "black is beautiful." The model of Willie Mays is powerful.

But the model of Willie Mays, the super-hero, is not readily converted into an ongoing way of life which is meaningful and satisfying to Luther. The Black Muslim who reaches him at the 600 school on Riker's Island is probably closest to offering a combination of pride in race and an organized way of life that Luther seeks. At the end of the story the author seems to suggest that this too is an interlude in Luther's life and that anger and revenge, his most powerful motivators, will erupt again.

springboards for inquiry

1. Why were Carter's attempts to befriend Luther doomed to failure?

2. What evidence is there that the angry avenging side of Luther will reappear?

3. Do you know of any educational programs which have been successful with students like Luther?

4. Read two books about the inner-city child in school.[1] Assess the accuracy of Neugeboren's story in terms of your research.

[1]Some books that deal with urban ghetto students are Herbert Kohl, *Thirty-Six Children* (New York: New American Library, 1968), and Jonathan Kozol, *Death at an Early Age* (New York: Bantam, 1970).

the teacher as counselor

This volume has depicted the teacher in many roles—as model, as adversary, as human being. A cursory review of these essays will indicate that the teacher is nearly all things to all children. The narrowest view of all is the teacher's role as counselor, if by "counselor" we mean simply one who guides the child into the proper courses or the college most suited to his needs and abilities. A better view relates the counselor to the total behavior of the school population, individually and collectively.

Programming the student wisely is of course important especially in these days of flexible scheduling and arena scheduling[1] when the counselor must evaluate every student's program with his counselee well in advance, for after the semester begins, it is difficult to make changes. Vocational and other educational aspirations are also crucial problems for adolescents. Sometimes the only adult who knows anything about the capabilities and aspirations of a student is the person who sits in an office marked, *Guidance Counselor*. Counselors who use their information to help the child realistically appraise himself are fulfilling a significant educational role and are often able to suggest avenues for the best use of a child's talents.

Although the counselor's role of programmer and evaluator is important, his most effective role is in the area of behavior modification. For example, when Amidon and Hoffman trained teachers to help rejected children reenter their schoolroom world, they were using teachers as counselors in the most philosophic and pragmatic sense.[2] Their final report indicates that teachers can help rejected children improve their status in classroom groups.[3] They note that teachers can, once they know which children are rejected by their peers, design group and individual strategies so that the rejected children may become more acceptable to their peers. If the role of teacher as counselor is seen only in the traditional one-to-one, teacher-student counseling relationship, the definition of counselor is greatly limited.

However, when the counseling role is seen as a three-pronged approach—the teacher as counselor to himself, as counselor to a group, and as counselor to individuals—the definition of the task matures.

Using the Amidon model as exemplified in his early work—the teacher as the person most able to mediate the breach between the child identified

[1]Arena scheduling is a high school's name for teacher and time selection similar to the way college students schedule themselves.

[2]Edmund Amidon and Carl Hoffman, "Helping the Socially Isolated or Rejected Child," *The National Elementary Principal*, 43, no. 2 (November 1963): 75.

[3]"Can Teachers Help the Socially Rejected?" *Elementary School Journal* (December 1965): pp. 149–54.

as the outcast or isolate and his peer group[4]—we observe that the teacher must first diagnose the climate he has created in his classroom (Role #1—teacher as counselor to himself) and set about correcting his own rejective behavior in accepting, perhaps even encouraging the group's isolation of a particular child—"People, do you see how John purposely holds up our recess by his behavior?"; next (Role #2—the teacher as counselor to a group), by assigning the isolate to work with others, by designing group games to include the isolate, and by using the class for general discussions of group behavior—"How can we, class, help those who are not good in games?"; and, finally (Role #3—the teacher as counselor to an individual), by conferring with the rejected child to help him more realistically evaluate himself or his particular dilemma—"John, what are some of the things you do to get others angry?" Here, then, is the teacher in the role of the total counselor.

The examination of one's own professional behavior, though difficult and often self-revealing, is an urgent necessity.[5] Accepting responsibility for one's influence upon a group and upon individuals for both their academic learning and the sociology of the group is awesome.[6] Helping the group to see itself as an organism, a creature that does affect those who are part of the group (and those who are not—such as the rest of the school, the bus driver) not as an irresponsible nonentity, is a crucial counseling role. Recognizing all of the individuals in the group as being an inherent part of anyone else's problem and counseling with each of those persons represents an especially significant counseling role.

Teachers often assume the role of counselors. A walk through any school in America will show teachers in a multitude of positive, therapeutic counseling stances. We recollect the sixth grade, mature girl who never failed to whisper quietly to her male teacher, "Martha has come again," and that if she acted bratty or stupidly he would understand. We recollect the high school teacher who helped a 17-year-old addict enter a treatment program. Everyone else thought Greg was just a sleepy TV addict. And we remember the heavy set college student who sat down in her professor's office to announce that she would be gone for a while to have an out-of-state abortion. In each case the student needed understanding, even a sense of humor. Like it or not, the American school teacher is a counselor.

---

[4]See p. 119 for our discussion of the Cunningham Sociogram for analyzing the social status of a child in his schoolroom. It may be well to note here that one of the reasons for the concern over children identified early as being rejected by their peers, is embodied in Dr. Jacob Moreno's "law of the social atom." A more detailed and challenging discussion of the contributions of sociometry may be found in Jacob L. Moreno, "Contributions of Sociometry to Research Methodology in Sociology." *American Sociological Review* 12, no. 2, (April 1947): 287–92. In brief, Moreno postulates that a child who is socially isolated early in his school career is likely to stay that way if he stays in the same ecosystem.

[5]In recent years college professors have had to face the frank evaluations of their students. Many have for the first time in their careers, been faced with the need to discover "where they are" vis-à-vis their teaching of late adolescents.

[6]This is now called "accountability." Unfortunately it usually applies only to the teacher's responsibility for the academic achievements of the class.

Fern Rives

Friday, thank god!

Don't she have a right to learn herself French? My Gloria's a bright girl—she's bright like her poppa, God rest his soul—and I want her to be a fine lady. Maybe she don't want to work but you have that for your job. You got to make her work!"

The morning air tasted stale as though the close-woven clouds cut off its customary tang, and glancing down at the sheaf of daffodils in her lap, Allison thought that their clear yellow pierced the murkiness like a light. If only that light on her desk would pierce the Monday gloom in her classes! She knew just what her students would be like, either lethargic and listless or full of the devil, according to their temperaments and degree of fatigue. As for the faculty—better forget it. She had often wondered if it were the same in all professions, if Monday were the born stepchild of the week. She would ask Ash this afternoon.

Approaching within a block of the school she saw by the increasing crowd of students that she was much later than usual, and sure enough her favorite parking place was pre-empted. By the time she had wangled her car into a difficult niche, walked the extra block, and fought her way through the near riot in the halls, the first bell had rung, so the week was definitely off to a bad start. As she was extracting the mass of Monday mail from her box, someone jolted her arm, precipitating late senior essays and textbook circulars in every direction, and then, as an exclamation point at

Reprinted by permission of G.P. Putnam's Sons from Friday, Thank God! *by Fern Rives. Copyright © 1943 by Fern Rives.*

the end of a bad fifteen minutes, great red letters leaped up at her from the Time Sheet. IMPORTANT. SPECIAL FACULTY MEETING IN STUDY B AT THREE-FIFTEEN. *THIS MEANS YOU.*

Mr. Ward's secretary called to her across the hubbub. "Mrs. Bourdet, there's a parent waiting to see you at your room—a Mrs. Zeiter! She seems perturbed."

Allison groaned, "Gloria's mother!" and Miss Billings laughed. "Right. Buck up! We're rooting for your side."

Then Allison saw Jeff Ward standing in his office door, his amused glance taking in everything and managing somehow one tiny flicker of a smile. She smiled back shakily with a devout prayer that no one had caught the expression on her face and hurried toward the noise which she knew must come from in front of her closed room.

This first period was sophomore French, an enormous heterogeneous class, which certainly did block traffic in the narrow hall. Miss Wilkes stood at her own door across the hall, her raised eyebrows proclaiming to all the world, which unfortunately was not listening at the moment, "I get to school by seven-thirty. My assignment is on the board and my students are working quietly in their seats instead of disturbing the entire building."

Mrs. Zeiter was certainly on a

rampage. Nothing lethargic about her. Ten yards away her shrill voice was quite audible, scolding her jolly, hulking daughter who wasn't in the least embarrassed to have the entire class as audience to this family fray. At sight of Allison, Mrs. Zeiter detached herself from her daughter and, to the delight of the class, projected her small, round body at Allison like a bullet, all the while talking at the top of her voice. "Why should my Gloria drop her study of French? Don't I slave my fingers to the bone that she should get herself an education? Don't she have a right to learn herself French? My Gloria's a bright girl—she's bright like her poppa, God rest his soul—and I want her to be a fine lady. Maybe she don't want to work but you have that for your job. You got to make her work!"

After several futile attempts to stem the tide, Allison gave up and made her way through the little path her students cleared for her with Mrs. Zeiter at her elbow, managed to unlock her door, and signaled to the class to go to their seats. Fortunately the assignment was already on the board, and the class was far too enchanted by this free show to be anything but perfectly silent. Allison took off her hat and hung it in the closet, hoping that her hair was in order, tried once more without result to turn the tide of invective, and gave up.

If only she could get her out in the hall again; but Mrs. Zeiter established herself in the chair at Allison's desk and proceeded to enjoy herself. "Gloria, come here," she said to her daughter, and Gloria, still smiling and unperturbed, left her seat and came up to the front of the room.

"Now then," Mrs. Zeiter demanded of Allison, "look at her."

Allison and the entire class obliged. "Isn't she a good big girl?" Certainly everybody agreed to that. "Hasn't she got a good head on them broad shoulders?" Well, thought Allison, there is room for debate on that point. Gloria's official I.Q. was 65, and although there was often reason to doubt the final validity of I.Q. results, in Gloria's case everything went to substantiate the findings of Terman. It was absurd that Gloria should have ever been allowed to tackle French, but Mrs. Zeiter had insisted and the counselor had been forced to O.K. her program of studies.

Suddenly Mrs. Zeiter stopped and demanded of Allison, "Well, why don't you say something? Why do you think I came here so early to wait for you?"

Allison wet her dry lips, saw from the corner of her eye that the class was waiting with concentrated interest to see how she was going to meet this crisis, and wished she were dead. She must say something and she obviously couldn't tell Mrs. Zeiter that her Gloria had a mind just a shade above that of a moron. On the other hand, the class knew the situation perfectly and would know it if she didn't tell the truth. At last she said, "You see, Mrs. Zeiter, some students are talented along lines other than purely scholastic"—she could see that these technical words impressed her interlocutor—"I understand that Gloria is very clever at dressmaking, so we thought that if she spent her time on something which may help her later on to earn her living instead of on French—"

Mrs. Zeiter exploded again, "You

think I want my daughter to be a dressmaker! You're crazy! You think I work in a laundry just to have my Gloria—" She stopped for breath and with an expansive gesture managed to scatter half a dozen daffodils across the floor.

For the first time, Gloria showed signs of perturbation, and as she stooped to recover the flowers she rebuked her mother sadly, "Now, Momma, see what you done."

Mrs. Zeiter sank down into her chair and answered meekly, "I'm sorry. Did I break any?"

"No," Allison assured her. "Besides, I have dozens of them and more at home. Gloria, would you like to choose a bowl and arrange them for me?"

"Sure," said Gloria, her face beaming. She gathered up the flowers with a swift sure gesture, selected a flat green bowl from those in the cupboard, and leaving the flowers on the work table left the room to bring water.

Allison seized that moment of calm to get the class started on the day's work and returned to a strangely chastened Mrs. Zeiter, whose eyes were so worried that Allison restrained a desire to comfort her by a handclasp as well as by her words, "I always have Gloria arrange flowers for me. She has a real knack with them."

"Sure, she gets that from me." When Mrs. Zeiter smiled she looked like a roguish pixie. "You know something, Mrs. Bourdet? I always wished I would 'a' worked in a flower place."

"That would be lovely," Allison agreed. "Your daughter has a talent for design, a natural feeling for what colors will blend and what lines are harmonious."

"That's right," the girl's mother admitted. "She's always been good with colors. We got some of her pictures she done when she was a kid—real pretty, with frames she made for them—and she's made her room real nice, too. Gloria's a good girl. She don't never cause me no trouble but only I can't get her to do her duty. Every night after supper I say, 'Gloria, do your homework,' and she says, 'O.K., Momma, just wait till I fix up this hat. I seen one like it in *Vogue.*' What can I do with such a girl?"

Allison reached over to pat her hand. "You see, Mrs. Zeiter, we all like to do the things we do well. Look at her now."

They stopped to watch Gloria arrange the daffodils with deft fingers and unerring taste.

"There isn't another student here who could do that."

"That's real pretty, all right, but"—her smile faded into a frown—"can she make her living by it?"

"Perhaps not arranging flowers but surely with the same talent. She might very well develop into a first-rate stylist or even a designer."

"A designer? What's that?"

"She might learn to draw the styles for dress patterns or plan color combinations for costumes. It's a fine profession and there is good money in it." Allison prayed that the Lord and Mrs. Zeiter would forgive her if Gloria merely developed into the neighborhood dressmaker. Certainly Gloria wouldn't mind.

"You think she might do that?"

"I do, indeed. Mrs. Malin, our dressmaking teacher, thinks she is splendid and would like very much to have her this first period to help out with some of the younger girls—give them advice in planning their work—and then that would give Mrs. Malin time to help Gloria with advance design."

Mrs. Zeiter looked doubtful. "But this first period she takes French."

"I know, but she really isn't doing very much with French and that period with Mrs. Malin would be so valuable to her."

There was a moment's tense silence when Allison feared that all this would come to naught, but suddenly the woman leaned over and gave her hand a hard squeeze. "I think maybe you're right and I am wrong. Will you excuse me please that I was so mean this morning when I came? I wasn't mad at you—I was worried and I didn't know what to do. Gloria is all I got and I want her to be a lady."

"Gloria is a lady," Allison assured her, "and I think she is an artist, too. Someday you will be proud of her."

Mrs. Zeiter rose and gave Allison her hand again, "You been very nice to me, Mrs. Bourdet, you put my mind to rest. Gloria says everybody wants to study with you and now I know why." She walked to the door. "Get your books, Gloria. You are dropping French. Mrs. Bourdet made me see what is best."

For a few minutes after they were gone, Allison just sat quietly, scarcely believing her good fortune and Gloria's. It might so easily have turned out the other way. Maybe the Monday jinx was broken.

The last half-hour of the recitation skimmed by so pleasantly and the students acquitted themselves so well that Allison experienced that rarest joy of the schoolteacher, the momentary conviction that she really was a good teacher, although she knew well that by tomorrow the class might be plunged again into abysmal ignorance and she would feel herself to be a failure.

After class, Alfred Swanson stopped shyly before her desk, and as always when she looked at this tall thin boy her heart smote her, he was so clean and patched, so pale, and so obviously undernourished. Early in the term she had made tentative suggestions that she place his name with the P.T.A. president so he might receive free milk at noon, but had been ever so gently repulsed by his quick pride.

He spoke very quietly and formally, but his luminous, speaking eyes, which always mirrored every passing emotion in the class, smiled down at her. "I beg your pardon, Mrs. Bourdet, but if it is possible, my mother wishes me to make an appointment for her to meet you."

"Surely your mother isn't worried about *your* French."

"Oh, no. She merely wishes to talk to you."

"I should love to meet your mother, Alfred. Tell her I can see her any day this week between two and two-thirty. Just tell me which day is best for her when you come to French."

As she watched him leave the room, she promised herself that she would have another try at giving him the free milk.

Just before the noon hour, which in the rush of events seemed to leap on her from ambush, Allison received two notes. One of them was from her friend, Ella Marshall, the Girls' Guidance Counselor, and she had to laugh as she took the beautifully printed card from the envelope, for pinned onto it was an old piece of red Christmas ribbon to which had been pasted a large gold star. The printed card read,

Allison Bourdet is hereby awarded *L'Étoile d'Honneur* in recognition of her valor and discretion under heavy fire.

At the bottom of the card was added in pencil,

Well, Al, how about giving your counselor a few private lessons in her duties? After two years of intractability, Mrs. Zeiter suddenly announces that Mrs. Bourdet has made her see the light and poor Gloria is saved from a fate worse than death—or am I being too hard on the irregular verbs? At any rate, I've recommended you to the Chief for a corporal's stripe!

Your admirer,
Ella

discussion

There are advantages in establishing a high school counseling department autonomous from subject area departments. This arrangement usually ensures that counselors do not interact with the students in a teaching role. There are times, however, as illustrated by this story, when the teacher can be the most effective counselor.

Allison Bourdet has obviously found the time to establish a relationship of trust with her students that allows her to assume the unique position of teacher-counselor. Despite the fact that the high school is strongly subject-matter oriented, Miss Bourdet was able to provide Gloria with satisfying experiences which had little to do with French. This teacher is not only resourceful but assumes responsibility for students beyond the subject area she teaches. Miss Bourdet assumes responsibility for her students as people. She has moved away from the "group-think" displayed by many teachers in an attempt to "individualize," a task which is demanding and time consuming.

Ella Marshall has been Gloria's counselor with little success. The setting of her office undoubtedly offers a good opportunity for parent and counselor to talk in confidence, but the setting does not always ensure success. In this case the hectic counseling session that took place in the classroom in front of the entire class and Gloria turned out well despite the adverse conditions. Miss Bourdet was able to demonstrate the concern and interest she has in Gloria, thereby helping Mrs. Zeiter to drop her defensive stance and to participate in more realistic planning for her daughter.

springboards for inquiry

1. Can you recall a teacher in your past who assumed a teacher-counselor role for you?

2. What do you think of Miss Bourdet's conference with Mrs. Zeiter? Would you have refused to talk to Mrs. Zeiter under these conditions?

3. Should teachers take responsibility for students' problems which go beyond their subject matter areas?

4. What do you think is an optimal relationship between teachers and counselors at the high school level?

5. Do you think that high school counselors should schedule regular appointments with all their students or should students initiate conference time with their counselor?

the teacher as adversary

Enough has been written so far to indicate that if anything represents the antithesis of what a good teacher should be, it is his role of adversary. We accept the teacher as questioner, pretender of ignorance, facilitator, even controller, but the thought of the teacher as the enemy is distasteful. It is true, however, that on rare occasions teachers have carried on vendetta-like crusades against individual students. Even these teachers are exceedingly rare.

For the most part the adversary behaviors of teachers are defined as personality conflicts. Occasionally, though rarely, a teacher is so annoyed by the behavior of a child that all of the children in the class can "feel" the resentment. More often a teacher communicates to a particular child that no matter what he does he will fail in the eyes of that teacher. Psychological studies of the "self" require only that the ratio of positive experiences to negative ones should be greatly in favor of the positive. It sometimes happens that because of some conduct disturbance, teachers may appear to be "picking on" a particular child. An occasional verbal blast is only human. A persistent negative response to any child is not good professional behavior because it is necessary, in the elementary school years particularly, to develop in all children a sense of industry, not a sense of inferiority.

It is often the case that the child who experiences the most frequent rejection by the teacher is the one who needs acceptance most. In the elementary school classroom the most frequently heard admonitions are "sit still," "stop talking," and "pay attention." The child who is repeatedly the target of this verbal and sometimes physical exasperation on the part of the teacher may be an emotionally needy child who does not have the inner calm to stay in his seat and concentrate for long periods of time. He may be a clinically hyperactive child who cannot screen out distracting stimuli, who is motorically and/or verbally always "in gear." The teacher's repeated scoldings are negative experiences to the child and frequently label him as a "bad child" among his schoolmates.

In the junior and senior high school years and particularly in the seventh, eighth, and ninth grades, the possibility of intense dislike for particular youngsters seems to be heightened. In junior high, during the early years of adolescence, personality traits are frequently found in some children which, while not full blown, are yet sufficiently aggravating to suggest more than just the mere early blossoming of repugnant traits. Physical abuse of students seems more common at this level than anywhere else in the school system. Much of this personal antagonism in junior high stems from complex sources. Junior high school teachers are frequently young and not where they want to be—in the senior high school. Thus, they bear a certain understandable resentment towards having to "put up" with a wide range of often repugnant adolescent verbal repartee and testing of limits. Also, junior high school teachers are very much more in a position to observe the omnipresent sexuality of the students which, to one near them in age, is often intolerable. In fact, there is a great deal of sexual attraction between junior high and high school teachers and their students which is often denied by the teacher as being unworthy of his professional status.

It is not unusual for male teachers in the junior high school to be challenged by the bursting physical development of the student at this age. In many cases the growth spurt occurs in the eighth and ninth grade making the junior high school male a very awkward, pimply yet powerful adversary. It is as if the junior high school child is overtaking his young teachers in his frantic rush towards full adolescence. Sometimes the clash occurs between the adolescent and a teacher in his late 30s or 40s who is experiencing the first pangs of a middle-age syndrome of anxiety and despair created by not being where he would really like to be. Some middle-aged teachers find it threatening to be subjected to daily evidence of their decline as they compare themselves with the energy and power of their young students. Under these circumstances it is possible for teachers to develop some very hostile attitudes towards individual students, especially those who epitomize the defiance of youth.

One usually becomes an adversary only to those over whom it is clearly possible to triumph. When it is perfectly evident that only defeat is possible, retreat rather than attack becomes the order of the day. In relationships between junior high school adolescents and their teachers, it is a foregone conclusion that the winners will almost always be the teachers. Junior high school students are virtually powerless to survive the verbal and nonverbal abuses of teachers who have full command of the lifespace and the "weaponry" to conquer those who inhabit it. Under these circumstances adversary-like behavior is more apt to develop and the gentle, euphemistic term "personality conflict" is just that—a way of not talking about the real relationships that can develop between students and teachers.

During adolescence, when the search for one's identity is fully under way, the child is very vulnerable to teachers who behave as adversaries. The youngster at this time in his life has not consolidated his wellsprings of personality, and thus he is very easy to hurt. The verbal exchanges that adversaries often indulge in seem harmless to the adults who blissfully banter them about. They are deadly stings to young people who are more unsure of themselves now than they will ever be again. Abraham Maslow's warning in *Motivation and Personality* is relevant here:

> Let people realize clearly that every time they threaten someone or humiliate or hurt unnecessarily or dominate or reject another human being, they become forces for the creation of psychopathology, even if these be small forces. Let them recognize that every man who is kind, helpful, decent, psychologically democratic, affectionate, and warm, is a psychotherapeutic force even though a small one.[1]

---

[1] Abraham H. Maslow, *Motivation and Personality*, 2nd ed. (New York: Harper & Row, 1970), p. 254.

Robert Graves

The abominable Mr Gunn

"Don't answer me back, boy! Why aren't
you working out that sum?'
'I have already written down the
answer, sir.'
'Bring your exercise-book here! . . .
Ah, yes, here is the answer, . . . —'but
where is it worked out?'

One Monday morning in September 1910, the abominable Mr J.O.G.
Gunn, master of the Third Form at
Brown Friars, trod liverishly down
the aisle between two rows of pitch-
pine desks and grasped the short
hairs just above my right ear. Mr
Gunn, pale, muscular and broad-
faced, kept his black hair plastered
close to the scalp with a honey-
scented oil. He announced to the
form, as he lifted me up a few
inches: 'And now Professor Graves
will display his wondrous erudition
by discoursing on the first Mission-
ary Journey of St. Paul.' (Laughter.)

I discoursed haltingly, my mind
being as usual a couple of stages
ahead of my tongue, so that my
tongue said 'Peter' when I meant
'Paul', and 'B.C.' when I meant 'A.
D.' and 'Crete' when I meant 'Cy-
prus'. It still plays this sort of trick,
which often makes my conversation
difficult to follow and is now read as
a sign of incipient senility. In those
days it did not endear me to Mr
Gunn . . .

After the disaster at Syracuse,
one Athenian would often ask
another: 'Tell me, friend, what has
become of old So-and-so?' and the
invariable answer came: 'If he is not
dead, he is school-mastering.' I can

*Reprinted by permission of Collins-
Knowlton-Wing. Copyright © 1953, 54,
55, 56, 57, 58, 59, 60, 62, 64 by Robert
Graves.*

wish no worse fate to Mr J.O.G.
Gunn—father of all the numerous
sons-of-guns who have since
sneered at my 'erudition' and cruelly caught at my short hairs—than
that he is still exercising his profession at the age of eighty-plus; and
that each new Monday morning has
found him a little uglier and a little
more liverish than before.

Me erudite? I am not even de-
cently well read. What reading I
have done from time to time was
never a passive and promiscuous
self-exposure to the stream of literature, but always a search for particular facts to nourish, or to scotch,
some obsessive maggot that had
gained a lodgement in my skull.
And now I shall reveal an embarrassing secret which I have kept from
the world since those nightmare
days.

One fine summer evening as I sat
alone on the roller behind the crick-
et pavilion, with nothing much in
my head, I received a sudden celes-
tial illumination: it occurred to me
that I knew everything. I remember
letting my mind range rapidly over
all its familiar subjects of knowledge; only to find that this was no
foolish fancy. I did know everything. To be plain: though conscious of having come less than a
third of the way along the path of
formal education, and being weak
in mathematics, shaky in Greek
grammar, and hazy about English

history, I nevertheless held the key of truth in my hand, and could use it to open any lock of any door. Mine was no religious or philosophical theory, but a simple method of looking sideways at disorderly facts so as to make perfect sense of them.

I slid down from the roller, wondering what to do with my embarrassing gift. Whom could I take into my confidence? Nobody. Even my best friends would say 'You're mad!' and either send me to Coventry or organize my general scragging, or both; and soon some favour-currier would sneak to Mr Gunn, which would be the end of everything. It occurred to me that perhaps I had better embody the formula in a brief world-message, circulated anonymously to the leading newspapers. In that case I should have to work under the bedclothes after dark, by the light of a flash-lamp, and use the cypher I had recently perfected. But I remembered my broken torch-light bulb, and the difficulty of replacing it until the next day. No: there was no immediate hurry. I had everything securely in my head. Again I experimented, trying the key on various obstinate locks; they all clicked and the doors opened smoothly. Then the schoolbell rang from a distance, calling me to preparation and prayers.

Early the next day I awoke to find that I still had a fairly tight grasp of my secret; but a morning's lessons intervened, and when I then locked myself into the privy, and tried to record it on the back of an old exercise-book, my mind went too fast for my pen, and I began to cross out—a fatal mistake—and presently crumpled up the page and pulled the chain on it. That night I tried again

under the bedclothes, but the magic had evaporated and I could get no further than the introductory sentence.

My vision of truth did not recur, though I went back a couple of times to sit hopefully on the roller; and before long, doubts tormented me, gloomy doubts about a great many hitherto stable concepts: such as the authenticity of the Gospels, the perfectibility of man and the absoluteness of the Protestant moral code. All that survived was an afterglow of the bright light in my head, and the certainty that it had been no delusion. This is still with me, for I now realize that what overcame me that evening was a sudden infantile awareness of the power of intuition, the supralogic that cuts out all routine processes of thought and leaps straight from problem to answer.

How easily this power is blunted by hostile circumstances Mr Gunn demonstrated by his treatment of one F.F. Smilley, a new boy, who seems, coincidentally, to have had a vision analogous to mine, though of a more specialized sort. Smilley came late to Brown Friars; he had been educated at home until the age of eleven because of some illness or other. It happened on his first entry into the Third Form that Mr Gunn set us a problem from Hilderbrand's *Arithmetic for Preparatory Schools*, which was to find the square root of the sum of two long decimals, divided (just for cussedness) by the sum of two complicated vulgar fractions. Soon everyone was scribbling away except F.F. Smilley, who sat there abstractedly polishing his glasses and gazing out of the window.

Mr Gunn looked up for a moment from a letter he was writing, and asked nastily: 'Seeking inspiration from the distant church spire, Smilley?'

'No, sir. Polishing my glasses.'

'And why, pray?'

'They had marmalade on them, sir.'

'Don't answer me back, boy! Why aren't you working out that sum?'

'I have already written down the answer, sir.'

'Bring your exercise-book here! . . . Ah, yes, here is the answer, my very learned and ingenious friend Sir Isaac Newton'— tweaking the short hairs—'but where is it worked out?'

'Nowhere, sir; it just came to me.'

'Came to you, F.F. Smilley, my boy? You mean you hazarded a wild guess?'

'No, sir, I just looked at the problem and saw what the answer must be.'

'Ha! A strange psychical phenomenon! But I must demand proof that you did not simply turn to the answer at the end of the book.'

'Well, I did do that afterwards, sir.'

'The truth now slowly leaks out.'

'But it was wrong, sir. The last two figures should be 35, not 53.'

'Curiouser and curiouser! Here's a Brown Friars' boy in the Third Form who knows better than Professor Hilderbrand, Cambridge's leading mathematician.'

'No, sir, I think it must be a misprint.'

'So you and Professor Hilderbrand are old friends? You seem very active in his defence.'

'No, sir, I have met him, but I didn't like him very much.'

F.F. Smilley was sent at once to the Headmaster with a note: 'Please cane bearer for idleness, lying, cheating and gross impertinence'— which the Headmaster, who had certain flaws in his character, was delighted to do. I cannot tell the rest of the story with much confidence, but my impression is that Mr Gunn won, as he had already won in his battle against J.X. Bestard-Montéry, whose Parisian accent when he was called upon to read 'Maître Corbeau, sur un arbre perché' earned him the name of 'frog-eating mountebank', and a severe knuckling on the side of the head. Bestard was forced to put a hard Midland polish on his French.

Mr Gunn, in fact, gradually beat down F. F. Smilley's resistance by assisuous hair-tweakings, knucklings and impositions; and compelled him to record all mathematic argument in the laborious way laid down by Professor Hilderbrand. No more looking out of the window, no more guessing at the answer.

Whether the cure was permanent I cannot say, because shortly before the end of that school-year the Chief of County Police gave the Headmaster twenty-four hours to leave the country (the police were more gentlemanly in those Edwardian days), and Brown Friars broke up in confusion. I have never since heard of F.F. Smilley. Either he was killed in World War I, or else he is schoolmastering somewhere. Had he made his mark in higher mathematics, we should surely have heard of it. Unless, perhaps, he is so much of a back-room boy, so much the arch-wizard of the mathematic-formula department on which Her Majesty's nuclear physicists depend for their bombs and piles, that the Security men have changed his name, disguised his features by plastic surgery, speech-trained him into alien immigrance, and suppressed his civic identity. I would not put it past them. But the mathematical probability is, as I say, that Gunn won.

discussion

In this story Robert Graves, the well-known English scholar, may have been writing about an occurrence out of his own early school experience. Although this took place in an English boarding school, teachers like Mr. Gunn appear in a number of classrooms in every country. They impose rules inflexibly and are particularly intimidated by the bright student who may respond to a problem or situation in an unorthodox manner. Graves, himself, and F.F. Smilley, the student he writes about, were undoubtedly gifted thinkers. They were able to leap "straight from problem to answer." Teachers who themselves are unable to conceptualize this kind of superior thinking may mistakenly view the student who rejects many plodding steps in the arrival at the solution to a problem as attempting to undermine their authority. Mr. Gunn's critical remarks are not only aimed at what he considers an incorrect answer. He gains satisfaction from attacking Smilley personally. To add to the psychological abuse, Mr. Gunn sends Smilley to the headmaster for physical abuse.

Adults who are particularly adept at verbalizing, and teachers who by the nature of their profession fall into this category, may be prone to use words to devastate others. This quick verbal parry is called sarcasm. It effectively sabotages communication between adult and child and therefore keeps the adult "one-up." When a student is stifled in this way he will often resort to vengeful fantasies as his only outlet. This form of communication is detrimental to the mental health of the student, because it lowers his self-esteem. Teaching is an art intended to foster self-esteem in young people.

springboards for inquiry

1. Discuss an experience from your own school years in which a teacher's behavior was clearly detrimental to the mental health of a child.

2. Write or role-play two situations in which the teacher takes the role of adversary to the student. Then write or role-play the same situation in a positive manner.

3. Students at either end of the learning spectrum, i.e. the gifted and the slow learner, are usually a source of frustration to the inflexible teacher. Describe the kinds of behaviors of gifted students and those of slow learning students that would antagonize such a teacher.

Robert Phillips

A teacher's rewards

"What'd you say your name was?" the old lady asked uncertainly, peering through the screen door to where he stood on the dark porch beyond.

"Raybe. Raybe Simpson. You taught me in the third grade, remember?"

"Simpson . . . Simpson. Yes, I suppose so," she said vaguely. Her hand remained firm on the latch.

"Of course you do. I was the little boy with white hair. I sat right in the front row. You always used to rap my knuckles with your ruler, remember?"

"Oh, I rapped a lot of knuckles in my time. Boys will be boys. Still, the white hair, the front row . . ." Her voice trailed off as she made an almost audible effort to engage the ancient machinery of her memory.

"Sure you remember," he said coaxingly. " 'Miss Scofield never forgets a name.' That's what all the older kids told us. That's what all the other teachers said. 'Miss Scofield never forgets a name.' "

"Of course she doesn't. I never forgot a pupil's name in forty-eight years of teaching. Come right in." She ceremoniously unlatched the screen door and swung it wide for him to enter. The rusty spring

Reprinted from The Land of Lost Content, *by Robert Phillips, by permission of the publisher,* The Vanguard Press, Inc. *Copyright © 1970, 1969, 1968, 1967, by Robert Phillips.*

All my life I've had a real calling for teaching. A real calling. I always said I would teach until I dropped in my tracks. It's such a rewarding field. A teacher gets her rewards in something other than money. . . .

creaked as the door opened and closed.

"I can't stay long, like I say. I was just in town for the day and thought I'd look you up. You were such a good teacher and all. I've never forgotten what you did for me."

"Well, now, I consider that right kindly of you." She looked him up and down through wire-rimmed spectacles. "Just when was it I taught you?"

"Nineteen thirty-eight. Out to the old school."

"Ah, yes. The old school. A pity about that fire."

"I heard something about it burning down. But I've been away. When was the fire?"

"Oh, years ago. A year or two before I retired. I just couldn't teach in the new brick schoolhouse they built after that. Something about the place. Too cold, too bright. And the classroom was so long. A body couldn't hardly see from one end of it to the other. . . ." She made a helpless little gesture with her hand. He watched the hand in its motion: tiny, fragile, transparent, a network of blue veins clearly running beneath the surface; the skin hung in wrinkles like wet crepe paper.

"That's rough. But you must have been about ready to retire by then anyhow, weren't you?"

Her watery blue eyes snapped. "I should say not. All my life I've had a real calling for teaching. A real calling. I always said I would teach until I dropped in my tracks. It's such a rewarding field. A teacher gets her rewards in something other than money. . . . It was just that new red-brick schoolhouse. The lights were too bright, new-fangled fluorescent lights, bright yellow. And the room was too long. . . ." Her gaze dared him to contradict her.

"I don't think much of these modern buildings you see all around either."

"Boxes," she said firmly.

"Come again?"

"Boxes. Nothing but boxes, that's all they are. I don't know what we're coming to, I declare. Well now, Mister—?"

"Simpson. Mister Simpson. But you can call me Raybe, like you always did."

"Yes. Raybe. That's a nice name. Somehow it has an honest sound to it. Really, the things people name their children these days. Do you know, the last year I taught, I had a student named Crystal. A little girl named Crystal. Why not name her Silverware, or China? And a boy named Jet. That was his first name, Jet. Or was it Astronaut? I don't know. Whatever it was, it was terrible."

"Sounds terrible," he said unenthusiastically. Then a shaft of silence fell between them. At last she smiled, as if to herself, and said cheerily, "I was just fixing to have some tea before you happened by. Would you like some nice hot tea?"

"Well, I wasn't fixing to stay long, like I said." He shuffled his feet to and fro.

"It'll only take a second. The kettle's been on all this time."

She seemed to have her heart set upon a cup of tea, and he was not one to disappoint. "Okay. If you're having some, I'll have some too."

"Good. Do you take lemon or cream?"

"Neither. Actually, I don't drink much tea. I'll just try it plain. With some sugar. I've got a sweet tooth."

"A sweet tooth, have you? Let me see. Is that one of the things I remember about you? Raybe Simpson, a sweet tooth? No, I don't think so. One of the boys I had always used to eat candy bars right in class. The minute my back was turned at the blackboard he'd sneak another candy bar out of his desk and start to chew away. But that wasn't you, was it?"

"No, it wasn't."

"I didn't think it was you," she said quickly. She was getting down two dainty cups with pink roses painted on them. She put them on a tin tray and placed a sugar bowl between them. The bowl was cracked down the middle and had been taped with yellowed Scotch tape. When the tea finally was ready, they adjourned to the living room.

"Well, how've you been, Miss Scofield?" he asked.

"Can't complain, except for a little arthritis in my hands. Can't complain."

"Good." He glanced around. "Nice place you got here." He took a sip of the tea, found it bitter, and added two more heaping spoons of sugar.

"Well, it's small, of course, but it serves me." She settled back in her rocker.

"You still Miss Scofield?"

"How's that?" She leaned forward on her chair as if to position her ear closer to the source.

"I said, your name is still Miss Scofield? You never got married or anything?"

"Mercy, no. I've always been an unclaimed blessing. That's what I've always called myself. An unclaimed blessing." She smiled sweetly.

"You still live alone, I take it."

"Yes, indeed. I did have a cat. A greedy old alley cat named Tom. But he died. Overeating did it, I think. Ate me out of house and home, pretty near."

"You don't say."

"Oh, yes, indeed. He'd eat anything. Belly got big as a basketball, nearabout. He was good company though. Sometimes I miss old Tom."

"I should think so." An old-fashioned clock chimed overhead.

"What business did you say you're in, Mr. Simp . . . Raybe?"

"I didn't say."

"That's right, you didn't say. Well, just what is it?"

"Right now I'm unemployed."

She set her teacup upon a lace doily on the table top and made a little face of disapproval. "I see. How do you get along?"

"Oh, I manage one way or the other. I've been pretty well taken care of these last ten years or so. I been away."

"You're living with your folks? Is that it?" Encouragement bloomed on her cheeks.

"My folks are dead. They were dead when I was your student. I lived with an aunt. She's dead now too."

"Oh, I'm sorry. I don't think I realized at the time—"

"No, I don't think you did. . . . That's all right, Miss Scofield."

You had a lot of students to look after."

"Yes, but still and all, it's unlike me not to have remembered or known that one of my boys was an *orphan*. You don't mind if I use that word, do you, Mr. . . . Raybe? Lots of people are sensitive about words."

"I don't mind. I'm not sensitive."

"No, I should think not. You're certainly a big boy now. And what happened to all that hair?" Looking at his bald head, she laughed a laugh as scattered as buckshot. "My, you must be hot in that jacket. Why don't you take it off? It looks very heavy."

"I'll keep it on, iffen you don't mind."

"Don't mind a bit, so long's you're comfortable."

"I'm just fine."

She began to rock in her chair and looked around the meager room to check its presentability to unexpected company.

"Well, now, what do you remember about our year together that I may have forgotten? Were you in Jay McMaster's class? Jay was a lovely boy. Always so polite. You can always tell good breeding—"

"He was a year or two ahead of me. You're getting close though."

"Of course I am. How about Nathan Pillsbury? He was in your class, wasn't he?"

"That's right."

"See!" she exclaimed triumphantly.

"He was in my class, all right. He was the teacher's pet, you might say." Raybe observed her over the rim of his bitter cup of tea.

"Nathan, my pet? Nathan Pillsbury? I don't remember any such thing. Besides, I never played favorites. That's a bad practice." She worked her lips to and fro.

"So's rapping people's knuckles." He laughed, putting his half-full cup on the floor.

She laughed her scattered little laugh again. "Oh, come now, Raybe. Surely it was deserved, if indeed I ever *did* rap your knuckles."

"You rapped them, all right," he said soberly.

"Did I? Did I really? Yes, I suppose I did. What was it for, do you remember? Passing notes? Gawking out the window?"

"It wasn't for any one thing. You did it lots of times. Dozens of times." He cleared his throat.

"Did I? Mercy me. It doesn't seem to me that I did. I only rapped knuckles upon extreme provocation, you know. Extreme provocation." She took a healthy swallow of tea to dismiss the matter.

"You did it lots of times," he continued. "In front of the whole class. They laughed at me." He made no effort to pick up his teacup again.

"I did? Goodness, what a memory! Well, it doesn't seem to have done you any harm. A little discipline never hurt anybody. What was it you said you've been doing professionally?"

"I've been in prison," he said with a pale smile. He watched her mouth draw downward in disapproval.

"Prison? You've been in prison? Oh, I see, it's a little joke." She tried to laugh again, but the little outburst wouldn't scatter this time.

"*You* try staying behind those walls for ten years and see if it's a joke." He fumbled in his pocket for

a package of cigarettes, withdrew one, and slowly lit it. He blew the smoke across the table.

"Well, I must say! You're probably the only boy I ever had that . . . that ended up in prison! I'm sure there were . . . circumstances . . . leading up to that. I'm sure you're a fine lad, through it all." She worked her lips together faster now, and her gaze traveled to the window that looked out upon the black of night.

"Yeah, there were circumstances, as you call it. Very special circumstances." He blew an enormous smoke ring her way.

The old woman began to cough. "It's the smoke. I'm not used to people smoking around me. Do you mind refraining?"

"Yeah, I do mind," he said roughly. "I'm going to finish this cigarette, no matter what."

"Well, if you must, you must," she said nervously, half rising in her chair. "But let me just open that window a little—"

"Sit back down in that chair!" he ordered.

She fell back into the rocker like a bundle of rags.

"Now, you listen to me, you old bitch," he began.

"Don't you call me names. Don't you dare. How dare you? No wonder you were behind bars. A common jailbird. No respect for your elders."

"Shut up, Grandma." He tossed the cigarette butt to the floor and ground it out on the rug beneath his feet. Her eyes bulged as if they would pop.

"I remember you very clearly now," she exclaimed, her hands to her brow. "I remember you! You were no good to start with. A troublemaker. Always making trouble. I knew just where you'd end up. You've run true to form." Her gaze was defiant.

"Shut your mouth, Grandma," he said quietly, beginning to unzip his jacket at last.

"I will not, I'll have my say. I remember the day you wrote nasty words on the wall in the supply closet. Horrible words. And then when I went back to get paper to distribute, I saw those words. I knew who wrote them, all right."

"I didn't write them."

"You wrote them, all right. And I whacked your knuckles good with a ruler, if I remember right."

"You whacked my knuckles good, but I didn't write the words."

"Did!"

"Didn't!" He squirmed out of the jacket.

"I never made mistakes of that kind," she said softly, watching him shed the jacket. "I knew just who needed strict discipline in my class."

He stood before her now, holding the heavy jacket in his hand. Underneath he wore only a tee shirt of some rough gray linsey-woolsey material. She was positive she could smell the odor of the prison upon him.

"I never made mistakes," she repeated feebly. "And now you'd better put that coat right back on and leave. Go back to where you came from."

"Can't do that just yet, Grandma. I got a score to settle."

"Score? To settle?" She placed her hands upon the rocker arms for support.

"Yeah. You're the one. You're the one that sent me to prison. I had a long time to figure it all out, see? Ten years to figure it out. Lots of nights I'd lie there on that hard old board of a bed in that puke-hole and I'd try to piece it all together. How I come to be there. Was it my aunt? Naw. She did the best she could without any money. Was it the fellas I took up with in high school? Naw, something happened before that, or I'd of never taken up with the likes of them. And then one night it came to me. *You* was the one."

"The one? The one for what?" Her lips worked furiously in and out like a bellows. Her hands tightly gripped the spindle arms of the rocker.

"The one that sent me there. Because you *picked* on me all the time. Made me out worse than I was. You never gave me the chance the others had. The other kids left me out of things because you were always saying I was bad. And you always told me I was dirty, just because my aunt couldn't keep me in clean shirts. You punished me for everything that happened. You even made fun of my name one day, and at recess all the boys called me "Raybe-Baby" and the name stuck. But the worst was the day of the words on the wall. You hit me so hard my knuckles bled. My hands were sore as boils for a week."

"That's an exaggeration."

"No it isn't. They're *my* hands, I ought to know! And do you know who wrote those words on the closet wall? *Do you know?*" he screamed, putting his face right down next to hers.

"No. Who?" she managed, breathless with fright.

"*Nathan Pillsbury,* that's who!" he shouted, clenching his teeth and shaking her frail body within his grasp. "Nathan Pillsbury! Nathan Pillsbury! *Nathan Pillsbury!*"

"Let me go," she whimpered into her sunken chest. "Let me go!"

"I'll let you go after my score is settled."

The old woman's eyes rolled upward toward the blank, unseeing windows. "What are you going to do to me?"

"Just settle my score, lady," he said, taking the hammer from his jacket. "Now, put your hands on the table top."

"My hands? On the table top?" she whispered.

"On the table top," he repeated pedantically. "Like this." He made two fists and placed them squarely on the surface. "*Like that!*" he yelled, wrenching her quivering hands and forcing them to the table top. Then with his free hand, he raised the hammer.

discussion

We are suspicious when an individual blames all his misfortunes on one event in his life. This kind of thinking is simplistic and one tends to assume that the person is rationalizing his predicament or projecting onto others or onto an event, happenings that were not completely out of his control.

In this story Raybe Simpson builds a very convincing case for the way in which Miss Scofield labeled and humiliated him at a very impressionable age. One cannot dismiss the influence teachers have in shaping a child's image of himself, particularly if that child has social or physical handicaps that separate him from the group. The teacher can make a critical difference in helping the child to overcome the handicap and "make it" with the other children. The teacher can also do the opposite and reinforce the problem, thus enlarging it and making acceptance by the peer group almost impossible. Raybe keenly felt Miss Scofield's negative value judgment of him.

It is interesting that Miss Scofield really did not perceive herself as a teacher who put children in compartments labeled "bad" and "good" based upon their degree of cleanliness and family background. Prejudices such as these are very subtle, and many teachers who practice some form of discrimination would probably vehemently deny that they do so. Most teachers see themselves as dedicated and impartial.

"A Teacher's Rewards" is a stunning reminder that a teacher's relationship with each child needs to be examined and reexamined throughout the period of their relationship. In the early years in particular children need adults who are supportive and perceptive of their special needs because the child is less able to find enhancing outlets for himself. The story states its theme with a good deal of reality. Raybe Simpson becomes a symbol of the irreparable damage that children can sustain from unfeeling teachers.

springboards for inquiry

1. Explain how Miss Scofield might have been the single most important factor in molding Raybe Simpson's career in crime. Then take the opposite point of view.

2. How could other school personnel such as a school social worker, a school psychologist, or a principal have been of help to Raybe Simpson?

3. If you were responsible for hiring teachers in your school, what personal and professional characteristics would you consider important to look for in the applicants? Devise a set of questions you would ask in conducting an interview for a teacher for either the early primary grades, intermediate grades, junior high school, high school, or special education.

teachers versus teachers

There are teachers' lunchrooms where Catholic teachers eat at one end of the table, Protestant teachers at the other end, and Jewish teachers, feeling unwelcome, stay away. Every once in a while a maverick comes along who either does not want to know, or does not know, or cares little for these arbitrary divisions, and breaks his bread with the "wrong" group. And that's the way it sometimes is. More often than not the cliques in school buildings are formed around departments, and it is the height of indignity for the English department faculty to lunch with the history people. If perchance some idiot does not know how to find out whom to go to lunch with, there are those who will enlighten him. In small elementary schools the senior teachers sometimes separate themselves from the newer staff members.

Since schools are social systems, these dichotomies fairly represent the way the outside world is. Variations upon the theme of shared interests are most common—the young often cluster while the old guard cluck. The females frequently gather in places where it is understood males just do not enter. There is one university in which a woman has not sat at the "bachelor" table in 20 years.

One can almost live with these divisions between professionals. Hardest of all, however, are those divisions between individuals who just do not like one another. Frequently these divisions arise from differences in discipline or grade standards. Often people avoid each other because their two body chemistries just do not mesh. The results are predictable. We have known faculty members who have not said "Boo!" to one another for a quarter of a century.

Although adults can learn to live and understand teacher conflicts, when teacher differences become, as they inevitably do, part of the world of the children, there are sometimes cruel and unjust consequences. When children sense the crossed swords of teachers, they often pit them against one another and aggravate the situation. Teachers are human, and conflicts will arise between individuals. It is to be hoped that young children never become the casualties of the battlefield.

Gretchen Finletter

From the top of the stairs

One day at Miss Spence's School, a teacher announced a plan which she said must last us our lifetime and through all the trials and ordeals that would come to us. The teacher was Miss Bovee, who taught a subject known as Elocution. Her demand was that even if her pupils were faced by a major operation, a war, or a proposal of marriage—much giggling from the little girls—they must be able, as members of Miss Bovee's Always Ready Club, should the surgeon, general, or lover cry "Recite!" to give immediately three poems without a single mistake, and *with expression.*

Miss Bovee was completely successful. I do not believe that I or any of the other girls in her classes have ever forgotten our three recitations, and under strange circumstances they rise to our lips, with expression.

The school of some three hundred girls had Elocution once a week, in classes of eight, for forty-five mintes. We were required to learn a minimum of sixteen lines a week and our range of selection was extremely limited. The schooner *Hesperus* was sunk some eighty times a term, a hundred more reciters brought the good news from Ghent to Aix, a further group made Abou Ben Adhem's tribe increase, or went Up the airy mountain, Down the rushy glen, with "The Fairies."

There must have been more interesting or modern verse but we did not know of it. We were bound by a purple book called *The Silver Treasury,* with five illustrations. After putting mustaches on the ladies' faces and scratching the name of our favorite college along the sides of the book, we settled down to a long career of recitations.

Miss Bovee sat at the end of a table with her class-book open in front of her, where all could see what marks were given. The pupil's name was called and, standing at the end of the room and facing Miss Bovee and her leering classmates, she recited. Miss Bovee closed her eyes, her lips moved silently, her facial expression changed constantly while she emphasized moods with a toss of her head.

At the conclusion, the trouble began. Miss Bovee would pick out the two most important lines and ask to have them repeated. Then she would stand up and give them herself the right way and shot with dramatics.

To the new pupil it was horrifying. She realized that to get a good mark she would have to be a damn fool; and even if she were willing to take that painful step, she did not understand the technique.

So Miss Bovee explained the "one, two, three." This meant that before the great line of the poem the pupil was to pause and count "one, two, three," and then give it everything. In "Abou Ben Adhem," the angel writes Abou's request.

The angel wrote, and vanished. The next night

Excerpt from From the Top of the Stairs *by permission of Thomas Finletter.*

It came again with a great wakening
  light,
And showed the names whom love of
  God had blessed,
And lo! [*one, two, three*] Ben Adhem's
  name led all the rest.

The "one, two, three" was at first
given audibly and it was always a
great struggle to say it silently, and
quite impossible not to move the
lips.

Miss Bovee broke down self-con-
sciousness. She insisted on varied
voices and much expression, but we
were never allowed to invent our
own. It must be as complete an imi-
tation of her style as possible. "The
Wreck of the Hesperus" was her
great favorite. It gave rare opportunity for a deep and a high voice in
the unhappy dialogue between the
father and his little daughter, and it
was full of "one, two, three's."

"O father! I see a gleaming light,
Oh say, what may it be?"
But the father answered never a word,
[*one, two three*] A frozen corpse was he.
                . . .
Then the maiden clasped her hands
  and prayed
That saved she might be;
And she thought [*one, two, three*] of
  Christ, who stilled the wave,
On the Lake of Galilee.

A recitation which we all learned
and for which Miss Bovee had a
profound admiration was a poem
by Ralph Waldo Emerson about the
mountain and the squirrel. It was
nineteen lines long and became a
basic "must" of the Always Ready
members. It contained many problems.

The first was the pronunciation

of the word "squirrel." As a little animal that skips up and down trees, it
remained a normal squirrel, but
when it had its famous and victori-
ous argument with the mountain, it
became a "squi-i-rrr-il"—and woe to
the girl who did not roll it out and
add an extra dot or two to the *i*'s.

The next demand was deeply
embarrassing. When the squirrel
spoke, we must resemble a squirrel.
This was to be accomplished with
merry eyes and an extremely roguish manner. We balked. Could we
suggest it in another way—say, by
simulating nuts in our cheeks? No,
we must twinkle. This was an unhappy period and the nearest I remember to mutiny. But teachers are
powerful. With sulky expressions
we figuratively waved our tails. Says
the squi-i-rrr-il:—

If I cannot carry forests on my back,
Neither can you [*one, two, three, twinkle,
  dimple, and with great archness*] crack
  a nut!

There was a deep rivalry between
Miss Spence, the principal of the
school, and Miss Bovee over Shakespeare. Miss Spence owned Shakespeare. She had an enormous class
once a week, where she read us the
plays and we learned the more famous speeches.

The classes were held in the Assembly Room. We sat on camp
chairs in long rows, each of us having a cloth-bound copy of the play.
Miss Spence stood high above us on
a platform, reading and acting and
having, I always felt, the time of her
life. With her there were no closed
eyes, no silently moving lips. She
flung herself into the parts, she
loved the drunken scenes full of bad
puns, but like Miss Bovee she insisted that what we learned must be

given in an exact copy of her style. At a certain moment we would be made to recite some passage in unison with identical inflection.

Miss Spence was particularly fond of *The Merchant of Venice*. For some reason which was never made clear to us, she insisted that in the opening line of Portia's great speech in the courtroom scene, the voice should rise at least an octave on the word "strained."

The quality of mercy is not strained,
It droppeth as the gentle rain from
   heaven
Upon the place beneath.

It was not just a slight lifting of the voice: it was an enormous vocal jump. The effect of ninety girls together making this very unnatural sound never disturbed her and she would lead us like an orchestra with a swoop of her arm.

In Shylock's speech we let ourselves go and fairly shrieked, "You call me misbeliever, cut-throat, dog?" but quickly Miss Spence raised her hand. The dog, like the squirrel, had become a different animal. He was no longer a friendly Dawg: he was forever a Dahk.

Miss Spence wore voluminous, bright-colored silk dresses which had a peculiar and penetrating rustle. I have never heard a dress since that could give quite the same crackle and hiss. For us the sound was a signal to sit in an unnaturally straight position and not to turn around, thereby showing a great concentration.

Miss Spence often showed the parents of prospective pupils through the school. Once she brought a visiting father and a mother into the elocution class. Miss Bovee had unfortunately been poaching on Miss Spence's territory and had been bootlegging us some Shakespeare. The decision had to be made quickly whether to bury Caesar Miss Spence's way or Miss Bovee's. We were flustered by our audience but we were loyal to Miss Bovee.

As Caesar loved me, I weep for him; as he was fortunate, I rejoice at it; as he was valiant, I honor him; but, as he was ambitious, I slew him.

Miss Bovee felt Brutus had killed regretfully, and our voices became hushed for "slew." Miss Spence listened to two girls, but it was like a red rag to her. She stood up herself and hurled out: "But, as he was ambitious, I *slew* him!" And there was no doubt that Brutus was delighted.

Miss Bovee thanked Miss Spence and Miss Spence swished out, followed by the startled parents, who apparently were not aware of how swords had crossed. But we left Brutus for the rest of the period, and Miss Bovee after a quick blow of her nose asked for volunteers of the Always Ready Club, and her closed eyelids were pink.

At this time E. H. Sothern and Julia Marlowe were giving a cycle of Shakespeare at the Empire Theater and we were all encouraged to go. We knew the plays so well that we had a sense of authorship. But when Sothern and Marlowe diverged from the interpretation of the school, we were unanimous that they were wrong. One mannerism of Sothern's, however, impressed me deeply: he never said "my"; he said "meh."

Signior Antonio, many a time and oft

In the Rialto you have rated meh
About meh moneys and meh usances.

This seemed to me fascinating and daring, and I was determined, in spite of Miss Bovee, that I would never say "my" again.

The fact that Sothern and Marlowe were married was romantic to us, and we used to search through their grease paint for some glint of the deep love that we knew must be burning between them. Sothern was a very dirty old Shylock with matted beard and sunken eyes, and Julia Marlowe a particularly Vassar-like Portia, and they met only once in the courtroom scene, but several girls would always claim that there had been a moment when Shylock had looked at Portia in a "married" sort of way.

I was never convinced of this phenomenon, but when they took their rather stately curtain calls together, first to the right, then to the left, then to the top balcony, and then to each other, surely at that moment there was a mild, connubial glow. That was the moment when all Miss Spence's pupils broke into their wildest applause.

At that time actors and actresses were mysterious and remote and no magazine ever divulged their weight, their love affairs, or how they did their manicures. But the interest in them was just as deep, and we assumed that as they were in their parts, so must they be in their private lives. Half the school worshiped Maude Adams. It was known then as a crush, but the joys of this jelly-like state were much enhanced if they were shared by a dozen others. Pictures of Peter Pan in his little house in the treetops appeared inside schoolbooks to be surreptitious-ly adored, and thimbles were worn for kisses, and Best and Company got out a little cap with feathers. Rows of girls who were older and should have known better excitedly waved very clean pocket handkerchiefs when Peter asked with that particular break in his voice, "Do you believe in fairies?" and the big ambition was to have been to *Peter Pan* a greater number of times than anyone else.

I belonged to a smaller and more organized group who loved William Gillette. He was then playing *Secret Service, Held by the Enemy,* and his great role of Sherlock Holmes. The advantage of the Gillette circle, as opposed to the Maude Adams party, lay largely in the fact that William Gillette was a man. Little girls of nine and ten adored Maude Adams. It was silly. To shiver over Sherlock Holmes in his silk dressing gown when he cried, "Quick, Watson, the needle!" bared his arm and stuck the hypodermic into the upper wrist, and then gazed out over the audience with that, oh, so tired look—that was a moment of mature experience in one's life. It made the Peter Pan goings on mere childish falderal.

We liked him best in his dusty uniform of the Union officer in *Secret Service;* in his smoking jacket; wearing his cap with the visor at each end; in his dressing gown; or as he looked when he lit his pipe. Many were the girls who at home of an evening wandered about the rooms in striped wrappers, holding imaginary pipes between their clenched teeth as they looked out wearily into the night solving little crimes.

But we were humble and we were timid. It would not have occurred to us to wait at the stage door to see William Gillette leave the theater.

Instead we combined on a second-tier stage box where, if we hung far out, we could see him standing in the wings before his entrance. There was revealed to each of us in turn, by changing seats rather noisily, not Holmes, the detective, but Gillette, the man. He was equally wonderful. He looked just as tired, just as misunderstood, and just as full of dope as when he was on the stage.

We were convinced he was a real drug fiend, and in the wonderful daydreams that we wove, we forced him to give up the terrible morphine. And then came the great scene when he thanked one for having rescued him. Somehow he shed the dressing gown, was in a dusty uniform, and lo, it was a beautiful love scene.

"But I am too old for you."

"No—no—"

It ended in a vague mist and we began all over again. It was very, very silly and we were very, very happy.

Admiration for Gillette affected my elocution badly, for Gillette had a dry, almost monotonous voice admirably suited to the great Holmes but somehow lacking in the timbre necessary for Robert Browning. I would recite:—

That's meh last Duchess painted on the wall

in an ancient and weary voice and with no expression. My marks shot down but I would not give in. I felt I was at last an actress creating a role.

[Years later,] during the war the office of Civilian Defense held one of its many air-raid rehearsals in which a shock feeding unit of which I was a member was asked to make a special test for speed, with all equipment. At the first wail of the siren, the group was to rush to a certain fire department and make coffee and revive the wounded firemen while doctors and first-aiders tended the other injured.

A Red Cross captain who had been sent to time us kept her eyes on her wristwatch and gave us all a real sense of panic. Four large firemen stretched themselves out on tables and cried out that they were in great agony and only a drink could save them. A little lady, a new member of the shock feeders, hidden by a too large helmet, feverishly started stirring the pot, which looked like an oversized garbage can. In it was suspended the coffee in a gauze bag surrounded by gallons of tepid water.

An elderly canteener of many courses and little experience proffered a great deal of advice. "You should have heated the water first in small quantities," she insisted.

"You've been eighteen minutes already!" announced the Red Cross captain.

"Hurry up, girls, we're bleeding to death!" yelled the firemen.

The lady, who had been murmuring some incantation at the great pot, now turned furiously.

If I cannot carry forests on my back, Neither can you ONE, TWO, and THREE crack a nut!

The water suddenly boiled. An unknown Alumna of the Always Ready Club had survived a crisis.

discussion

On the surface this story chronicles the idiosyncratic styles of two dedicated but feuding teachers. Like two great battleships they levy guns over Shakespeare. On a more significant level the story reveals the discomfort students suffer when teachers feud. The students must calculate the risks of snubbing either Miss Bovee or Miss Spence, each of whom insists upon her own interpretation of Shakespeare. Although ludicrous in this case, when students are forced to regurgitate opinions in the exact manner of their teachers, there is a betrayal of real learning.

Undoubtedly the enjoyment of Shakespeare for these girls will always be tinged with the competitiveness of their teachers. In addition Miss Bovee and Miss Spence have sabotaged the students' right to speculate upon Shakespeare's intent and to make their own choices about interpretation.

The purposes of education are distorted when students must make decisions based on teacher power rather than on acquired knowledge. It is no wonder that students become cynical about educational institutions when they must adjust to their teachers' biases in order to "make it" in the system.

springboards for inquiry

1. How would you respond to a teacher like Miss Spence or Miss Bovee who insists on her own interpretation of subject matter?

2. How can the school counselor assist students who are caught between feuding teachers? For what reasons might students hesitate to involve counselors in conflicts with their teachers?

3. Are you consciously aware of teacher biases? How might students react to these biases in order to improve their grades or status?

4. Does self scheduling[1] deter teachers from conducting practices in the classroom that the students find objectionable?

---

[1]This refers to student selection of classes and teachers at registration.

References

AMIDON, EDMUND. "Can Teachers Help the Socially Rejected?" *Elementary School Journal* (December 1965): pp. 149–54.

AMIDON, EDMUND, and HOFFMAN, CARL. "Helping the Socially Isolated or Rejected Child." *The National Elementary Principal* 43, no. 2 (November 1963): 75.

ASHTON-WARNER, SYLVIA. *Spearpoint—Teacher in America.* New York: Knopf, 1972.

———. *Teacher.* New York: Bantam, 1971.

BHAERMAN, STEVE, and DENKER, JOEL. *No Particular Place to Go.* New York: Simon and Schuster, 1972.

BRUCE, JOYCE AND WEIL, MARSHA, *Models of Teaching.* Englewood Cliffs, N.J.: Prentice-Hall, 1972.

DENNISON, GEORGE. *The Lives of Children.* New York: Random House, 1969.

GRAUBARD, ALLEN. *Free the Children.* New York: Pantheon, 1973.

HERBST, JURGEN. "The Anti-School—Some Reflections on Teaching." *Educational Theory* 18 (Winter 1968): 15.

HOWES, VIRGIL M. "Quest for Self." In *Individualization of Instruction: A Teaching Strategy.* New York: Macmillan, 1970.

ILLICH, IVAN. *Deschooling Society.* New York: Harper & Row, 1971.

JERSILD, ARTHUR T. *When Teachers Face Themselves.* New York: Bureau of Publications, Teachers College, Columbia University, 1955.

KOHL, HERBERT. *The Open Classroom.* New York: Random House, 1970.

KOHL, HERBERT. *36 Children.* New York: Signet Books, New American Library, 1967.

KOZOL, JONATHAN. *Death at an Early Age.* Boston: Houghton Mifflin, 1967.

———. *Free Schools.* New York: Houghton Mifflin, 1972.

LANE, HOWARD, and BEAUCHAMP, MARY. *Human Relations in Teaching.* New York: Prentice-Hall, 1955.

MASLOW, ABRAHAM H. *Motivation and Personality,* 2nd ed. New York: Harper & Row, 1970.

———. "Some Basic Propositions of a Growth and Self-Actualization Psychology." In *Perceiving, Behaving, Becoming.* Washington, D.C.: Association for Supevision and Curriculum Development, 1962.

MORENO, JACOB L. "Contributions of Sociometry to Research Methodology in Sociology." *American Sociological Review* 12, no. 2 (April 1947): 287–92.

NEILL, ALEXANDER S. *Summerhill.* New York: Hart, 1960.

PURKEY, WILLIAM W. *Self Concept and School Achievement.* Englewood Cliffs, N.J.: Prentice-Hall, 1970.

RATHS, JAMES; PANCELLA, JOHN R.; and VAN NESS, JAMES S. "The Model of Good Teaching." In *Studying Teaching.* Englewood Cliffs, N.J.: Prentice-Hall, 1967.

RATHS, LOUIS E. "What Is a Good Teacher?" *Childhood Education* 40, no. 9 (May 1964): 451.

———; HARMIN, MERRILL; and SIMON, SIDNEY B. *Meeting the Needs of Children.* Englewood Cliffs, N.J.: Prentice-Hall, 1972.

———. *Studying Teaching.* Englewood Cliffs, N.J.: Prentice-Hall, 1967.

———. *Teaching for Learning.* Columbus: Merrill, 1967.

———. *Teaching for Thinking.* Columbus: Merrill, 1967.

———. *Values and Teaching.* Columbus: Merrill, 1966.

REIMER, EVERETT. *School Is Dead.* New York: Doubleday, 1972.

ROGERS, CARL R. *Client-Centered Therapy.* Boston: Houghton Mifflin, 1951.

———. *Education For What Is Real.* New York: Harper, 1947.

———. *The Workshop Way of Learning.* New York: Harper, 1951.

———. "Toward Becoming a Fully Functioning Person." In *Perceiving, Behaving, Becoming.* Washington, D.C.: ASCD, 1962.

———, and STEVENS, BARRY. *Person to Person: The Problem of Being Human.* Moab, Jordan: Real People Press, 1971.

SKINNER, BURRIS F. *The Technology of Teaching.* New York: Appleton, 1968.

SILBERMAN, CHARLES E. *Crisis in the Classroom.* New York: Random House, 1969.

SILBERMAN, MELVIN L. "Behavioral Expression of Teachers' Attitudes Toward Elementary School Students." *Journal of Educational Psychology* 60 (1969): 402–7.

———, ed. "Teachers' Attitudes and Actions Toward Their Students." In *The Experience of Schooling.* New York: Holt, Rinehart and Winston, 1970.

TABA, HILDA. *Curriculum Development: Theory and Practice.* New York: Harcourt Brace Jovanovich, 1962.

———. *Teachers Handbook for Elementary Social Studies.* Reading, Mass.: Addison-Wesley, 1967.

TORRANCE, PAUL. *Guiding Creative Talent.* Englewood Cliffs, N.J.: Prentice-Hall, 1962.

The Learner

Educators can devise strategies for teaching—and they have. Teachers can spend their summers (and they do) planning interest centers or pageants— even next year's Christmas play! Professors can march into (and one we know did) junior high English classes armed to the teeth with subject matter knowledge. It is possible, even probable, that all of these preplanned scenarios may be doomed to failure if their originators do not realize that the learner and his "set," "motivation," "culture," etc., will permit him to interact with the teacher's plans.

Educators think it is axiomatic that knowing the learner and appreciating his growth and development is the key to understanding how and what to teach him. There are three fundamental principles which are still widely accepted, though not without refutation by distinguished authorities.[1] These are seeking, self-selection, and pacing. Each is a basic proposition which, within limits, describes the learner.

Seeking: Humanistic psychology tells us that individuals want to learn, want to become, want to progress. Ignorance is not bliss. Even ignorant humans worry. Blissfulness is not man's state. Man is not satisfied to be somnolent. He attacks his environment with vigor and shapes it to his needs. The child-learner does not want to be left alone in his original state of ignorance. He seeks information and the good life. He organizes his world no matter where he is. He seeks the condition of homeostasis—a tendency towards the maintenance of both a psychological and physiological stability. This means that he will seek experiences (learning) that will assure his own comfort. The learner does not accept the world but becomes a seeker in his world. And so man has learned to understand atomic power and gravity and to create art and literature. From a plethora of viewpoints man searches for explanations and interprets the world.

Self-Selection: Research on nutrition has clearly demonstrated that children old enough to feed themselves will, when given a free and wide choice of good foods, select for themselves a diet as nutritionally sound as any devised by trained technicians.[2] Learners, too, select from their environment—i.e. books, articles, concepts, and ideas—what they feel they need.

---

[1]One of those distinguished authorities is David P. Ausubel. His discussion of readiness, maturity, and self-selection refute the contentions advanced here and are indispensable reading for those wishing to enlarge their horizons about teaching and learning. His "Viewpoints from Related Disciplines: Human Growth and Development," in *Teachers College Record* 60, no. 5 (February 1959): 245–54, is a classic in the field. Briefly, he refutes the notion that (a) readiness is maturation and says that maturation is a function of development irrespective of experience while readiness is solely a function of prior learning experience. Then (b) he refutes the idea that because the child self-selects his diet, he can, ipso facto, select his own curriculum plan of study. Incidentally, even though Ausubel's article is 15 years old it is "must" reading for all who are interested in open and alternative education.

[2]Willard C. Olson, *Child Development* (Boston: D. C. Heath, 1959), p. 50.

They reject that which is inappropriate to their homeostatic condition. Ausubel disagrees. He says, "because the child is sensitive in early childhood to internal cues of physiological need we cannot conclude that he is similarly sensitive to cues reflective of psychological and other developmental needs; even in the area of nutrition, selection is a reliable criterion of need only during early infancy."[3]

Critics of Ausubel conclude that he has too narrowly extrapolated the concept of self-selection. The real meaning of self-selection is precisely what it says—the learner chooses to ignore or attend to what his teacher thinks he ought to learn on the basis of what is relevant or interesting in the light of his needs at the moment. This is not to say that since he self-selects, he is therefore able to select what it is he should learn in school in order to meet his long term needs. Nevertheless, no matter what he is given in school, he will select to learn that which he feels he wants to learn. A desirable plan for teachers to follow, therefore, is to give their learners a choice of equally valuable learning topics, so that what they select to learn will likely be approached with more alacrity and assiduousness.

Pacing: Much of today's emphasis on individualizing learning through programmed instruction, interest centers, and contractual performance is based upon the idea that each learner proceeds to learn at his own speed and in his own fashion. He cannot be forced either to relax or to accelerate that pace without affecting his learning. It should be mentioned here, however, that pace, as valid and important as it is, is but one factor of modern instruction. Learning styles, individual interests, motivational devices, etc., must also be considered when instruction is tailored to the individual. Pace, of course, is far easier to design into a lesson plan than are the other facets of individuality. Differences in learning style are too rarely a factor in curricular design.

A discussion of the learner would be incomplete without focusing upon certain other "core" propositions about human growth and development. If seeking, self-selection, and pacing are philosophical topics, the two other topics to be outlined may be more properly referred to as developmental. These are Erik Erickson's neo-freudian, psychoanalytic socialization model and Piaget's psychological formulations. Erikson, presently at Harvard, has described the socialization of man in eight stages. He uses each stage to describe the type of learning that goes on at the various levels of human development. Each stage culminates with the individual overcoming or resolving that psychosocial crisis that is necessary to allow the learner to negotiate the next stage. Erikson's model goes from infancy through maturity in adulthood. In Figure 1 the eight stages are represented architecturally, since Erikson sees man's progress through life as a set of building blocks with each stage resting and depending upon the earlier stages. An understanding of this pyramid-like structure is essential to full comprehension of the model.

In Erikson's first three stages (trust, autonomy, and initiative) which cover psychosocial development during infancy and the pre-school years, con-

---

[3]Ausubel, "Viewpoints from Related Disciplines," p. 251.

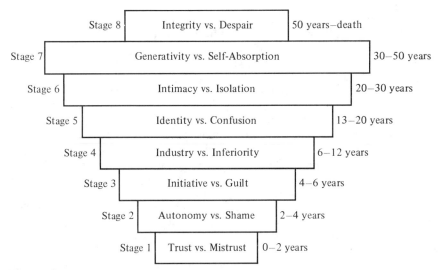

Stage 8	Integrity vs. Despair	50 years–death
Stage 7	Generativity vs. Self-Absorption	30–50 years
Stage 6	Intimacy vs. Isolation	20–30 years
Stage 5	Identity vs. Confusion	13–20 years
Stage 4	Industry vs. Inferiority	6–12 years
Stage 3	Initiative vs. Guilt	4–6 years
Stage 2	Autonomy vs. Shame	2–4 years
Stage 1	Trust vs. Mistrust	0–2 years

Figure 1

tinuous effort is made by the individual, through early nurturance, to develop a trusting relationship with the external world and to become self-directing and seeking before entering school. While Erikson's model parallels Freud's psychosexual one, the major difference is that whereas Freud saw the nondevelopment at any stage as a fixation to be resolved only through psychoanalysis, Erikson believes that failure to develop fully in any stage makes success later on more difficult but not impossible. In fact, Erikson presumes that in every stage of life the developmental tasks of all previous stages are remet. Thus, all through one's life an individual's trust is tested, his autonomy threatened, etc. Having quite successfully navigated any and all of these earlier, a person finds his present crisis easier to resolve.

Most learners entering nursery school, kindergarten, or first grade have been reasonably successful in passing through stages 1 and 2. If, however, the learner has, instead of developing a sense of trust and a feeling of autonomy in his first three or four years of life, developed mistrust and shame, entrance into nursery school may be fraught with problems. Trust and autonomy refer to the feeling of security and a basic optimism accompanied by pride in the child's newfound abilities to control his motor and physical needs. In the nursery school, he will broaden his skills through play. He will learn to cooperate, to lead, and to follow. He will, if he is in a good school, find that his initiative is encouraged yet limited. A good experience for a pre-schooler paves the way for his elementary school years when he must learn more formal skills. He will better learn to relate to peers, to play according to rules, to master cognitive knowledge such as social studies, English, and mathematics. He will learn to be industrious. Again, if he has successfully resolved his earlier psychosocial crises and is a trusting, autonomous, and exploratory-minded person, he will more easily learn to be zealous and industrious. Should the opposite be the case, then he will be mistrustful and filled with shame and guilt which will inhibit his elementary school progress and result in the experience of inferiority, the precursor of alienation.

The learner, then, is in no sense a *tabula rasa* or blank slate standing ready to be etched upon, nor is he an empty vessel waiting to be filled. The junior high, high school, and college years are faced by an individual who in every way is bubbling with the failures or successes of his earlier days. Whether or not he successfully finds his identity over this seven or eight year span of time depends largely upon what has occurred earlier. The answer to the questions, "who am I?" "what am I doing here?" "whither shall I go?" and "what may I become?" are part of the adolescent's search for identity. These experimental years, especially for middle-class children, have been called by Erikson a "psychosocial moratorium." Adolescents in search of their identity play games "for fun," games in which they can get their marbles back if they lose. Hopefully, in the mid-twenties, the experiment with different roles is nearly over, allowing the adolescent to consider settling down to a relationship of intimacy as well as a sense of worth in work.

The learner is not a machine to be programmed. He is not a complicated pigeon. He is a human being who has had a vast experience in just growing up. He does not park his psychosocial self outside the schoolhouse door. He does not tether his lifespace to an educational hitching post. He brings his self into the learning situations created by his teachers. An inadequately socialized child cannot learn. A child brought up with mostly the negative aspects of his socialization reinforced (the adjectives in Figure 1 following the word *versus*) approaches the formal learning of the schools with diffidence. The learner needs to be seen through the psychosocial lens as well as the more structured cognitive prism.

Jean Piaget, the Swiss psychologist whose theories about learning have swept the psychological world, describes three stages of cognitive development beyond infancy which concern the learner as he is schooled in institutions other than the home. What people do with the learner once he is in an educational institution may be greatly affected by Piaget's theory regarding the development of expectancy-probability in children. Piaget refers to a developmental continuum that may be divided into three or four phases. It is worth noting that Piaget postulates this development of cognition regardless of experience and individual differences. The phases are:

1. the sensorimotor (birth to age two)
2. the pre-operational (age three to six)
3. the concrete-operational (approximately age seven to ten)
4. the formal-operational (eleven or twelve through fifteenth year)

In the pre-operational stage, about the time the child enters pre-school or kindergarten, there is egocentric thinking. Language is used for simple communication, and some experience with symbolism is evident. The child is tied to actions, not symbols in his everyday life. True concepts cannot be formed. The child tends to reason from particular to particular with no generalization. During this time children link ideas together even though they are not really related. The learner also thinks that what he sees is seen in exactly the same way by everyone else. Further, children at this stage believe that the world is maintained by what people do. There is evidence of thinking and reasoning but not of operational thinking. There is an awareness of certainty, probability, possibility; and simple chance. Finally, during the last part of elementary school and into the early high school years, there is the period of formal operations or logical development. At this time abstract concepts can be mastered. It is important for the prospective teacher and parent to realize that the full and mature development of each of these cognitive stages is possible but not inevitable for each learner. Use of this schema as an absolute guide for adult expectations about the learner would be a serious breach of understanding. Some children may zip through Piaget's stages of cognitive development in grand style; others will pass through incompletely yet be able to function quite adequately. Any rigid expectations based on the age of the child are as inappropriate with Piaget as with Erikson.

The learner is a many-splendored thing. We have some knowledge of what impels or inhibits him. We also know how and through what steps he acquires knowledge. Erikson's ideas lead rather nicely into a discussion of the concept of self. This self-evaluation which everyone makes is either positive or negative depending upon the nature of his social experience. Thus, if he has learned mistrust, shame, guilt, and inferiority and is not at all sure of his sexual or personal identity, then his self-concept is low. Bernard says, "the self-concept is built up slowly through experience, especially with people, and concerns the kind of being that the individual conceives himself to be and the kind of person he believes himself capable of becoming."[4]

In the psychology of expectancy and self-fulfilling prophecy we find the most important implications of the self-concept.[5] Children tend to become what they are expected to become. Learners whose input from meaningful adults indicates that they are delinquents, hoods, and incapable of learning become as they are described. We tend to live the roles into which we are cast. Rosenthal and Jacobson[6] report that when teachers expect students to "spurt," they actually do so. Despite some objections to their study, we may still conclude that adults' expectations can erode or enhance the concept of self.

[4]Harold W. Bernard, *Child Development and Learning* (Boston: Allyn & Bacon, 1973).

[5]The most significant book on theory and research in the area of self-concept is Ruth Wylie, *The Self-Concept* (Lincoln: The University of Nebraska Press, 1961).

[6]Robert Rosenthal and Lenore Jacobson, *Pygmalion in the Classroom* (New York: Holt, Rinehart and Winston, 1968). In an article, "A Patient by Any Other Name . . . : Clinician Group Difference in Labeling Bias," by Ellen J. Langer and Robert P. Abelson in the *Journal of Consulting and Clinical Psychology* 42, no. 1 (February 1974): 4–9, the same expectancy based upon a label is evident even amongst highly trained Ph.D.s.

Recently educators have become more cognizant of the effects of race, status, and class upon the self-concept of learners. Children with a negative consciousness of their poverty or color tend to develop low concepts of themselves. One's social class status (SCS) deeply influences one's view of oneself. The terms *disadvantaged, culturally deprived* or *different* have today become educational bywords. So, too, have *welfare kids, hoods* and *junkies* become part of the nation's vocabulary. Each label, often libelous, sears the self-concept.

The learner is the child. The child is father to the learner. The lifespace of the child shapes his possibilities as a learner. The learner approaches the tasks of learning armed with everything that has happened to him in his family and in the world that has nurtured him. He learns what he has lived. If he has lurked in infinite corridors of despair, he learns little. If he has basked in the light of acceptance and love, he learns avidly.

the first day
of school

The child of five or six has been the center of attention in his family. Every day has been a great day, especially if he is an only child. What he did in the park, at the zoo, at his friend's house—all of these things are very important to his parents. He is the great participant as it were. If anything goes wrong he can usually count on his mother being just around the corner. In short, he has had about a half dozen years of glorious one-to-one attention.

Suddenly, on September 12 of a certain year he finds himself getting up on a clear fall day which separates all the yesterdays from a vastly new future. For one thing, time suddenly seems very important. It appears that he has to be somewhere at a very specific time. It cannot be any old time. He must be exactly on time. No dawdling this morning. No skipping to the usual early morning places—only one place to go—to school and by 8:30 A.M. (or 9:00 or whatever time the tardy bell rings). And the clothes he's dressed in! For the last five years or so, even until just yesterday he usually wore whatever seemed to be about. If it was torn or frayed or a little too large or small it was really quite O.K. Not today! Everything is laid out, it's clean and stiff (not soft because he wore it yesterday and six yesterdays before!) It's new. It's shiny. And it must be worn.

Another strange thing. Yesterday breakfast wasn't all that important. Today there seems to be a desperate urgency about eggs, toast, juice, and that isn't all. His mother seems to be particularly concerned that he eats enough to last till some mysterious hour when he may eat again. Only yesterday he could toddle home at any old time and eat from a great variety of goodies in the refrigerator or on the shelves. Where could one be going that demands the relinquishing of all the familiar, comfortable habits in exchange for a rigid routine ahead?

To school, of course.

For those who have already been a part of this rite of passage its trauma has nearly disappeared. If it hasn't, they may be among those who assiduously avoid 7:45 A.M. classes. But for the child on his way to the first day of school, there is a very marked difference compared with all the other days he has experienced. For the oldest child especially, with no model to follow, the first day of his public, parochial, or private education may be his first real encounter with a society which has been telling him how much it loves him for six years, but which suddenly demands a conformity to time and motion heretofore only observable on TV serials. This regimentation, now, at age six seems utterly incomprehensible, yet it is happening.

Off he goes, then, on this lovely morning when the world still seems so friendly and personal—off to a bus perhaps or to a school a few blocks away. Bus rides were possibly a novelty, and one always had a parent with him. But now there are over 40 other kids in their very stiff and new duds, each with the same stunned looks of abandonment. In some communities a percentage of the children either do not have the same flesh tint or do not talk the same language. But all are headed for the same place . . . a cavernous monster of brick with an unquenchable desire to imbibe busload after busload of similarly startled scholars.

"Scholars?" you say. Yesterday they were but children. Today they will perhaps start pecking away at a book which forces them to draw lines from one picture to another and having successfully done "x" number of pages at their own pace, they will move to a book with still a prettier cover and perhaps spend more time doing exactly what they just finished doing. Or, if they are a bit luckier, the teacher will read stories to them and then want to know if they understand what she has read.

And there will be appointed hours. One of these will be "recess"—when, whether they need to or not, children will be marched to a shiny, tiled room and told to use the toilets then instead of asking to be excused during class time. Boys may have their first introduction to urinals at this time. Girls whose toilet training has included fastidious cleanliness may have some difficulties using school toilets, especially in situations where some children look under the stalls or invade privacy in other ways.

After interminable hours of doing things in concert with others, the children wearily trudge or bus home, where upon their arrival mothers want to know what they have learned! Learned? Why for the past five years and up until yesterday, a return home was an occasion of hugs and kisses and bits of apple, a time to clean up and rejoin the family. And now, instead of being able to relax, the child must describe his cognitive experiences!

That's about what the first day of school is for many children—not exactly a place of children's freedom nor a reformatory.[1] It is, to be sure, a place where the child may first sense that he is not the center of the universe. And it seems reasonable to assume that this introduction to the school world in which he will live for the next decade or two of his life will be filled with stress and difference.[2]

There are two other significant classes of people who need to be concerned about the first day of school. They are the parent and the teacher. We shall deal only briefly with both.

If the child's experience of his first day of school has been exaggerated, it was only to make the point that some of the "culture shock" the mythical

---

[1]We have undoubtedly been somewhat unfair in picturing a child's first school experience as being so rigid and lacking in freedom. Nonetheless, with the exception of certain private schools (and in some instances public schools as well) while both freedom and license prevail, the average kindergarten youngster faces about what we have depicted. For those students who have become particularly intrigued with the issue of schools or freedom, see Ray Hemming, *Children's Freedom: A. S. Neill and the Evolution of the Summerhill Idea* (New York: Schocken Books, 1973).

[2]The general topic of stress in children is not the subject of much special attention. The most significant general book is Hans Selye, *Stress of Life* (New York: McGraw-Hill, 1956). A more specific volume is Ronald C. Doll and Robert S. Fleming, *Children Under Pressure* (Columbus: Merrill, 1966). Even more recently, Ved. P. Varma, ed., *Stress in Children* (New York: Crane, Russak and Co., 1973), which pays particular attention to handicapped, slow learning, adopted, immigrant, and injury-prone children in school. Each of the contributors is British; thus they speak from the point of view of the English school.

learner faced could have been, at least in part, avoided by parents who were alert to the imminent situation. It is important for parents not to wait until the day before school to "prepare" the child for the following day's first school experience. However, verbal admonitions and descriptions not tied to the concrete (recollect what Piaget had to say about the thinking of children at age five or six) will be of little value. It is important that in the pre-school years every child will have had some ever-widening experiences so that, in fact, the first day of school would be less painful. Where buses were to be used for whatever reason, the child could have at least ridden on a city bus or even be brought to the busyard to see where the behemoths are stored. For a small child to step into a bus for the first time and to be transported miles from home can be a very unsettling experience. A gradual desensitization to this new experience would be wise. If busing is not in the picture, then the neighborhood school surely is. So, whether or not there are older siblings in that school, a summer visit with parents to the building is very important. If parents feel at all that the separation anxiety will be of any consequence to the child, a number of visits would be in order with the last visit being as close to the opening day of school as possible.

For teachers the first day of school is crucial to the future success of the class. A wise teacher does not teach the whole term's work on that first day, but he goes all out to make that first learning contact an unforgettable one. Whether the first day of school means the first day ever or the first day again, it is very important that all learners return home anxious to return the next day because that first day was terrific! Alas, this is rarely the case. But children who want to return are well on their way to a good school experience.

Many teachers start with a tight rein so that they can ease up rather than tighten up as time goes by. A tight rein does not mean abject silence or Hitler-like discipline. All human beings respond to laughter and love. Both must be in evidence. In the upper grades these two, plus a love for the subject to be taught, make an ideal combination. When children return home and tell of teachers who seem to care, the children are anxious to return the affection. The teacher who really believes he must scare the devil out of the heathens finds that there is an equitable reaction to his threats. Setting up the laws of the class too soon before the rules are broken practically guarantees broken rules. In no sense are children like colts.

It is true, however, that while children on a one to one basis may be perfectly manageable, as a group they may become formidable opponents. Teachers, therefore, need sureness of purpose, appreciation for the group's anxiety, and humor to dissolve that anxiety. Teachers need to communicate standards which are fair and realistic. In the most threatening of schools and under the most disadvantaged regime the teacher who emits messages of affection and high spirits cracks the first day anxiety barrier.

William Saroyan

The first day of school

He was a little boy named Jim, the first and only child of Dr. Louis Davy, 717 Mattei Building, and it was his first day at school. His father was French, a small heavy-set man of forty whose boyhood had been full of poverty and unhappiness and ambition. His mother was dead: she died when Jim was born, and the only woman he knew intimately was Amy, the Swedish housekeeper.

It was Amy who dressed him in his Sunday clothes and took him to school. Jim liked Amy, but he didn't like her for taking him to school. He told her so. All the way to school he told her so.

I don't like you, he said.

I don't like you any more.

I like *you*, the housekeeper said.

Then why are you taking me to school? he said.

He had taken walks with Amy before, once all the way to the Court House Park for the Sunday afternoon band concert, but this walk to school was different.

What for? he said.

Everybody must go to school, the housekeeper said.

Did you go to school? he said.

No, said Amy.

Then why do I have to go? he said.

You will like it, said the housekeeper.

He walked on with her in silence, holding her hand. I don't like you, he said. I don't like you any more.

I like you, said Amy.

Copyright by William Saroyan, 1936, 1964.

Miss Binney, the teacher of the first grade, was an old lady who was all dried out. The room was full of little boys and girls. School smelled strange and sad. He sat at a desk and listened carefully.

Then why are you taking me to school? he said again.

Why?

The housekeeper knew how frightened a little boy could be about going to school.

You will like it, she said. I think you will sing songs and play games.

I don't want to, he said.

I will come and get you every afternoon, she said.

I don't like you, he told her again.

She felt very unhappy about the little boy going to school, but she knew that he would have to go.

The school building was very ugly to her and to the boy. She didn't like the way it made her feel, and going up the steps with him she wished he didn't have to go to school. The halls and rooms scared her, and him, and the smell of the place too. And he didn't like Mr. Barber, the principal.

Amy despised Mr. Barber.

What is the name of your son? Mr. Barber said.

This is Dr. Louis Davy's son, said Amy. His name is Jim. I am Dr. Davy's housekeeper.

James? said Mr. Barber.

Not James, said Amy, just Jim.

All right, said Mr. Barber. Any middle name?

No, said Amy. He is too small for a middle name. Just Jim Davy.

All right, said Mr. Barber. We'll try him out in the first grade. If he doesn't get along all right we'll try him out in kindergarten.

Dr. Davy said to start him in the

first grade, said Amy. Not kindergarten.

All right, said Mr. Barber.

The housekeeper knew how frightened the little boy was, sitting on the chair, and she tried to let him know how much she loved him and how sorry she was about everything. She wanted to say something fine to him about everything, but she couldn't say anything, and she was very proud of the nice way he got down from the chair and stood beside Mr. Barber, waiting to go with him to a classroom.

On the way home she was so proud of him she began to cry.

Miss Binney, the teacher of the first grade, was an old lady who was all dried out. The room was full of little boys and girls. School smelled strange and sad. He sat at a desk and listened carefully.

He heard some of the names: *Charles, Ernest, Alvin, Norman, Betty, Hannah, Juliet, Viola, Polly.*

He listened carefully and heard Miss Binney say, Hannah Winter, what *are* you chewing? And he saw Hannah Winter blush. He liked Hannah Winter right from the beginning.

Gum, said Hannah.

Put it in the waste-basket, said Miss Binney.

He saw the little girl walk to the front of the class, take the gum from her mouth, and drop it into the waste-basket.

And he heard Miss Binney say, Ernest Gaskin, what are *you* chewing?

Gum, said Ernest.

And he liked Ernest Gaskin too.

They met in the schoolyard, and Ernest taught him a few jokes.

Amy was in the hall when school ended. She was sullen and angry at everybody until she saw the little boy. She was amazed that he wasn't changed, that he wasn't hurt, or perhaps utterly unalive, murdered. The school and everything about it frightened her very much. She took his hand and walked out of the building with him, feeling angry and proud.

Jim said, What comes after twenty-nine?

Thirty, said Amy.

Your face is dirty, he said.

His father was very quiet at the supper table.

What comes after twenty-nine? the boy said.

Thirty, said his father.

Your face is dirty, he said.

In the morning he asked his father for a nickel.

What do you want a nickel for? his father said.

Gum, he said.

His father gave him a nickel and on the way to school he stopped at Mrs. Riley's store and bought a package of Spearmint.

Do you want a piece? he asked Amy.

Do you want to give me a piece? the housekeeper said.

Jim thought about it a moment, and then he said, Yes.

Do you like me? said the housekeeper.

I like you, said Jim, Do you like me?

Yes, said the housekeeper.

Do you like school?

Jim didn't know for sure, but he knew he liked the part about gum. And Hannah Winter. And Ernest Gaskin.

I don't know, he said.

Do you sing? asked the housekeeper.

No, we don't sing, he said.

Do you play games? she said.

Not in the school, he said. In the yard we do. He liked the part about gum very much.

Miss Binney said, Jim Davy, what are you *chewing?*

Ha ha ha, he thought.

Gum, he said.

He walked to the waste-paper basket and back to his seat, and Hannah Winter saw him, and Ernest Gaskin too. That was the best part of school.

It began to grow too.

Ernest Gaskin, he shouted in the schoolyard, *what* are you *chewing?*

Raw elephant meat, said Ernest Gaskin. Jim Davy, what are *you* chewing?

Jim tried to think of something very funny to be chewing, but he couldn't.

Gum, he said, and Ernest Gaskin laughed louder than Jim laughed when Ernest Gaskin said raw elephant meat.

It was funny no matter what you said.

Going back to the classroom Jim saw Hannah Winter in the hall.

Hannah Winter, he said, *what in the world* are you *chewing?*

The little girl was startled. She wanted to say something nice that would honestly show how nice she felt about having Jim say her name and ask her the funny question, making fun of school, but she couldn't think of anything that nice to say because they were almost in the room and there wasn't time enough.

Tutti-frutti, she said with desperate haste.

It seemed to Jim he had never before heard such a glorious word, and he kept repeating the word to himself all day.

Tutti-frutti, he said to Amy on the way home.

Amy Larson, he said, *what, are, you, chewing?*

He told his father all about it at the supper table.

He said, Once there was a hill. On the hill there was a mill. Under the mill there was a walk. Under the walk there was a key. What is it?

I don't know, his father said. What is it?

Milwaukee, said the boy.

The housekeeper was delighted.

Mill. Walk. Key, Jim said.

Tutti-frutti.

What's that? said his father.

Gum, he said. The kind Hannah Winter chews.

Who's Hannah Winter? said his father.

She's in my room, he said.

Oh, said his father.

After supper he sat on the floor with the small red and blue and yellow top that hummed while it spinned. It was all right, he guessed. It was still very sad, but the gum part of it was very funny and the Hannah Winter part very nice. Raw elephant meat, he thought with great inward delight.

Raw elephant meat, he said aloud to his father who was reading the evening paper. His father folded the paper and sat on the floor beside him. The housekeeper saw them together on the floor and for some reason tears came to her eyes.

discussion

Many adults can remember their first day of school. Fear of the strange and new, a potent emotion, and a prominent one on this important day in every child's life, makes it hard to forget. Only a few children go off to school on their first day entirely willingly. Some, along with being fearful, may be down right angry like Jim. His reaction is very normal. There is no love even for a mother, if she is the one who forced you into this new situation.

At least Amy's forecast for his first day in school is accurate. Many parents tell their children they will learn to read and write. Children who do not understand time sequences are very unhappy when they come home without having used a pencil or held a book that whole first day. Amy seems to react to school as strongly as Jim does. When children react with a great deal of crying and refuse to leave Mother at the kindergarten door, it is not unusual for the mother to be enduring a painful separation anxiety as well. In fact, frequently, but not always, the child who cannot be separated from his mother on the first day of school has a mother who cannot be separated from her child.

Jim immediately likes his classmates. He is much more aware of them than he is of the teacher or the school program. For some children like Jim it is their first extended contact with peers. By school age most children are ready and eager to play with their age mates. (In pre-school years children frequently play alongside their agemates but do not interact in play).

The teacher and school program should hold interest for the student. Even though many children will answer "nothing" to the question "what did you do in school today?" kindergarteners in particular usually like school activities because the activities involve play and art materials, which are new and fun to use. The teacher is also an important and positive force in the new student's life. Boys and girls alike will send love notes and speak warmly of their teacher who is the important adult in their lives now. Parents are told how Miss So and So wants things done, and they now consider her way the right way. For the first time parents take the back seat to another adult.

Miss Binney, Jim's teacher, is probably not going to be the recipient of love notes from Jim. Maybe some very conforming little girls will like her, but not a little girl like Hannah Winter. Particularly in the first years of school, the teacher should be an adult the child cares for. Later on in the school years respect and admiration are good substitutes for the early dependent-love relationship. Teachers do not have to be young to get love notes from the little boys in her class. Teachers who are gentle and nurturant are seen as beautiful even if near retirement age.

We are particularly sorry that Jim Davy will not have a particularly pleasant memory to recall in his life—a cherished first teacher.

springboards for inquiry

1. Recall your first teacher, or your first pleasant memory of a teacher. Describe your memories of a first unpleasant teacher.

2. What is your overall impression of your elementary school years and high school years?

3. Should children in elementary school remain with a teacher they particularly dislike because "in life you have to take the good and the bad" or should a parent act to have the child's class changed?

4. Are there some things a teacher should do on the first day of school at any level of education? If you were a teacher at the elementary school level preparing for the first day of school, what would you be sure to plan to do and say to promote good feeling with your students? How would you plan for the first day in a junior high or high school?

discipline

One day in 1915, A. S. Neill the founder of the Summerhill School was chastised by a school inspector who said, ". . . discipline, which is kindly, might be firmer, especially in the Senior Division, so as to prevent a tendency to talk on the part of the pupils whenever the opportunity occurs."[1] Earlier in the inspector's report he had found the children "to be intelligent and bright under oral examination"[2] and Neill wondered why, if the inspector was impressed with their brightness, did he want them to be silent?

Nietzsche once said, "If we have a degenerate and mean environment, the fittest will be the man who is best adapted to degeneracy and meanness: he will survive."[3]

Until the advent of John Dewey and his progressive theories, schools kept control in many inhumane ways. The thinking was that the child was naturally evil and needed to be disciplined harshly in order to prevent the eruption of negative behavior.

Those who misunderstood Dewey as they now do Neill, thought that progressivism meant license to do whatever one pleased. People who have felt the most oppressed and have been brought up under the heel of authoritarianism often break with their past in a markedly opposite way, seeing, for example, Neill's ideas on freedom as being dictums about anarchy. Thus Neill was dismayed when a female teacher extrapolated his libertarian doctrine to mean that it was permissible for her to bathe in the nude with her pupils!

The ethos of democracy at home and at school has bred concepts of discipline which smack of an egalitarianism that is detrimental to school discipline. In 1968–1970 an hysterical wave of antiauthoritarianism swept through academia. On the university level, professors were forced to consult their students about course content, tenure, retention of professors, and pay scales. John Ciardi, who was visiting professor of poetry at an eastern university, was confronted by a student who said that he expected that he knew as much about poetry as Ciardi, and he did not think Ciardi could teach him anything!

Pupils want and need discipline appropriate to their maturational level, and the teacher creates the emotional climate which prevails in the schoolroom. However, it is foolish to place the full onus of discipline in a school or classroom on the shoulders of the teacher alone. The larger society and the home have influenced the climate and parameters for discipline before the child reaches the school, and he does not leave the ideals and behaviors learned elsewhere at the schoolhouse door.

Parental ferment in the Brownsville section of New York where, justifiably or not, parents were stirred up enough to demand the removal of Cau-

---

[1]Quoted from Ray Hemming, *Children's Freedom* (New York: Schocken Books, 1973), p. 12.
[2]Ibid., p. 12.
[3]Ibid., p. 13.

casian teachers and administrators, communicated to school children strong racial feelings in their homes and community.

Reports of black students making demands of predominantly white faculties are not unusual. These nonnegotiable "requests" have ranged from the demand for black history classes to all-black student lounges. Community antagonism toward "honky" teachers has resulted in overt physical and emotional struggles between white teachers and black students. Where moderate adult blacks have intervened, they, too, have been punished. In a recent case, the black superintendent of schools of Oakland, California was fatally shot as he left the administration building.

Let us cite an example of discipline that comes from the experience of one of the editors of this book. It was not unusual at the junior high in which he taught (J.H.S. 52, The Bronx, New York City) to frisk (search for weapons) the kids as they came into class each morning. Aha! Authoritarian, police state, counterproductive you may exclaim. When one considers that in the early 1950s the school was (as it still is) located in the midst of a community drenched in drugs, rife with gang warfare (but not militant in the 1970s sense) and that the children came to class out of this cauldron of neighborhood dysfunction, it appears that these measures were not as oppressive as they might appear. In a school where more than one murder occurred on the school's premises, precautions against weapons (not unlike airport security procedures in effect in 1974) were wise and prudent. Yet, there was a general esprit de corps in that school that was beyond description. It's nickname was "The Friendly School" and it was just such a place once some of the hardware was stacked for the day.

In general, mental health authorities today acknowledge that an atmosphere of therapeutic discipline should prevail in the schools. To the extent that it is possible to maintain an atmosphere in which dignity, autonomy, and inner-directed control may prevail, teachers should strive to create such a climate of therapeutic discipline. The ultimate aim of discipline is to help create human beings who can reach their maximum potential as Homo sapiens intellectually and socially, without trampling upon the rights of others.

The widely held belief that teachers should impose "the minimal degree of external control necessary for socialization, personality maturation, conscience development, and emotional security" is not to be construed to mean that there should not be "external constraints, standards and direction, or freedom from discipline as an end in itself."[4] Ausubel makes the point that too many educators automatically assume that only democratic pupil-teacher relationships are compatible with positive mental health and personality development in children.

Harold W. Barnard in speaking of discipline said: "The teacher's aim in classroom control is to make himself unnecessary—obsolete. The successful

---

[4]Quoted from David Ausubel, "Some Misconceptions Regarding Mental Health Functions and Practices in the Schools," in George J. Mouly, ed., *Readings in Educational Psychology* (New York: Holt, Rinehart and Winston, 1971), p. 184.

teacher is one whose pupils no longer need him to control their conduct or to help them to pursue their learning."[5]

Today the theories of Harris, Glasser, and Ginott[6] in transactional analysis, reality therapy, and talking with children, seem to be very popular. Each, however, has its own merits and its own deficits when used as the only answer to discipline at home or at school.

Research has made it clear that either extreme authoritarianism or permissiveness in school or at home has unwholesome results. Rather than adopting either pole, teachers need to examine wise, sensible and down-to-earth ways of dealing with classroom misbehavior. Yet teachers should not look at discipline as the way of dealing with misbehavior. Discipline is more nearly all that transacts in a classroom which characterizes the tone of that classroom. Teachers who wait for trouble and do not see that discipline is the atmosphere that prevails are doomed to become disciplinarians. In fact, one may assume that those who react only to breaches of conduct are likely to be punishers. The effects of punishment have been the subject of intense research and deserve special attention from prospective teachers.[7]

Since the works of B. F. Skinner and the host of behaviorists who have followed him, many specific behavioral techniques have been developed both to attack specific behavior problems and to develop a classroom "attitude" on the part of the teacher which would insure a peaceful atmosphere. Odgen R. Lindsley, the father of precision teaching, has developed a technique which calls for children and teachers to record the frequency of negative behavior.[8] Then through curriculum changes the teacher and children discover which format is most successful in decreasing the frequency of this negative behavior. Lindsley says that Skinner's greatest discovery was the use of "frequency as a measure of behavior."[9] Lindsley is now able to chart not only overt behavior but also inner feelings such as anxiety, compassion, and love.

Skinner's philosophy requires that teachers acknowledge good behavior and ignore poor behavior. Thus, when children do things that teachers ordinarily approve of such as sitting quietly, thinking well, helping others, instead of merely passing off this good behavior as if it were simply expected, teachers need verbally to reinforce the positive to assure it will be repeated.

---

[5]*Child Development and Learning* (Boston: Allyn & Bacon, 1973), p. 446.

[6]Thomas A. Harris, *I'm O.K.: You're O.K.: A Practical Guide to Transactional Analysis* (New York: Harper & Row, 1969). William Glasser, *Reality Therapy* (New York: Harper & Row, 1963). Also *Schools Without Failure* (1969), *Mental Health or Mental Illness: Psychiatry for Practical Action* (1970), and *The Identity Society* (1972); and Haim G. Ginott, *Teacher and Child* (New York: Macmillan, 1972).

[7]Kenneth L. Witte and Eugene E. Grossman. "The Effects of Reward and Punishment Upon Children's Attention, Motivation and Discrimination Learning," *Child Development* 42 (1971): 537–42. Also for a more popular treatment of adult punishment see Karl Menninger, *The Crime of Punishment* (New York: Viking, 1968).

[8]"Precision Teaching in Perspective: An Interview with Ogden R. Lindsley" *Teaching Exceptional Children* 3 (Spring 1971): 114–19. See also entire issue.

[9]Ibid., p. 116.

Teachers should be especially alert to all behaviors of which they approve, and be certain they laud these so that they are likely to be repeated by the children who, after all, want to please their teachers. Good behavior is good discipline.

Eugene Burdick

The quiet school

"You evil, evil boy," Mrs. Maurer was shouting at her son. "You rotten, foul little bastard, you. Spitting on the nice teacher."

Toni paused at the door of the room in which the mothers were drinking coffee. She could see them holding the thick white mugs with their initials painted on them in red fingernail polish. In the dim room the bright initials were clearer than the faces of the mothers: A.M. which would be Anne Moriarty, wife of Professor Moriarty in chemistry; H.D., which would be Hildebrande Donovan, wife of the associate professor of Germanic languages; P.Q., which would be Phyllis Quick, wife of full-Professor Quick, of philosophy.

Toni walked on down the corridor thinking that in a few days she would have a mug with T.M. on it . . . which would stand for Toni Moore, wife of Instructor in Physics Henry Moore. She wondered for a moment if she would be the only wife of an instructor in the cooperative nursery.

At the end of the corridor, leaning against the doorjamb, was Miss Henry, the one full-time teacher employed by the nursery. Each of the mothers served as a volunteer one day a week. In this way costs

From A Role in Manila *by Eugene Burdick. Copyright © 1966 by The Estate of Eugene Burdick. Reprinted by arrangement with The New American Library, Inc., New York, New York.*

were kept down and the big gray Victorian building in which the nursery was held was the only expense.

Miss Henry was thin and gaunt, with a face that would have been mannish with its thin gray-mustached lip and its bony cheek, but its lines were slack because her mouth never came completely closed so that she looked like a somewhat indolent, elderly woman. Actually she was only thirty-five.

From the open doorway Toni looked out at the sixty children in the yard. Behind the quadrangle of wire fence the different age-groups went about their different pleasures. A line of four-to-fives crept in a patient, wormlike queue up the steps of the slide and then came swooping down as individuals again; three-to-fours played in the sandpile, intently shaping the sand into figures and then smashing them; fives and sixes swarmed over the swings and the jungle bar. In a corner a boy stood quietly crying, his legs apart, his pants stained dark. A cooperating mother came swiftly across the yard, her arms held out but her face showing the slight disgust that foreign urine always generates, so that Toni knew the boy was not her own child.

The yard was yellow with dust and the rich sunshine that California produces in early spring.

Beyond, San Francisco Bay glittered in hard blue chips and a gray Navy transport edged through the water. "They have so much fun, don't they?" Toni said.

Miss Henry turned and passed her hand across her forehead as though to brush a strand of hair out of her eyes, although her hair was cropped short in the new fashionable cut. Her eyes lit up automatically, registering enthusiasm and a greeting at the same time.

"Yes, don't they? Especially when the weather is good. Have you met the other mothers yet?"

"No," Toni said slowly, wanting to postpone it.

"Well, you shall right now," Miss Henry said.

They walked back down the hall and into the coffee room where the cooperating mothers escaped from the children during the mornings.

"Dexedrine may not affect you very much at first," a carrot-topped woman was saying. Her cup bore the letters P.M., which meant she was Priscilla Maurer, wife of an associate professor in the Econ department. "But its effect is cumulative. After a few weeks you find that you can't sleep and then you get jumpy in the mornings and finally you are touchy all day. It really can be serious."

"It seems unnatural to kill your appetite with a drug that—" another woman started to say. Priscilla Maurer went on talking.

"Exercise is the only way, the only really safe way to take off weight," she said. "Walking a few miles a day is the best; sitting-up exercises when you get up in the morning can start your metabolic rate spurting ahead too fast. Walking is the best thing."

"Ladies, this is Mrs. Henry Moore," Miss Henry cut in. "She

and Betty, her three-year-old, just joined the nursery today. She'll cooperate on Tuesday mornings. She will also help the Toy Repair Group on Thursday evenings."

The mothers looked up at Toni. A few of them nodded. Toni walked across the room and poured herself a cup of coffee, using one of a small stack of unmarked cups. Miss Henry went out. Toni sat down at an empty table.

The mothers were all dressed in play clothes. Some of them were wearing halters and shorts, others were in pedal-pushers, a few wore slacks. But they looked oddly alike. Whatever they had on was made of either denim or a kind of Mexican monk's cloth that Toni knew was quite expensive. And none of them wore make-up; their lips seemed thin and pale, oddly incongruous with the middle-aged, lumpy bodies.

Mrs. Maurer was talking again.

"Gesell is really not a creative psychologist," she said. "He is really a sort of clerk who just took notes on a lot of children. Of course, it is nice to know that your child is not abnormal, so that makes him worthwhile."

The mothers talked energetically of Gesell and several other child psychologists. One of the study groups was going to have a lecture tomorrow night from a visiting social scientist on "A Psychology for Parents." It was the general opinion that the university's Department of Psychology had a very conservative approach to child psychology.

"What is interesting is that a conservative approach today is really just the opposite of common sense," Mrs. Hildebrande Donovan laughed. "What children need is a lot of love and then a chance to develop their own potential . . . especially in a democratic society." She glanced quickly around the room with a challenging look and a quick movement that swung her heavy breasts in their loose halter.

"Self-development in an atmosphere of real love," two of the mothers said at once . . . echoing one another. All the mothers laughed.

"We all heard the same lecture last week by a Yale psychologist," Mrs. Donovan brayed at Toni.

Toni nodded. She reached into her purse and brought out her cigarettes. She fumbled for a match, feeling brittle and exposed. She knew she was much overdressed. Her lipstick felt thick on her mouth.

Mrs. Maurer threw Toni a book of matches.

"I'll give you a light if you 'Shop Co-Op,' " she said.

Toni looked at the book of matches and saw that they were labeled SHOP CO-OP and were decorated with three modernistic pine trees. She smiled tentatively at Mrs. Maurer but Mrs. Maurer only looked resolute.

They began to talk again of child psychology. Toni thought of the Co-Op store downtown. She had shopped there a few times, but it was crowded with women in slacks who drove up in jeeps converted into station wagons and who bought enormous amounts of food, and in the end she had resorted to a quiet little store where you told the owner or his wife—they had no clerks— what you wanted and they brought it to you pleasantly and efficiently. Turning the matchbook over she read that she was entitled to dividends and could go square-dancing.

"It is interesting that Freud said that it was impossible to affect love," Mrs. Maurer was saying when the crash came down the hall. "The child always knows when it is not loved. A loving environment must be *Real.*"

The crash was not loud, nor was it really a crash. It was a break in the steady drone of noise from the yard. To Toni it sounded like a crash because it was accompanied, shockingly, by an adult voice raised in anger or fear or surprise.

The mothers all put their cups down carefully and leaned forward, listening, and then as a group stood up. Mrs. Maurer and Mrs. Donovan were the first two out into the corridor. The others came in a solid clot of denim and Mexican cloth, bare flesh, white faces. They rushed to the door opening on the yard and Toni trailed behind. They stood for a moment, eyes blinking, getting used to the sudden sunlight.

All the children in the yard seemed arrested in mid-motion, staring one way. They were looking at Miss Henry. Miss Henry was facing a boy of about six who was sitting on top of the fence, well above her head.

"It's Tommie Maurer," Toni heard one of the younger women say. Toni looked at Mrs. Maurer. Her face was taut and her long upper lip quivered like that of a scenting rabbit.

"Come down, Thomas," Miss Henry said. Her voice rose shrill and rigid, the words clipped with the precision of bits of metal falling from a cutting machine. "Come off that fence and quit spitting."

The boy grinned down at her. His lips were juicy with the green stain of the grass that he had in his mouth. He chewed with relish and then he opened his mouth and spat at Miss Henry. She quivered.

"Goddam you, Tommie Maurer," Miss Henry said with even greater precision. It was the weird exactness that only voices in extreme duress can assume.

"She should not talk like that to the children," said Mrs. Smith, the wife of an assistant professor in Professor Maurer's department. "After all," Mrs. Smith said, "she studied at Iowa under Lewin; she should have more patience."

The wife of another assistant professor said urgently, "We really should stop her. She is upsetting the children."

Toni glanced at the children, looking for Betty. She could see only upturned faces, unfamiliar and not at all childlike, rapt with attention, delight, expectancy.

"For the last time, Tommie," Miss Henry said dreadfully, "I order you to stop that this minute and come down." The shoulders of her white linen blouse were spattered with green saliva. Tommie chewed steadily, grinned, and then sprayed her between closed teeth.

With the agility of a cat Miss Henry suddenly leaped into the air, caught the surprised boy by an ankle, and jerked. He came down with a thud, the wind pounded out of his lungs, his grass-green mouth opening. Miss Henry stepped forward with her hand raised.

With Miss Henry's leap the cooperating mothers had moved as a single unit. They started at a quick walk but broke into a trot when they were halfway across the yard. Toni could hear some of the mothers start to breathe very deeply and one of them, it may have been young Mrs. Moriarty, was chanting in a flat voice, "Goddam . . . ungrateful . . . ungrateful . . . wretch . . . ungrateful wretch." Toni felt a catch of excitement as she trotted with the group of mothers; a quick impulse of solidarity; an antagonism against Miss Henry. She was relaxed for the first time that morning.

"Terrible thing to do," Toni said. "Really terrible. No group sensitivity in it at all. Very bad example."

"Terrible thing. No group cooperation," two or three of the younger mothers said, correcting Toni. By the time the group of cooperating mothers reached Miss Henry and the fallen boy they were moving with a quick, smooth rush. They were moving so fast that things seemed to blur.

Miss Henry was suddenly before Toni. Quite instinctively she reached out to restrain Miss Henry. She grabbed the dry, pebbly arm that came out of the white linen blouse and pulled it down with savage strength. Mrs. Moriarty and Mrs. Engels, wife of Assistant Professor Paul Engels, also laid hands on Miss Henry. They pulled her back in a series of skidding jerks, their feet slipping on the graveled earth, falling and stumbling against her, seeming to squeeze out of her an odor of chalk, hand paint, old talc.

Suddenly the little group realized that they had become separated from something larger and they stood still.

"You evil, evil boy," Mrs. Maurer was shouting at her son. "You rotten, foul little bastard, you. Spitting on the nice teacher."

Her hands flicked out at him, slapping him across the head with blows so fast that they could not have been strong. The boy stared up at her blankly, his head rocking with the blows. The rest of the cooperating mothers surged around the two, some shouting at the boy and striking out at the air with quick, irritated gestures.

"Antisocial," one of the mothers said. "Antisocial, nasty little fellow."

The boy twisted once, like a baited animal. The mothers closed in around him.

The three around Miss Henry shifted and glanced at one another. They gave Miss Henry awkward and apologetic smiles, their hands falling away. Then in unison, and as if their futures depended on it, they walked with quick, firm steps to the circle of cooperating mothers around the boy.

discussion

Eugene Burdick, who taught at the University of California at Berkeley, may have had first hand experience with the cooperative nursery school in his story. The cooperative nursery school movement in California is a vigorous and well organized system of community pre-school education. The cooperative nature of the school means that it is composed of mostly middle class families. Mother (or father) must be able to afford to work at school at least one half day a week while other children are left with a babysitter. The cooperative focuses on parent education, usually a class one evening a week. Since the schools are community organizations, it is not surprising that at the cooperative in Berkeley, mentioned in this story, the mothers having coffee are the college-educated wives of the university faculty.

This pre-school experience provides many opportunities for children to experience varied materials, play with well designed equipment, and interact with other children of their own age. Many cooperative nursery schools, realizing the advantages of this experience, are combining with Head Start programs (pre-school education for economically disadvantaged children) to include some Head Start children in their classes.[1]

Burdick pokes fun at the women intellectualizing about the upbringing of children. Some of the mothers seem so sure of what is right, and within the group there seems to be unanimity of opinion. The incident seems like a caricature of highly cerebral people who permit their basic emotions to take over only when a shocking incident cuts through their highly controlled response to a situation. These mothers, who must always act in unison or "cooperation," watch for the correct signal, for they are not sure whether to swoop down on the teacher or the child.

springboards for inquiry

1. Do you think middle class parents are less spontaneous than lower class parents? When is the intellectual approach desirable? How spontaneous should teachers be in their reaction to the class?

[1]In San Mateo, California a Head Start Auxiliary has formed to act as surrogate parents to participate in the nursery school program (as is a requirement in cooperative schools) because so many pre-school children whose parents work and/or cannot provide transportation would otherwise miss the opportunity to participate in the program.

2. Why are nursery schools a good experience for children?

3. Many problems in school could be totally avoided if teachers knew when a child needed special handling and when he needed to be made to conform. What guidelines should a teacher use to make such a distinction?

"And what has to be done to a child who sucks his thumb?"

Hayyim Bialik

Aftergrowth

Two years passed at the *heder* without my profiting any too greatly from the Hebrew reading. Then the teacher introduced me to the *Humash*, the Pentateuch; and may he be blessed for so doing. The prayerbook had grown stale for me, and its letters I now looked upon as long dead. You could compare the state of affairs to somebody chewing and munching away at husks and shells and peel. This was not the case with the *Humash*. Here fresh lattices and loopholes into the world of fantasy were opened for me. To begin with there was the little *aleph*. I found the little fellow at once, sitting at the very beginning of the book of Leviticus, awaiting my arrival. As for his comrades, little fellows like himself, we were old acquaintances from the sections in smaller type in the prayerbook, and I could give them greetings in the name of the others. Then again, there were the flocks and the herds and the fowl; ox, sheep, goat, dove and pigeon. All these were things with which I was well-acquainted and in which, it might almost be said, I had a share.

From Aftergrowth and Other Stories *by H. N. Bialik. Reprinted by permission of The Jewish Publication Society of America.*

The goat and the calf grazed in the pasture behind our house at the end of the suburb, and I spent my time with them when I could. As for the doves, they came from the dovecote of our neighbor Truchim, and had the right of entry into our courtyard. When I went off to *heder* in the morning, they would come strutting towards me, puffing out their chests and cooing, *toor toor toor.* I had already fixed my eye on a pair of them, and at the coming of Hanukkah, when I would be rich, God willing, I would, if only it were possible, purchase that pair for good money.

And when I reached those passages which talk of head and fat, innards and shanks washed in water, "and he shall set them on the wood which is on the fire," twisting the head and breaking the wings of the bird, "crop and contents," squeezing out the blood, an offering in a pot, a frying pan and so on and so forth, it immediately brought to my mind my mother's kitchen on the eve of a festival. My mother and the girl would have aprons tied round and sleeves rolled up to the elbow, standing armed with rolling pins, and rolling dough on the board, breaking and mixing eggs in a dish, pouring gleaming oil into hollows sunk in mounds of meal. The cat was here as well; it lay in wait round the salting board, its eyes on the "caul above the liver," on the loin-fat and the kidneys and the crops and shanks lying in salt with a red fluid oozing from them. From time to time the girl would throw him a piece of intestine or a white bladder from the inside of a fish, or the "contents of the crop" and the like, giving him something to do for the moment in order to divert his attention from the meat. The mortar and pestle gave voice, saying, "Pound well and fine, fine and well pound," just as described in the Mishna. The pleasant, revivifying smell of things baking in an oven and of an offering of meal mixed with oil and white of egg mounted in my nose; my ears caught the burble and bubble of pancakes floating in fat in their frying pan, and the frying of "dipped" offerings and other kinds of pastry, the cutting up of dough into fine strips like noodles for making puddings and hard cake with raisins and saffron and cinnamon. The word "dipped" is the one that most appetized me, so that my temples ached and my cheeks drew in. I was overcome by a sudden rush of hunger, my mouth began to water and my thumb made its way without my knowledge between my teeth.

"Where's the place?" the teacher suddenly asked me, his strap in hand.

All the pupils became silent and watched me. My little finger wandered amid the lines, wandering blind and fearful. My eyes turned tearfully now to the *Humash* and now to the teacher's strap. The letters danced in a blur before me.

The teacher's hand rose. My right shoulder also rose and twisted in fear. In my fright I forgot to take my thumb out of my mouth.

"Berele!" the teacher suddenly said to one nimble child, "jump up and run along to Nahum the cobbler and fetch me a little pitch from there. At once. Say the teacher asks for it."

Berele jumped up and went out. The children round the table began to whisper to one another, stealing glances at me and laughing, stealing glances afresh and laughing all over again. What was it they saw in me? And why were the laughing?

Berele brought back a bit of pitch on a splinter, and put it down on the table in front of the teacher.

"Come down!" ordered the teacher.

Down I came.

"Come here to me . . . "

I took one tiny step towards him.

"Closer . . . "

Another even tinier step forward.

"Still closer . . . "

And I stood caught between the teacher's knees. Lord of the Universe, what did he propose to do to me?

And the teacher jerked his thumb back so that at the joint with the other fingers there appeared a small fold. This he filled with snuff, raised it to his nostrils, breathed deep, rose and suddenly sneezed straight in my face, "Atishoo!"

After which deed his mind cleared and he came to the matter in hand. He pulled my thumb out of my mouth and held it up for all the children to see, waving it in the air and asking, like a teacher using the sensory method:

"Children, what is this?"

"A thumb, a thumb . . . "

"And what's this?" he now asked about the pitch.

"Pitch, pitch . . . "

"And then what is this?"

"Snuff, snuff . . . "

"And what has to be done to a child who sucks his thumb?"

This was a hard one for the children. They remained silent. The teacher's eyes demanded a response. Suddenly one child, a stutterer, jumped up. His eyes were as bright as though the Holy Spirit shone through them, while he stuttered in his excitement:

"I-I-I-I Kn-n-now . . . "

"Tell me, tell me," the teacher urged him.

"C-c-c-c-cu . . . "

"Cut off the thumb!" his comrade got it out ahead of him.

The cleverer children burst out laughing, and the teacher also grinned. The stutterer felt ashamed. There was silence once again.

"Well?" asked the teacher, lowering his eyelids.

"Tie a rag round it," carefully ventured one child.

"Give him a beating," decided another.

"Nay!" the teacher shook his head. "You don't know. When a child sucks his thumb, this is what you do to him."

And he began showing the children, slowly and without haste, adding deed to word, exactly how this matter is attended to:

"First take pitch . . ."

And he took pitch.

"And spread it on the thumb . . ."

And he spread it.

"Then take snuff . . ."

And that as well the teacher took.

"And sprinkle it on the pitch . . ."

And he sprinkled.

"And now," he finished at the top of his voice, "let him go and suck . . ."

From that day forth I was weaned as far as thumbsucking was concerned. When my evil desires attacked me, I would bite my fingernails instead. . . .

discussion

Hayyim Bialik was the national poet of Israel. He died in 1934 after spending the last ten years of his life in Israel. This excerpt is from one of only five pieces of prose Bialik wrote. Like most of his poems, the story is autobiographical and represents an attempt to escape back to dreams of the author's childhood in the Ukraine.

Bialik was extremely imaginative and spent a great deal of time building his own world of fantasy. Even as he was taught the letters of the alphabet in his first year of schooling, his imagination turned the letters into visions of soldiers marching, goats and calves grazing, or doves and pigeons. In the chapter preceding this excerpt Bialik explains that for him the Hebrew letter for "I," "ל . . . was clearly nothing but a stork stretching out its neck and standing on one leg." On some days the letters would appear to Bialik in one form, and then his fantasy would turn them into something else the next.

It is probably a fact that many children sitting in classrooms today are for some part of the day many miles and adventures away from what the teacher and his classmates are talking about. When a child has a particularly vivid imagination and makes associations that lead him into his own fantasies as Bialik did, there is a good chance that he will not be able to respond appropriately when called upon by a teacher. Teachers today do not keep a strap in the classroom to punish such lapses, but verbal ridicule is not uncommon and can be humiliating and psychologically painful. In this episode the teacher's asking the class for suggestions for punishment is done with mockery. However, teachers do sometimes ask the class to suggest procedures for disciplining. Interestingly, as they do in this story, the students will frequently suggest extreme penalties. Why is it that children are not compassionate with their classmates in meting out punishments when the next day they may be on the receiving end?

Most children are not able to empathize with the child-offender. They are not developmentally ready or have not been taught to put themselves in another's shoes. They identify instead with the person with power and get carried away with their new weapon. Power-oriented discipline is so frequently the example for children that they tend to use this method of discipline as adults in the role of parents or teachers. The way to set the pendulum in motion toward positive and humanistic methods of discipline is to teach parents and teachers more positive ways of communicating with children. Dr. Thomas Gordon,[1] Haim Ginott,[2] and Elliott Landau[3] have written books and newspaper articles to help adults set better examples of compassion and dignity as they help children acquire more acceptable behavior patterns.

Too many classrooms today are not very different from the one depicted by Bialik. Hopefully teachers will learn to reward on-task behavior periodically so that children's attention will not wander. In addition, class structure should allow children to work at their own pace and at their own achievement level rather than requiring that they listen to long class recitations by teachers or other students. When the teacher sits in front of the class while the students take turns reading from the same text as they did in Bialik's "heder," discipline will remain the teacher's number one problem.

springboards for inquiry

1. List and comment upon each of the forms of discipline that the teacher used in this excerpt. Is aversive punishment always a poor procedure?

2. Cite studies that reveal the differences that socioeconomic status and culture impose on the forms of discipline to which children are subjected.

3. Read Section IV of John B. Krumboltz and Helen B. Krumboltz, *Changing Children's Behavior* (Englewood Cliffs, N.J.,: Prentice-Hall, 1972) and discuss their approach to discipline.

[1]Thomas Gordon, *Parent Effectiveness Training* (New York: Wyden, 1970).
[2]Haim Ginott, *Between Parent and Child* (New York: Macmillan, 1965).
[3]Elliott Landau, *You and Your Child's World* (Salt Lake City, Utah: Deseret Press, 1967).

peer influences

A Juvenile Court judge recently expressed rage at a fifteen year old whose only answer to his question, "Why did you torment the old man?" was "Everyone was doin' it." Although no sensitive human being would condone inhumane behavior, psychologists explain that peer group influence upon children is so strong that children will sometimes abandon their own values in favor of the group's.

It is probably safe to say that when immediate role models and decisions are needed, children choose their peers rather than their parents.[1] In the matter of long-run decisions, however, even during adolescence, the child who comes from a cohesive family will value his family's decisions over those of his peers.

As children grow and develop, they spend more and more time with peers. Until about the age of three, the major influence on the child is his immediate environment—his home, his parents (especially his mother). Usually until this age most play is highly egocentric and parallel. In the first two years a child is very content to be with himself and his TV set. He talks to himself, seeks his mother as companion, but has relatively little interest in his age mates. Recent research data supports the idea that as early as age three, children begin to communicate with other children.[2] Though there may be little real exchange of information, there is what has been termed "collective monologue"—providing the simple pleasure of affective communication without any real responses to what the other child had just finished saying.[3]

The younger the child, the less direct contact he has with peer group influence. An early study by Wright indicates that as one grows older, he spends more time in community settings rather than in a family environment.[4] Thus from about the age of three onward, as children grow away from their parents, the teacher can expect that what the peer group thinks and values the individual child will too. Bernard seems to place the time for the development of strong peer pressure in the first grade. He says, "even the first grader may be concerned about what his classmates think if his mother brings him to school and holds his hand as they cross the street, or when he sucks his thumb."[5]

By the time the child is eight or nine there is "an anxiety about peer ac-

---

[1]See Clay V. Brittain, "Adolescent Choices and Parent-Peer Cross-Pressures," *American Sociological Review* 28 (1963): 385–91 and Daniel Solomon, "Influences on the Decisions of Adolescents," *Human Relations* 16 (1963): 45–60.

[2]Betty Rowen, *The Children We See* (New York: Holt, Rinehart & Winston, 1973), p. 151.

[3]There is some strong evidence that when adult "conversations" are qualitatively analyzed, the follow-up on what was just said is often very poor. Hundreds of my students who have been specifically directed to study adult conversation have reported that in over 60% of casual adult conversation, the "next thing said" did not follow what "was just said."—EDL

[4]Herbert Fletcher Wright, "Psychological Development in the Midwest," *Child Development* 27 (June 1956): 265–86.

[5]Harold W. Bernard, *Child Development and Learning* (Boston: Allyn & Bacon, 1973).

ceptance that is painful to contemplate."[6] Peer group acceptance is strongest at this age. Then from about age ten the importance of peer group acceptance diminishes gradually until late adolescence. At ages eight, nine, and ten, children form very close friendships. Most of these friendships are between children of the same sex. The "best friend" relationship often drives teachers consciously to separate children under the misguided notion that this separation will help classroom discipline. What, in fact, happens is that long-distance signals, notes, gesticulating, and even verbal communication start and add considerably to the discipline problems of the teacher. Teachers often design campaigns to split the chums instead of building upon the strength of the friendships.

It is important to remember that selecting a very special peer person is further preparation for developing the close and long-lasting relationships essential to adolescence and later to marriage. Though there are modernists who frown upon the idea of childhood being a preparation time, nevertheless, the middle grades (four to six) do provide the intensity, even ferocity of attachments, separations, "make-up" time, and reattachments which must be experienced before life-long, meaningful, enduring adult relationships can be formed.

If there is any exception to the chronological pattern of separation from one's parents and reliance upon the peer group for norms, it is probably among children of the poor. Undoubtedly Wright's study of psychological development in the Midwest[7] did not take into account the accelerated development with respect to peer group influence of children in slum homes where mothers too often "respond to their children's requests with 'shut up' and 'leave me be,' despite clear evidence elsewhere of love for their children. . . ."[8] Hunt concludes that it should not be surprising to learn that in the slum subculture children turn to their peer group for acceptance and companionship very early in their lives. Hunt says, "moreover, with both parents often absent from slum homes much of the time, these peer groups go unsupervised. . . . It is from these unsupervised peer groups, therefore, that the children of the poor learn their values and standards. As pre-adolescents they copy the adolescents of the local delinquent gangs."[9]

It is important for teachers to know that the child's self-concept will be heavily influenced by the degree of acceptance or non-acceptance he achieves with his peer group. And his self-concept is correlated highly with achievement in school. Coopersmith,[10] Hill and Sarason,[11] and Walsh[12]

[6]Rowen, *The Children We See*, p. 190.

[7]Wright, "Psychological Development in the Midwest."

[8]Joseph McVicker Hunt, "Parent and Child Centers: Their Basis in the Behavioral and Educational Sciences," *American Journal of Orthopsychiatry* 41, no. 1 (January 1971): 24–25.

[9]Ibid., p. 24.

[10]Stanley Coopersmith, "Self-Esteem and Need Achievement as Determinants of Selective Recall and Repetition," *Journal of Abnormal and Social Psychology* 60 (1960): 310–17.

[11]Kennedy T. Hill and Seymour B. Sarason, "The Relation of Test Anxiety and Defensiveness to Test and School Performance over the Elementary School Years: A Further Longitudinal Study," *Monographs of the Society for Research in Child Development* vol. 31 (2), no. 104 (1966).

[12]Ann M. Walsh, *Self-Concepts of Bright Boys with Learning Difficulties* (New York: Teachers College Press, 1956).

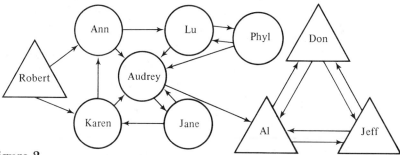

Figure 2

have all done research which bears upon the fact that underachievement is directly related to self-perception. Finally, Wattenberg and Clifford[13] found that measures of self-concept taken in kindergarten were predictive of reading achievement two and a half years later.

Since the etiology for some part of failing school behavior may, in fact, be related to a child's non-acceptance by his peer group, one of a teacher's never-ending tasks is the continual and persistent monitoring of peer group interaction. In the Cunningham sociogram shown here Robert is chosen by no one in the group. Thus he is termed an isolate. At the other extreme Audrey is chosen by five people and thus qualifies to be called a "star." There are other instances of mutual choices meaning that everyone in the group but Robert was picked by someone; every child except Robert had a modicum of acceptance. Robert's total rejection by his peer group might seriously deflate his self-image. The research data shows that this negation of self may affect Robert's academic performance.

A sociogram backed up by teacher observation may serve to get the educational team moving in the direction of ameliorating an isolate's position. Personal counseling, regrouping of children so that those who seem most likely to accept the isolate will be near him, and talking with a group in the absence of the isolate—all of these may contribute greatly to the "rehabilitation" of the rejected child.

Human beings need to function in social settings which accept them. Few humans can survive the ordeal of isolation.[14] Viewing the classroom as a social microcosm, part of the teacher's function is to arrange the conditions of the environment so that, barring personal wishes to be "let alone," each child enjoys and has open access to his peer group. The seeds of violent behavior are rooted in a climate of low self-esteem and rejection by age mates.

[13]William W. Wattenberg, and Clare Clifford, "Relation of Self-concepts to Beginning Achievement in Reading," *Child Development*, 35 (1964): 461–67.

[14]Recently, a graduate of one of our U.S. military academies was interviewed regarding a virtual isolation (freeze) he endured for nearly two years. It is fortunate that his particular gene pool allowed him to survive relatively unscathed. In the case of many others, the "silent treatment" was too much and they left the institution.

H.C. Branner

Iris

And whether it was because Alice had been aware that Iris had been looking at her all the time, or because Iris had stood so humbly at the outside of the circle around the powder case—anyway, their eyes met, and a peculiar look flickered over Alice's cat face, a look that seemed to hint that the two of them had something in common.

The seventh graders met in the schoolyard after the summer holiday, and it became apparent that great silent changes had taken place. Alice and Ruth who couldn't stand each other came there suddenly and were friends—before the vacation it had been Alice and Erna, but now Erna was standing a bit to the side and smiling feebly while Alice and Ruth clung close together and waltzed around the yard three times to show what bosom friends they were. And there was one who had never before been taken into account who had suddenly blossomed out and was now considered important, and someone else had returned home from England the day before and was telling about it in a weary voice as if it were nothing. But fat Margrete was the same fat Margrete from previous years, rushing up with great zeal to show the schedule and what class they'd be in, and have you heard that there's somebody new?

And when the bell rang, and the girls stormed giggling in to fight about who should have which desk, the newcomer was already sitting there with a pencil case and sharpened new pencils, and her mother was with her in the classroom. So

"Iris" by H.C. Branner from Two Minutes of Silence *is reprinted by permission of The University of Wisconsin Press.*

they just stood there all of them, and the fight about the desks had to take place surreptitiously—a sneer and an angry glance and a pinch in a dress. But the name of the new girl was Iris, and Iris' mother was a small person in a black suit, with a timid smile.

"Yes, I'm Iris' mother," she said to the girls, "and I hope you'll get along nicely with Iris."

Nobody said anything further to that, of course, just a cautious yes and a smile here and there, but her words had given that first damning impression.

"I'm Iris' mother," Alice said at morning recess, and it curved around the corners of her mouth like a fish of prey lurking among the rushes. And Ruth could tell that the suit that Iris' mother was wearing had been dyed—and black knit gloves with a hole in the index finger—and Iris herself: grrr, ordinary, dull—long asparagus legs in wool stockings and a home-knit sweater and her hair combed into two rigid pigtails.

"Her head looks like an upside down egg, and she has such a stupid smile."

Alice made her front teeth protrude to show what Iris looked like. And Alice herself had become one summer vacation more sophisticated with lipstick and her own perfume and black eyelashes, and in the boys' Senior High there was someone—Alice remembered him well from last year, but this year he had a tailored suit and a new bike with gearshift, and of course he was just a boy, but someone to fool around with a bit, "and as a substitute for—you know, Ruth." And Ruth nodded with great emphasis and was the one who knew about Hornbaek* and the law student, and at the long recess she was going to hear more. Ruth was actually thin, with a gray complexion and no feminine charm, but so was Erna, all of Alice's friends were, and why not? "Why bother," Margrete and the others had said to Erna a year ago, and "Why bother," they were saying to Ruth this year. But Ruth did. She had a share in Hornbaek and another in the law student.

Iris had no share in anything, she was grrr, dull and stood by herself on long unsteady asparagus legs and wouldn't fit in. The fact that Iris' mother was still around and always wanted to drop over and tell her Iris something—something about the food and about a coat for recess—probably did something, too.

"Gee, mom," Iris twisted and turned, "if you'd just leave me alone."

But that was the one thing Iris' mother didn't want to do, she bustled in and out of doors in her black suit and saw the principal and saw the home-room teacher and couldn't make herself let Iris plunge in alone. And perhaps that was nothing to wonder at. Iris' mother had been forty when she married and forty-two when she got her only child Iris, and since then neither

Iris' mother nor Iris' father nor Iris herself had been away from one another as much as one day. Iris' father was a sexton, he sat in his room and registered births and marriages and deaths and grew quiet and serious, and Iris herself had been delicate, with asthma and a tendency to bronchitis even in infancy. For this reason she had had her schooling at home until she was thirteen, with special permission from the authorities.

Yes, Iris was a homebody, homespun and home-taught, you could tell that at a glance. When her name was called in class, she got up, red and pale and panting, and the first days the class giggled and whispered each time she had the question, for what she knew was always something very different from what they knew. Her arithmetic problems were correctly solved all right, but they were correct in a queer way, and in history she made out something different from what actually had happened, and when there were protests all around her, she stalled completely and just stood there stupidly smiling with two front teeth pushing out. Iris wasn't actually ugly, but that smile was such that the class writhed under it, and the teachers didn't know what to do about it. One teacher let her eyes pass over Iris' head and swoop down on someone else, and another wrote something in a book, and fat Margrete who was sitting next to Iris asked plump in the middle of one class: "What's so funny, Iris?" And that question released a howl from the whole class, and the teacher had to take the side of those who laughed. But Iris' front teeth merely pushed out a little further, and it was an unnatural smile.

*A famous seaside resort.—*Translator's note.*

In all fairness, fat Margrete hadn't asked to be seated next to Iris. For several years she had had the privilege of sitting alone at a double desk because she was fat Margrete and after a while was simply called Fatty, and if this nickname had ever made her cry, she now responded to it cheerfully and underscored it herself by making everything topple over and by sweeping books and pencil case down from the desks and taking up much more room than she had to. But she was the best student in the class, and even if she was a nuisance and answered back in class, she still couldn't hide the fact that she was the brightest one in the room, and therefore Iris was put next to her. The first day Iris settled happily with her sharp new pencils and neat new books within her half of the desk, but already the next day she was sitting like a shadow all the way out on the edge of her seat, and eight days later there was a strange thud in the middle of the Danish class, and there was Iris sitting on the floor with her long asparagus legs sprawling before her, and the whole class laughed, and then Iris too laughed with her front teeth. But the Danish teacher had no discipline, and fat Margrete was the one who spoke up first, so Iris was directed to the single desk up in the front row, and the whole incident was smoothed over. The next recess Iris moved with all her books and her pencil case, and when the home-room teacher asked why she had moved, she merely smiled her smile.

Yes, Iris was in deep water, and it was of no avail that Iris' mother sat in during the morning prayer nodding from the other side of the auditorium, and complaints and meddling would only make matters worse. So Iris merely answered "fine" when they sat at the supper table and talked about how it was going, but when she came up to her room to do her homework, she locked her door. She had never done that before, and she really didn't know why she did it now. But there she sat and was at last all by herself and very, very quiet, and it was September and it was October, and a big tree outside the window lost its leaves, and they had turned on the heating system in school, and Alice munched nuts in class. Alice. And one day it was splendid sunshine and all the girls linked arms forming a long chain and jumped across the schoolyard singing along, and they were one summer vacation and one fall older, and here and there a round budding form was already bouncing up and down inside a blouse and most noticeably under Alice's smooth tight dress. But Iris was not a part of the chain, she just sat at night behind a locked door and saw them dance around and around the big chestnut with the benches surrounding it, and in the center danced Alice's round impudent cat face with the grey-green eyes and the freckles over the bridge of her nose. And the whole chain was just like a pair of wings that was carrying her away.

Now, Iris might easily have been among the virtuous ones from whom the others copied essays and assignments—the Salvation girls Alice called them, and at recess they had a corner of their own where they discussed their homework and quizzed each other. Iris might easily have joined that corner, and she didn't know herself why she didn't go there. But one day Alice was standing in the middle of a conspiratorial crowd and had something to show again, an elegant case with a powder compact and a puff, and Alice let the puff dance deftly over her cat face and only once sent a quick glance in the direction of the guard—and then there was Iris who had stolen up close and was standing at the outer edge of the circle.

"What's the joke, Iris?" Ruth asked, for this had become a wise-crack whenever Iris was around, but Alice held the powder puff away from her face and frowned and said: "Ruth!" and then Iris was left alone.

And in the next period during the recitation, Alice's eyes wandered through the class and all the girls were bent over their books, but not Iris. And whether it was because Alice had been aware that Iris had been looking at her all the time, or because Iris had stood so humbly at the outside of the circle around the powder case—anyway, their eyes met, and a peculiar look flickered over Alice's cat face, a look that seemed to hint that the two of them had something in common. It might not have been what she meant at all, but to Iris that was what she had meant—for the first time since she began school she came home with a "hallo!" and "great!" she said at supper when they were talking about how the day had been. And she took the stairs to her room in three leaps and turned the key emphatically against her parents, and at night she stayed awake a long time and thought of the secret that she shared with Alice; and "Ruth!" she said out in the dark, "Ruth!" And she said it in Alice's voice, only much sterner, for after all Alice had said it to help her, to help Iris against the others.

"Ruth! Leave Iris alone—come Iris, sure, you can look too. No, come, let's go there—you know! We don't want the others too. Come Iris, you and I . . ."

This was something Iris faked and made up, for Alice would never have spoken that way, of course. Alice and Iris—never! And yet it was only three days when Alice actually did say this and much more still. A wild tremendous happiness befell Iris with the protruding front teeth.

Iris' single desk wasn't the only one in the room, there was also one in front of the second row, and there, one morning, sat Ruth and looked thin and gray and dreary in a way she had never been before. And at the rearmost desk that until then Ruth and Alice had been sharing, Alice was now making herself at home alone, and her cruelly innocent cat face knew nothing and couldn't help anything, and anyway she was all indifference. But fat Margrete was fat Margrete and knew all about it and rasped out the story at recess: it was about him, Eigil, over in the boys' Senior High—and he was writing letters to Alice, and Alice had him address them to Ruth, and when Ruth opened them there was just an envelope with "Alice" inside. But last night Ruth's dad had opened both letters and called up Alice's father and read to him what Eigil had written. But according to Alice, her own dad was sheer indifference and treated the whole story as of no account, and all it had led to was that Ruth was now sitting in solitary confinement and wouldn't learn riding with Alice, and wouldn't go with Alice to Hornbaek next year.

"So there you can see what sort she is!" Margrete said with stern eyes, dealing out justice for all of them.

And sure, it wasn't Ruth's fault, and sure, they all felt that friendship with Alice was very dangerous and unreliable and led straight to disaster. And Iris was standing at the outer edge of the circle and felt it also, but she felt it like a warm, sweet fear—aah, Alice with the round cat face and the freckles over the bridge of her nose. And when Alice soon after came slouching past, she met a wall of cold indignation, but not from Iris, not from Iris. And Alice was aware of this and sought Iris with her eyes, and "my, they're silly!" she said with the same expression as before in the history class, and "my, they're silly!" Iris replied with the same expression and went unreservedly over to the enemy. Sure it was dangerous, and sure it was only because Alice didn't have anyone else at the moment, but Iris went over nonetheless—a flood dam burst within her, and her small cramped being with the locked door and the bookcase and the homework and everything else that had been hers, floated off at random like a piece of driftwood, and reality was the dreams at night and the empty place at Alice's desk. Come Iris, let's go there—you know! We don't want the others to come, too. Come Iris, you and I . . .

And after only ten minutes of lunch recess Margrete, her eyes as round as balls, was telling that Iris with the teeth was sitting with Alice in the corner behind the gym, and the others wouldn't believe it and sneaked out one by one to see if it was true. But it was true. They were sitting on the trash can, where before Alice and Ruth used to sit, and Iris was sitting way out on the edge and didn't dare to eat her food or to smile her smile and hardly even to breathe. And in the fourth period Alice got up and asked: "Teacher, may Iris sit next to me?" and it was the Danish teacher and she nodded her consent to avoid trouble, and Iris moved at once with her books and pencil case.

"Why bother," fat Margrete whispered when Iris went past her desk, but Iris did—it was enough that the others noticed her and what she did.

And the rest of the hour it was Alice's grey-green eyes and Alice's small nose with the freckles very close by—oh, all too blindingly close—and Alice's voice whispering like a small flame right into Iris' ear and asking and telling straight through the recitation and everything.

"Alice and Iris! If you can't be quiet, Iris will have to come up here again!" the teacher called rapping her desk, and to Iris this was the baptism of fire, the first scolding.

"Alice and Iris!"

Oh, she drew herself up proudly under it and tried to look injured like Alice. And when the period was over Alice and Iris stayed in their seats "because I want you to see some pictures from last summer—but let the others get out first." And when they were chased out anyhow, Alice put her arm under hers.

"Come, let's go down there again."

And Iris walked as if in a fog, and Iris saw pictures and had no idea what Alice was saying, and Iris read one of Eigil's letters and didn't understand a word, but at the last recess she promised to come home with Alice and drink tea after school.

"You can call your mother from the bake-shop."

But Iris didn't dare to say that they had no telephone in her home, nor did she dare to say no, so she said to heck with it, and it didn't matter. But it did matter, and all during the last period Iris' heart was heavy at the thought of her mother and father, and the homebody Iris, little good-as-gold Iris hated her mother and dad and crunched them between her teeth. But let them say what they would, let them go to the principal and spoil everything—they aren't going to keep me away from Alice, anyway.

And after school Alice hooked her arm under Iris' and pressed her hip against Iris' and led her far from her home with its grandfather clock and her small black parents. And two boys on shining bikes flashed up against the sidewalk like sharks and slammed on the brakes, and Alice slouched with her school bag and walked in a peculiar, loose-jointed fashion. And one of the boys was a big, strapping lad with his voice breaking and a plump face full of pimples—not one bit attractive, Iris thought, and he and Alice just kept arguing and coming out with strange words and expressions that Iris didn't understand. Yes, sure it was dangerous to be a friend of Alice's. And now they turned onto a path behind the building grounds, and there the big fellow started to push Alice, and they began to fight and Alice got hold of his cloth cap and threw it up in a tree. And Iris couldn't understand that this was the fellow who was called Eigil and who wrote "my beloved Alice." On the whole Iris understood almost nothing that happened that day, for it was all too much and everything went too fast, and when she later tried to think it over there were great gaps as in a dream. And Alice's home was almost all gaps, for it wasn't a home, it was a castle and a whole city. But she did remember

the living-quarters of the chauffeur, they were as large as her dad's place, and greenhouses and Alice's hand patting a big riding horse on the neck, and patting two long shining cars as if she owned them. And then a room where there were trees growing, and an enormous silent rug that made Iris' shoes look very shabby, and Alice's hand pressing a button, and a door disappearing without a sound into the wall—everything was silent in that house, and not a soul to be seen. And then Alice's room—ooh, Alice's room with furniture in white finish and a balcony, and Alice's hand again pressing a button and a black-and-white maid came in with cocoa and cookies on a tray. And Alice didn't even say thanks. Alice with her round cat face and the freckles around her nose, here she owned cars and riding horses and grown-up people, and would the teachers dare to scold her if they knew about it? And Alice munched sweets and pushed the box over to Iris, and there was as much as they'd ever want. But Iris only took one piece, for it was four o'clock and her heart was heavy at the thought of her mother and dad. And what were they sitting there waiting for, she thought with hatred, and now her own attic room with the bookcase meant nothing any more.

"Maybe our chauffeur can take you home," Alice said pressing a button, and Iris said nothing but only wished he wouldn't be able to, and thank God, he wasn't able to.

"Well, bye Alice and thanks for today!" But she didn't start running until she couldn't be seen any more from Alice's balcony.

No, Iris didn't remember much of what had happened that day, but she remembered coming home, that burned into her memory: her dad's full black beard with the dark-red lips and the church voice behind it, and why did her mother always have to go around in black and look so worried, and everything in the house was black on black, and Alice's bright white room and no and no! Iris lied her way out of all the black and far away from her mother and dad—it was the softball practice that had been changed from three to four. And when the red mouth kept jumping up and down behind the black beard wanting to know who and how and why, she stamped and threw up a wall of weeping and fury, and up the stairs and the key around in the lock! And flung herself flat on her bed and bit her teeth into the bedspread, and it was a full black beard she was biting into. But that night there was much weeping in the dark around Iris' bed, and Iris' mother sat with her timid pale face and got the true story out of her Iris. And "Forgive me, mom!" and two pairs of clasped hands, and "Now I lay me down to sleep, I pray the Lord my soul to keep." And Iris was back home again, and at breakfast everything was as before, and Iris went to school transfigured. But Eigil's letters and the meeting with the two boys she had kept silent about.

And the weeks flew past with Iris' stormy happiness. Every morning at a quarter of nine she stood at the school entrance looking for Alice, and every morning Alice didn't come until the last minute. And during morning recess they walked closely entwined to show what bosom friends they were, but at the long recess they sneaked behind the gym and over the fence and out forbidden roads to meet Eigil and

Knud. And in the construction area it was stormy fall weather with trees blowing, and Eigil and Knud were in a fighting mood and roared in their breaking voices and both wanted to walk next to Alice. But Alice always let Knud walk behind with Iris, and Iris fought to keep her teeth in place in her mouth, and when she said anything it always was something about Alice, and what Alice said and did, and she exaggerated on purpose and effaced herself in the glory reflected from Alice. But when Knud once told something that made them both laugh and Iris doubled up and became loose-jointed the way she had seen Alice—well, then Alice was suddenly there and tucked a hand under Knud's arm, and Eigil was left to walk behind with Iris. And after that Iris didn't laugh, because she was scared to death of Eigil with his coarse voice and fat pimpled face.

On the whole Iris was terribly scared of these meetings, and she was scared stiff that she might be late getting home and would have to lie to her dad and have to lie in class, and she only agreed to it all because she was even more afraid of losing Alice. All her happiness was one great fear, and every morning she was anxiously on the lookout fearing Alice to come arm in arm with a new girl friend. For what did Iris have to give more than an occasional peep, a feeble obligato to Alice's rich music, and that couldn't be enough, and it must be wrong, too, that she got A's when Alice was just passing, and could answer in class when Alice couldn't. But when one morning she greeted Alice in exultant terror, telling that she hadn't done her homework—well, then

Alice pulled her arm out of hers and frowned. Was she crazy? One of them had to do it. And that way you never knew where you had Alice. But from that day on Iris was letter-perfect in her homework, and she sat glowing on her post and whispered to Alice, and she passed little notes over to Alice, and blissfully anxious she stood on guard in front of the bicycle shed where Alice sat copying her homework.

"Why do you bother!" fat Margrete said, but the others were silly and weren't going to go with Alice to Norway to ski in the Christmas vacation. But at home Iris talked for hours with her mother, and one morning she came to school transformed, wearing a new dress and new shoes and with a gold brace around her front teeth to force them back.

November came with its dark, and they had to eat lunch inside in the corridor, and the secret meetings with Eigil and Knud were automatically dropped. And anyway they were just boys, Alice had long been tired of them, and now it was Herr Højer with whom all the High School was in love, and whenever Herr Højer went past, Alice got a distant look and her cruel cat eyes became deep and veiled, for that was the way to win *him*. And in honor of Alice Iris, too, fell in love with Herr Højer, and they wrote his name everywhere and had small signs and code words that all referred to him. And in other ways too they walked more closely entwined than ever, and during lunch recess they had their own corner where they ate far away from the others, and Alice had pictures from Norway, "and that's me standing there, and that's me in the middle of

a jump." And there was a picture of the hotel with a cross marking Alice's window, "but you and I are going to have one of the big rooms with a balcony. And on December seventh is my birthday, just wait. I'm not going to say anything, just wait. . . ."

And Iris waited, thinking of December seventh, and one morning there was a letter in the mailbox: Alice Eierman requests the pleasure of Iris' gracious company for dinner on Friday December seventh at eight o'clock. Dress formal. And it was on a printed card with deckled edges, and the whole thing was in print except the name of Iris, "and there you see, mom!" And Iris' mother smiled transfigured and was touched by her Iris, and whispering at length they made plans for an apple green silk dress, "and now I'll talk with dad." That morning Iris wasn't content to stand waiting at the school entrance, she went to meet Alice, waving and calling from far away, and the whole morning they sat in fever about how many they were going to be, and who was going to come, and what they'd have to eat, and Alice's dress, and the gentlemen were going to be in black tie. . . .

And then the world had to collapse that very day.

The fifth period was arithmetic, and nothing happened until the last ten minutes when Herr Højer distributed their papers. But when he came to Alice's and Iris' desk he took a long stride past them, there were no math books for them. And Alice looked at Iris and raised her eyebrows and was all indifference, and Iris looked at Alice and thought of the party and clung to this, and even when together with Alice she was standing in front of the teacher's desk, and the two blue books lay there open and the whole class was whispering in anticipation, she still thought of the party and the gentlemen in black tie, and anyway she had already made up her mind.

"Well, my ladies," Herr Højer began, and there was a cruel smile in the corner of his mouth, and first he asked Iris and then Alice what four and three was. Seven, of course.

"Then how do you explain that you both made it eight?"

Silence. Alice stood with deep veiled eyes, for that was the way to win Herr Højer. But Herr Hojer wasn't won over that way, all he wanted to know was who had copied whom.

"For you aren't trying to tell me, are you, that you've both made the same mistake?"

And then there was Iris who had made up her mind—small, homespun Iris stepped forward and said it was she who had copied Alice. And to be sure her voice trembled as she said it, but the martyr's flame was strong in her, and Alice nodded yes when asked if it was true, and the world hadn't collapsed yet. But the silence was heavy in the class, and Herr Højer looked from Alice's bold innocent cat face to Iris' scarlet face, and from Alice's shining silk stockings to Iris' thick wool stockings, and he compared Alice's *passing* with Iris' *excellent*, and there was still a cruel smile in the corner of his mouth.

"When did you do your math?" he suddenly asked Alice.

"Last night."

"When?"

"At eight."

"That can't be right!" "Yes!" "No, you're lying!".

Ooh, the class curled fingers and toes during this cross examination, for now Alice wasn't the cat any more, Alice was the mouse scurrying from one hiding-place to the next, and in the end she had to admit that what Iris had said was a lie, and that what she had said herself was a lie, and that it was she who had copied Iris—all of the worldly wise lady Alice had caved in in front of the class and become a fourteen-year-old schoolgirl with tears of shame and fury in her eyes. And the rest was a matter of three extra assignments for Alice and Iris and staying one hour after school, and then the bell rang in the middle of it and that was it. The class dispersed.

But still, Iris had done what she could, and the world hadn't yet collapsed. And when Iris hugged Alice around her neck and wanted to comfort her, and Alice tore loose saying, "Scram, you!" and ran away and didn't show up until the last period began—well, the world sank, of course, but not completely, not irreparably, because, after all, Iris had done what she could, and surely Alice would come to think better of it. The whole last hour Iris sat cringing as she faced Alice's hostile back, and when Alice needed a pencil she quickly handed her own over. But Alice pushed it away. And when the bell rang, Alice got up at once and went to the detention hall with her assignments, and up there not a sound was tolerated, and you sat at separate desks. And when the long, strict silence was over and the teacher said "Okay!" Alice had already packed up and was out the door, and Iris had to run after her down the corridor and the stairs and way out on the street.

"Alice!" she called standing with

two helpless hands, "Alice! You know I couldn't . . ."

But Alice turned with ten claws and a white twisted cat face, and there was venom spouting from her: "What couldn't you, and what did you have to act noble for, and what are you running after me for, you smart little stupid-head. Scram! Run home and cry in your mama's skirts. . . . Mama's little Iris. . . . Watch out so your teeth don't fall out of your mouth. . . . And don't take the trouble to come to my birthday party, you numskull!"

Well, the world did collapse, but Iris didn't say anything at home. Nothing to her black dad with the black beard around his red mouth, and nothing to her little black mother with the pale worried face. For they were the ones who were to blame, not Alice. Alice was not to blame for anything. And Iris didn't hate Alice for what she had said, ooh, she loved Alice with two sorrowful hands, loved her with burning tears for what she had said. Alice with her round cat face and grey-green eyes and freckles by her nose.

"Numskull!" Iris said behind her locked door, "you stupid little brat, you numskull!"

And she said it in bed at night and said it in Alice's voice, and each time she said it, her mouth broadened and trembled with crying, and it was as if Alice were stepping on her and kicking her and spitting at her, and Iris' pillow became burning hot and damp. And in the morning she woke to a great terrible darkness and a tiny little hope in that darkness, for after all, she had only done what she could, and maybe Alice would have thought better of it by now; and she went to school early and waited in the yard, for then it was up to Alice herself what she wanted. But Alice didn't want anything. However, that day was the first of December, and the room was decorated with a Christmas tree and there was a feeling of the Christmas holiday in the air, and then perhaps Alice would? . . . But when Iris came up to class, Alice had already moved her belongings to the front desk, the same single desk where Iris had been before, there Alice sat twisting one silkstocking leg around the other and knew nothing and couldn't help anything and was all indifference. And yet Iris didn't give up hope entirely, for there was the card, a certain solemn printed card of invitation, and Alice would have to say something, wouldn't she? Something more. And two and three and four days went past, and Iris tried on her apple green silk dress and smiled bravely into the mirror and kept hoping, and not until the sixth, in the afternoon, when the bell had rung its three long signals, and Alice's steps lost themselves down the corridor and nothing had been said, was the little tiny light in the dark put out.

On December seventh Iris woke with an aching head and body, and she turned out to have a temperature of 102. The doctor was called and he diagnosed influenza, and the little black mother was inconsolable and nursed and timidly tucked her Iris in, and her Iris lay with her face to the wall and wanted only to die. And in the evening her temperature rose to 104, and most of the night Iris' mother and father both sat by the bed, but Iris didn't even recognize them and "Stupid brat!"

she called to them in delirium. And they sought each other's hands in their great fear that Iris' lungs had been infected. . . .

It wasn't pneumonia, but even so it was serious enough—for the better part of a month Iris lay there listless, and she kept throwing up, and although she dozed away the days there was no real recovery in it. Not until January, when Christmas was over, did she begin to get better.

On the first of February Iris came back to school, and during the two months that she had been away great, silent changes had taken place. One girl had left and a new one had come, and one girl came in a grown-up dress and pinned-up hair, and Alice and fat Margrete had made friends—Iris stood some distance away and watched them waltz around the schoolyard arm in arm to show what bosom friends they were. And they shared desk and wrote little secret messages to each other and had a lunch corner to themselves, and fat Margrete stood guard in front of the bike shed, where Alice sat copying her homework.

"Why bother!" Erna and Ruth and the others said.

But fat Margrete did.

discussion

The need for peer approval becomes extremely important by the middle school years. Since Iris had spent so little time with her peer group because of home teaching, her need for acceptance was overwhelming. Her chances to succeed in making friends were dimmed by her intrusive mother and her own awkwardness. Sometimes a new student becomes the object of positive attention, but Iris is too far from the norm in her appearance and in the appropriateness of her school work to warrant even a swift flurry of attention as the "new girl." When the teacher is also inclined to laugh at her, Iris is in further jeopardy. Yet Iris will not settle for the more conforming and lackluster group of girls. Probably her humdrum existence with her parents makes the prospect of acceptance into the "in" group more tantalizing.

Her attraction to Alice is intense and is probably her first "crush." In early adolescence it is not unusual for a student to feel a particular attraction to a popular teacher or even to an older student of the same sex. Iris' attachment to Alice seems to fall into that category. She is a willing instrument in Alice's hands. The reward of Alice's interest and attention is sufficient to compensate for Iris' fear of transgressing school regulations by meeting the high school boys at lunch or permitting Alice to copy her homework. The enhancement of being Alice's best friend dominates her life.

Despite Iris' predictable downfall, analysis of the situation seems to indicate that Iris gains more than Alice from their association. Iris' exposure to Alice's escapades gives Iris some confidence in herself with boys and teachers. She is no longer the object of ridicule by the other boys and girls. She gains status within the peer group even though it is short lived.

For Iris, Alice's friendship was an important step away from her oppressive parents, although the consequences were devastating, physically as well as psychologically. At the end of the story Alice repeats her controlling peer relationship. Hopefully Iris will find a new friend who will value rather than exploit her loyalty.

springboards for inquiry

1. The learner is obviously not an entity divorced from the reality of childhood. Describe Iris' intense desire to become part of the "in" crowd.

2. Is there some relevant role a teacher could play in helping an "outsider" crack the social barriers?

3. The joy of acceptance by at least one individual in the peer group is beautifully described in this story.

   a. Which section describes Iris' ecstasy upon returning home after a full school day with Alice?

   b. Trace the fall of Iris from the moment Herr Højer discovers their collusion and observe how the terror of rejection actually sends her home ill.

4. Recall an important friendship from your own childhood. What age were you? In what ways did this relationship influence your speech, dress, food preferences, handwriting, or other aspects of your behavior?

the individuality of the learner

There is sufficient evidence to indicate that even in the first week of life there are individual differences between newborns. These differences have been classified in terms of "easy babies," "difficult babies," and "a little of each" babies. Despite the fact that the babies were in the same environment (the children were all observed in the same nursery for the first few days after birth) they clearly reacted to life in individual patterns which were attributable to heredity only.[1]

Taking this fact as a given in life's equation, we may expect that each learner's specific gene pool regulates his response to his learning environment. The ancient $S \longrightarrow R$ (Stimulus yields Response) paradigm is now redesigned and looks like this: $S \longrightarrow O \longrightarrow R$. The SOR model (Stimulus acting upon a specific Organism yields a Response) more nearly corresponds to reality. Using the technique of the semanticist known as subscripting,[2] it is even more accurate to design the learning model to show that a given stimulus (S) acting upon a classroom of organisms (O^1, O^2, O^3, O^4, etc.) will yield a variety of responses (R^1, R^2, R^3, etc.).

Translated into learning theory Figure 1 means that the teacher and his lesson are perceived by each learner in a unique way and each learner's responses will be individualized. Some literature in developmental psychology calls this individualized perception and response the student's learning style.[3] In general children learn in at least four different ways—one, through the concrete or abstract; two, structured or informal; three, inductive or deductive; four, direct confrontation or sequenced approach.

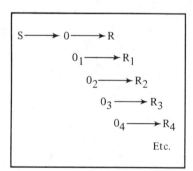

Figure 3

[1]Stella Chess; Alexander Thomas; and Herbert Birch, "Characteristics of the Individual Child's Behavioral Responses to the Environment," *American Journal of Orthopsychiatry* 29 (1959): 791–802.

[2]See the works of Korzybski, Whorf, Hayakawa, and others for more complete details.

[3]See Gerald Weinstein and Mario D. Fantini, *Toward Humanistic Education: A Curriculum of Affect* (New York: Praeger, 1970).

Good teaching requires a reasonable knowledge of learning styles so that, when possible, a particular learning experience can be made most meaningful to an individual either by using all four methodologies or by discovering which one fits the learner best for the particular problem at hand. It is important for teachers to have an arsenal of methodology available so that each learner is approached with the method most nearly suited to his learning style(s). However, individuals are not limited to one learning style. If a teacher labeled a learner with a single style and tried to teach him all things with the same methodology, he would undoubtedly meet with frustration. Labels are libelous. Even if a child is a "concrete" learner in many or most situations, he may not be a "concrete" learner in specific instances. When the student obviously does not respond to the method being used, the teacher must be sensitive to the problem and try a different approach. Thus, if a child fails to respond to a lesson describing the principle of mathematical addition using some real materials (e.g. 15 pingpong balls), it is possible that an abacus or even a small calculator will reach him. To give up teaching a concept because one method does not work would be the height of folly. An armamentarium of methodology should capitalize on every possible learning style of the child.

The four learning styles reflect different fundamental assumptions:

1. *Concrete versus Abstract*—Piaget tells us that abstract thinking occurs around the age of 12 or so. Therefore, the wise teacher generally uses the concrete approach in which things are manipulated and objects are used to show what concepts really mean. However, some children can understand abstract ideas at an earlier age.[4] Therefore the teacher must consider the individual status of the particular learner and may need to intersperse the abstract approach with the concrete. The art of teaching requires the teacher to be able to move quickly from concrete descriptions (e.g., of the principle of condensation) to an abstract one which might just capture the imagination of the child. Thus, a drawing of droplets of vapor becoming drops of water might possibly be more effective than the "real" thing.

2. *Structured versus Informal*—The learning that is described as taking place in the Informal Schools[5] in England best exemplifies the assumptions of informal learning. When a teacher says, "I used to order 35 copies of a book—now I order 35 different books!"[6] one may be reasonably sure that informal rather than structured learning is occurring. Structured learning more nearly approaches the typical world-model of a teacher presiding

---

[4]In R.A. Hinde and J. Stevenson-Hinde, *Constraints on Learning* (London: Academic Press, 1973), an article by S.J. Hutt called, "Constraints upon Learning: Some Developmental Considerations," says, "In similar vein, the long-standing claim by Piaget that children cannot combine information inferentially until eight years of age could be shown to be false . . . Bryant has elegantly shown that children can combine information inferentially, several years earlier than Piaget has supposed, provided they have access to the data upon which the information must be based." (p. 458.)

[5]For detailed description of informal teaching read Maurice Kogan, ed., *Informal Schools in Britain Today* (New York: Citation Press, 1972).

[6]Ibid., p. 375.

over 30+ children of similar ages who will all be asked to do the same thing at about the same time.

3. *Inductive versus Deductive*—When children learn inductively, they reason from the particular to the general. They are said to be reaching a conclusion about all members of a class by observing only some of them. For example, they are told that gold, silver, and iron are metals. Gold, silver, and iron are heavier than water. All metals are heavier than water. The semanticists have warned us against the use of the word "all" in such situations. This induction about metals, based on examination of gold, silver, and iron became faulty when potassium was discovered because potassium is lighter than water. On the other hand, deductive learning, which we more consciously teach, draws conclusions from evidence. Reasoning is from the general to the particular. Children are given general rules for solving mathematical problems, scanning poetry, or setting the margins on a typewriter. Then they are told to apply the theories to specific tasks.

4. *Direct Confrontation versus Sequenced Approach*—The sequenced approach to learning completely negates any ideas of student individuality. Exemplified best by the concept of programmed instruction, it reduces any area of knowledge to specific short steps, one building upon the other and providing instant feedback to the learner so that he knows immediately when and what he did wrong. Every program is identical for every child regardless of anything that is known about the child. Hundreds of children are put into programs which take every child through every lesson in precisely the same order. The only provision made for any individuality is that each learner proceeds at his own pace and may do as much as he can regardless of where his peers are. In contrast to the sequenced approach, the direct confrontation approach provides teacher-designed experiences with the subject and allows the learner to work his way through the experiences learning those facts and/or concepts which present themselves to him. Thus, a tenth grade class may be learning about "power" in the sociological sense. Confrontation techniques may suggest a visit to the mayor's office to discover how a local level decision about garbage collection or fuel allocation is reached. The "facts" about community power will slowly come to a student as he confronts reality. The same material based upon what is already known, tried and tested could be sequenced. The evaluation of the learning experience in either case is, of course, a matter of philosophy.

In addition to the individuality of learning styles, students have many other aspects of individuality. Differences in intelligence, cultural background, family lifestyles, and personality are of great significance.

In a very real sense each student presents to his teacher the possibility for multi-dimensional understanding. It seems self-evident that, though children may be in the same age-placement class, their differing intellectual abilities would dictate at least minimal provisions for the individualization of instruction. For example, certain children might have the details of a homework assignment lessened so that they could do that part of the work that is within the scope of their own abilities. Shorter assignments, even more complex ones (for those with high I.Q.s) may be in order. So too are different assignments on the same subject important when the individual intellectual competence of students is used as a guideline for more sensible teaching.

Children from culturally different backgrounds present challenges, too. In one school, children from very poor Croatian families were suddenly mixed with an elite economically and culturally rich Anglo-Saxon group. The usual conversations on Monday morning about pheasant hunting weekends or sports car racing were highly inappropriate. In one sixth grade class the problem was considerably lessened by the WASPs inviting the Croatians to share some of those weekend adventures. In a town where dozens of Navajo children attend the public schools, the teachers were distressed that Navajo culture teaches children not to talk about what they did or about their families. Navajo women, unlike most other American women, do not wear their often magnificent turquoise and silver belts over their blouses but tuck them under so they are not the objects of attention. Verbal behavior normally expected from non-Indian children is alien to Navajo youth. Teachers who attributed Navajo reticence about participating in early morning discussions of home and family life to dullness or stubbornness did not understand the Navajo culture.

More and more children are being brought up in one-parent homes. Teacher indifference to this fact may result in embarrassing silences when talk of mothers and fathers gets heavy. In one school, a report from the principal's office to the teachers indicated that nearly three out of four children were not living with the same father and mother they were born to. The family lifestyle of one-parent families is different from the typical nuclear family (mother-father-children) arrangement that once dominated the family scene. Children from communal families, open-style families, and even polygamous[7] families present problems if teachers assume that all families are alike.

In addition to intellectual, cultural, and family differences between children there are personal, economic, and social differences which need to be considered. There is a very blurred line of difference between many of these terms. For instance, having just discussed cultural differences in terms of the Navajos and their particular culture, a discussion of social differences could also focus on the same point. Understanding this overlapping will help the reader to realize that the terms "economic," "personal," and "social differences" are not categories that have been completely absent from our discussion thus far.

When a biologist was asked why the nature versus nurture controversy still existed in humans when it was solved in studies of the fruit fly and the mouse, he replied that the behavior and misbehavior of 48 chromosomes in each human cell was vastly more complicated than the two chromosomes in the fly. The personal differences between children of the same age and sex, etc., are nearly infinite. Even the slightest pretense at generalization is sus-

[7]In parts of Arizona, Utah, Idaho, Wyoming, California, New Mexico, and Montana there are still pockets of polygamous family life representing dissident and excommunicated adherents of the Mormon faith.

pect. It is true that there are some common behaviors expected in fourth graders. Even these are subject to the personal stamp affixed by each individual member of that fourth grade class. Not every family in the same culture is predictable. The predictable unpredictability of even those who share the same heredity and ostensibly the same culture is axiomatic. In fact, the breadth of understanding necessary to really comprehend the child is almost incomprehensible. One of the peculiar joys of teaching is the endless opportunity to focus on a child and reconstruct the knowns and unknowns of his past and present. The task of teaching is filled with complexities. There is no system available for feeding the variables of any human child's lifespace into some computer such that a ready formula for teaching that child will spew forth.

If all human behavior is caused and if the teacher understands the causes behind a child's behavior, does this knowledge of cause excuse all behavior? Actually, the single cause theory is outmoded. Behavior has many causes. Does a God-like comprehension of even multiple causation necessitate teacher toleration of all behavior? While teachers may know about causation, they should nonetheless expect certain levels of responsible behavior. No changes in behavior come about simply because etiology is known. In spite of what is known about cause it is particularly important for those who teach to expect behavior and learning that on the surface seem impossible to expect. The personal philosophies of the teachers expressed in *The Real Teachers* reinforces this position.[8] In this exciting volume of interviews with thirty dedicated inner-city teachers, the idea of always considering individual circumstances yet expecting progress from children recurs throughout:

> Your first impulse is to shower the children with love and to let them run all over you as a sign that you love them. I learned very quickly that that's not the way . . . I give everybody a good dose of tender loving care, but at the beginning I'm very stern. . . . I'm precise, I give children definite boundaries.[9]

Even in the very touchy realm of race relations where Alan Kellock, a white, taught African history to all black classes, he learned that there were times when a direct confrontation about certain taboo words was better than making believe the words didn't exist:

> The object of attack (in a class discussion without the teacher there) was a kid who'd been going to some of the Muslims' religious-education, political-education classes. He was arguing against the diehard, very emotional Christians—not too effectively because he was so much in the defensive that he was shouting and antagonizing people. I took a real deep breath and said, "Explain the difference between a black man and a nigger." The kid jumped . . . he's about five ten and he's all set to go.
>
> But the fascinating thing was that the guy who [earlier had] pulled the gun on

---

[8]Philip Sterling, ed., *The Real Teachers* (New York: Vintage Books, 1972).
[9]Ibid, p. 150.

me . . . swarmed up and intervened. "You don't understand what he means. By getting angry you're only showing your disrespect for yourself," which is one use of the term "nigger" among blacks.[10]

"Our recognition of the provision of a wise Creator that every human being should be different from every other human will surely lead teachers . . . to desist from teaching toward similarity and conformity and turn to the preoccupation of the talent scout helping children learn to know themselves and like it, and helping each one to find his valued roles to play among the people of his world."[11]

Donna van Tassell

Home thoughts

"Where was my father," I wondered. "Was he working or was he drunk somewhere."

Half darkness gradually fading into dawn hung like fog in my room. If a pin dropped, I'd be its only witness. If a word was spoken, it was my own. The freshly starched white pillow on which I rested my head only accented my aloneness. I tossed and turned and retossed with self-pity.

Days came and left, leaving me silent. Each morning I awoke sure of my next movement. My mother would be rolled in her bed covers unaware that a new day had come and that the cat needed to be let in from out back where my step-father chained him according to his custom shortly before work. I freed the cat and hurried to the greasiness of the kitchen to scramble eggs before it was too late and I'd go hungry again. No breakfasts had been

"Home Thoughts" from Talking About Us *is reprinted by permission of the author and Mr. Herbert R. Coursen, Jr.*

allowed after seven-thirty ever since my mother's remarriage and I dared not alter her rule. Besides, the school bus was due at eight and unless I caught that I'd be trapped at home all day.

There was no mad rush to put on my coat, pick up my books, and bang out the door, as one normally expects. I was much too eager to leave not to be already on my mark and set to go.

A mile trip to school on rough and twisting road through the woods only takes a few minutes. Often I arrived in class with the words of my mother still ringing in my ears, "Aren't you ever going to get out of here?" or even more often, "Where's that damn bus?"

By the end of the first class I had usually lost myself and my problems in a book or a discussion and by the last class I secretly began dreading the three o'clock bell. I didn't need a

[10]Ibid, pp. 384–85.
[11]Howard Lane and Mary Beauchamp, *Human Relations in Teaching* (New York: Prentice-Hall, 1955), p. 130.

clock to tell me what time it was, something inside of me forewarned me.

Kitchen smells rarely greeted me as I idled through the front door but even less frequent was a word from anyone to assure me that human existence wasn't altogether foreign to that house, that surprisingly was by some few considered home. Perhaps the clatter of tin plates and plastic ones, the ring that glasses make, and the jingle jangle of silverware being sloshed in water was my welcome home each night. Or perhaps the sound of one foot pressing upward always ahead of the other as I climbed the stairs leading to my bedroom was my only assurance that I was home.

Turning at a right angle from the stairs, walking mechanically to the big wooden dresser near my bed, flinging my books down in a nearby chair, and methodically changing my clothes were all ordinary movements on my part. Sometimes I found myself wondering what I would have done had someone rearranged those few pieces of furniture to which I turned every night.

Before supper I usually sprawled out on my cot with a book. And so I would read until either boredom or some particular words within my book made me drift off into some distant memory.

"My Lord, I think I saw him yesternight."

"Saw? Who?"

"My Lord, the King your father."

"Where was my father," I wondered. "Was he working or was he drunk somewhere." I looked down at my watch; it was five-thirty—five-thirty—just four years ago I would have known where he was. He'd be home with mama and me up on the hill where we used to live. We'd all be sitting round the kitchen table eating and talking. It was always a good life back then before the divorce. I can't remember having any real problems then but now . . . now it was all changed. We never talked anymore; mama was always too busy or too tired. My step-father rarely spoke. It was almost like he was a complete stranger and the only thing I really knew about him was his face. Each night he came home from work, puttered with the familiar chores, sat down in his wooden rocking chair with his pipe tucked in his teeth and slept until supper. After supper he always returned to his chair or else mama and he went up the road to visit with his mother. Even there he slept. Rage and laughter looked bad on him. Whenever he put them on, I felt uncomfortable because they seemed unreal.

What would life have been like if I didn't know this man, my unwanted step-father? If only things hadn't changed and my real father was the man downstairs. But no, it was best not to think about it and so I forced myself to think of other things. I looked again at my book but my thoughts quickly returned to my family. I asked the question—"What would it be like?" Before the divorce there was carefreeness. I had a kitten for a pet and a back yard swing, and I'd chased June bugs, caught tadpoles, and hunted wild flowers. I went barefoot, picked berries, and rolled in clover that made my clothing sweet with scent. Even now I can close my eyes and picture life as it was. Now at twelve I wanted the things that twelve-year-olds are supposed to have. I wanted pretty dresses, not hand-me-downs; curls in my hair and jewelry just because everyone had them. I wanted to invite friends over to my house after school or go to theirs. Maybe even have a boyfriend.

A voice from my past urged me onward, to get up and conquer, to be that twelve-year-old of my dreams. I started up, pressed down the wrinkles from my clothing with my hands, started for the mirror to comb my hair, got there, and as the comb took its first sweep, the words of my mother came exploding in the air, "Get downstairs, supper's ready." I dropped the comb, walked to the door, turned back for just a moment, then went slowly down those stairs.

discussion

This well written story represents the thoughts of a real twelve-year-old girl, a student in a specially funded compensatory education program called Upward Bound. If each child in any classroom wrote down his "home thoughts" how many stories would be similar? The exact circumstances may differ, but feelings of loneliness and desperation may be a surprisingly common theme. For many children, silence is the only greeting they receive when they return from school, for the one parent in the household is still at work. In Donna's case the alienation is heavy even when the parent is at home at the end of the school day.

She dreams of life before her parents' divorce. Since the number of divorces is mounting, the proportion of children who are from broken homes, even in suburban schools, may reach as high as one-third of the class, particularly on the East and West coasts. A child who is unhappy with his present circumstances may fantasize about his changed life pattern. Some of the memories may be glorified in order to make life tolerable. For Donna the past was supportive enough to provide her with the incentive to arouse herself from fantasy and to face today resiliently.

Teachers who are working hard to cover curriculum requirements for their grade level are aware that some of their students are having difficulty because the circumstances of their life outside of school hinders concentration and the will to learn. Luckily for Donna, school was a place in which she could lose herself and her problems. A book or discussion did not solve her problems but helped to postpone thinking about them. For many other students, schoolwork is not as satisfying. Sometimes poor skills in reading, spelling, and math keep them from participation with their age mates. Reading problems in particular affect performance in every subject area, and the school day may become a series of frustrations. Teachers may feel that many of their students are poor learners because they are psychologically damaged human beings. What is the school's responsibility in these cases? Philosophically there are two major and differing points of view.[1] Carl Rogers, the advocate of humanistic education, says "the inner world of the individual appears to have more significant influence on his behavior

[1]This discussion of educational objectives is based on William D. Hitt, *Education as a Human Enterprise* (Worthington, Ohio: Charles A. Jones, 1973).

than does the external environmental stimulus." He would expect the school to take a major role in building the students' character by helping students to develop a strong self concept, a sense of responsibility, the ability to reason and to be independent in their thinking. Behaviorists like B.F. Skinner consider the school environment responsible for shaping the student in keeping with objectives prescribed by the educator with little or no emphasis upon the student's inner thoughts or feelings. Using Skinnerian philosophy, teachers would attempt to construct appropriate graduated learning assignments based upon the child's learning style. The learning experience would then be a successful one and school would be perceived as reinforcing.

springboards for inquiry

1. To what extent do you think schools should feel responsible for a student's learning and adjustment in school when the home environment does not support school success?

2. Plan a lesson for a student in the age range of your interest in any subject area using one of the learning styles described in this chapter.

3. Whose philosophy appeals to you most—that of Carl Rogers or the philosophy of B. F. Skinner?

motivation
for learning

There are experiments and a wealth of data on motivation, running the gamut from discussions of psychological hedonism to achievement motivation. A chapter in a recent text book discusses motivation theory in this purely psychological manner without accounting for what appears to be a major force for motivation to learn—culture.[1]

The motivation to learn appears to be related to the influence of the learner's progenitors and the lifespace he occupies. This influence may be termed the "outside1" culture.[2] There is also the "outside2" culture—the culture of the school which includes the teachers and principals. The motivation created by the school culture may support the "outside1" culture or it may run counter to it.[3] Should the "outside2" culture resist the explicit needs and ways of the "outside1" culture, a battle is sure to shape up. Where there is a convergence of opinion and should this agreement be in the direction of high motivation for learning, we may expect such excellence as is evident in the Bronx High School of Science and the High School of Music and Art in New York City.

A recent article in the *American Psychologist* attributes Sarason's motivation to learn to his Jewish background.[4] He maintains that the motivation for learning he grew up with was part of the fabric of intellectual accomplishment valued by everyone he knew in his Jewish world. He says, "I do not have to relate more anecdotes to make the point that being Jewish was inextricably interwoven with *attitudes* [italics ours] towards intellectual accomplishment. To separate one from the other was impossible. This did not mean that being Jewish meant that one was smart or capable of intellectual accomplishments, but it meant that one had respect for such strivings."[5] Sarason also attributes his motivation, in part, to the knowledge that he lived in a hostile world. About this he says, "now to another aspect of Jewishness to which I have alluded: the knowledge (it is not a feeling, it is

[1]Guy L. Lefrancois, *Of Children: An Introduction to Child Development* (Belmont, Ca.: Wadsworth, 1973).

[2]Two interesting volumes which further demonstrate this thesis are: Sue Stanley and N. N. Wagner, *Asian-American Psychological Perspectives* (Ben Lomond: Science and Behavioral Books, 1973), and Isao Fujimoto, *Chinese-Americans: School and Community Problems* (Chicago: Integrated Education Assoc., 1972).

[3]Paul W. Jackson, *Life in Classrooms* (New York: Holt, Rinehart & Winston, 1968), Seymour B. Sarason, *The Culture of the School and the Problem of Change* (Boston: Allyn & Bacon, 1971), and Robert Rosenthal and Lenore Jacobson, *Pygmalion in the Classroom* (New York: Holt, Rinehart & Winston, 1968).

[4]Seymour B. Sarason, "Jewishness, Blackishness and the Nature-Nurture Controversy," *American Psychologist* 28, no. 11 (November 1973): 962–71.

[5]Ibid., p. 964.

phenomenologically a fact) that one is in a hostile world. This was crystal clear in my parents' and grandparents' generations."[6]

Too frequently critics who discuss the problem of motivation for learning are in ethereal realms bandying about terms such as cognitive dissonance, physiological needs, and arousal-bound integration. All of these concepts have a sound research base but they call to mind a Zen Buddhist saying "Don't mistake the finger pointing at the moon for the moon." When children come to school unmotivated, it is "finger pointing" to blame their I.Q. scores on their laziness. Motivation springs from culture—ethnic, home, and community.[7] Until blacks were prodded into seeking after their origins by militant ghetto groups, they were content to let their local schools rant on about the equator passing through the center of Africa. Similarly, until Chicanos, Jews, and American Indians awoke to the fact that their respective cultures were unknown to their children they did not strive for more ethnic consciousness. From this awareness on the part of the adult community, came the motivation on the part of their children to learn about origins.

Because there is an intrinsic relationship between the meaning of the terms *ethnic subgroups* and *socioeconomic status* (social-class status) and a high degree of correlation between the two factors, it is desirable (and necessary) to determine the socioeconomic status of the child so that this important variable is to be accounted for in the evaluation of experimental data.[8] Any discussion of motivation for learning in the schools would be irrelevant without reference to the type of children studied. Havighurst and Taba and Hieronymus were early researchers in this area.[9] Since then it is rare to find the variable of socioeconomic status absent in the literature.[10] In general data on social class show that despite ethnicity and ethnic subgroup, when children of the same or approximately the same social class are stud-

[6]Ibid., p. 965.

[7]Wallace A. Kennedy, *Child Psychology* (Englewood Cliffs, N.J.: Prentice-Hall, 1971), uses the term *ethnic subgroup* instead of the broader word *culture* used here. Still, the intention is the same as in Sarason's article—to point out that ethnic subgroupings are highly correlated with achievement and motivation. Further hard research findings may be found in Gerald S. Lesser, Gordon Fifer, and Donahld H. Clark, "Mental Abilities of Children from Different Social Class and Cultural Groups," *Monographs of the Society for Research in Child Development* 30 (4) no. 102 (1965).

[8]Cf. Mary Alice White and Jan Duker, "Suggested Standards for Children's Samples," *American Psychologist* 28, no. 3 (August 1973) where social class is listed ninth in a list of twenty-two standard characteristics which ought to be included in any data reported when children are used as a sample.

[9]Robert J. Havighurst and Hilda Taba, *Adolescent Character and Personality* (New York: John Wiley & Sons, 1949); A. N. Hieronymus, "A Study of Social Class Motivation: Relationships Between Anxiety for Education and Certain Socio-Economic and Intellectual Variables," *Journal of Educational Psychology* 42 (1951): 29–45.

[10]In a survey of 207 articles in four psychological journals, 31 percent reported social class (although in only 2 percent of the articles was there any report on the scale or measure used to arrive at the social class labels). White and Ducker, "Suggested Standards for Children's Samples," p. 781.

ied, the results are almost identical. That is, the middle class family, ethnicity notwithstanding, values education and encourages children to study and learn. Although the gap between social classes is closing,[11] it still seems plausible even in 1976 to state that it is income and occupational level,[12] rather than race or culture which almost predetermines one's motivation for learning.

The psychological basis for high motivation has produced hundreds of studies. Recent researchers generally believe that people are motivated by the need to achieve and that this need is motivated much by parental aspirations and at-home parental behavior.

Believers in the cognitive dissonance theory of motivation believe that people will be motivated to behave in a manner which will stop an emotional conflict caused by pursuing two conflicting courses of behavior. The exploratory theory for the motivation of human behavior simply says that humans are curious and wish to explore their environment.

Behaviorists say that students are motivated because of the reinforcement (or lack of it) they receive from their surroundings for what they do. If the classroom teacher rewards exploratory behavior (he may applaud it, give prizes for it, assign grades for it) then the class is more likely to be motivated in the direction of exploring.

The arousal-based school of motivation is predicated on the theory that human beings do things which arouse their physiological/psychological alertness. They postulate an optimal level of arousal where humans behave with exceptional keenness. A sleeping person's level of arousal is lowest; therefore, his effectiveness of behavior is low. On the other end of the arousal spectrum, panic (as in restaurant and theater fires) motivates ineffective behavior because the level of arousal is so high that there is, in fact, a deterioration of behavior.

Finally, there is the motivational theory based upon needs. In general, this theory states that once our physiological needs are met reasonably well, we are motivated to fulfill higher and higher needs; and the highest of these is to be motivated to become the most self-actualized beings possible. In other words, when a person is reasonably well satisfied in terms of basic needs, free from hunger and thirst, enjoying feelings of safety, love, and self-esteem, then he is able to concentrate on becoming whatever he is capable of, developing his identity through self-fulfillment.

What motivates the child to learn? There are many theories. The teacher's role is to be especially sensitive to any success with children who usually appear unmotivated. When motivation does not come to school with the child, the teacher needs to explore every conceivable possibility for motivating the child himself.

[11]Urie Bronfenbrenner, "Socialization and Social Class Through Time and Space," in *Readings in Social Psychology*. 3rd ed., ed. Eleanor E. Maccoby, Theodore M. Newcomb, and Eugene L. Hartley (New York: Holt, Rinehart & Winston, 1958), pp. 400–25.

[12]The latter is still the most significant difference between social class levels.

Virginia Moriconi

Simple arithmetic

*"Simple Arithmetic" by Virginia Mori-
coni is reprinted by the kind permission of
the author.*

Geneva, January 15
Dear Father:
Well, I am back in School, as you
can see, and the place is just as miserable as ever. My only friend, the
one I talked to you about, Ronald
Fletcher, is not coming back any
more because someone persuaded
his mother that she was letting him
go to waste, since he was extremely
photogenic, so now he is going to
become a child actor. I was very surprised to hear this, as the one thing
Ronnie liked to do was play basketball. He was very shy.
The flight wasn't too bad. I mean
nobody had to be carried off the
plane. The only thing was, we were
six hours late and they forgot to
give us anything to eat, so for four-
teen hours we had a chance to get
quite hungry but, as you say, for the
money you save going tourist class,
you should be prepared to make a
few little sacrifices.
I did what you told me, and when
we got to Idlewild I paid the taxi
driver his fare and gave him a fifty-
cent tip. He was very dissatisfied. In
fact he wouldn't give me my suitcase. In fact I don't know what
would have happened if a man
hadn't come up just while the argument was going on and when he

Dear Stephen:
. . . No examiner is going to find
himself favorably impressed by
"charactor" or "instructer" or "villan" or
"riserved" or similar errors. You will
have to face the fact that in this world
we succeed on our merits, and if we are
unsuccessful, on account of sloppy
habits of mind, we suffer for it.

heard what it was all about he gave
the taxi driver a dollar and I took
my suitcase and got to the plane on
time.
During the trip I thought the
whole thing over. I did not come to
any conclusion. I know I have been
very extravagant and unreasonable
about money and you have done the
best you can to explain this to me.
Still, while I was thinking about it, it
seemed to me that there were only
three possibilities. I could just have
given up and let the taxi driver have
the suitcase, but when you realize
that if we had to buy everything
over again that was in the suitcase
we would probably have had to
spend at least five hundred dollars,
it does not seem very economical.
Or I could have gone on arguing
with him and missed the plane, but
then we would have had to pay
something like three hundred dollars for another ticket. Or else I
could have given him an extra twenty-five cents which, as you say, is just
throwing money around to create
an impression. What would you
have done?
Anyway I got here, with the suitcase, which was the main thing.
They took two week-end privileges
away from me because I was late for
the opening of School. I tried to explain to M. Frisch that it had nothing to do with me if the weather was
so bad that the plane was delayed

for six hours, but he said that prudent persons allow for continjensies of this kind and make earlier reservations. I don't care about this because the next two week-ends are skiing week-ends and I have never seen any point in waking up at six o'clock in the morning just to get frozen stiff and endure terrible pain even if sports are a part of growing up, as you say. Besides, we will save twenty-seven dollars by having me stay in my room.

In closing I want to say that I had a very nice Christmas and I apreciate everything you tried to do for me and I hope I wasn't too much of a bother. (Martha explained to me that you had had to take time off from your honeymoon in order to make Christmas for me and I am very sorry even though I do not think I am to blame if Christmas falls on the twenty-fifth of December, especially since everybody knows that it does. What I mean is, if you had wanted to have a long honeymoon you and Martha could have gotten married earlier, or you could have waited until Christmas was over, or you could just have told me not to come and I would have understood.)

I will try not to spend so much money in the future and I will keep accounts and send them to you. I will also try to remember to do the eye exercises and the exercises for fallen arches that the doctors in New York prescribed.

Love,
STEPHEN

New York, January 19
Dear Stephen:
Thank you very much for the long letter of January fifteenth. I was very glad to know that you had gotten back safely, even though the flight was late. (I do not agree with M. Frisch that prudent persons allow for "continjensies" of this kind, now that air travel is as standard as it is, and the service usually so good, but we must remember that Swiss people are, by and large, the most meticulous in the world and nothing offends them more than other people who are not punctual.)

In the affair of the suitcase, I'm afraid that we were both at fault. I had forgotten that there would be an extra charge for luggage when I suggested that you should tip the driver fifty cents. You, on the other hand, might have inferred from his argument that he was simply asking that the tariff—i.e. the fare, plus the overcharge for the suitcase—should be paid in full, and regulated yourself accordingly. In any event you arrived, and I am only sorry that obviously you had no time to learn the name and address of your benefactor so that we might have paid him back for his kindness.

I will look forward to going over your accounting and I am sure you will find that in keeping a clear record of what you spend you will be able to cut your cloth according to the bolt and that, in turn, will help you to develop a real regard for yourself. It is a common failing, as I told you, to spend too much money in order to compensate oneself for a lack of inner security, but you can easily see that a foolish purchase does not insure stability, and if you are chronically insolvent you can hardly hope for peace of mind. Your allowance is more than adequate and when you learn to make both ends meet you will have taken a decisive step ahead. I have great faith in you and I know you will find your anchor to windward in your studies, in your sports, and in your companions.

As to what you say about Christmas, you are not obliged to "apreciate" what we did for you. The important thing was that you should have had a good time, and I think we had some wonderful fun together, the three of us, don't you? Until your mother decides where she wants to live and settles down, this is your *home* and you must always think of it that way. Even though I have remarried, I am still your father, first and last, and Martha is very fond of you too, and very understanding about your problems. You may not be aware of it but in fact she is one of the best friends you have. New ideas and new stepmothers take a little getting used to, of course.

Please write me as regularly as you can, since your letters mean a great deal to me. Please try too, at all times, to keep your marks up to scratch, as college entrance is getting harder and harder in this country, and there are thousands of candidates each year for the good universities. Concentrate particularly on spelling. "Contingency" is difficult, I know, but there is no excuse for only one "p" in "appreciate"! And *do* the exercises.

Love,
FATHER

Geneva, January 22
Dear Mummy:

Last Sunday I had to write to Father to thank him for my Christmas vacation and to tell him that I got back all right. This Sunday I thought I would write to you even though you are on a cruze so perhaps you will never get my letter. I must say that if they didn't make us write home once a week I don't believe that I would ever write any letters at all. What I mean is that once you get to a point like this, in a place like this, you see that you are supposed to have your life and your parents are supposed to have their lives, and you have lost the connection.

Anyway I have to tell you that Father was wonderful to me and Martha was very nice too. They had thought it all out, what a child of my age might like to do in his vacation, and sometimes it was pretty strenuous, as you can imagine. At the end the School sent the bill for the first term, where they charge you for the extras which they let you have here and it seems that I had gone way over my allowance and besides I had signed for a whole lot of things I did not deserve. So there was a terrible scene and Father was very angry and Martha cried and said that if Father always made such an effort to consider me as a person I should make an effort to consider him as a person too and wake up to the fact that he was not Rockefeller and that even if he was sacrificing himself so that I could go to one of the most expensive schools in the world it did not mean that I should drag everybody down in the mud by my reckless spending. So now I have to turn over a new leaf and keep accounts of every penny and not buy anything which is out of proportion to our scale of living.

Except for that one time they were very affectionate to me and did everything they could for my happiness. Of course it was awful without you. It was the first time we hadn't been together and I couldn't really believe it was Christmas.

I hope you are having a wonderful time and getting the rest you need and please write me when you can.

ALL MY LOVE,
STEPHEN

Geneva, January 29

Dear Father:

Well it is your turn for a letter this week because I wrote to Mummy last Sunday. (I am sure I can say this to you without hurting your feelings because you always said that the one thing you and Mummy wanted was a civilized divorce so we could all be friends.) Anyway Mummy hasn't answered my letter so probably she doesn't aprove of my spelling any more than you do. I am beginning to wonder if maybe it wouldn't be much simpler and much cheaper too if I didn't go to college after all. I really don't know what this education is for in the first place.

There is a terrible scandal here at School which has been very interesting for the rest of us. One of the girls, who is only sixteen, has gotten pregnant and everyone knows that it is all on account of the science instructer, who is a drip. We are waiting to see if he will marry her, but in the meantime she is terrifically upset and she has been expelled from the School. She is going away on Friday.

I always liked her very much and I had a long talk with her last night. I wanted to tell her that maybe it was not the end of the world, that my stepmother was going to have a baby in May, although she never got married until December, and the sky didn't fall in or anything. I thought it might have comforted her to think that grownups make the same mistakes that children do (if you can call her a child) but then I was afraid that it might be disloyal to drag you and Martha into the conversation, so I just let it go.

I'm fine and things are just the same.

Love,
STEPHEN

New York, February 2

Dear Stephen:

It would be a great relief to think that your mother did not "aprove" of your spelling either, but I'm sure that it's not for that reason that you haven't heard from her. She was never any good as a correspondent, and now it is probably more difficult for her than ever. We did indeed try for what you call a "civilized divorce" for all our sakes, but divorce is not any easy thing for any of the persons involved, as you well know, and if you try to put yourself in your mother's place for a moment, you will see that she is in need of time and solitude to work things out for herself. She will certainly write to you as soon as she has found herself again, and meanwhile you must continue to believe in her affection for you and not let impatience get the better of you.

Again, in case you are really in doubt about it, the purpose of your education is to enable you to stand on your own feet when you are a man and make something of yourself. Inaccuracies in spelling will not *simplify* anything.

I can easily see how you might have made a parallel between your friend who has gotten into trouble, and Martha who is expecting the baby in May, but there is only a superficial similarity in the two cases.

Your friend, is, or was, still a

child, and would have done better to have accepted the limitations of the world of childhood—as you can clearly see for yourself, now that she is in this predicament. Martha, on the other hand, was hardly a child. She was a mature human being, responsible for her own actions and prepared to be responsible for the baby when it came. Moreover I, unlike the science "instructer," am not a drip, I too am responsible for *my* actions, and so Martha and I are married and I will do my best to live up to her and the baby.

Speaking of which, we have just found a new apartment because this one will be too small for us in May. It is right across the street from your old school and we have a kitchen, a dining alcove, a living room, two bedrooms—one for me and Martha, and one for the new baby—and another room which will be for you. Martha felt that it was very important for you to feel that you had a place of your own when you came home to us, and so it is largely thanks to her that we have taken such a big place. The room will double as a study for me when you are not with us, but we will move all my books and papers and paraphernalia whenever you come, and Martha is planning to hang the Japanese silk screen you liked at the foot of the bed.

Please keep in touch, and *please* don't forget the exercises.

Love,
FATHER

Geneva, February 5
Dear Father:

There is one thing which I would like to say to you which is that if it hadn't been for you *I* would never have heard of a "civilized divorce,"

but that is the way you explained it to me. I always thought it was crazy. What I mean is, wouldn't it have been better if you had said, "I don't like your mother any more and I would rather live with Martha," instead of insisting that you and Mummy were always going to be the greatest friends? Because the way things are now Mummy probably thinks that you still like her very much, and it must be hard for Martha to believe that she was chosen, and I'm pretty much confused myself, although it is really none of my business.

You will be sorry to hear that I am not able to do any of the exercises any longer. I cannot do the eye exercises because my roommate got so fassinated by the stereo gadget that he broke it. (But the School Nurse says she thinks it may be just as well to let the whole thing go since in her opinion there was a good chance that I might have gotten more cross-eyed than ever, fidgeting with the viewer.) And I can not do the exercises for fallen arches, at least for one foot, because when I was decorating the Assembly Hall for the dance last Saturday, I fell off the stepladder and broke my ankle. So now I am in the Infirmary and the School wants to know whether to send the doctor's bill to you or to Mummy, because they had to call in a specialist from outside, since the regular School Doctor only knows how to do a very limited number of things. So I have cost a lot of money again and I am very very sorry, but if they were halfway decent in this School they would pay to have proper equipment and not let the students risk their lives on broken stepladders, which is something you could write to the Bookkeeping Department, if you felt like it, because I can't, but you could, and it might do some good in the end.

The girl who got into so much trouble took too many sleeping pills and died. I felt terrible about it, in fact I cried when I heard it. Life is very crewel, isn't it?

I agree with what you said, that she was a child, but I think she knew that, from her point of view. I think she did what she did because she thought of the science instructer as a grownup, so she imagined that she was perfectly safe with him. You may think she was just bad, because she was a child and should have known better, but I think that it was not entirely her fault since here at School we are all encouraged to take the teachers seriously.

I am very glad you have found a new apartment and I hope you won't move all your books and papers when I come home, because that would only make me feel that I was more of a nuisance than ever.

Love,
STEPHEN

New York, February 8
Dear Stephen:

This will have to be a very short letter because we are to move into the new apartment tomorrow and Martha needs my help with the packing.

We were exceedingly shocked by the tragic death of your friend and very sorry that you should have had such a sad experience. Life can be "crewel" indeed to the people who do not learn how to live it.

When I was exactly your age I broke my ankle too—I wasn't on a defective stepladder, I was playing hockey—and it hurt like the devil. I

still remember it and you have all my sympathy. (I have written to the School Physician to ask how long you will have to be immobilized, and to urge him to get you back into the athletic program as fast as possible. The specialist's bill should be sent to me.)

I have also ordered another stereo viewer because, in spite of the opinion of the School Nurse, the exercises are most important and you are to do them *religiously*. Please be more careful with this one no matter how much it may "fassinate" your roommate.

Martha sends love and wants to know what you would like for your birthday. Let us know how the ankle is mending.

Love,
FATHER

Geneva, February 12
Dear Father:

I was very surprised by your letter. I was surprised that you said you were helping Martha to pack because when you and Mummy were married I do not ever remember you packing or anything like that so I guess Martha is reforming your charactor. I was also surprised by what you said about the girl who died. What I mean is, if anyone had told me a story like that I think I would have just let myself get a little worked up about the science instructer because it seems to me that he was a villan too. Of course you are much more riserved than I am.

I am out of the Infirmary and they have given me a pair of crutches, but I'm afraid it will be a long time before I can do sports again.

I hope the new apartment is nice and I do not want anything for my birthday because it will seem very funny having a birthday in School so I would rather not be reminded of it.

Love,
STEPHEN

New York, February 15
Dear Stephen:

This is not an answer to your letter of February twelfth, but an attempt to have a serious discussion with you, as if we were face to face.

You are almost fifteen years old. Shortly you will be up against the stiffest competition of your life when you apply for college entrance. No examiner is going to find himself favorably impressed by "charactor" or "instructer" or "villan" or "riserved" or similar errors. You will have to face the fact that in this world we succeed on our merits, and if we are unsuccessful, on account of sloppy habits of mind, we suffer for it. You are still too young to understand me entirely, but you are not too young to recognize the importance of effort. People who do not make the grade are desperately unhappy all their lives because they have no place in society. If you do not pass the college entrance examinations simply because you are unable to spell, it will be nobody's fault but your own, and you will be gravely handicapped for the rest of your life.

Every time you are in doubt about a word you are to look it up in the dictionary and *memorize* the spelling. This is the least you can do to help yourself.

We are still at sixes and sevens in the new apartment but when Martha accomplishes all she has planned it should be very nice indeed and I think you will like it.

Love,
FATHER

Geneva, February 19
Dear Father:

I guess we do not understand each other at all. If you immagine for one minute that just by making a little effort I could imaggine how to spell immaggine without looking it up and finding that actually it is "imagine," then you are all wrong. In other words, if you get a letter from me and there are only two or three mistakes well you just have to take my word for it that I have had to look up practically every single word in the dictionary and that is one reason I hate having to write you these letters because they take so long and in the end they are not at all spontainious, no, just wait a second, here it is, "spontaneous," and believe me only two or three mistakes in a letter from me is one of the seven wonders of the world. What I'm saying is that I am doing the best I can as you would aggree if you could see my dictionary which is falling apart and when you say I should *memmorize* the spelling I can't because it doesn't make any sence to me and never did.

Love,
STEPHEN

New York, February 23
Dear Stephen:

It is probably just as well that you have gotten everything off your chest. We all need to blow up once in a while. It clears the air.

Please don't ever forget that I am aware that spelling is difficult for you. I know you are making a great effort and I am very proud of you. I just want to be sure that you *keep trying.*

I am enclosing a small check for your birthday because even if you do not want to be reminded of it I wouldn't want to forget it and you must know that we are thinking of you.

Love,
FATHER

Geneva, February 26

Dear Father:

We are not allowed to cash personal checks here in the School, but thank you anyway for the money.

I am not able to write any more because we are going to have the exams and I have to study.

Love,
STEPHEN

New York, March 2

NIGHT LETTER

BEST OF LUCK STOP KEEP ME POSTED EXAM RESULTS LOVE

FATHER.

Geneva, March 12

Dear Father:

Well, the exams are over. I got a C in English because aparently I do not know how to spell, which should not come as too much of a surprise to you. In Science, Mathematics, and Latin I got A, and in French and History I got a B plus. This makes me first in the class, which doesn't mean very much since none of the children here have any life of the mind, as you would say. I mean they are all jerks, more or less. What am I supposed to do in the Easter vacation? Do you want me to come

to New York, or shall I just stay here and get a rest, which I could use?

Love,
STEPHEN

New York, March 16

Dear Stephen:

I am *immensely* pleased with the examination results. Congratulations. Pull up the spelling and our worries are over.

Just yesterday I had a letter from your mother. She has taken a little house in Majorca, which is an island off the Spanish coast, as you probably know, and she suggests that you should come to her for the Easter holidays. Of course you are always welcome here—and you could rest as much as you wanted—but Majorca is very beautiful and would certainly appeal to the artistic side of your nature. I have written to your mother, urging her to write to you immediately, and I enclose her address in case you should want to write yourself. Let me know what you would like to do.

Love,
FATHER

Geneva, March 19

Dear Mummy:

Father says that you have invited me to come to you in Majorca for the Easter vacation. Is that true? I would be very very happy if it were. It has been very hard to be away from you for all this time and if you wanted to see me it would mean a great deal to me. I mean if you are feeling well enough. I could do a lot of things for you so you would not get too tired.

I wonder if you will think that I

have changed when you see me. As a matter of fact I have changed a lot because I have become quite bitter. I have become bitter on account of this School.

I know that you and Father wanted me to have some expearience of what the world was like outside of America but what you didn't know is that Geneva is not the world at all. I mean, if you were born here, then perhaps you would have a real life, but I do not know anyone who was born here so all the people I see are just like myself, we are just waiting not to be lost any more. I think it would have been better to have left me in some place where I belonged even if Americans are getting very loud and money conscious. Because actually most of the children here are Americans, if you come right down to it, only it seems their parents didn't know what to do with them any longer.

Mummy I have written all this because I'm afraid that I have spent too much money all over again, and M. Frisch says that Father will have a crise des nerfs when he sees what I have done, and I thought that maybe you would understand that I only bought these things because there didn't seem to be anything else to do and that you could help me some how or other. Anyway, according to the School, we will have to pay for all these things.

Concert, Segovia	
(Worth it)	16.00 (Swiss Francs)
School Dance	5.00
English Drama	
(What do they mean?)	10.00
Controle de l'habitant	
(?)	9.10
Co-op purchases	65.90
Ballets Russes	
(Disappointing)	47.00
Librairie Prior	59.30
Concert piano	
(For practicing)	61.00
Teinturie	
(They ruined everything)	56.50
Toilet and Medicine	35.00
Escalade Ball	7.00
Pocket Money	160.00
77 Yoghurts	
(Doctor's advice)	42.40
Book account	295.70
Total	869.90 (Swiss Francs)

Now you see the trouble is that Father told me I was to spend about fifty dollars a month, because that was my allowance, and that I was not to spend anything more. Anyway, fifty dollars a month would be about two hundred and ten Swiss Francs, and then I had fifteen dollars for Christmas from Granny, and when I got back to School I found four Francs in the pocket of my leather jacket and then I had seventy-nine cents left over from New York, but that doesn't help much, and then Father sent me twenty-five dollars for my birthday but I couldn't cash the check because they do not allow that here in School, so what shall I do?

It is a serious situation as you can see, and it is going to get a lot more serious when Father sees the bill. But whatever you do, I imploar you not to write to Father because the trouble seems to be that I never had a balance foreward and I am afraid that it is impossible to keep accounts without a balance foreward, and even more afraid that by this time the accounts have gone a little bizerk.

Do you want me to take a plane

when I come to Majorca? Who shall I say is going to pay for the ticket?

Please do write me as soon as you can, because the holidays begin on March 30 and if you don't tell me what to do I will be way out on a lim.

Lots and lots of love,
STEPHEN

Geneva, March 26

Dear Father:

I wrote to Mummy a week ago to say that I would like very much to spend my Easter vacation in Major-ca. So far she has not answered my letter, but I guess she will pretty soon. I hope she will because the holidays begin on Thursday.

I am afraid you are going to be upset about the bill all over again, but in the Spring term I will start anew and keep you in touch with what is going on.

Love,
STEPHEN

P.S. If Mummy doesn't write what shall I do?

discussion

Stephen does exceedingly well at school despite his parents' marital problems and their obvious desire to lead their own lives. Their attitude toward him probably strengthens rather than weakens his coping skills as he is left no choice but to stay at school. Stephen's father applies a great deal of pressure for Stephen to succeed. He writes very sincere letters to ensure that Stephen "makes something" of himself. Fortunately, Stephen has the intellectual capacity to be a good student. School fills his time while he "waits not to be lost." Stephen is a perceptive youngster who has warm feelings for others and has insight into his own situation. He knows how to ask for what he needs although he does worry when the bills arrive.

Stephen's success in school seems to stem from many sources, all of which are well documented motivators. He is doing what is culturally expected of him by his father, who is well educated himself. His father backs his demands for good performance by documenting the realities of college entrance exams. Stephen's father chronicles the tragedy of those who do not "make the grade." He then puts the responsibility for "making the grade" right on Stephen's shoulders. He seems to talk to Stephen on an adult level making it very clear that he cares and that he expects Stephen to do well. In addition to the cultural expectation, Stephen is intrinsically rewarded by his studies and extrinsically by his good grades.

springboards for inquiry

1. What are some qualities that make Stephen an achieving student? Which traits do you believe are learned?

2. There are many instrinsic and extrinsic rewards for being a good student. List as many as you can.

3. Do you think the future bodes well for Stephen? Explain.

the culturally
different

Teaching the culturally different means teaching those whose group traditions differ from the teacher's traditions. Bunker and Adair say, "Culture can be a tyrant. Our own set of ways of looking at what we may consider the set ways of strangers may prevent us from really seeing the peoples we encounter."[1] The clash between teacher and student culture can result in pain, frustration, and a deep sense of failure in both teachers and students.

Unfortunately a wide variety of labels have been used to describe the culturally different. Many of these such as *culturally deprived* and *culturally disadvantaged* have left teachers with the feeling that there was a certain inferiority inherent in those who were so labeled. Labels are libelous, and while economic deprivation is common among members of America's minority groups, it is sheer fabrication and misunderstanding that allows one to equate a low pecuniary status with a lack of culture. "Culturally different" is just that and nothing more. A difference in lifestyle, beliefs, and values should imply neither inferiority nor superiority.

The following description by Salisbury of the plight of the Eskimo child as he faces a typical middle-class Caucasian teacher clarifies the nature of the difference in cultural attributes:

> His teacher is likely to be a Caucasian, who knows little or nothing about his cultural background. He is taught to read the *Dick and Jane* series. Many things confuse him: Dick and Jane are two gussuk (white) children who play together. Yet, he knows that boys and girls do not play together and do not share toys. They have a dog named Spot who comes indoors and does not work. They have a father who leaves for some mysterious place called "office" each day and never brings any food home with him. He drives a machine called an automobile on a hard covered road called a street which has a policeman on each corner. These policemen always smile, wear funny clothing and spend their time helping children to cross the street. Why do these children need this help? Dick and Jane's mother spends a lot of time in the kitchen cooking a strange food called "cookies" on a stove which has no flame in it.
>
> But the most bewildering part is yet to come. One day they drive out to the country which is a place where Dick and Jane's grandparents are kept. They do not live with the family and they are so glad to see Dick and Jane that one is certain that they have been ostracized from the rest of the family for some terrible reason. The old people live on something called a "farm," which is a place where many strange animals are kept—a peculiar beast called a "cow," and some odd looking birds called "chickens," and a "horse" which looks like a deformed moose. . . . The native child continues to learn this new language which is of

---

[1] Robert Bunker and John Adair, *The First Look at Strangers* (New Brunswick, N.J.: Rutgers University Press, 1959), p. 150.

no earthly use to him at home and which seems completely unrelated to the world of sky, birds, snow, ice, and tundra which he sees around him.[2]

The Eskimo child, by age seven, has internalized the living patterns of his parents' culture, and when he brings this culture with him to school, it often conflicts with what he reads, sees, and hears from a curriculum oblivious to his world.[3]
A further and perhaps more scholarly example of this contrast between the beliefs and values held by children and those espoused by the books they have used is found in Evvard and Mitchell's chart.

Beliefs and Values of the Scott-Foresman Basic Reading Series Contrasted with Beliefs and Values of the Navajo Children[4]

Middle-Class, Urban	Navajo
Pets have human-like personalities.	Pets are distinct from human personality.
Life is pictured as child-centered.	Life is adult centered.
Adults participate in children's activities.	Children participate in adult activities.
Germ-theory is implicitly expressed.	Good health results from harmony with nature.
Children and parents are masters of their environment.	Children accept their environment and live with it.
Children are energetic, outgoing, obviously happy.	Children are passive and unexpressive.
Many toys and much clothing is an accepted value.	Children can only hope for much clothing and toys.
Life is easy, safe, and bland.	Life is hard and dangerous.

In the examples of the Eskimo and Navajo child and their problems in learning to read from materials foreign to their culture, it is fairly obvious that no one can reasonably proclaim that having grandparents live at home, for example, is a cultural negative, or that having many toys and much clothing is better than having few toys and clothing. Differences in culture are neither positive nor negative in and of themselves. In middle-class society, loquaciousness is a decided asset. When Navajo children are

[2]Lee H. Salisbury, "Teaching English to Alaska Natives," *Journal of American Indian Education* 6 (January 1967):5 as quoted in Miles V. Zintz, *Education Across Cultures* 2nd ed. (Dubuque: Kendall-Hunt Publishing Co., 1969).

[3]It is axiomatic that children do not leave their home and community culture at the schoolhouse door and thus enter the world of the school as a *tabula rasa* or blank slate ready to be etched by the cultural "finesse" of the typical middle-class school.

[4]Evelyn Evvard and George C. Mitchell, "Sally, Dick and Jane at Lukachukai," *Journal of American Indian Education* 5, no. 5 (May 1966): 5.

taught to be passive and unexpressive, all we may correctly say is that those attributes will not get them very far in an Anglo culture.

Zintz lists obvious differences between Native Americans and Anglos:

1. He must place a value on competitive achievement and climbing the ladder of success.

2. He must learn *time orientation* that will be precise to the hour and minute, and he must also learn to place high value on looking to the future.

3. He must accept the teachers' reiteration that there is scientific explanation for all natural phenomena.

4. He must become accustomed to change and must anticipate change. (The dominant culture teaches that "change," in and of itself, is good and desirable!)

5. He must "trade" his shy, quiet, reserved, and anonymous behavior for socially approved aggressive, competitive behavior.

6. He must somehow be brought to understand that he can, with some independence, shape his own destiny, as opposed to the tradition of remaining an anonymous member of his society.[5]

Those who plan to teach people whose culture is different from their own need to make every effort to accept the children from differing cultures as they are and for what they are.

It is said that the melting pot theory of American culture is in disfavor these days. In the early 1900s it was fashionable to expect that the Irish, Jews, Italians, and Poles who immigrated to America would melt into the Yankee culture and be absorbed by the Anglo-Saxon majority. This process of assimilation did occur in many cases. In other cases, pockets (ghettos) of ethnic minorities developed, and much to the disturbance of the cities, the minorities did not lose their cultural identities. And so Chinatowns, Little Italies, and Jewish ghettos flourished but were held in contempt by the "real" Americans. Today, while the dominant culture still favors assimilation, the minority cultures are more prone to take pride in preserving, if not all, at least some of their cultural differences. While this pride has ofttimes been evident purely in the political[6] realm, the activities of La Raza, AIM (American Indian Movement), BLM (Black Liberation Movement), and others have raised the level of consciousness[7] of the culturally different.

---

[5]Miles V. Zintz, "Indian Children Are Different," *The New Mexico School Review* 40 (October 1968):26–27.

[6]Norman Podhoretz in, "Now, Instant Zionism," *New York Times Magazine* (February 3, 1974), p. 11, describes the Jews in America as having been converted to Zionism by the events of the Yom Kippur war of October, 1973. On American campuses the once quiescent, sometimes struggling Hillel Foundation which operates on several hundred American campuses, was unprepared "for the massive and unprecedented response by Jews on campuses in the October war."

[7]Recollection of the protest of the IAL (Italian-American League) over the image that movies like "The Godfather" tended to project of Italians as being mafia-type gangsters, indicates further that pride in cultural difference is new and "in."

While it is the aim of educators to provide all students with curricula which will be relevant to their future needs, teachers need to be sensitive to the additional needs of the culturally different, who bring home from school a second culture which they, their family, and the schools must help the student to reconcile.

Florence McGehee

Good boy

"We have nothing to bring, Señora," Jesús defended them. "Only tortillas. We are poor people. And the other children laugh at tortillas. That makes us ashame'. Think of it! No, we will not bring tortillas to school. We will not have lunch."

Day was at morn and the year at the spring, and all along the levee that paralleled the too low Sacramento violent swirls of dust arose and wrestled with Jesús. A strong north wind had come up in the night to whip the river and the dry fields beyond, where peas and beets and asparagus thirsted. In his bare feet Jesús scuffled up the white powdery dust, abetting its fury, bucking his head to the wind and rubbing his eyes. They smarted. He rubbed harder and kicked harder in the dirt. Just around the next corner was the little schoolhouse toward which he was making his none too eager way, and where "Ticher" sighed heavily every time she looked at him.

Ticher was small, fair, and firm, and filled with an incredible zeal for action. You no sooner got one task done, than she had two others ready for you. Nor would she leave you in peace in the performance thereof. You must hold the chalk in your right hand and you must make one

"Good Boy" from Please Excuse Johnny *by Florence McGehee is reprinted by permission of the author.*

letter (always the first) bigger than any of those that followed. You must write on the lines and you must not chew the end of your pencil. You must not wipe your nose on your sleeve (for this she had pretty little soft pink papers in a box on her desk) and you must not spit upon the blackboard even if there wasn't an eraser handy. You must not put down the answers to problems unless you had looked at the other numbers first.

She wanted everything to be just right, but she still had a little difficulty with his name. When he had come to the school a few months ago, along with Mary and Lupe and Conchita and Salvador and Ramón and Elvira and Concepción, and had handed her his report card, she had given a little squeal and had said in a voice, as if she were afraid, "Gee-sus! But you can't be called *that!* Why, that's terrible! Why, the idea!"

He had been patient with her, as he had had to be with other teachers. He had told her over and over again that he was not "Gee-sus" but "Hay-soos." She had considered him levelly through puzzled blue eyes for a long uncomfortable moment before she had said, "Very well, Hay-soos."

He was late again—only a little, but still late. The children were gathered in a circle about the flagpole in the yard, with their hands held stiffly at their foreheads in the quaint morning exercise they did first of all every day. He slipped unobtrusively between two of them, whipped off his hat, and clamped it between his legs before he joined them in the chant: "I pledge a legion to the flag of the United Stakes of America and to the republic for Richard Strand, one naked individual with liberty and justice for all."

There was a Richard Schmaltz in the school. Jesús wondered vaguely who Richard Strand was. He tried to slink past Ticher, who waylaid him in the doorway.

"Good morning, Jesús. I've already said it to all the other boys and girls, but you, of course, are late again. What's the matter with your eyes?"

He had been rubbing the dust out of them again.

"I don't know, Ticher."

"Look at me. Jesús, you haven't the pinkeye, have you? They look awfully red. Tell me this minute, have you the pinkeye?"

"Maybe," he said, hopefully. "Yes, I think so. Always we have lots of pink eyes in our family."

"You go straight back home," said Ticher, excited, as she always was. There was no rest in the woman. "I'll send the school nurse later."

Jesús sped away with greater alacrity than he had come, albeit his spirit was a bit dampened by the reference to the school nurse. He dawdled the happy day away on the riverbank, skipping rocks in the water, ambushing a ground squirrel, idly watching the activity of a dredger. At noon he allayed a faint inner gnawing with an orange he had picked up in flight. It had been just sitting there alongside one of the tin buckets in a row on the schoolhouse porch. Nobody had been with it, so it was his by right of discovery.

The school nurse, a large matter-of-fact woman, as calm as Ticher was excitable, was completely unimpressed by his asserting that there were always many pink eyes in his family, and, after examination, ordered him back to school next day.

"But I cannot go, señorita. See, I have no shoes! I am barefoot. Nobody else is barefoot. I am ashame'."

"*Verdad,*" his large soft mother confirmed him. "*No tiene zapatos.*" She laid a loving hand upon her son's head and smiled upon him tenderly, as though his having no shoes was some peculiar virtue of which she was particularly proud.

She drew him to her fondly, jostling the babe at her bosom so that it lost its tenacious hold and nuzzled and whimpered complainingly. Jesús noted how much whiter was the nipple area it released than any other part of his parent's body. The rest of her was the dull gray color of the levee. He pulled himself out of her caress.

"No shoes. See, my mother says so!"

But the nurse was prepared. He was appalled by her next action. She pulled a large grocery box filled with shoes from the back of her car and spent an enervating twenty minutes pulling footgear on and off Jesús' unwilling, grimy feet. Jesús himself was singularly uninterested. He reclined limply against the doorjamb, quite unable, it seemed, to brace himself or even to stiffen his knee joints against the onslaught. The nurse began to show signs of annoyance.

"Straighten up here, boy!" she commanded.

"I cannot, señorita. The pain I suffer in my knee! Think of it!"

At length she was satisfied, and Jesús was the not too happy possessor of an almost new pair of plain black shoes.

"There. Now you have shoes. And there's nothing the matter with your eyes, either. You be at school tomorrow—and on time."

"Good boy," said his mother sweetly, meaning to commend not her son, but the nurse, who was pouring a solution out of a small bottle onto her hands with something of the air of one who was shaking the dust of a place off her feet.

At length the woman was gone, and Jesús and his mother contemplated the new shoes through melancholy dark eyes. Came, too, Mary and Lupe and Conchita and Salvador and Ramón and Elvira and Concepción, who, until now, had stayed at a safe distance lest they, too, be fitted to shoes. Came, too, from somewhere, his father and his elder brother Manuel, and they all looked solemnly at the feet of Jesús, fettered by the hand of authority against the delights of springtime.

There was no help for it: he and the shoes must go to school. He would carry them, however, until he came within actual sight of the schoolhouse. Stopping to put them on delayed him so that he was a little late. The last of the children, including his own brothers and sisters, had filed into the room, and he was forced to make a lone and conspicuous entry. Ticher leaped upon her prey.

"Jesús, this simply will not do! This is the fourth time you have been late this week. Now why can't you be less shiftless and get up early? Why can't you do as the others do, and get here on time?"

Jesús put his hand on his heart. "It was a little bird, señorita."

"A little bird?"

"It had fallen from its nest, and crying so. I had to put it back."

Ticher's eyes softened behind the dark-rimmed glasses.

"Well—but you should start early enough to allow for emergencies. Take out your reader."

Jesús took out his reader, a primer devoted to large gay pictures and sprightly comment about the doings of Jackie and Janie. It seemed utterly unimportant to Jesús, big boy that he was, that Jackie and Janie liked to go down the "slicky slide." In sheer boredom he cut a large half-moon in the top of his desk. He was relieved when Ticher announced that the time had come for folk dancing. Along with the other big boys, he pretended to scorn this part of the program, and had to be dragged from corners to participate, but secretly his soul delighted in the seductive rhythms. As always, he was paired with Reiko Nasamura, because she, of all those present, did not seem to mind being his partner. The phonograph whined its way to top speed, and the dance was begun. The spectacle of a Mexican boy and a Japanese girl solemnly tramping their way through a Swedish polka seemed no more ludicrous to Jesús than it did to Ticher.

Presently there was another dance whose dominant feature was a frequent change of partners. At long last Jesús came abreast of a pert little golden-haired creature in a stiff pink dress. She looked like the angels in Elvira's book. Jesús had long looked upon her with eyes of devotion. He made a more than usually courtly bow and reached for her hand. She slapped him away with a furious, "Don't you dare touch me, you old—you old—thing, you!"

Ticher interfered with heavy-handed diplomacy, and the physical education period was declared over. But the boy's troubles were not. Yet another very clean little girl, who sat behind him, presently tiptoed to the desk and ostentatiously whispered in Ticher's ear. Ticher looked startled, and requested the presence of Jesús in the anteroom. There, with squeamish fingers, she explored his dark, rebellious head. She sent him home.

The school nurse came again that night, to be welcomed with happy anticipation by Jesús' mother, whose dull days were lightened by these frequent visitations. Jesús felt resentment stir in his soul as the woman took firm hold on his head and afterward on those of Mary and Lupe and Conchita and Salvador and Ramón and Elvira and Concepción, all of whom had formed a disconsolate homecoming queue behind him that afternoon. What was there about this to cause such a fuss? A few little creatures in the head! They did not hurt anybody—itched a little sometimes, but one or the other or all of the young Aranyos had always had them and been quite comfortable about it.

The sensitive soul of Jesús shrank within him. Somehow, he had gained ill repute with his fellows be-cause of this affair of the head. He would stay at home a few days so that they would miss him.

Evidently they did miss him, for at the end of the third day a neighbor stopped in to say that Ticher had declared she wanted him back at school again and that nothing, *nothing*, was to keep him away. He was pleased. They had done wrong, and they were sorry. Jesús was not one to harbor a grudge. With him, bygones were always bygones.

Carrying his new shoes, he set out for school next morning only a half-hour behind his brothers and sisters, and filled anew with loving-kindness. But he was delayed by this and that en route, and when he entered, cringing a little, a group of boys and girls were already at their social studies. Just as he entered, Ticher was saying something about the Aztecs. Her eye pounced upon him.

"Jesús can probably tell us," she said to the others. "He may have heard his parents or his grandparents speak of them. Jesús, what do you know about the Aztecs?"

He flinched at the implied accusation. A moment ago he had been happy; now he was sad again, threatened and suspected.

"Nothing, señorita," he said, "I do not have them any more now."

The children shouted with laughter. He crimsoned.

"Oh, Jesús, you don't *have* them," Ticher said, sharply. "Do you know anything about them? It's people."

"I do not know them or have anything to do with them."

Ticher shook her head and said, "Tck, tck," as she so often did when he answered her questions.

The day, so inauspiciously begun, did not go well. Even Reiko

Nasamura avoided him, and a cloud fell upon his spirit. At noon he and his brothers and sisters huddled together in an ell of the building while other boys and girls in groups of two and three and five ate their luncheons, talking and laughing with mouths too full, gaily swapping sandwiches. The young Aranyos never brought lunch. This was a source of disturbance to Ticher, who liked to know reasons for everything. Often she reproved Jesús and Mary and Lupe and Conchita and Salvador and Ramón and Elvira and Concepción, who wounded, backed up against the schoolhouse wall with their flat stomachs, melancholy dark eyes, and apologetic mannerisms. Didn't they know they needed nourishment?

Yes, Ticher.

Did they forget their lunches?

No, Ticher.

Would one of them like this nice ham sandwich? This piece of chocolate cake?

No, thank you, Ticher.

What did their mother have to say for herself about this lunch situation?

Yes, Ticher.

Ticher said she would find out about this. Jesús had no doubt she would. He was wearied of this talk about food every noontime. He would stay at home a few days. Perhaps it would all be forgotten then, and again they would be sorry he was gone and send for him to come back.

But that sad day had its happy ending, for when the children arrived at home, hours after leaving the mile-away schoolhouse, their mother beckoned them into the one room where all the Aranyos did their collective living, and invited them to behold. Their father was there, and Manuel, and the four who were yet too young to go to school. In the center of the room that was guiltless of other furnishings stood the white, gleaming electric refrigerator they had all talked about for so long—theirs at last. A man came sometimes and gave his father a piece of paper which his father turned into things like flour and corn meal and gasoline and a guitar. The man said something about "relief," and Jesús dimly understood that the Aranyos had a benevolent godfather somewhere who paid his father for not doing things his father would not have done anyhow. The refrigerator was somehow a gift from that man.

They were all admiringly exclamatory. Their mother laughed happily, and slammed the door over and over again, and at length brought forth a bowl of frijoles which she set solemnly in the very center of the lowest shelf. Manuel showed how he had connected the machine to the little wires that had been in the small house when they came there. The man had said that would keep it always cold.

Jesús, for a joke, stuck his head inside as far as it would go and said that it *was* cold. They all laughed. His father ran a caressing hand over the gleaming white surface of their new treasure. Jesús did likewise, his hand lingering in pleasure at the smoothness and the coolness of it. All the little ones stroked it tenderly. His mother even unhooked the baby from her bosom to smack its limp dirty little hand upon the pretty thing.

Jesús was sated with happiness. He wandered out into the starlight to sit in the tomato patch, where he thought how fortunate they all were to come into possession of this splendid cold thing. Down in Mexico, when he was very little, they had never— This was a good place. He ate a half dozen greenish tomatoes and repaired to the house, where he lay down on the floor between Manuel and Mary, pulling a convenient gunny-sack around his shoulders as preparation for the night.

They stayed at home next day to admire the new refrigerator. They did not mention it as the reason for not going to school. But when they had all risen and eaten from the bowl of beans that had chilled all night, and when the upward sweep of the sun heralded the probable hour of departure for school, good little Concepción discovered a stomach-ache.

"Concepción must not go to school, then," said Mary, speaking with the firmness becoming in the eldest daughter. "And I, too, shall stay at home with her. Maybe, some way, I can help her."

"And I," said Jesús. "I feel a stomach-ache, too. How it aches me! Think of it!"

Salvador and Ramón now discovered twinges, and all the others decided to stay at home to sympathize with those who were afflicted. Their large soft mother approved. This was kindness they were showing to one another. They could always go to school, and tomorrow was another day. She blessed them. They strolled outdoors, where they partook of early tomatoes and lolled in the dirt beside the door, bound to one another by ties of love.

Late afternoon brought a new lady. I did not smile, and I spoke with authority. In clear ringing tones, I wanted to know what was the meaning of all this truancy. Manuel and his father disappeared; the mother beamed and murmured, "Good boy, good boy," repeatedly to welcome me, the stranger. Jesús saw that he must take charge.

"My stomach, señora," he began. "Or, no—it was the stomach of my sister, Concepción. Or was it Ramón? Anyhow we are sick. We have stomach-ache very bad. Think of it!"

"Who has stomach-ache?"

"All of us," said Jesús, proud of their unity.

"Nonsense," I said. "You can't all have stomach-ache. That is, unless you've eaten something. By the way, what did you have to eat today?"

"Frijoles," said Mary.

"Beans," corrected Jesús.

"Cold," supplemented Conchita.

"Good," said Concepción.

Its door was open, and I looked into the new refrigerator. I turned to their mother.

A lively debate then ensued between us, with the Aranyos taking the affirmative side of the question that cold beans were, of all things, the most to be desired for the building of bodily strength and beauty. Having got off to a good start on the subject of food, I was loath to leave it. I mentioned accusingly the fact that the children did not bring lunch to school.

"We have nothing to bring, señora," Jesús defended them. "Only tortillas. We are poor people. And the other children laugh at tortillas. That makes us ashame'. Think of it! No, we will not bring tortillas to school. We will not have lunch."

I declared that tortillas made a highly desirable luncheon as opposed to nothing at all. The young

Aranyos looked doubtful, even when assured that henceforth the other children would not laugh. When the assurance was passed on to their mother through Jesús, she too looked doubtful. Jesús knew it was a good deal of trouble to put up lunches for so many, and since nobody ever got really hungry at noon there was no sense in it. He knew how his mother felt about it, and he did not blame her. He knew, too, how obdurate she could be. She was going to be that way now. He waited, admiring, for the demonstration.

It came. Mamacita gave forth a regular pyrotechnical display of staccato "No's," calling upon the Virgin to witness that she would never burden her dear children with packages that they must carry all that long way to school! Never!

Jesús interpreted, and I took up the challenge.

"Now, Mrs. Aranyo, this has gone far enough. These children have been out of school for every conceivable reason, good, bad, and indifferent. The law requires them to attend. If they do not attend, we shall have to hold the parents responsible. On the occasion of the very next absence, we shall have to take Mr. Aranyo into court—maybe into jail. Do you understand, Jesús? Tell your mother what I say."

Jesús told his mother. At the end of two minutes of lively oratory he announced, "She says 'all right.'"

"All right! All right, what? All right to put your father in jail?"

"Yes, señora."

I sped away, the very bounce of my car as it leaped into low gear expressing my exasperation.

The father did go to jail, for the community stomach-ache of the

young Aranyos continued another week; and though the school doctor pronounced it mythical, they felt a vast disinclination for education, and clung to their vague symptoms. Señor Aranyo rode away stoically enough with the big man who came for him, resplendent in the bright green shirt that Mary had risen early to iron for the occasion. They watched the car out of sight, each volubly disapproving. They missed their father, of course, but Jesús noticed during this time that his mother wore a relaxed look he had never seen on her face before.

And then in a few days the family was reunited. They had a brave supper of peppers and beans and tomatoes that night, and they all sat down at once while they listened to the wonderful experiences the father recounted. He had met an old friend in the jail, a man he had not seen since happy days in Guadalajara, and they had enjoyed much speaking together. Another fine fellow—detained because he had merely held a hot iron against his wife's cheek when she lied to him— had lent him a guitar, and their evenings had been pleasant with music. There had been coffee and good stew. As a crowning touch, the father had won $2.60 in a game of chance.

For proof, he placed $1.90 on the table to delight their eyes. Haltingly, Jesús, who could count, called attention to the discrepancy between story and cash in hand. But yes, the father had bought a little medicine, of a kind he much liked and often wanted. Reaching into his hip pocket, he brought forth a bottle of Vegetable Compound. Each took a long sip, and rejoiced with him.

Probably it was not necessary to

go to school now. Their father had expiated their sin in staying away by going to jail. And had I not given them their choice: school or jail? They had chosen the latter. Feeling singularly carefree and absolved, Jesús spent a long delicious day idling along the riverbank. He shouted encouragement to the engineers aboard Uncle Sam's dredger, busy deepening the channel. He caught three illegal fish, and thought how beautiful they would look all alone in the big refrigerator. He picked an armful of pussywillow for Ticher, just in case he ever should go back to school again. He lay on his back watching the clouds until the rhythm of their passing lulled him to sleep.

It was almost dark when he arrived home, and his mother, strangely enough, wanted some kindling wood. It was seldom she cooked, and yet more seldom that she made demands upon her children, but tonight she said the two older boys must chop some wood and bring it into the house.

Manuel, lolling in the doorway with a cigarette, declined the menial task, delegating it to Jesús. Jesús, a little chilled and irritable from his long nap in the sand, would have none of it. If it was not a manly task for Manuel, it was not a manly task for him. The brothers argued, their words waxing hotter. Manuel struck Jesús, and the two clinched, stumbled, and rolled to the ground, where they bit and clawed and pummeled each other. The younger children stood, an interested semicircle, at a safe distance.

But the mother did not like to see her sons engaged in this unbrotherly conflict. She did have one stout stick of wood, and when she saw Jesús reach for the small hunting knife he always carried she sprang into the fray, the baby at her breast bouncing and wailing at being thus unceremoniously detached from sustenance, and laid about her impartially and with surprising vigor. A sharp whack on the knuckles sent the knife slithering away out of reach of Jesús. But Manuel fared worse. His mother brought the stick, through which a long nail had been driven, smartly down upon his forehead, so that an ugly jagged tear appeared and blood spurted between his eyes.

Through surprise, hurt, and shock, Manuel appeared to have given up the ghost. He rolled over on his side and lay very still, his eyes shut. Jesús gallantly arose and stood, panting, over his fallen brother. Their mother remembered to deposit the baby carefully upon a soft pile of manure before she dropped to her knees beside her firstborn, weeping loudly and wiping his bloody face with her skirt.

This was the unhappy moment chosen by the Fates for a visit from me, with my strange notions about going to school or to jail. From the knife (which Jesús had forgotten to retrieve), from the bloody wound, from the loud wails of the mother, I pieced together my own story.

I went away from there quickly, and in less than an hour Jesús found himself in rough masculine hands en route to the Detention Home, while Manuel, in the county hospital, lay for the first time in his life between sheets.

Jesús stayed a whole week in the Detention Home, during which time he would not remove his hat, excepting just once during those few shocking moments when the big man made him wash himself all over. When they had locked him in at night, he slept on the floor, eschewing the white iron bed and its soft covers.

He heard himself described as "incorrigible," whatever that might mean. He had knifed his own brother (they said), and he would not go to school. They did not seem to know that it was his mother who, with her stick of wood and amazingly strong arm, had inflicted the damage upon Manuel, and he was not the one to tell them. He admired Mamacita. He would keep silent.

He was outraged at the accusation that he would not go to school. Gregarious, he loved school, but they were so fussy there, insisting upon shoes and lunches, disapproving his gallantry to the girls, suspecting him of being in league with some strange family called the Aztecs, when he had never even seen the people, being intolerant about little things in his hair, never liking the numbers he put down for answers even when he filled a whole sheet of paper on both sides. So he would not go to school! Why, he had been sent home more times than he could remember.

For the first time he began to feel sullen and resentful as he gazed around the room at the half dozen grave strangers who had come to question or accuse him. His parents were there, his mother not understanding one word but smiling and nodding at intervals, his father not disposed to interfere in what was obviously his son's own affair. Neither spoke a word during the hearing.

Ticher was there, too, looking strangely disturbed and inclined to disagree with all the other people. At length she came and stood beside him, put a hand on his shoulders

and said good words about him to these others, much better words than she had ever used to him in the schoolroom. She smelled very nice. Suddenly he liked her very much. He did not know that Ticher had got the true story of the affair of the brothers from little loose-tongued Lupe and that, ever a lover of justice and chivalry, she was according him a new respect. She wanted him to be set free. She said so.

"And furthermore," the big man was saying, "unless you take better care of these children, Mrs. Aranyo"—he shook an admonishing finger at her—"I'm greatly afraid someone will come and take some of them away from you!"

"Good boy," said his mother, aware of nothing but her name and the finger wagging.

Jesús interpreted, and there ensued a lively bit of oratory.

"What does she say?" the stern man asked at length.

"She says all right. She don't care. She got too many kids anyhow. How many you take?" said Jesús.

Ticher laughed. She looked very pretty with all her white teeth showing and her blue eyes dancing with new lights. Everyone else was stricken dumb. Ticher's laughter was pleasant in the gloomy room. He liked her even more.

Jesús was given over to his parents with orders to behave himself in future. That was easy to promise. He always behaved himself. His father stalked majestically from the room. His mother lingered behind to smile a goodbye on each person present, not bothering to detach the greedily sucking youngest Aranyo from her drooping brown bosom.

Back at home, Manuel, a once-white bandage around his head, grinned welcome to Jesús and offered him a cigarette. It was the first time Jesús had ever got a cigarette from Manuel without prolonged bargaining, though he had been smoking since he was eight. The brothers leaned against the side of the building and smoked together in silent camaraderie.

It had been a good day. Ticher had laughed and he was free again and here was good tobacco. Reflecting, he rubbed a hand along his jawbone and across his upper lip. Strong black hairs resisted his touch. His heart leaped. Maybe when they worked in the beets this summer, his father would let him keep enough of his money to buy a razor. Maybe!

He went to school happily next day, and was only twenty minutes late. He showed Ticher the black hairs on his lip, and she said, yes, indeed, that was very nice. She let him pass the wastebasket, and at noon said nothing at all about lunch.

Returned home, he found his mother moving listlessly along the rows in the tomato patch. She seemed thoughtful. Waiting for her to speak, he squatted on the ground and bit into a none too ripe tomato. At length she wondered, a shade wistfully, if the big man who had shouted so yesterday would take Tita and Rosa and Miguel and José (who were all too young to pick fruit or top beets anyhow) and keep them for a while as he had suggested. Not for always, she hastened to add, for she loved her children, but just until they got big to earn a little money, for it was necessary to feed the body that the soul might live, no?

Jesús, new in wisdom, patted her soft arm. "The big man does not want the little ones, Mamacita. No, we will keep all of them, and by and by they will go to school with me. School is a nice place now. I passed the wastebasket today, and tomorrow—if I am not late—I will run the flag up on its pole. Everybody will see me do it. Think of it!"

His mother's face relaxed. Pleased that her son had won recognition at last, she tore the baby firmly from her person, deposited it on the ground, and embraced Jesús.

"Good boy," she said.

discussion

In Jesús' eyes, school is filled with do's and don't's which are uncompromising and incomprehensible. The gap between home and school is a chasm, and Jesús looks with relief upon any opportunity to be sent home. Jesús' parents are not anxious for him to adapt. They do not see school as preparation for a better life than their own. They are rooted in the everyday problems of feeding their family rather than in planning and hoping for the individual futures of their children.

There is pride and love in the Aranyo family. There is also an understanding of the difference between the roles of father and mother. The school has little insight into the culture of this family in much the same way that the Aranyos are unable to comprehend the Anglo culture. The story details the many incidents which humiliate Jesús and his family. Through the teacher's eyes we can realize how exasperating the problems can be. How can home and school be brought together in a situation like this?

Many minority children are uncomfortable in schoolrooms where teachers are unacquainted with their particular cultural differences. If a classroom contains one Japanese child, one Moslem child, one Jewish child, or one child from any subculture, the teachers should be alert to the facts about holidays, foods, and other customs that are unique in the home of this child. Of course the teacher should not single out a child to tell the class about "his holiday." Often this is a humiliating experience for the child who is very sensitive to being different from his classmates. When the teacher reveals a knowledge of the custom to the child privately, however, she may build a good relationship with him. A good example of a well meaning teacher using poor judgment is the incident in which the teacher asks Jesús what he knows about the Aztecs. Knowledge of Jesús' family background would have helped this teacher avoid humiliating Jesús in front of his classmates.

Other children sometimes make life very difficult for children who have odd sounding names, a different skin color, or who bring different foods to school for lunch. Many teachers would like to see groups of black or Mexican-American or Tonganese children eating and intermingling at recess with the Caucasian children, but frequently ethnic groups will remain together during free time. We do not know all the strategies for helping children to feel pride in their ethnic heritage and yet feel comfortable in a heterogeneous society. In California 56 percent of the students are from minority ethnic groups while 80 percent of teachers are Caucasian. Obviously the teachers have a lot to learn. It is necessary for them to continue to learn about ethnic minorities through seminars and in-service education in ethnic studies. It is also necessary for them to keep in touch with the students and parents of ethnic minority groups so that there is open communication with home and school. Unless the ethnic population is very large, many schools tend to ignore the problem, some claiming that there is no problem. But for the child who is called a burned taco or who goes without lunch, as Jesús and his sisters and brothers do, the problem is a very real one.

springboards for inquiry

1. In many ways there is a communication gap between the Anglo community and Jesús' family. Carefully study two instances of miscommunication and describe the nature of the gap in each case.

2. Define the term *machismo*. Find an example of it in this story. Discuss.

3. "Ticher" redeems herself in Jesús' eyes. What is it that she does that accomplishes this? Why is Jesús impressed with the behavior?

4. The thrust of the entire story is not so much the "communication gap" but the cultural chasm which separates the two communities. Detail this chasm using more than one incident to exemplify it.

5. What do the "experts" recommend when trying to accommodate cultural differences within an elementary school classroom? A high school?

Donald Gropman

The heart of this or that man

Mr. Shapiro fumbled with the window pole. Nine C would be here in a few minutes for its weekly session and he was not prepared. Open the window, remove his jacket, set out the jars of paint and the brushes he argued for each week.

"Now Allan," Miss Katz would say. "I don't know if this request is covered by any rule. After all, I'm the art teacher and you teach English."

"Well, Miss Katz," he would say, "if you don't tell anyone, and I don't tell anyone, it will be our little secret. You know," and here he would smile, a little less broadly each week, "it's like giving an anonymous donation to the CJA or Red Feather. You and I help these kids, but we don't brag about it. Inside we know we are doing something good."

"Well, all right, Allan, what somebody doesn't know won't hurt him. Now remember to have them wash the brushes and wipe down the jars. Your boys are awfully messy. And by the way, do you really need so much paper?"

He still fumbled to fit the metal hook into the slot at the top of the window. He had read somewhere that an open window provides fresh air and inspiration. Through the high many-paned window he could see the street below him. The pale

Reprinted from The Literary Review *(Autumn 1967, Volume 11, Number 1), published by Fairleigh Dickinson University, Rutherford, N.J. by the kind permission of the author.*

"We live in a room with four other families. Every month we change places in the room. This month is our turn in the middle. I want to hang my painting but I have no wall."

lemon light of a two o'clock winter afternoon drifted down from a silent and spent sky, but did not seem to fall on the brown heaps of snow and slush.

A policeman walked by and Mr. Shapiro noticed that he could not see the small balloons of breath puff out over the policeman's shoulder. Was it warmer, what was it, March? Or April already? Snow on the streets in April? No matter. He liked to watch the breath balloons and fill them in. For policemen he inserted things like: *I am a policeman, sometimes I'm your friend; I like to find robbers 'cause I'm partners with them.* The policeman crossed the street. Mr. Shapiro looked over and saw Jaime sitting in a doorway. He was looking up at the empty sky and started up when the policeman burst into his sight. The policeman leaned over and Jaime waved his arms, shook his head, and pointed at Mr. Shapiro. No, Mr. Shapiro thought, he is pointing at the whole school. The policeman now shook his head and crossed back to the school side of the street with Jaime. The policeman disappeared at the side of the window and Jaime disappeared beneath it. Did the policeman invoke me, Mr. Shapiro thought, to make Jaime come to class and stop being truant?

The bell rang to start the last class as Mr. Shapiro was folding his suit jacket over the back of his chair. He had read somewhere that a teacher in shirtsleeves provokes less resistance in these students. The students started to drift into the room, singly or in twos. Mr. Shapiro had a moment of panic. What am I doing here? I should be home reading, getting my Ph.D., getting laid, getting money. What good can I do, help these poor underprivileged bastards become privileged so they can assimilate, have appliances and not live on welfare, and use toilet paper to wipe their asses instead of *El Diario de Nueva York,* so that in the final end they'll fill me with loathing like all the rest of the smug, consuming bastards. Shapiro's law of human nature, not too romantic I hope, says, a human being evinces more interesting manifestations while being consumed than while consuming. A contemporary aesthetic: What is the most beautiful thing in the world, the ultimate perfection? A young girl dying of consumption? No. A whole ethnic group being consumed.

Am I merely stupid, or expiating guilt? Anyway, why do these kids call me Mr. Shapiro? Everyone else calls me Allan, in the army they called me kike, my wife calls me *schmouk,* my professors call me dummy, although I never heard them.

Hey Al baby, what's shakin'? Man, this is a wise scene and you a real wig. Catch some pot Al, it's just a fifty pinney joint, but like it's all I carry. You not like those other teachers, they hard bastards, but you okay man, you got it everywhere, and the boy would use his index finger as a wand to touch his own temple, his chest, and his sex. The monologue elated Mr. Shapiro even though he could not recognize the student in the daydream.

On Friday afternoon the class

with Nine C always went well. Four times a week Mr. Shapiro tried to teach them English. They wrote compositions and read *Silas Marner.* They had spelling quizzes and tried to parse sentences on the board. Whenever his wife, or anyone else not connected with the school, asked him about the class, Mr. Shapiro had one stock answer, "They just don't give a shit." But one thing did seem to interest them and that was the Friday session.

Mr. Shapiro had decided it would be a good idea to read them poems and let them paint what the poems meant to them. This would serve several functions: they will hear some poetry, they will express themselves in the paintings and, maybe, Mr. Shapiro hoped, I can get through to them. In September he had found a box of gold stars in his desk, the only trace left of the teacher before him. Each week he pasted a star on a painting, trying to give the star where he felt it would do the most good.

He tried to select poetry from the high school reader that would appeal to them. This afternoon he was going to read some Robert Frost. He felt it would make sense to them, offer them images they could instinctively grasp.

While he sat on his desk thinking, the students took paper and jars of paint. Two of them went into the hall to fill the water pitchers, for they had finally accepted the fact that the paints worked better if they were thinned. Most of the class was busy mixing paint when Jaime walked in. He didn't look at Mr. Shapiro. He went to his seat and sat down.

Mr. Shapiro leafed through the reader, but he watched Jaime. The boy was probably older than he looked, perhaps fifteen or sixteen, but he was no bigger than a twelve-year-old. He always left the two top buttons of his shirt open and he wore no undershirt, so Mr. Shapiro could see the middle of his pale honey-colored chest, the skin pulled taut across the knobby clavicles.

Jaime didn't move. He sat staring at his desk, his thin fingers buried themselves in his matted black hair.

Mr. Shapiro walked up the aisle. "Don't you have any paints, Jaime?"

Jaime looked up at him. Mr. Shapiro saw a bleached face. The black eyes seemed gray, the hirsuteness on the upper lip seemed white. Mr. Shapiro's legs felt suddenly weak, he felt a large parching knot in his throat.

"What's wrong?" he asked, his voice much softer than he had intended.

"Nothing, Mr. Shapeiro. There's nothing is wrong."

"Come with me, I'll help you get some paints and a piece of paper." He felt foolish mouthing these words, silly words about bottles of paint and empty paper, but he could think of nothing else.

Jaime was seated again, his paints before him on his desk. Mr. Shapiro waited until he was ready, smiled at him and began to read. As he read the first words of "Mending Wall" they too sounded silly to his ears. He felt embarrassed and knew that his face was turning red. The volume of his voice dropped from the pitch it started at, he mouthed the words as quickly as he could, droning them out like some primitive and unyielding chant. He looked up from the book while mouthing fa-miliar phrases and saw the class looking at him strangely.

"Am I reading too quickly?" he asked, trying to control his fluster, restraining himself from hurling the high school reader through one of the many-paned windows and leaving the school and the students forever. "Am I reading too quickly for you to follow me?" He despised himself for the touch of condescension in his voice, but he would have augmented it if a student hadn't answered.

"Yes, Mr. Shapeiro, much too fast." It was Jaime. He was still sitting with his elbows on his desk and his fingers buried in his matted black hair.

"Sounds like the IRT," another student said, and there was general laughter, even from Mr. Shapiro.

"I guess you're right, I was going a little fast. I'll begin again."

Something there is that doesn't love a wall,
That sends the frozen-ground-swell under it
And spills the upper boulders in the sun,
And makes gaps even two can pass abreast.

Mr. Shapiro read the whole poem, slowly and with emotion. Now that the poem was fresh in his mind he recited most of it from memory. Before him at the rows of desks he could see the pale honey-colored faces, some with dark eyes on his face, others staring at the book in his hands. Jaime had not changed his position. Mr. Shapiro could still see where the boy's fingers started to disappear into his black hair. He repeated the last line twice,

He says again, "Good Fences make good neighbors."

The class stirred itself. Mr. Shapiro had an ephemeral sense of accomplishment. Maybe there was a contact, he thought, maybe I had their attention, that is the start of a dialogue. "Any questions?" he asked.

One boy asked why the wall was there anyway if it didn't do any good, and Mr. Shapiro started to answer. He started to explain the significance of New England stone walls, how they originated when the farmers had to pick the stones out of the soil in order to plant a crop, and how they have become a tradition in that part of the country. He started to explain further the irony of the dialogue between the two farmers, and felt he was losing the class again, so he cut it short, "Any other questions?"

"Yes, Mr. Shapeiro." It was Jaime again. "Can you read that part again where they carry rocks like wildmen?"

Mr. Shapiro picked up the book:

I see him there,
Bringing a stone grasped firmly by the top
In each hand, like an old-stone savage armed.
He moves in darkness as it seems to me,
Not of woods only and the shade of trees.

"What did you want to know about them, Jaime?"

"Nothing, Mr. Shapeiro, I just wanted to hear you read them again."

"All right. All right, class, we'll begin painting now. It wasn't a long poem and it didn't take up much time. Maybe there will be time enough for two paintings."

It was Mr. Shapiro's practice not to bother the students while they were painting, he felt his looking over their shoulders might inhibit or intimidate them. He took his jacket and went to the teachers' room for a cigarette. It was not the standard procedure, leaving a class alone, especially Nine C, but he had done it before on Fridays and there were never any complaints from the adjoining rooms.

The lounge for male teachers was next to that for female teachers. At the door he saw Miss Katz. He didn't want to talk to her. He didn't even want her to see him.

"Allan, you naughty, have you left your class unattended? And with poster paints yet! I hope you don't have any trouble," Miss Katz said, walking up to him. She had an empty cup in her hand. Mr. Shapiro knew that if it was wet she was leaving the lounge and if it was dry she was just arriving. But Miss Katz held the cup upside down and he couldn't tell. At first he didn't hear her words. He was convinced she was holding the cup that way just to keep him from knowing if it was wet or dry. "I hope you've never left them before, this could raise a problem for you."

"No," Mr. Shapiro said, "I haven't. I had to go to the bathroom." He had wanted to say *I had to take a wicked leak,* or *I suddenly, for no reason at all, felt like puking,* but he only said, and repeated, "I had to go to the bathroom." He hated himself again, for not saying what he wanted to say, for putting the bathroom excuse in some vague past tense, as if everyone didn't have to empty out at least once a day. He thought of the kids in the room, their honey-colored faces screwed up over their paintings, dreaming in their heads of orchards and fields, and he blurted out, "Do you know, Miss Katz, they are really more ginger-colored than honey-colored," and he leaped into the male lounge.

When he returned to the classroom it was just as he'd imagined. He saw rows of heads, almost every one of the heads covered with very black hair, bent over the desks. He felt pleased, he forgot all about Miss Katz and the probability that she was at that moment telling some other faculty member what he had said to her. When Mr. Shapiro thought about this in the lounge he tried to re-create Miss Katz's language. "You know, Louise, we were talking about his leaving his class unattended, and he was looking strange to begin with, staring at my teacup, and suddenly he shouted at me something about ginger and honey. Then he flew into the men's lounge and slammed the door. Don't you think he's disturbed?" He had ground his cigarette out on the floor of the lounge, and Miss Katz with it.

He stood at the window looking out. The sun was still shining, but it really wasn't shining, he thought, that is too active a description. The sunlight is drifting down, it is settling like a cloud of pale dust, it is

falling because of gravity. He glanced at the students and saw Jaime. His head was bent over his desk, but both his hands were buried in his hair. Mr. Shapiro walked over to him. "What's wrong, Jaime, don't you feel like painting today?"

"Yes, Mr. Shapeiro, I'm all done."

Mr. Shapiro looked at the painting on Jaime's desk. There were two huge figures, manlike but inanimate, facing each other. Both figures had their arms raised high above their heads and in their hands held stones. There were bright carmine streaks on their heads, faces and shoulders. Between them was a black wall that began in the absolute foreground of the painting and ran right through the depth and off the paper. Mr. Shapiro looked more closely and saw a third figure, a smaller one, crouched in a blob of gray on the wall. He felt the same weakness in his legs and the knot in his throat that he had when he looked into Jaime's face at the start of the class.

"What does it mean?" His voice was gruff, almost angry. Two or three of the other students looked up at him, then turned back to their paintings.

"Nothing."

"It can't mean nothing. Everything means something. It has to mean something." His voice was more insistent, hatred for himself ran through his body like a chill. "What does it mean?"

"Nothing," Jaime said, looking up at him with the gray eyes and white hirsuteness on his upper lip. "It don't mean nothing."

Mr. Shapiro straightened up, he looked at the painting again from his new and more distant perspective. The two large figures were both all green. He hadn't noticed that before. And the sky was watery yellow. The ground, where there was grass in the poem, was grape-purple. His eyes were drawn to the small blotted figure crouched on the wall. He leaned over again to have a closer look at it. "Who is that little figure supposed to be, the one on the top of the wall?"

Jaime looked up at him for a moment, then slid his fingers back into his hair and started to look at his painting again.

Mr. Shapiro looked at the clock over the door. There were only ten minutes left to the class. Ten minutes and the day was over, and the week. "All right, class, let's start cleaning up. While you clean the brushes and wipe off the jars I'll come around and pick the star-winner for today."

Most of the paintings tried to show the two farmers standing by the wall, and most of them had green grass and blue skies. But Mr. Shapiro could not think about any of them. He looked at them all, made a comment here, gave a word of encouragement there, but his imagination wasn't in it.

He walked up the aisle Jaime sat in. He paused a little longer at each painting as he got closer to Jaime. When he got to him he walked right by.

The brushes were all washed and standing in a jar, the bottles of paint were all cleaned on the outside, the empty water pitchers stood beside them. Mr. Shapiro looked at the clock. The bell would ring in two minutes. He had to announce a winner. "All right, class, the best paint-

ing today was done by Jaime Morales. Come up, Jaime, and I'll give you your gold star." The usual practice was to exhibit the best painting at the front of the room, and explain why it was the best. But today Mr. Shapiro didn't do this. He only announced the winner, and when Jaime didn't come forward he repeated, "Jaime, come up and I'll give you your star."

He looked at Jaime. The boy was still sitting as he had sat for all the time Mr. Shapiro saw him in class. He saw the top of his head, the thin fingers buried in the thick black hair. But now the fingers were clutching at Jaime's scalp. He was crying.

A few of the students around him looked at him, and then looked at Mr. Shapiro. Mr. Shapiro looked back at them vacantly. Jaime started to cry louder. Mr. Shapiro saw the bony clavicles in Jaime's pale honey-colored chest jerk in and out, he saw the boy's forehead and cheek muscles clench up to hold back the tears. "What the hell is wrong?" he shouted, running up the aisle. "What's wrong now, what did I do?" The whole class was staring at them now, at Jaime and Mr. Shapiro. "What's wrong? Answer me!" he shouted. He didn't care that he was shouting, or that the whole class was watching him. Jaime looked up at him. Now his gray eyes were flecked with red. He stopped crying. "Nothing is wrong, ever."

The bell rang. Mr. Shapiro was still standing over Jaime. Some of the class got up, others waited for Mr. Shapiro to dismiss them. "Okay," he said, his voice cracking and weary, "you can all go now."

Mr. Shapiro was still leaning over

Jaime. He was looking at the painting. He was still drawn to the small gray figure.

"What's wrong, Jaime, you can tell me now, everyone is gone."

"There's nothing wrong."

"Come on," Mr. Shapiro said, his confidence returning, "you can tell me."

"I have nothing to tell."

"Well, in that case, how about helping me carry the supplies back to the art room?"

Mr. Shapiro felt that he had suppressed whatever it was that made his legs weak and made him shout. Together, in two trips, they returned all the supplies. Now the week was over, but Mr. Shapiro knew something in it was unfinished. He wanted to know why Jaime had cried. He wanted to know because he wanted to help the boy. He wanted to understand him, to communicate with him and thereby comfort and help him. He could be honest with himself again, now that he had himself in control, and he could admit that he also wanted to know just for the sake of knowing.

"C'mon, Jaime, I go your way, I'll walk you home." They started out the door, "Wait a minute, you forgot your painting." Jaime went back to get it. Mr. Shapiro remembered the open windows and began to close them. The pale lemon light of an hour ago had turned to grayish-yellow. The sun seemed to be drawing into itself, absorbing its light back from the world.

He turned from the window and saw that Jaime was crying.

The slush had hardened on the sidewalk. Mr. Shapiro could see breath balloons when Jaime exhaled, but he could think of no words to fill them. "I'll buy you a coke, or a hot chocolate," he said, and they went into a Nedick's. Jaime had his painting rolled up, and he put it on the floor beside him. They both ordered hot chocolates and Jaime put two teaspoons of sugar into his. They blew into their cups without talking. Jaime took a sip of his chocolate and smacked his lips. It was too hot.

"Do you want to know why I cried?"

"Yes, if you want to tell me."

"I want to tell you, Mr. Shapiro, but it's not easy. It's hard."

"Start at the beginning, then, take it slow." Mr. Shapiro felt very comfortable sitting at the counter in Nedick's on a Friday afternoon with one of his students. Before Jaime started to talk, he already felt a sense of accomplishment.

"It's account of my painting."

Mr. Shapiro was mildly disappointed. "How could that painting make you cry? And anyway, you won the star this week. It was the best painting. You should be proud of it." Mr. Shapiro had not yet tasted his chocolate, but he felt warm inside. He said again, "You should be proud of it."

"I am, I am, I wanted to win a star but now I don't have anything to do with it."

Mr. Shapiro was hardly listening. He felt expansive inside himself. The questions that had nagged at him earlier in the day seemed resolved. He knew why he was here, why he was teaching and not doing something else, why he was teaching in this particular school. He knew why he was teaching students like Jaime. He was helping them. He would never despise them for assimilating or becoming bourgeois. He was their friend, not their critic. He understood them. They needed him. "What did you say, Jaime?"

"I don't have anything to do with it now, nothing at all."

"Why don't you keep it in your wallet as a memento, so you can look at it and feel good when you want to."

"What do you mean, Mr. Shapeiro, it can't fit in my wallet, it's too big."

"Oh, you're talking about the painting. I thought you meant my gold star."

"The painting, that's what I can't do anything with," Jaime said, his voice cracking, and he started to cry again.

Mr. Shapiro was upset. "What is it, Jaime, you're not telling me everything. What is it? I have a right to know."

"I'm proud of my painting, Mr. Shapeiro, I'm glad I got the star today." Jaime huddled up on his stool, he crouched over his hot chocolate and held the cup in both his hands. "We live in a room with four other families," he said, and he looked at Mr. Shapiro. Mr. Shapiro didn't want to hear what Jaime was saying. He looked at the boy's eyes. They were black now, and shining. Tears rolled like pebbles down his smooth face. Mr. Shapiro blew into his chocolate. He drank some, it scalded and stuck in his throat. "Would you like a doughnut?" he sputtered.

"We live in a room with four other families. Every month we change places in the room. This month is our turn in the middle. I want to hang my painting but I have no wall." Jaime stopped. He was still looking at Mr. Shapiro. "I have no wall!" he shouted into Mr. Shapiro's face, and ran out of the Nedick's.

Mr. Shapiro sat at the counter. He looked down and saw Jaime's painting on the floor. He picked it up. A chill ran up his arm and down his back. He pushed his cup of chocolate aside and unrolled the painting. One end of the black stone wall drilled into Nedick's countertop, the wider end thrust at him.

When he first saw the painting in the classroom he knew what it was about, but he had tried to fool himself. Now his eyes fell on the green figures planted on the grape-purple grass. So he thought, so I've come to this.

He glanced around Nedick's, but nothing seemed as real as the green men stiffly raging on the purple lawn beneath the streaked and watery sky.

He folded the painting and stuffed it into his coat pocket. He lit a cigarette and sipped some chocolate. Miss Katz's teacup, dry or wet, what was the difference? Why had he let it matter?

He felt sorry.

Mr. Shapiro slapped the edge of the countertop with his fingers. The countergirl asked what he wanted, but he did not look up. It has always been walls, he thought. Hearts of men sometimes pushed against walls. But the heart of this or that man, he thought, is the heart of this or that man ever strong enough to force the issue, to burst the walls and let the outside pour in?

He did not know. He was sorrier now, for his brain had failed him. *Kike* they called him, *schmouk, dummy*. They may be right. He nestled deeper into his shame. But it was more bitter than that. He knew now, with a fierce hatred for all mankind, that he did not have the heart to reject his own sorrow.

discussion

Mr. Shapiro is the unusual teacher who dares to try some innovative ideas with a difficult class. It takes courage, a love of poetry, and a commitment to deprived students to dare poetry reading during the last period on the last day of the school week. Only a free-spirited individual can break out of the traditional mold to combine painting with poetry reading. Mr. Shapiro's Friday program is successful. The children like being in Mr. Shapiro's class and can work at their paintings without his overseeing them. For this measure of trust he gives the students, Mr. Shapiro is criticized by his colleagues. Mr. Shapiro is used to scorn and criticism. He has been the butt of derision in the Army, at school, and with his wife. Mr. Shapiro is hurt by the critical attitude of the adults around him, yet he remains true to his own convictions. He is the kind of person who spends a great deal of time with his own thoughts and enjoys the wanderings of his mind. This makes him appear unworldly and even foolish or naive to others, but since he is not judgmental, other people become angry at him because he will not confirm their prejudices.

Mr. Shapiro is a sensitive man, perhaps too sensitive. Unlike other professionals such as pediatricians or psychologists, teachers do not spend enough time in their training discussing objectivity. Nor do teachers have enough opportunity to discuss their problems of over-involvement in the personal circumstances of their pupils. Yet unlike the professionals who see their clients once a week in their own offices usually far away from the child's own neighborhood, the teacher has contact with his students daily and is always aware of the environmental conditions which make his students disturbed or hyperactive. Knowing a student's background can be particularly upsetting to sensitive teachers like Mr. Shapiro, whose concern for Jaime is genuine. His difficulty in reaching students causes him much pain and questioning. The incident at the end of the story illustrates the immovable wall of poverty with which Jaime and therefore Mr. Shapiro must coexist. Perhaps the gray figure on the wall that Jaime paints is Jaime or Mr. Shapiro, both of whom are overshadowed by large immovable forces.

springboards for inquiry

1. How do you interpret Jaime's picture? For what reasons does he cry?

2. What do you think of Mr. Shapiro's Friday paint and poetry sessions?

3. Would Mr. Shapiro's students be more comfortable with a teacher with the same ethnic and cultural background as theirs? Why?

4. Is Mr. Shapiro too sensitive and self pitying to work well in this school setting which is marked by the deprivation of its students? Explain.

school phobia

In most school districts, the school team composed of principal, teacher, school psychologist, and/or counselor will deal with several children a year who experience more or less severe symptoms of school phobia. Johnson, Falstein, Szurek, and Svendsen were the first authors to use the term school phobia recognizable by the intense terror associated with leaving home to attend school.[1] The feeling of fear is usually accompanied by somatic symptoms used as a device to remain at home.

A typical case history might be that of Susie, six years old, and in first grade. One morning Susie refused to go to school. She complained of a stomachache, nausea, and an overwhelming feeling of being afraid. She cried and screamed as her mother attempted to put her into the car in an effort to bring her to school. Unable to force her to enter the car, Susie's mother kept her home and called school to say that Susie had an upset stomach. Mother noticed that Susie's symptoms disappeared as she played happily about the house. After three days of the same early morning trauma Mother called the school to explain that it seems a case of Susie refusing to go to school rather than a stomach upset. Susie's mother said the situation was particularly upsetting to her because in three weeks she was expecting to accompany her husband for the first time on a business trip out of town.

The school principal called the school psychologist and counselor to jointly interview the parents and to help formulate a plan to get Susie back into school. The interview revealed circumstances which are quite typical in cases of young school-phobic children. Mother is a woman who takes great pleasure in catering to her child's every need. She mistrusts the ability of anyone else to look after Susie and she tends to feel lonely and uncomfortable when Susie is in school. It was decided that for the next week Father rather than Mother would bring Susie to school, despite any complaints on Susie's part of stomachache or nausea. The counselor would be on hand to greet Susie as she arrived each morning, to welcome her, and to reassure her that she would be at school if Susie wished to talk to her during the day. The teacher was helped to feel comfortable in being firm about keeping Susie in school despite tearful demands to go home. The counselor suggested that Susie might need reassurance during the day that Mother was all right at home while Susie was in school. The teacher knew the services of the counselor were available to Susie if she wished to talk to her. For the next two weeks the daily support and individual attention that Susie received helped her to adjust to school. By the time her parents went on their business trip, Susie was able to come to school comfortably.

The psychologist continued to discuss the dynamics of the problem with the parents. In this case psychotherapy was recommended for Susie's mother to help her to resolve her own dependency problems. Susie, whose symptoms of school refusal were handled immediately and successfully was

[1]A. M. Johnson, E. J. Falstein, S. A. Szurek, and M. Svendsen, "School Phobia," *American Journal of Orthopsychiatry* (1941) 702–11.

not considered a candidate for further intervention from an outside agency.

Susie's case exemplifies the young child whose school phobia is a manifestation of separation anxiety between mother and child.[2] In an older child school refusal is frequently of a more serious nature. It is usually precipitated by an unpleasant school experience. It may be a teacher who criticizes the student in front of the class, or involve a humiliation like being forced to shower or undress in the presence of other students. The precipitating incident will usually involve some threat to the child's sense of adequacy.[3] These children have unrealistic self-images, and they are hypersensitive to any threat to their fragile sense of personal adequacy. This child is usually powerful and controlling at home and the strategies employed to return the child to school must be carefully designed to counteract the child's resistant maneuvers.

The cooperation of the parents and possibly an outside consultant are usually needed to successfully resolve the student's fears and to return the child to school.

Once a pattern of school refusal becomes established, it tends to recur with detrimental effects upon normal personality development. The child who is sheltered at home because of school refusal lags behind his agemates in developing self reliance. He falls behind in his studies as well as in social skills which enhance self esteem. It is important for teachers to realize that school phobia is not merely a "spoiled child" reaction to school. The child's feelings of panic and somatic complaints like nausea or stomachache are real.

Because of the far reaching consequences of school refusal, all treatment approaches focus on returning the child to school as soon as possible. The usual treatment has been psychotherapy which is based upon a psychoanalytic model and attempts to explore the separation anxiety that is rooted in the interaction between a dependent child and an overprotective mother.[4] A more recent approach to the problem of school phobia is behavior therapy. Behaviorists treat the school refusal through systematic reduction of fear caused by the school situation.

Treatment involves both the "neutralization" of fear-arousing school stimuli through desensitization and reinforcement of school attendance.[5] Behavior therapists also take into consideration the observable reactions on the part of parents toward the child's school refusal and attempt to eliminate their behaviors which may be encouraging the child to stay at home.

---

[2]For a discussion of school refusal as an expression of separation anxiety, see S. L. Smith, "School Refusal with Anxiety—A Review of Sixty-Three Cases," *Canadian Psychiatric Association Journal* 15: (1970) 257–64.

[3]A prominent non-psychoanalytic explanation of school phobia is based on the child's need to maintain an unrealistic self-image. This theory is described in T. Leventhal and M. Sill, *Orthopsychiatry* 34 (1964): 685–95.

[4]S. Waldfogel, J. C. Coolidge, and P. B. Hahn, "The Development, Meaning and Management of School Phobia," *American Journal of Orthopsychiatry* 27 (1957):754–76.

[5]A. A. Lazarus, G. C. Davison, and D. D. Polefka, "Classical and Operant Factors in the Treatment of School Phobia," *Journal of Abnormal Psychology* 70 (1965): 225–29.

Some therapists instruct the parents as behavioral engineers. In a case reported in the literature the parents of a thirteen-year-old girl were shown that by allowing their daughter to avoid facing the demands of school they may have inadvertently strengthened school refusal.[6] To help reinforce school attendance they were instructed in a series of behavior-shaping, school-approach hierarchies which started with a brief school visit and ranged to attendance all day.

In difficult cases, especially those of older children whose phobia is long-standing with other neurotic behaviors present in the child and/or family, more intensive treatment is likely to be necessary.

Schools have within their structure practices or personnel that may cause or aggravate symtoms of school phobia. It is important for teachers to be alert to children whose frequent absences may be part of a pattern of school avoidance. Working with other school personnel they can be helpful in identifying as well as helping the school-phobic child.

Jesse Stuart

The moon child from wolfe creek

"I don't want to tell on anybody," Vennie McCoy whispered to me, "but I think you ought to know Don Crump didn't come all the way to school. He started with us but he didn't get here."

"Where did he go?" I asked. Vennie stood beside me and moved his left bare foot on the pine-board floor of the Lonesome Valley schoolhouse. "Is he playing hooky?"

"He's up there on the mountain-top," Vennie said. "Go to the door and look toward the sky and you'll see 'im."

From A Jesse Stuart Reader by Jesse Stuart. Copyright © 1963 by McGraw-Hill Book Company. Originally published by Curtis Co. Used with permission of McGraw-Hill Book Co.

And one of the first decisions I had to make in my teaching career was what to do with him. *If they run him down and tie his hands and feet and bring him down here,* I thought, *that won't tame him. That will make him wilder than ever.*

"What's he doing up there?" I asked in low tones. My Lonesome Valley pupils looked at one another and then at me as they listened to our conversation. "Why doesn't he come on down to school?"

"He's afraid, Mr. Stuart," Vennie whispered.

I walked to the door and looked toward the peak.

"See 'im yander," Vennie said. He pointed to a tall boy who was walking across a clearing. Just above him on the ridgeline a flock of white clouds floated on a sea of July blue. I watched this tall, slender boy walk back and forth across the little clearing. He would walk first to the tall timber on one side and then he would walk back to the other. His long, lean, restless body was etched

[6]J. A. Tahmisan, and W. T. McReynolds, "Use of Parents as Behavioral Engineers in the Treatment of a School Phobic Girl," *Journal of Counseling Psychology* 18 (1970): 225–28.

against the white clouds. This was hard for me to understand, since it was my first day of teaching in Lonesome Valley.

"Where does Don Crump live?" I asked Vennie as I stood wondering what to do.

"He lives on Wolfe Creek."

"Any other family live near him?"

"Nope."

"How long is Wolfe Creek?"

"Five or six miles long."

"What does Don do at home?"

"He helps his pappy with the croppin' during the season," Vennie explained. "All winter long he hunts and traps. That's the way the Crumps make some money. They sell hides. Don is a good hunter. He can put his nose down to a dirt hole and tell if there's anything in it. And if there's something in the hole he can tell you what it is."

"Are you sure he can do that?" I laughed.

"Oh, yes he can, Mr. Stuart," said Birch Caudill, a small redheaded fifth-grade pupil. "I've seen him do it. Once I saw him lay flat on his stummick and put his face in a water-seap hole and he sniffed and sniffed like a hound-dog, and he says to me when he took his head out of the hole: 'Birch, he's back there. It's a possum.' And we started diggin'. We followed the water-seap hole, a-diggin' through rocks and roots until we come to a big possum a-layin' there asleep in a dry bed of leaves. I'd as soon trust Don Crump as I would the best hound-dog in these parts."

Several of the boys and girls looked at one another and smiled as I, their seventeen-year-old teacher, stood in the door watching the restless figure walk back and forth like a trapped animal in a cage. I wondered why he didn't walk under the tall timber and hide. I wondered if he looked down toward the Little Lonesome schoolhouse, deep down in the narrow-gauged valley, and saw me standing in the door watching him. I tried to reason what to do with him. I wondered why he didn't walk up the steep slope to the ridgetop and into one of the white clouds that were floating lazily along the calm sky. While I stood there, I wondered why a boy of his wild restless nature, afraid of people and of school, would let the tall timber and the white clouds fence him within the semicircle of clearing where somebody pastured cattle and sheep.

"You want us to get 'im for you, Mr. Stuart?" Vennie asked.

"How would you get 'im?" I asked.

"Run 'im down and tie his hands and feet and fetch 'im to you," Vennie replied.

"Maybe you could do that," I said.

"He's fast as a rabbit but we could do it," Vennie bragged. "We've played fox and dog with him and he's faster than any of us, but if enough of us go after 'im and go up every side of the mountain and surround him, he can't get away."

"Yep, we can ketch 'im for you, Mr. Stuart," said Tom Adams, a blue-eyed shaggy-haired seventh-grade pupil. "We can go up the mountain in different directions and hide in the green timber all around the clearin'. Then somebody can give a signal and we can run out into the clearin' and ketch Don. I could almost slip up on 'im myself. I've slipped up on rabbits a-settin' and ketched 'em with my bare hands. I once ketched a ground hog that way. Nabbed 'im by the neck so he couldn't bite me."

Then all of the pupils laughed. Don Crump's being up there on the mountain had disturbed all of us. Everybody who had started to school had come but Don. And one of the first decisions I had to make in my teaching career was what to do with him. *If they run him down and tie his hands and feet and bring him down here,* I thought, *that won't tame him. That will make him wilder than ever.*

Another thought flashed through my mind. I remembered how my father had tamed cattle when they went wild in our big pasture. When we put them on grass in late March and left them alone, except for occasional visits to salt and count them, many went wild. My father finally tamed the wild ones until he had them licking salt out of his hand.

"Want us to go after 'im?" Vennie was impatient. "We'll fetch 'im in."

"Shore will," Tom Adams said.

They're wanting to get out too, I thought.

"No, leave him alone," I said. "If he likes it up there that's quite all right with me. I don't believe in roping a boy hand and foot and carrying him inside a schoolhouse. You can tell him when you see him again the school here is a fine place. Tell him we have a good time playing and that you believe he will like it. Tell him to come on down. Tell him we don't have anything here that will hurt him."

Many of my pupils looked quietly at each other and smiled. I took my last look at Don, who was still walking around in the clearing, up near the white clouds. I turned and walked back down the aisle with Vennie.

At the first recess, when my pupils played The Needle's Eye, I looked up to the high hill in the clearing and I didn't see Don Crump. Not at first. But I finally located Don sitting on a stump looking down in the valley toward the school. He was watching the pupils play. Don Crump sat there on the stump during the fifteen-minute recess (we let it run a little overtime) and looked on. Not one of my pupils paid any attention to him now. They were too busy playing. I did pay attention to him but he didn't know it. I didn't want Don to know I wanted him in school.

At the noon hour we, teacher and pupils, sat on the crumpled roots of the giant sycamores that grew all around the schoolhouse and ate our lunches. These sycamores with their massive canopy of leaves stood betwixt us and the hot July sun. My pupils hurried to eat their lunches so they could play The Needle's Eye. Just as they were choosing sides to play, I looked toward the clearing to see if I could see Don Crump. He walked from the tall timber on the east side.

During the noon hour, I played The Needle's Eye with my pupils. Often, I looked up. Don was back on the stump where he had sat that morning. When Vennie McCoy saw him, before the noon hour was over, he came to me and wanted to get all of the boys in the school and chase him. But I wouldn't let him. I told him to leave Don alone. If Don wanted to come to school that was all right. If he didn't he could stay away. This was hard for Vennie McCoy, Tom Adams, Ova Salyers and Guy Hawkins to understand. They couldn't understand why they were in school and Don Crump was sitting on a stump, high upon the mountainside in the clearing, watching us play.

On the second day of school, Don Crump, in the early hours, walked back and forth in the clearing shade. This was before recess. During recess he sat on the same stump and watched us. At the noon hour he came from the tall timber on the east side of the clearing and watched us playing in the valley below. In the afternoon he disappeared again. At the afternoon recess he emerged from the shade of the tall timber to watch us. He had a little world of his own up on the mountainside. He had found something to interest him. That was watching us. And I was watching him too.

"Don brings his dinner in a lard bucket," Vennie told me on the third day. "His pappy thinks he comes to school. But he goes to the woods, as you know, Mr. Stuart. You want me to go to Wolfe Creek and tell his pappy what he's doin'?"

"No, whatever you do, don't tell his father anything," I said. "Leave Don Crump alone. When he wants to come to school, he'll come."

Takes a long time to tame cattle with salt, I thought. *Maybe Don will finally get here. He's a little closer now.*

For on this third day Don had moved down the mountainside by a hundred yards or more. He was getting closer, where he could see us better from the new stump he'd found. He could hear us sing and shout as we played The Needle's Eye. He could see us better as we ran foot races and played "anti-over the schoolhouse," with a twine ball.

On the last day of the first week, Don came still closer. He was, perhaps, within a quarter of a mile of the schoolhouse now. But he was getting closer, and that pleased me. There was something about the place where the pupils played and had a good time that attracted Don. There was life, laughter and play among us. He must have realized that he was on the outside of all this. He must have craved association, play and laughter with us.

In the second week of school he moved down to a wild blackberry patch where there was a big rock covered with gray lichen moss. He sat on this big rock and watched us.

"I was tellin' Pappy and Mammy about Don Crump," said Tom Adams, as he walked over and stood beside me on the noon hour of the first day in the second week. "Pappy said he was teched. Mammy said he was a moon child."

I stood and looked at Tom.

"What is a moon child?" I asked.

"Born when the moon is tilted in the sky," he explained. "All people are strange that are born when the moon is tilted. Funny in some way or another, so Mammy and Pappy say."

"There's not anything wrong with Don," I said. "He is just not ready to come to school."

"Funny he don't like school," Tom said. "It's a wonderful place. Wouldn't miss it for nothin'."

Then Tom raced back and joined the circle playing The Needle's Eye.

During the second week, Don Crump moved from rock to stump and shade to shade until he was within one hundred yards of the schoolhouse. I warned my pupils not to talk to him, or about him, or even notice him. I told them to go ahead with their play as if Don Crump were not near the schoolhouse, and they did. Don was close enough now to see everything. He could hear the wild, high laughter of my pupils. He could watch the two teams, that had been chosen in the game of The Needle's Eye, pull against each other. He could see one team outpull the other and the pupils spill on the schoolyard and get up and brush the dust from their clothes. He could hear them laugh louder than the wild wind he had so often heard in the lonely treetops. Don sat upon the slope and smiled. This play fascinated him. On the last day of the second week, he walked onto the school-yard, though he stood a safe distance away from the pupils. He kept a good distance away from me.

In the beginning of the third week, Don Crump walked down the little, narrow, winding valley road with the pupils. Then I got my first good look at this tall, blue-eyed, handsome, intelligent-looking boy. His hair, blond as frost-bitten crab grass, came about to his shoulders. He came onto the schoolyard but he wouldn't come inside the school-house. I never tried to get him in-side. He sat on a gnarled root in the sycamore shade while school went on inside the house. He must have listened to what we said inside. When I had the chance, at recesses and noon, I looked at him and smiled, though I never approached him. My pupils left him alone too. For during the beginning of this third week, he stood nearby and watched the pupils at play. He stood and watched and clapped his hands and laughed loudly at times. He kept getting closer to the circle of pupils marching around and around singing The Needle's Eye. Before the week was over, he joined the circle and played with the pu-pils. But, never once did he venture inside the schoolhouse.

While the rest of us were inside,

Don Crump played around the schoolhouse. Often he sat on the sycamore root and whistled. He whistled a tune like the wind was playing in the sycamore leaves above. Ova Salyers told me once that he had whistled like the wind so much, while he was alone in the woods, that he could whistle the tune of any wind. This was hard for me to believe, until once I walked outside the school-house and lis-tened to Don's whistling on the syca-more root below, the tune of the wind in the sycamore leaves above him. He was whistling the tune of the wind all right. But, to leave this boy outside the schoolroom, while the rest of us were inside, caused considerable talk among the school patrons of my district. Many of the patrons accused me of having a "pet," one I let do as he pleased. Of course, many of my pupils didn't understand what I was trying to do and they went home and told their parents about Don Crump and what I had told them about leaving him alone. Several of the parents dis-missed Don Crump and said he should not be allowed to go to school, since he was a moon child. A few of the parents thought I was afraid of him.

But on Monday afternoon, of my first month at Lonesome Valley, Don Crump came inside the school-house. He walked inside, looked quickly at all the pupils, at the win-dows, then at the door. He held a cap in his hand when he sat down on a back seat. He acted as if he were ready to run. My pupils were naturally excited when he came in-side, and started looking at him. I motioned for them to look toward my desk and to keep quiet and pay no attention to Don Crump. The stray one had finally come because of his hunger and thirst. His was the eternal hunger and thirst of youth for laughter, play, recreation, association and enjoyment upon this earth. Don had come to us. We hadn't run him down, tied his hands and feet and brought him to us either. He had come of his own accord.

discussion

The author indicates in his introduction to this story that the experience with Don Crump was drawn from his own teaching career. He asks if he was right in dealing with the boy in the manner he devised. Although the author was only 17 at the time, he could not have been more sophisticated in his approach to the problem. His process of progressive desensitization to the feared object (attending school), which he carried through following his intuition and memory of his dad taming cattle, would probably agree almost entirely with methods devised by behavior therapists today. Although the application to humans of a method of changing behavior that works with animals may seem repugnant, psychologists have learned a great deal about the human learning process by observing animal behavior. B. F. Skinner is the noted psychologist whose observations of animal behavior have been the basis of a new form of therapy which is being used successfully to change behavior in children and adults.[1] Joseph Wolpe is a therapist who has devised a successful method of curing phobias such as the school phobia described in this story through a behavioral approach.[2] He uses progressive desensitization to the feared object almost precisely as did the author who discovered it for himself.

Mr. Stewart, realizing that Don Crump's greatest fear was coming to school, uses the children to improve Don Crump's image of the school experience. He encourages them to say positive things about the school to Don. In talking to the children, Mr. Stewart is careful to avoid any mention of himself or how much he wants the boy to return to school, as he does not want to introduce another possible frightening component—the fear of the teacher, an unknown adult. He attempts to deal with his fear in another way. Mr. Stewart plays with the children at noon so Don Crump can see him from a safe distance and form a positive impression of him.

The teacher is patient. He never hurries the process. He knows instinctively that Don will approach the situation little by little as he is ready. It is difficult for Mr. Stewart to pursue his patient strategy as parents and children criticize him for not being strict and insisting that Don attend school immediately. However, by insisting that the children not report Don's nonattendance at school to Mr. Crump, Mr. Stewart keeps Don's parents from pushing him into the fearful situation. As Don moves down the mountainside closer to school, Mr. Stewart knows his nearness to the children's fun and laughter will help him to feel less frightened.

---

[1]James G. Holland and B.F. Skinner, *The Analysis of Behavior* (New York: McGraw-Hill, 1961).

[2]Joseph Wolpe, *The Practice of Behavior Therapy* (Elmsford, N.Y.: Pergamon Press, 1969).

As Don sees school as a place that the other children enjoy, his own healthful need to play and learn with children of his own age replaces his fear, and he enters the school yard to play and then the school room to learn. The process takes one month's time. Today's behavior therapist could probably not accomplish Mr. Stewart's plan of desensitization in less time and surely not with less expense.

springboards for inquiry

1. If you were the teacher in this story, how would you have enticed Don Crump to come to school?

2. React to two studies which use behavior therapy to help the school phobic child. (Use the references in the essay on school phobia.)

3. React to two studies which use a therapeutic approach as intervention for school refusal.

4. Do you think the public school system can afford to help an individual child with school phobia considering the amount of time and varied school personnel required?

References

AUSUBEL, DAVID. "Some Misconceptions Regarding Mental Health Functions and Practices in the Schools." In *Readings in Educational Psychology,* ed. George J. Mouly. New York: Holt, Rinehart and Winston, 1971.

————. "Viewpoints from Related Disciplines: Human Growth and Development." *Teachers College Record* 20, no. 5 (February 1959): 245–54.

BERNARD, HAROLD W. *Child Development and Learning.* Boston: Allyn & Bacon, 1973.

BRITTAIN, CLAY V. "Adolescent Choices and Parent-Peer Cross-Pressures." *American Sociological Review* 28 (1963): 385–91.

BRONFENBRENNER, URIE. "Socialization and Social Class Through Time and Space." In *Readings in Social Psychology.* 3rd ed. Ed. Maccoby, Eleanor E., Newcomb, Theodore M., and Hartley, Eugene L. New York: Holt, Rinehart and Winston, 1958.

BUNKER, ROBERT, and ADAIR, JOHN. *The First Look at Strangers.* New Brunswick, N.J.: Rutgers University Press, 1959.

CHESS, STELLA, THOMAS, ALEXANDER, and BIRCH, HERBERT. "Characteristics of the Individual Child's Behavioral Responses to the Environment." *American Journal of Orthopsychiatry* 29 (1959): 791–801.

COOPERSMITH, STANLEY. "Self-Esteem and Need Achievement as Determinants of Selective Recall and Repetition." *Journal of Abnormal and Social Psychology* 60 (1960): 310–17.

DOLL, RONALD C., and FLEMING, ROBERT S. *Children Under Pressure.* Columbus: Merrill, 1966.

EVVARD, EVELYN, and MITCHELL, GEORGE C. "Sally, Dick and Jane at Lukachukai." *Journal of American Indian Education* 5, no. 5 (May 1966): 5.

FUFIMOTO, ISAO. *Chinese-Americans: School and Community Problems.* Chicago: Integrated Education Assoc., 1972.

GINOTT, HAIM G. *Teacher and Child.* New York: Macmillan, 1972.

GLASSER, WILLIAM. *Mental Health or Mental Illness: Psychiatry for Practical Action.* New York: Harper & Row, 1970.

————. *Reality Therapy.* New York: Harper & Row, 1963

————. *Schools Without Failure.* New York: Harper & Row, 1969.

HARRIS, THOMAS A. *I'm O.K.: You're O.K.: A Practical Guide to Transactional Analysis.* New York: Harper & Row, 1969.

HAVIGHURST, ROBERT J., and TABA, HILDA. *Adolescent Character and Personality.* New York: Wiley, 1949.

HEMMING, RAY. *Children's Freedom: A. S. Neill and the Evolution of the Summerhill Idea.* New York: Schocken, 1973.

HIERONYMUS, A. N. "A Study of Social Class Motivation: Relationships Between Anxiety for Education and Certain Socio-Economic and Intellectual Variables." *Journal of Educational Psychology* 42 (1951): 29–45.

HILL, KENNEDY T., and SARASON, SEYMOUR B. "The Relation of Test Anxiety and Defensiveness to Test and School Performance over the Elementary School Years: A Further Longitudinal Study." *Monographs of the Society for Research in Child Development* 31 (2), no. 104 (1968).

HINDE, R. A., and STEVENSON-HINDE, J. *Constraints on Learning.* London: Academic Press, 1973.

HUNT, JOSEPH MCVICKER. "Parent and Child Centers: Their Basis in the Behavioral and Educational Sciences." *American Journal of Orthopsychiatry* 41 (January 1971): 24–25.

JACKSON, PAUL W. *Life in Classrooms.* New York: Holt, Rinehart and Winston, 1968.

JOHNSON, A. M., FALSTEIN, E. J., SZUREK, S. A., and SVENDSEN, M. "School Phobia," *American Journal of Orthopsychiatry* 11, no. 4 (October 1941): 702–11.

KENNEDY, WALLACE A. *Child Psychology.* Englewood Cliffs, N.J.: Prentice-Hall, 1971.

KOGAN, MAURICE, ed. *Informal Schools in Britain Today.* New York: Citation Press, 1972.

LANGER, ELLEN J., and ABELSON, ROBERT P. "A Patient by Any Other Name . . . : Clinician Group Difference in Labeling Bias." *Journal of Consulting and Clinical Psychology* 42, no. 1 (February 1974): 4–9.

LAZARUS, A. A., DAVISON, G. C., and POLEFKA, D. D. "Classical and Operant Factors in the Treatment of School Phobia." *Journal of Abnormal Psychology* 70 (1965): 225–29.

LEFRANCOIS, GUY L. *Of Children: An Introduction to Child Development.* Belmont, Ca.: Wadsworth, 1973.

LESSER, GERALD S., FIFER, GORDON, and CLARK, DONALD H. "Mental Abilities of Children from Different Social Class and Cultural Groups." *Monographs of the Society for Research in Child Development* 30 (4), no. 102, 1965.

LEVENTHAL, T. and SILL, M. "Self-Image in School Phobia." *American Journal of Orthopsychiatry* 34 (1964): 685–95.

MENNINGER, KARL. *The Crime of Punishment.* New York: Viking, 1968.

MCKEACHIE, WILBUR J. "Student-Centered versus Instructor-Centered Instruction." *Journal of Educational Psychology* 45 (1954): 148.

MOULY, GEORGE J. *Readings in Educational Psychology.* New York: Holt, Rinehart and Winston, 1971.

OLSON, WILLARD C. *Child Development.* Boston: D. C. Heath, 1959.

PETERSON, JOHN. "Mousepack Mayhem." *The National Observer* 12, no. 51 (December 22, 1973): 1.

PODHORETZ, NORMAN. "Now, Instant Zionism." *New York Times Magazine* (February 3, 1974), p. 11.

"Precision Teaching in Perspective: An Interview with Ogden R. Lindsley." *Teaching Exceptional Children* 3 (Spring 1971): 114–19.

ROSENTHAL, ROBERT, and JACOBSON, LENORE. *Pygmalion in the Classroom.* New York: Holt, Rinehart and Winston, 1968.

ROWEN, BETTY. *The Children We See.* New York: Holt, Rinehart and Winston, 1973.

SARASON, SEYMOUR B. *The Culture of the School and the Problem of Change.* Boston: Allyn & Bacon, 1971.

_____. "Jewishness, Blackishness and the Nature-Nuture Controversy." *American Psychologist* 28, no. 11 (November 1973): 962–71.

SELYE, HANS. *Stress of Life.* New York: McGraw-Hill, 1956.

SMITH, S. L. "School Refusal with Anxiety—A Review of Sixty-Three Cases." *Canadian Psychiatric Association Journal* 15 (1970): 257–64.

SOLOMON, DANIEL. "Influences on the Decisions of Adolescents." *Human Relations* 16 (1963): 45–60.

STANLEY, SUE and WAGNER, N. N. *Asian-American Psychological Perspectives.* Ben Lomond, Ca.: Science and Behavioral Books, 1973.

STERLING, PHILIP, ed. *The Real Teachers.* New York: Vintage Books, 1972.

TAHMISAN, J. A., and McREYNOLDS, W. T. "Use of Parents as Behavioral Engineers in the Treatment of a School Phobic Girl." *Journal of Counseling Psychology* 18 (1970): 225–28.

VARMA, VED P. *Stress in Children.* New York: Crane, Russak, 1973.

WALDFOGEL, S., COOLIDGE, J. C., and HAHN, P. B. "The Development, Meaning and Management of School Phobia." *American Journal of Orthopsychiatry* 27 (1957): 754–76.

WALSH, ANN M. *Self-Concepts of Bright Boys with Learning Difficulties.* New York: Teachers College Press, 1956.

WATTENBERG, WILLIAM W., and CLIFFORD, CLARE. "Relation of Self-Concepts to Beginning Achievement in Reading." *Child Development* 35 (1964): 461–67.

WEINSTEIN, GERALD, and FANTINI, MARIO D. *Toward Humanistic Education: A Curriculum of Affect.* New York: Praeger, 1970.

WHITE, MARY ALICE, and DUKER, JAN. "Suggested Standards for Children's Samples." *American Psychologist* 28, no. 3 (August 1973): 700–703.

WITTE, KENNETH L, and GROSSMAN, EUGENE E. "The Effects of Reward and Punishment upon Children's Attention, Motivation and Discrimination Learning." *Child Development* 42 (1971): 537–42.

WRIGHT, HERBERT FLETCHER. "Psychological Development in the Midwest." *Child Development* 27 (June 1956): 265–86.

WYLIE, RUTH. *The Self-Concept.* Lincoln: University of Nebraska Press, 1961.

ZINTZ, MILES V. *Education Across Cultures.* 2nd ed. Dubuque: Kendall/Hunt, 1969.

———. "Indian Children Are Different." *The New Mexico School Review* 40 (October 1968): 26–27.

Teaching the Exceptional Child

One of the basic ideals of a free society is to provide each individual the opportunity to develop to his full capacity. This was articulated in *The Pursuit of Excellence,* the Rockefeller Report on Education. John Gardner, the senior author, stated,

> The greatness of a nation may be manifested in many ways—in its purposes, its courage, its moral responsibility, its cultural and scientific eminence, the tenor of its daily life. But ultimately the source of its greatness is in the individuals, who constitute the living substance of the nation.[1]

The field of special education is devoted to developing the potential of those children who represent the extremes of exceptionality, the gifted and handicapped. With early and specialized intervention it is hoped that all individuals in our society can realize a future as fulfilled and productive as possible.

For educational purposes exceptional children have been defined as those with disabilities in the physical, mental, social, behavioral, or learning areas as well as those with superior abilities in the intellectual areas. The most widely accepted definition of exceptionality is given by Lloyd Dunn who defines exceptional children as those:

1. who differ from the average to such a degree in physical or psychological characteristics

2. that school programs designed for the majority of children do not afford them opportunity for all-round adjustment and optimum progress

3. and who therefore need either special instruction or in some cases special ancillary services, or both, to achieve at a level commensurate with their respective abilities.[2]

The child who is mentally retarded, sensorily impaired, or who has a language handicap needs special instruction. Those entering the field of education may question the need for national professional organizations such as the Council for Exceptional Children to concern themselves with the gifted as well as with children who are physically or mentally handicapped.

[1]*The Pursuit of Excellence: Education and the Future of America,* Rockefeller Brothers Fund, (New York: Doubleday, 1958).

[2]Lloyd M. Dunn, ed. *Exceptional Children in the Schools* (New York: Holt, Rinehart and Winston 1973).

Dunn's definition of exceptionality points up the fact that children who fall in the upper two percentiles of the population in intellectual ability differ significantly from the norm and therefore also need special instruction. The chapter on the gifted expands further on the identification, characteristics, and instructional needs of these exceptional children.

Education for the exceptional child is more expensive than education for the normal child because the pupil-teacher ratio should be close to one to ten. Specialized materials are usually necessary for optimum learning. Ancillary personnel are needed, particularly for the handicapped, because a team approach to their problems is more productive. A skilled psychologist assesses the capabilities of children who may be multi-handicapped. The school team may also include a social worker and a nurse who must work closely with the child's physician and family to insure a coordinated approach to his education.

Traditionally, centers for diagnostic services and education for the handicapped were established in large institutions located in outlying areas. This removed the handicapped from view. Today the community takes a more enlightened view of its responsibility for the handicapped population. The trend is toward regional diagnostic and treatment centers within large metropolitan areas.

Education for the exceptional child is also undergoing major changes. There is a movement away from special schools for specific handicaps and special self-contained classrooms within the neighborhood school. Spogen is concerned about the disability labels which stigmatize handicapped children. "These labels, coupled with a homogeneous classroom design, have assured many children of isolation from their school peers, isolation from many learning activities, and separation from their own communities. Academically, they may be given a short instructional day, an extended bus route, and a poor achievement record."[3]

On the basis of research, some authorities in the field of special education are recommending the resource room concept.[4] Handicapped students are now being integrated or mainstreamed into the regular classroom with free flow of children between the classroom and the resource center where each receives specialized instruction to meet the needs of his particular handicap. The Santa Monica Madison School Plan is one such innovative model which combines time in the regular classroom with time spent in a learning center.[5] The educators who devised this plan have established categories of readiness which the child must give evidence of having met before progressing to longer periods in the regular classroom.

There is growing interest in working with exceptional children as a professional specialty. Because the exceptional child is in so many respects like the so called "normal child," it is helpful for the prospective teacher to have

[3]David Spogen, "Take the Label Off the Handicapped Child." *Education Digest* (September 1972): 44–46.

[4]"Symposium No. 8," *Journal of Special Education* 6, no. 4 (Winter 1972): 335–89.

[5]Michael Soloway, and Frank D. Taylor, "The Madison Plan," *Instructor* 82, no. 3 (November 1972): 94–95.

experience with normal children so that he can put the specialized needs of the exceptional child in proper perspective. Ray Barsch, a well-known investigator in the field of special education, reminds professionals of the need to establish good rapport with the parents of the handicapped child.[6] The parents of the handicapped child necessarily occupy a more central role in the upbringing of a child with special needs. Grief and trauma have usually been associated with the child's earliest years. Since the family will continue to play a more significant role in this child's school years, it is important that home and school work together for the benefit of the child.

---

[6]Ray H. Barsch, *The Parent of the Handicapped Child* (Springfield, Ill.: Charles C. Thomas, 1968), p. 15.

the learning disabled

The learning-disabled child is frequently identified withint the first few days of his initial school experience. Typically he[1] is hyperactive, unable to stay in his seat and persist with a task or listen to a story, tends to have temper tantrums, has difficulty in relating to other children, and is unusually clumsy on the playground and/or in small motor tasks such as cutting, pasting, and coloring. With more knowledge about the learning disabled child, the teacher is no longer apt to call him "spoiled." Instead she will refer him to the school psychologist.

In the 1960s a new category of the exceptional child was defined, the *learning-disabled child*. For several years the terms *minimal cerebral dysfunction* or *selective brain injury* were used in connection with the learning-disabled child, but these labels of etiology have been discarded because in most cases actual brain damage is impossible to verify.[2] Kirk, who initially defined learning disability, revised his original statement. It now reads, "A learning disability refers to a specific retardation or disorder in one or more processes of speech, language, perception, behavior, reading, spelling, writing or arithmetic."[3]

Detection of children who are likely to have learning difficulties can be done at the preschool level. Dr. Richard L. Masland, head of the neurology department at Columbia University College of Physicians and Surgeons suggests that "physicians should be made more knowledgeable in this field."[4] "Soft" neurological signs such as failure to touch fingers rapidly and in sequence with the thumb of the same hand, difficulty in walking along a narrow line, accentuated extension of the arms when walking on tiptoe, along with lags in developmental milestones, are a signal to the physician that a child may exhibit problems in learning when he goes to school. Adkins calls for the establishment of more early learning centers so that parents, physicians, psychologists, and educators can work together to detect learning disabilities early.[5] The parent who has had the benefit of counsel concerning her child's early signs of developmental lag can take advantage of preschool intervention. This can eliminate secondary emotional problems which may stem from a first school experience marked by frequent scoldings for misbehavior (e.g., hyperactivity and distractibility), and a sense of failure because the child cannot accomplish school tasks as well as

[1]We use the pronoun *he* advisedly, because the learning disability syndrome is more prevalent among boys than girls.

[2]Herbert H. Birch, ed. *Brain Damage in Children* (Baltimore: Williams and Wilkins, 1964) pp. 4–5.

[3]Samuel A. Kirk, "The Illinois Test of Psycholinguistic Abilities: Its Origin and Implications," in *Learning Disorders*, vol. 3, ed. Jerome Hellmuth. (Seattle: Special Child Publications, 1968).

[4]"Minimal Brain Dysfunction," *Medical World News* (May 22, 1970).

[5]Patricia G. Adkins, "A Call for Early Learning Centers," *Academic Therapy* 7 (Summer 1972): 447–50.

his age-mates (incoordination of gross or small motor functioning). A pattern of child-parent disharmony frequently ensues when parents who receive adverse reports about their child from school attempt to teach the child at home. Out of frustration the labels *stupid* and *lazy* are often applied to these children who actually cannot learn with conventional methods. Taichert directs her therapy to the learning disabled child's educational disability as well as to the family dysfunction which so often occurs when the child's learning disability goes undetected and untreated.[6]

By far the most severely affected academic skill in the learning disabled child is reading. Failure to learn to read may be associated with a number of difficulties such as disturbance in visual perception (seeing b for d, for example), inability to recall sound sequences of letters, or difficulty in sound blending. The psychologist, through a series of tests, can help in pinpointing areas of greatest weakness and strength so that a program of remediation can be devised.[7] Some of the most commonly used tests are the Stanford-Binet and the Wechsler Intelligence Scale for Children. The latter is preferred because the discrepancy among the ten subtest scores yields useful information for remediation. The Bender Visual-Motor Gestalt Test or the Frosting Developmental Test of Visual Perception (for detection of visual perceptual disturbances) are also used along with the Wepman Test of Auditory Discrimination, the Illinois Test of Psycholinguistic Abilities, and various personality tests. It is important for the psychologists to determine whether a child is learning disabled, emotionally disturbed, or mentally retarded. In young children especially there may be some overlap among these three categories.

Most school districts now provide special education for the learning disabled child. This may be accomplished through self-contained classes, special groupings, or resource rooms as described earlier. With any arrangement, one of the most important keys to success is the disposition and preparation of the teacher who works with these special children. The teacher must be trained to work with the psychologist to develop educational prescriptions to remedy the children's learning problems. [8] Specialized techniques of behavior management are often utilized to reinforce learning in small increments and to encourage on-task learning behavior.[9]

In view of the short time that knowledge of learning-disabled children has been available to educational and health care professionals, a remarkable amount of progress has been made. The home, school, and medical profession have been brought together in a closer relationship to deal with developmental problems of children. Much more needs to be done in order to salvage more children from mislabeling and mismanagement.

---

[6]Louise C. Taichert, *Childhood Learning, Behavior and the Family* (New York: Behavioral Publications, 1973).

[7]Lester Tarnapol, ed., *Learning Disabilities* (Springfield, Ill.: Charles C. Thomas, 1969).

[8]Robert E. Valett, *Programming Learning Disabilities* (Belmont, Ca.: Fearon, 1969).

[9]Frank Hewett, "A Hierarchy of Educational Tasks for Children with Learning Disorders," *Exceptional Children* 31 (1964), pp. 207–14.

Forrest Rosaire

The pod of a weed

The interview with the principal had taken only five minutes but when Mr. Jackson came across the junior high school yard to the isolated bungalow at the far end, the place was a bedlam as usual. The boys seemed to be milling and scrambling, and the softball shot across the window. Mr. Jackson lumbered like an ungainly Newfoundland up the stairs, took the rolled newspaper he always carried in his pocket, and belabored the open door with it like a drum.

"Silence! Silence!" he shouted at the top of his voice.

Yacob was standing in the rear aisle with his cap on. Mr. Jackson whacked it off like a golfball off a tee. Gibby the Goon shot up an arm, fielded the cap neatly, and sailed it out the door. Yacob, without paying any attention to his cap, leaped headlong for Gibby. The two boys rolled pummeling in the aisle.

"Swats! Swats!" chorused the boys gleefully.

Mr. Jackson reached down and got Gibby by the belt—he had long since learned that a hold by the collar merely ripped the poor stuff of their shirts—and heaved him like a bale of hay toward the front of the room.

"Get in the printing room," he said.

The printing room was a cubicle off the front of the bungalow which

First published in Esquire *Magazine.*

"Ah, bushwah," said Charlie. "That's all you guys are full of, bushwah. What's the use of a guy like me? What can I ever do? You know there ain't nothin' in them drawings. They're just somethin' you can brag about, to show what a guy with fits did."

contained a broken chair, a hand press, and a quantity of hopelessly mixed type. It had been the original intention to occupy these special disciplinary cases with constructive hand work, but after the boys had daubed printer's ink on each other and had a free-for-all with the type, the project had been abandoned. The room was now a kind of solitary detention ward, where, on sufficient provocation, Mr. Jackson dealt out "swats" with a thirty-inch strap of harness leather.

If there was one thing Mr. Jackson loathed in the world, it was swats. If for any reason he could defer them, or ignore their necessity, he invariably did so; and that undoubtedly represented one great pole of his pedagogic failure. At the moment, however, he had no need of inventing any excuse to himself about the swats due Gibby, for the interview with Mr. Sparkman was so stunningly with him that he forgot the harness strap completely.

Of course Mr. Sparkman hadn't said, "Jackson, you're a cinch for the job." But the inference was clear enough. If the visit of the Superintendent went off satisfactorily this afternoon, Mr. Jackson was very likely slated for the senior high school vacancy.

He picked up the ball where it had rolled in the corner and replaced it in the cupboard.

"Get to work," he said.

Work, in the connotation of the

bungalow, meant doing anything they cared to so long as the boys kept quiet. This represented the other pole of Mr. Jackson's failure. Of course nobody—nobody with any experience of such boys, that is—expected him actually to teach them anything. They were the dregs of a tough harbor school system, the truants, thieves, subnormals and incorrigibles collected from three junior high schools, corralled here for Mr. Jackson to police.

But he had expected something of himself. When he first came here, a year ago, he had been full of real and honest fervor. He had thought something could be done with the boys; he had sweated like a galley slave to inch them just a hairsbreadth, just a millimeter, along the educational branch. Now the lines were deeper in his pouchy, drooping face, and the gaping ring of his coat collar showed how much more stooped his ungainly shoulders were. But the physical signs were no index of the capitulation, the exhaustion of his soul. He was at the nadir of any conception of his job. He had slipped downhill to the minimum that was required of him—to keep some modicum of order, not to bother Mr. Sparkman with disciplinary problems, and to stage, on the occasion of the Superintendent's visit, a certain convincing show of activity.

His mind clutched at the prospect of the high school like a starving man after bread. Everything depended on the Superintendent's visit this afternoon. If he could put over some simulation of successful teaching, the job was probably his. He felt a contraction through all his muscles with the very desperation

of his longing. To be out of this. To be through with this sickening travesty in the bungalow, these twelve impossible, brutalized, heartbreaking boys, these dozen millstones of failure that hung around his neck and had broken the very spirit in him. He had to get the high-school job. He had to. It meant life to Mr. Jackson, it meant escape from defeat, it meant a new, clean, finer page, a page with bright and normal young faces on it, looking up at him with hope and aspiration and intelligence in their eyes.

He sat staring at the dull impervious clay out of which he had to produce some telling effect this afternoon. There was Tony, with the pocked face and large, liquid, sleep-glazed eyes. He was, in fact, asleep at this moment, sitting bolt upright with his mouth open. Mr. Jackson could hardly blame him for that, for he had probably been up all night helping his father make Italian pastry in the bakery.

There was Cookie, the colored boy, who put his shoes in his desk and sat in his bare feet all day. Cookie was the brightest boy there, a mischievous, grinning mulatto who could steal an automobile without a key and perform multiplication and division on the blackboard. Mr. Jackson would have to lean very heavily on Cookie this afternoon.

There was Marco, with the wild look on his face, always ready to burst into laughter or uncontrollable rage. Marco with the wild dramatic sense, who delighted in telling pointless anecdotes and howling at them immoderately. He could not read two consecutive lines, but he had been over the story at the beginning of the fourth reader, called *The Giant with the Hundred Heads*, so many times with so many teachers that he could recite it by heart.

There was Charlie Catfits, the worker. Mr. Jackson felt a quick glow when he looked at Charlie. He was a blond, pimpled boy who kept his nose to his desk all day and worked with savage intensity. It was something extraordinary, as freakish in reverse as the lumpishness of the others, a kind of hammering fury, like a man running for a railroad crossing before the train got there. Charlie made drawings of leaves. Of tree leaves and weed leaves, of any leaf you brought him, every vein and crenelation executed with architectural precision. He kept his drawings in a cigar box at home.

They would be, of course, the pearl of this afternoon's inspection, and all semester Mr. Jackson had encouraged him with this eventuality in mind.

There was Yacob, who had precipitated the scuffle. Yacob the Lithuanian boy, with the livid scar on his forehead and the horrible burns on his hands that mangled his entire forearms. Yacob had a shock of hair like a palm tree and a rapt, inward look. You would have thought he was concerned with some tremendous idea, except that he had an I.Q. of fifty-five and could not spell his own last name.

There was Baptiste, the parolee from reform school, with the shoulders like a piano mover, who could hit a home run holding the bat in one hand. There were Chendo and Guppy and Maxie and the Root Toot and the Steckna twins, who had put a teacher in the hospital for five weeks. Mr. Jackson took a deep breath and gathered himself together. He rapped on the desk.

"Pay attention to what I say," he said. "Something very important is going to happen this afternoon. You are going to have a visitor. It is going to be Mr. Kedgery, the Superintendent."

A belligerent murmur arose.

"What for?"

"I know that fat squab."

"What's he comin' here for?"

"He's coming to see what you're doing," said Mr. Jackson. His mind cast desperately for some subterfuge to induce order this afternoon. "When he comes here, if he doesn't think you're doing anything, he's going to send you off to the reform school."

The boys blinked at him. They moved uneasily. They didn't like the idea of the reform school. Here, in this halfway house, there was an out-at-the-elbows freedom, a kind of camaraderie with Mr. Jackson, who was not such a bad scout. He let you play softball for an hour at a time and when Maxie had lost the three bucks to get his abscessed tooth pulled, Mr. Jackson had given it to him. The teachers at the reform school, according to Baptiste, carried billies in their pockets and you got in or out of your seat when they blew a whistle.

"When Mr. Kedgery comes," said Mr. Jackson, "I want this room absolutely quiet. I want every boy with a book in his hand, caps out of sight, and no papers on the floor. Do you understand that?"

Under the reaching paw of the reform school, they seemed to.

"Charlie, when you come back at lunch time, bring your cigar box of drawings with you. The rest of you are going to have your arithmetics open at page ten. You, Cookie, are going to do that problem for Mr. Kedgery."

"Kahee, k'hee-hee," said Cookie. "Punks, look me over."

Mr. Jackson took the newspaper

truncheon from his pocket. "Get up to the board now."

It was a simple problem involving the distance around a square, and Cookie could do it with his eyes closed. With a strut and a shuffle he went up and drew a square on the blackboard. "Y' see," he said, "y' take this yeah side, supposin' it's th'ee inches, see, and all y' do is tams it by foah . . ."

"Hold on there."

A solo by Cookie was not enough. There had to be much more than this. Co-operation. Class participation. Questions. Volunteering from the group.

"You, Marco, when he finishes drawing the square, ask him, 'Isn't that like our softball diamond?' "

"Gee, it is if you turn it around," said Guppy.

"That's it," pounced Mr. Jackson. "You say that, Guppy. You say, 'It looks like our softball diamond if you turn it around.' Do you get that?"

Guppy emitted a lip-tittering blast of derision. "Why should I ask him that? Gee, this is goofy. What's the idea of askin' him them questions?"

"You don't have to bother about the idea," said Mr. Jackson. He leaned forward, his jaw clenched. "Just do it, that's all. And you, Chendo, say, 'Why, the distance around that square is just like a home run.' "

He labored tooth and nail for the next five minutes, pounding their roles into the boys, assigning parts to the ones he could reasonably count on, trying to develop a situation that would make it look as if the class, not Cookie, solved the problem. The other boys grew immediately restless. The Root Toot cut two pieces of chalk to size and dotted them with ink for dice. Yacob

scraped a handful of soft mud off his shoe and leaned over to plaster Charlie Catfits with it. Mr. Jackson glimpsed this from the corner of his eye and yanked Yacob from his seat.

"Get in the printing room," he said.

He had forgotten all about his previous incarceration of Gibby. He had sucked a lungful of air to launch into his second rehearsal when a violent racket broke out in the printing room.

Mr. Jackson revolved on his heels and started in that direction. He threw open the printing-room door and saw Yacob and Gibby going at each other like wildcats. He saw the blanched, fear-stiff look on Gibby's face, the flash of the knife in Yacob's hand. Mr. Jackson, flinging out his arms like an ungainly cormorant, grabbed Yacob from behind. He pinned the boy's arm to his side and twisted the knife from him.

Gibby plunged out the door, baying, "He pulled a chive! He tried to murder me!"

Mr. Jackson swung around to the room. His voice was hoarse, panting. "Get out to recess. All of you. Get out of the room."

He went back in and closed the door of the printing room.

Yacob was sitting in the broken chair, twirling his cap, looking at Mr. Jackson with unblinking steadiness. Mr. Jackson stood in front of him, his shoulders sagging, suddenly engulfed in the most utter helplessness he had ever felt in his life. What was the use? What was the use? It was so horribly, so absolutely futile. What, in heaven's name, could anybody do with a situation like this? He looked at the knife in his hand and closed the blade. It was a scaling knife, which still reeked of fish.

"Where'd you get this?"

"I kiped it from my uncle."

"What's the idea of pulling a knife on Gibby?"

"Because I'm a killer."

"Who put that into your head? What kind of a rotten sneak are you? It started out as a fist fight, didn't it? Are you afraid of him?"

Yacob lifted his lip. "I ain't afraid of nobody."

"Then what did you pull a knife on him for?"

"Because I'm a killer."

At the second repetition his voice was more strident and his eyes had a feverish brightness. "Just keep out of my way, that's all. You know what I done. Everybody knows what I done. I'm a killer."

"Will you shut up with that talk? What do you mean, I know what you've done? Are you trying to tell me you killed somebody?"

Yacob stopped twirling his cap. His burn-welted, twisted hands hung motionless. A kind of slow shock struck through him.

"They ain't told you about it?"

"Who?"

"Everybody. My uncle." He burst out with loud, pounding excitement. "He was there. He seen it. He gave me this sock on the head, see, where I got the scar. Cheez did he sock me, it nearly bust my skull, it laid me in the hospital for two weeks, so I don't remember nothin'. But my uncle was there. He seen it. He said I was a born killer."

Mr. Jackson stood with his jaw hanging and his hands on his hips.

"Who did you kill?"

There was a strained, bluish whiteness around the boy's pupils.

"My cousin. I was over at my aunt's house. She was hangin' washin' in the back yard. Me and Sasha was playin' in the kitchen. He was a

little squirt and horsing around and he made me sore. I shoved him in the washtub of boiling water."

"You shoved him in the washtub of boiling water?"

"Yeah." His mouth opened and he breathed noisily through it. "I killed him, see. I killed him! That's the kind of guy I am."

"I don't believe it," said Mr. Jackson.

Yacob got out of the chair, his eyes enormous. "You don't believe it? You don't believe it?"

"No," said Mr. Jackson. "You couldn't have got burned like that from pushing him in. Why, your arms are mangled up to the elbows. You pulled him out, you fool, that's how you did that to yourself."

Yacob stared at his hands in a foolish, arrested way. He pulled up one sleeve and looked at the beef-colored, knotted flesh. For a second or two it seemed as if he had never seen it before. He dropped his hands to his sides and looked at Mr. Jackson with a peculiar vacuity. There was nothing in his face, nothing but a tortured reaching toward an impossible realization.

The sobs caught him from within, like a paroxysm, jerking him, flinging him like a figure on strings. They erupted from his throat, harsh, tearing sounds, hammering him forward, doubling him. He fell into the chair, letting go blindly, mashing his cap against his face. The words came from him in the shuddering inhalations of his breath, blurred gasping shards of sound.

"Cheez, Sasha . . . I all the time figgered . . . I killed you."

Mr. Jackson did not know what to do. There was nothing to do. He put both hands out twice. He would have liked to put his arms around the boy, but he was too shy of this terrible, this private grief. He went out of the printing room and closed the door.

Mr. Sparkman came in when recess was about over.

"How's it going?"

"Oh, pretty well," said Mr. Jackson. "I think I'll have something to show him."

"Good," said the principal. He washed his hands briskly, a gesture he had, an encouraging, let's-get-it-done gesture. "I think you've got that high-school job in a bag, if you can put on a good front. How about that kid that draws the leaves? Has he got something?"

Mr. Jackson walked down the aisle to where Charlie Catfits was working on a milkweed pod. It was, without doubt, his masterpiece, showing the feathery seeds ranked in perfect symmetry inside the opened shell. Charlie, however, was sitting idle. He was rubbing one dirt-incrusted hand across his pimply forehead.

"What's the matter, Charlie?"

"I don't feel so good."

Mr. Jackson felt a flash of pure horror at the idea of the absence of his star pupil. "Come on, Charlie, you're not really sick, are you? Where do you feel bad? Is your throat sore? Does your head ache?"

"No."

"What is it then?"

"Just a funny feeling."

"Oh, come, you're not going to let a little thing like that make you quit, are you? Why, you've got the drawing practically done. All you've got to do is finish the top, see? Come on now, stick with it and see if you can't get it done before noon."

Charlie heaved up his shoulders and made a wry face.

"Okay," he said.

After the boys came in Mr. Jackson labored with his trained seals again. It was harder than ever now, because the boys were excited from their exercise. Mr. Jackson yelled until he was hoarse and battered the newspaper to a ragged pulp. Sometimes he thought he must crack, that the halves of his brain would split down the middle if he went on another instant. Then he would think, "Maybe I'll never see them again. Maybe I'll be through with them. Maybe this is the last time." It gave him strength to gather himself together like the paralyzed fingers of a fist and plunge in again.

Within an hour or so he began to see some sign of the colloquy's rounding into shape. It had to round into shape. Time was creeping up on him. The forenoon was about gone.

He ran a finger around his wilted collar and swatted the newspaper on the board.

"One more time, Cookie. Get up to the board. Get up there! You, Guppy, remember you follow Marco. Come on now, Marco,—'Doesn't that look like our softball diamond?'

It was the frozen, dumbstruck look on Marco's face that made him turn around. Charlie was getting out of his seat. He had hold of the desk with both hands and he wrenched it completely from the floor. He staggered down the aisle, his eyeballs rolled up, a gurgling cry coming from his lips. The cry increased, became something ghastly, indescribable, a toneless roar.

The boys, with a single impetus, dropped books, chalk, erasers, and bolted out the door. Mr. Jackson found himself standing with his knees shaking, rooted like a senseless image. He saw Charlie fall, with no effort whatever to save himself, face forward on the floor.

With the perspiration pouring down his back and his knees wobbling like rubber, Mr. Jackson approached the boy. He had never seen an epileptic seizure before, had never known it could have such frightful physical manifestations. The boy's nose was bleeding where it had struck the floor. He took his handkerchief mechanically from his pocket and staunched it. His mind realized in a fumbling way that Charlie's "funny feeling" had been the aura, the premonitory symptom that warns an epileptic of an attack.

On the floor lay the drawing of a milkweed pod, mashed by somebody's foot, a huge gouge down the middle where the drawing pencil had slipped off the paper.

Mr. Jackson remained for some moments with his eyes closed and his lips quiveringly compressed. To the first cautious head that appeared in the door he said, "Get Mr. Sparkman."

When the principal arrived Charlie was stirring a little, over on his back now and making swallowing sounds.

"This is too bad," said Mr. Sparkman, "this is too bad." He washed his hands nervously. "It's the first time he's ever had one in school. What's his name—Charlie, isn't it?" He leaned down. "How do you feel, Charlie? Anything we can do for you?"

Charlie lay with his arms across his face. From beneath the ragged sweater sleeves tears leaked down. He moved his head back and forth in slow negation.

The two men stood helplessly and looked at him. "Have you got any place for him to lie down here?" asked Mr. Sparkman.

"No."

"I guess maybe you'd better take him home."

"I guess maybe I better had."

The two men carried him out to the parking shed behind the bungalow and put him in Mr. Jackson's car. He sat up unassisted and kept his head in his hands.

"Feel all right, Charlie?"

"Yeah."

His home was only a matter of four blocks away. It was a rickety cottage standing in a muddy plot behind an overturned garbage can. A woman in an apron with a tired face answered the door.

"Charlie got sick at school," said Mr. Jackson. "I thought maybe I'd better bring him home."

"Oh. All right."

There were a couple of chairs on a scuffed carpet and a lumpy couch by the open window. Charlie sat down on the couch.

"I think he'd better stay home for a day or two," said Mr. Jackson.

The woman nodded, twisting her hands in her apron.

Something welled up in Mr. Jackson, something driving and enormous, a wild desire to say something, do something, just one crumb of palliation in the starkness of the room. It collapsed futilely inside him. There was nothing to say or do. You could only close the door and forget it.

He hesitated in the doorway. "Oh—uh—that cigar box of Charlie's. The box he keeps his drawings in. May I have it?"

The woman stared at him openmouthed a second, went off, and came back with the cigar box.

"Lemme see which ones they are," said Charlie.

Mr. Jackson reached out the box. Charlie grabbed it from him, cocked his arm, and hurled the box out the window. It hit the garbage can, burst flimsily, and spewed mud-splattered drawings over the ground.

"That's all you care about," cried Charlie. "The drawings. The drawings. Just so you can show off this afternoon. That's all you are, a showoff. I heard Sparky tellin' you about puttin' on a front so's to get into the high school. So that's what I was pluggin' for, that's what I bust a gut for, that's what you was soapin' me along for, eh? Cripes, what a sap I was, thinkin' maybe I was good or somethin', when all the time all I was doin' was helpin' you."

Mr. Jackson felt as if he had been hit with a mallet. How he got into the chair he had no conception, but he found himself sitting in it with his mouth slackly open. He sat and stared at the boy.

"You're right, Charlie," he said, and did not recognize his own voice. "You're the one to tell me off, all right. You're right, you were helping me. More than you'll ever know or I'll ever know. You were showing me someone with a man's heart inside him, not a sham."

"Ah, bushwah," said Charlie. "That's all you guys are full of, bushwah. What's the use of a guy like me? What can I ever do? You know there ain't nothin' in them drawings. They're just somethin' you can brag about, to show what a guy with fits did."

Mr. Jackson covered his face with his hands. When he took them away the palms were cold with sweat.

"No, Charlie. Never say that about those drawings. They're the best drawings I ever saw. I'll be proud to pick them out of the mud. I'm going to take them back and show them anyway. If it's the last

thing I ever do, I'm going to make you proud of them too."

The visit of inspection, at two o'clock that afternoon, went off with surprising smoothness. Cookie drew the square on the board, Guppy and the others asked their questions, and if the colloquy sounded a little stilted it could no doubt be put down to shyness before a stranger. The rest of the boys sat like Mrs. Jarley's waxworks.

The drawings made a deep impression on Mr. Kedgery.

"Hang them in the high school?" he said. "Why, certainly I'll have it done. I'm going to arrange for the art department to provide him with materials. I think the boy has an extraordinary talent."

There was only one moment of crisis, when Marco, with his wild dramatic sense, volunteered to read something for the visitor. He got up and with galloping declamation delivered *The Giant with the Hundred Heads*. Mr. Kedgery, because he did not wish to see it, did not observe that the reader in his hand was upside down.

At the three-minute recess the two men walked across the schoolyard toward Mr. Kedgery's car at the curb. "I think you have done very creditably," said the Superintendent. "I know what a difficult, hopeless problem the bulk of these boys represent."

They passed the parking shed, where Yacob, with a dirty cloth in his hand, was awkwardly wiping off Mr. Jackson's car. A hundred feet or so further on, at his own car, Mr. Kedgery stopped with his foot on the running board.

"Mr. Jackson," he said, "there is an opening for an eleventh-grade teacher of mathematics. How would you like to teach at the high school?"

"Thank you," said Mr. Jackson. He looked at the drawing in his hand, half a milkweed pod, the seeds ranked in exquisite perfection almost to the top, where a pencil line gouged sharply downward across the paper. "I . . . Thank you very much, but the fact is, I'd rather stay here."

"What?" said the astounded Superintendent. "You prefer to stay here?"

"Yes, I . . . believe I do."

When Mr. Kedgery had driven up the block Mr. Jackson went back to the bungalow. The boys had returned and bedlam had broken out again. Mr. Jackson leaned against the door, a stooped, ungainly man who had missed his golden opportunity. He took the rolled newspaper from his pocket and began beating it on the door. "Silence! Silence!" he shouted at the top of his voice.

discussion

Mr. Jackson's class is real. Many school districts put students from several schools who are resistant to learning together in a small class with little regard for the etiology of their resistance. This class is usually located in rooms at the end of the corridor or in an isolated bungalow but always at some distance from the office. The special class is sometimes moved yearly to whichever school in the district has a vacant classroom. The teacher often changes with the room location, for the teaching life expectancy of such classes is very short.

Poor Mr. Jackson! Using special methods, materials, and manpower had not been part of his expertise or expectation. After a first burst of enthusiasm based on good feeling toward children in need, Mr. Jackson resigned himself to the job of policeman. He represents the many new teachers for whom assignment to a special class of reluctant learners is the first rung on the ladder to a position teaching "regular" children.

Despite Mr. Jackson's decision at the end of the story to stay on with his boys, we doubt that he will be able to put down his rolled newspaper and stop futilely calling, "silence, silence." He may have built more trusted pathways of communication with some of his boys, but he is still without the basic tools to make time in that classroom worthwhile for the boys and himself. Unless his school district is committed to giving him some time and money, he is still doomed to failing the boys' needs and his own needs as a teacher. Mr. Jackson needs training in how to teach each of his students. It may very well be that each student needs a different approach to improving his reading skills. Mr. Jackson needs time to enlist community support to plan trips for his students, many of whom may learn best by having firsthand experiences. He also needs community support to gather together materials and manpower to help each boy begin to acquire vocational and recreational skills, and Mr. Jackson needs a great deal of help from a psychologist, counselor, or social worker both to keep in touch with his own feelings and frustrations and to adjust his expectations for each of his students. It is too easy for the teacher to declare all these students academically uneducable, untalented, or unskilled. Yet to learn about each boy's potential and to work around all the factors inhibiting that potential is too large a task for one person. Mr. Jackson needs the help of specialists to create individual programs and provide needed services for each boy and his family.

Mr. Jackson has just begun to explore the reasons that Yacob is hostile and presently a danger to others. There is so much more to be done with skilled therapy for him. An I.Q. score of 55 is probably highly misleading in light of his Lithuanian background and emotional trauma. Charlie needs medical treatment and emotional counseling for his epilepsy. His compulsive but beautiful drawings may be the touchstone for fulfillment in the future.

Should the school district try to meet all the needs of these children? School districts must assume responsibility for the students who are most troubled academically and socially. Although they may pay heavily in terms of appropriate services during these children's years in school, society pays far more heavily when these students leave school without such services. It is known that a large percent of young people, particularly boys in state-supported reform schools have reading levels several grades below their chronological age. Fortunately, legislators are becoming aware that schools are the place for early identification of multi-problem children and families. Nevertheless, even with more specialized help, Mr. Jackson's job with ten or twelve students with such differing and inclusive problems will still be difficult, and progress will be very slow.

springboards for inquiry

1. Give several reasons why the printing room was a particularly inappropriate project for this class.

2. Read and react to the use of a token economy (reward system) to motivate on-task behavior and facilitate learning in a class like this.[1]

3. Outline in some detail what a counselor, psychologist, and social worker could do to help Mr. Jackson. You may wish to interview these pupil personnel workers in a school district to answer this question.

4. If you were assigned a class like this, what would be some of your goals for your students and how would you carry them out?

5. Select one student from this class and describe how you would go about analyzing his learning problems and how you would go about remedying them.

---

[1]Frank M. Hewett, *The Emotionally Disturbed Child in the Classroom* (Boston: Allyn & Bacon, 1968).

the physically handicapped

Physically handicapped children are those with impaired vision or hearing, children with speech handicaps or orthopedic handicaps, children with neurological impairment such as cerebral palsy, and those with chronic health problems.[1] Educationally, these children probably will not all need school programs adapted to their handicap, but most will need personal and vocational counseling in order to better understand their disabilities and utilize their abilities.

The child who has been protected in the environment of his home where families make special provision for the disability will suddenly and repeatedly have his deviance brought to his attention as soon as he reaches school age and associates with age-mates. Johnson stresses the need for early positive action to help a child accept and compensate for his limitations.[2] Although some physically handicapped children will be protected through the school years with some form of special education, they cannot live in a handicapped society all their lives, and they must be taught to cope effectively in the broader nonhandicapped society.

Education for the physically disabled child used to be offered exclusively in residential schools. The trend since World War II toward the community day school has been promoted by well-organized parent groups, by professional and lay organizations interested in the welfare of the physically handicapped, as well as by agencies within state departments of education specially created to meet the needs of the handicapped child.

The distribution of educational and diagnostic services is still problematic. Resources for early diagnosis and education are overtaxed in large urban areas and nonexistent in rural areas. Children in sparsely populated areas have no choice but to attend residential schools in order to receive the treatment and education they require.

There is an urgency about developing programs for earlier identification and treatment of particular categories of physical disability. Children who have speech problems related to physical irregularities such as cleft palate, cleft lip, and voice disorders are in need of extensive early speech training. The hearing-impaired child must also be identified early. Current research indicates the critical period for language learning is age one to four.[3] Concept formation is inadequate when early preschool training is unavailable to children with this handicap. Some world famous centers in

[1]William M. Cruickshank, "The Physically Handicapped Child," in *Education of Exceptional Children and Youth*, ed. William M. Cruickshank and G. Orville Johnson (Englewood Cliffs, N.J.: Prentice-Hall, 1967).

[2]G. Orville Johnson, "Guidance for Exceptional Youth," in *Education of Exceptional Children and Youth*.

[3]Edgar Lowell, "Psycho-Educational Management of the Young Deaf Child," in *Deafness in Childhood*, ed. Freeman McConnell and Paul H. Ward (Nashville: Vanderbilt University Press, 1967).

the United States such as the Tracy Clinic and the Lexington School for the Deaf provide diagnosis, training, and counseling for parents, but there are not nearly enough resources for the deaf child.

Education for the visually handicapped child used to be carried out in sight-saving classrooms. Since the admonition to conserve sight as a therapeutic measure is no longer accepted, many blind and partially sighted students are integrated into regular classrooms and receive additional help from a special teacher in a resource room for some period of time during the school day.

Controversy continues regarding special day schools in the community as opposed to mainstreaming physically handicapped students into regular classrooms with periods of help from a teacher with special training. Soldwedel and Terill did a sociometric study of the integration of the physically handicapped child into the regular school.[4] Putting the handicapped child in close physical proximity with the normal child does not insure social acceptance. Factors such as the personality of the handicapped child, the composition of the class, and the sensitivity of the teacher account for the success of mainstreaming versus grouping in special schools or classes.

Instead of applying either of these philosophies to all handicapped children, each child's case should be assessed to determine the best educational arrangement for the child. The child and his family, as well as school personnel, should be included in decision making.

Hortense Calisher

A wreath for Miss Totten

"What's your name?" she said.
"Ull—ee." The word came out in a glottal, molasses voice, hardly articulate, the *l*'s scarcely pronounced.
"Lilly?"
The girl nodded.

Children growing up in the country take their images of integrity from the land. The land with its changes is always about them, a pervasive truth, and their midget foregrounds are criss-crossed with minute dramas which are the animalcules of a larger vision. But children

Reprinted by permission of Robert Lantz-Candida Donadio Literary Agency, Inc. Copyright © 1951 by Hortense Calisher.

who grow in a city where there is nothing greater than the people brimming up out of subways, rivuleting in the streets—these children must take their archetypes where and if they find them.

In P.S. 146, between periods, when the upper grades were shunted through the halls in that important procedure known as "departmental," most of the teachers stood about chatting relievedly in couples;

[4]B. Soldwedel, and I. Terrill, "Sociometric Aspects of Physically Handicapped and Non-Handicapped Children in the Same Elementary School," *Journal of Exceptional Children* 23 (1957): 371–83.

Miss Totten, however, always stood at the door of her "home room," watching us straightforwardly, alone. As, straggling and muffled, we lined past the other teachers, we often caught snatches of upstairs gossip which we later perverted and enlarged; passing before Miss Totten we deflected only that austere look, bent solely on us.

Perhaps with the teachers, as with us, she was neither admired nor loathed but simply ignored. Certainly none of us ever fawned on her as we did on the harshly blonde and blue-eyed Miss Steele, who never wooed us with a smile but slanged us delightfully in the gym, giving out the exercises in a voice like scuffed gravel. Neither did she obsess us in the way of the Misses Comstock, two liverish, stunted women who could have had nothing so vivid about them as our hatred for them. And though all of us had a raffish hunger for metaphor, we never dubbed Miss Totten with a nickname.

Miss Totten's figure, as she sat tall at her desk or strode angularly in front of us rolling down the long maps over the blackboard, had that instantaneous clarity, one metallic step removed from the real, of the daguerreotype. Her clothes partook of this period too—long, saturnine waists and skirts of a stuff identical with that in a good family umbrella. There was one like it in the umbrella stand at home—a high black one with a seamed ivory head. The waists enclosed a vestee of dim but steadfast lace; the skirts grazed narrow boots of that etiolated black leather, venerable with creases, which I knew to be a sign of both respectability and foot trouble. But except for the vestee, all of Miss

Totten, too, folded neatly to the dark point of her shoes, and separated from these by her truly extraordinary length, her face presided above, a lined, ocher ellipse. Sometimes, on drowsy afternoons, her face floated away altogether and came to rest on the stand at home. Perhaps it was because of this guilty image that I was the only one who noticed Miss Totten's strange preoccupation with Mooley Davis.

Most of us in Miss Totten's room had been together as a group since first grade, but we had not seen Mooley since down in second grade, under the elder and more frightening of the two Comstocks. I had forgotten Mooley completely but when she reappeared I remembered clearly the incident which had given her her name.

That morning, very early in the new term, back in Miss Comstock's, we had lined up on two sides of the classroom for a spelling bee. These were usually a relief to good and bad spellers alike, since they were the only part of our work which resembled a game, and even when one had to miss and sit down there was a kind of dreamy catharsis in watching the tenseness of those still standing. Miss Comstock always rose for these occasions and came forward between the two lines, standing there in an oppressive close-up in which we could watch the terrifying action of the cords in her spindling gray neck and her slight smile as someone was spelled down. As the number of those standing was reduced, the smile grew, exposing the oversize slabs of her teeth, through which the words issued in a voice increasingly unctuous and soft.

On this day the forty of us still

shone with the first fall neatness of new clothes, still basked in that delightful anonymity in which neither our names nor our capacities were already part of the dreary foreknowledge of the teacher. The smart and quick had yet to assert themselves with their flying, staccato hands; the uneasy dull, not yet forced into recitations which would make their status clear, still preserved in the small, sinking corners of their hearts a lorn, factitious hope. Both teams were still intact when the word "mule" fell to the lot of a thin colored girl across the room from me, in clothes perky only with starch, her rusty fuzz of hair drawn back in braids as tightly sectioned as if a strong, pulling hand had taken hold of the braids.

"Mule," said Miss Comstock, giving out the word. The ranks were still full. She had not yet begun to smile.

The girl looked back at Miss Comstock, soundlessly. All her face seemed drawn backward from the silent, working mouth, as if a strong, pulling hand had taken hold of the braids.

My turn, I calculated, was next. The procedure was to say the word, spell it out and say it again. I repeated it in my mind: Mule, M-u-l-e. Mule.

Miss Comstock waited quite a long time. Then she looked around the class, as if asking them to mark well and early her handling of the first malfeasance.

"What's your name?" she said.

"Ull—ee." The word came out in a glottal, molasses voice, hardly articulate, the *l*'s scarcely pronounced.

"Lilly?"

The girl nodded.

"Lilly what?"

"Duh—avis."

"Oh. Lilly Davis. Mmmm. Well, spell 'mule,' Lilly." Miss Comstock trilled out the name beautifully.

The tense brown bladder of the girl's face swelled desperately, then broke at the mouth. "Mool," she said, and stopped. "Mmm—ooo—"

The room tittered. Miss Comstock stepped closer.

"*Mule!*"

The girl struggled again. "Mool."

This time we were too near Miss Comstock to dare laughter.

Miss Comstock turned to our side. "Who's next?"

I half raised my hand.

"Go on." She wheeled around on Lilly, who was sinking into her seat. "No. Don't sit down."

I lowered my eyelids, hiding Lilly from my sight. "Mule," I said. "M-u-l-e. Mule."

The game continued, words crossing the room uneventfully. Some children survived. Others settled, abashed, into their seats, craning around to watch us. Again the turn came around to Lilly.

Miss Comstock cleared her throat. She had begun to smile.

"Spell it now, Lilly," she said. "Mule."

The long-chinned brown face swung from side to side in an odd writhing movement. Lilly's eyeballs rolled. Then the thick sound from her mouth was lost in the hooting, uncontrollable laughter of the whole class. For there was no doubt about it: the long, coffee-colored face, the whitish glint of the eyeballs, the bucking motion of the head suggested it to us all—a small brown quadruped, horse or mule, crazily stubborn or at bay.

"Quiet!" said Miss Comstock.

And we hushed, although she had not spoken loudly. For the word had smirked out from a wide, flat smile and on the stringy neck beneath there was a creeping, pleasurable flush which made it pink as a young girl's.

That was how Mooley Davis got her name, although we had a chance to use it for only a few weeks, in a taunting singsong when she hung up her coat in the morning or as she flicked past the little dustbin of a store where we shed our pennies for nigger babies and tasteless, mottoed hearts. For after a few weeks, when it became clear that her cringing, mucoused talk was getting worse, she was transferred to the "ungraded" class. This group, made up of the mute, the shambling and the oddly tall, some of whom were delivered by bus, was housed in a basement, with a separate entrance which was forbidden us not only by rule but by a lurking distaste of our own.

The year Mooley reappeared in Miss Totten's room, a dispute in the school system had disbanded all the ungraded classes in the city. Here and there in the back seat of a class now there would be some grown-size boy who read haltingly from a primer, fingering the stubble of his slack jaw. Down in 4-A there was a shiny, petted doll of a girl, all crackling hair bow and nimble wheel chair, over whom the teachers shook their heads feelingly, saying, "Bright as a dollar! Imagine!" as if there were something sinister in the fact that useless legs had not impaired the musculature of a mind. And in our class, in harshly clean, faded dresses which were always a little too infantile for her, her spraying ginger hair cut short now and held by a round comb which circled the back of her head like a snaggle-toothed tiara which had slipped, there was this bony, bug-eyed wraith of a girl who raised her hand instead of saying "Present!" when Miss Totten said "Lilly Davis?" at roll call, and never spoke at all.

It was Juliet Hoffman who spoke Mooley's nickname first. A jeweler's daughter, Juliet had achieved an eminence even beyond that due her curly profile, embroidered dresses and prancing, leading-lady ways when, the Christmas before, she had brought as her present to teacher a real diamond ring. It had been a modest diamond, to be sure, but undoubtedly real, and set in real gold. Juliet had heralded it for weeks before and we had all seen it—it and the peculiar look on the face of the teacher, a young substitute whom we hardly knew, when she had lifted it from the pile of hankies and fancy note paper on her desk. The teacher, over the syrupy protests of Mrs. Hoffman, had returned the ring, but its sparkle lingered on, iridescent around Juliet's head.

On our way out at three o'clock that first day with Miss Totten, Juliet nudged at me to wait. Obediently, I waited behind her. Twiddling her bunny muff, she minced over to the clothes closet and confronted the new girl.

"I know you," she said. "Mooley Davis, that's who you are!" A couple of the other children hung back to watch. "Aren't you? Aren't you Mooley Davis?"

I remember just how Mooley stood there because of the coat she wore. She just stood there holding her coat against her stomach with both hands. It was a coat of some pale, vague tweed, cut the same length as mine. But it wrapped the wrong way over for a girl and the revers, wide ones, came all the way down and ended way below the pressing hands.

"Where you been?" Juliet flipped us all a knowing grin. "You been in ungraded?"

One of Mooley's shoulders inched up so that it almost touched her ear, but beyond that she did not seem able to move. Her eyes looked at us, wide and fixed. I had the feeling that all of her had retreated far, far back behind the eyes, which, large and light and purposefully empty, had been forced to stay.

My back was to the room but on the suddenly wooden faces of the others I saw Miss Totten's shadow. Then she loomed thinly over Juliet, her arms, which were crossed at her chest, hiding the one V of white in her garments so that she looked like an umbrella tightly furled.

"What's *your* name?" she asked, addressing not so much Juliet as the white muff, which, I noticed now, was slightly soiled.

"Jooly-ette."

"Hmm. Oh, yes. Juliet Hoffman."

"Jooly-ette, it is." She pouted creamily up at Miss Totten, her glance narrow with the assurance of finger rings to come.

Something flickered in the nexus of yellow wrinkles around Miss Totten's lips. Poking out a bony forefinger, she held it against the muff. "You tell your mother," she said slowly, "that the way she spells it, it's *Juliet.*"

Then she dismissed the rest of us but put a delaying hand on Mooley. Turning back to look, I saw that she had knelt down painfully, her skirt hem graying in the floor dust, and,

staring absently over Mooley's head, she was buttoning up the wrongly shaped coat.

After a short, avid flurry of speculation we soon lost interest in Mooley and in the routine Miss Totten devised for her. At first, during any kind of oral work, Mooley took her place at the blackboard and wrote down her answers, but later Miss Totten sat her in the front row and gave her a small slate. She grew very quick at answering, particularly in "mental arithmetic" and in the card drills when Miss Totten held up large manila cards with significant locations and dates inscribed in her Palmer script, and we went down the rows, snapping back the answers.

Also, Mooley had acquired a protector in Ruby Green, the other Negro girl in the class—a huge, black girl with an arm-flailing, hee-haw way of talking and a rich contralto singing voice which we had often heard in solo at Assembly. Ruby, boasting of her singing in night clubs on Saturday nights, of a father who had done time, cowed us all with these pungent inklings of the world on the other side of the dividing line of Amsterdam Avenue, that deep, velvet murk of Harlem which she lit for us with the flash of razors, the honky-tonk beat of the "numbahs" and the plangent wails of the mugged. Once, hearing David Hecker, a doctor's son, declare, "Mooley has a cleft palate, that's what," Ruby wheeled and put a large hand on his shoulder in menacing caress.

"She ain't got no cleff palate, see? She talk sometime, roun' home." She glared at us each in turn with such a pug scowl that we flinched, thinking she was going to spit. Ruby giggled. "She got no cause to talk, roun' here. She just don' need to bother." She lifted her hand from David, spinning him backward, and joined arms with the silent Mooley. "Me neither!" she added, and walked Mooley away, flinging back at us her gaudy, syncopated laugh.

Then one day, lolloping home after three, I suddenly remembered my books and tam and above all my homework assignment, left in the pocket of my desk at school. I raced back there. The janitor, grumbling, unlocked the side door at which he had been sweeping and let me in. In the mauve, settling light the long maw of the gym held a rank, uneasy stillness. I walked up the spiral metal stairs feeling that I thieved on some part of the school's existence not intended for me. Outside the ambushed quiet of Miss Totten's room I stopped, gathering breath. I heard voices, one surely Miss Totten's dark, firm tones, the other no more than an arrested gurgle and pause.

I opened the door slowly. Miss Totten and Mooley raised their heads. It was odd, but although Miss Totten sat as usual at her desk, her hands clasped to one side of her hat, lunch box and the crinkly boa she wore all spring, and although Mooley was at her own desk in front of a spread copy of our thick reader, I felt the distinct, startled guilt of someone who interrupts an embrace.

"Yes?" said Miss Totten. Her eyes had the drugged look of eyes raised suddenly from close work. I fancied that she reddened slightly, like someone accused.

"I left my books."

Miss Totten nodded and sat wait-ing. I walked down the row to my desk and bent over, fumbling for my things, my haunches awkward under the watchfulness behind me. At the door, with my arms full, I stopped, parroting the formula of dismissal. "Good afternoon, Miss Totten."

"Good afternoon."

I walked home slowly. Miss Totten, when I spoke, had seemed to be watching my mouth, almost with enmity. And in front of Mooley there had been no slate.

In class the next morning, as I collected the homework in my capacity as monitor, I lingered a minute at Mooley's desk, expecting some change, perhaps in her notice of me, but there was none. Her paper was the same as usual, written in a neat script quite legible in itself but in a spidery backhand that just faintly silvered the page, like a communiqué issued out of necessity but begrudged.

Once more I had a glimpse of Miss Totten and Mooley together, on a day when I had joined the slangy, athletic Miss Steele, who was striding capably along in her Ground Grippers on the route I usually took home. Almost at once I had known I was unwelcome, but I trotted desperately in her wake, not knowing how to relieve her of my company. At last a stitch in my side forced me to stop, in front of a corner fishmonger's.

"Folks who want to walk home with me have to step on it!" said Miss Steele. She allotted me one measuring, stone blue glance and moved on.

Disposed on the bald white window stall of the fish store there was a rigidly mounted eel that looked as if only its stuffing prevented it from growing onward, sinuously, from either impersonal end. Beside it were several tawny shells. A finger would have to avoid the spines on them before being able to touch their rosy, pursed throats. As the pain in my side lessened, I raised my head and saw my own face in the window, egg-shaped and sad. I turned away. Miss Totten and Mooley stood on the corner, their backs to me, waiting to cross. A trolley clanged by, then the street was clear, and Miss Totten, looking down, nodded gently into the black boa and took Mooley by the hand. As they passed down the hill to St. Nicholas Avenue and disappeared, Mooley's face, smoothed out and grave, seemed to me, enviably, like the serene, guided faces of children seen walking securely under the restful duennaship of nuns.

Then came the first day of Visiting Week, during which, according to convention, the normal school day would be on display but for which we had actually been fortified with rapid-fire recitations which were supposed to erupt from us in sequence—like the somersaults which climax acrobatic acts. On this morning, just before we were called to order, Dr. Piatt, the principal, walked in. He was a gentle man, keeping to his office like a snail, and we had never succeeded in making a bogey of him, although we tried. Today he shepherded a group of mothers and two men, officiously dignified, all of whom he seated on some chairs up front at Miss Totten's left. Then he sat down too, looking upon us benignly, his head cocked a little to one side in a way he had, as if he hearkened to

some unseen arbiter who whispered constantly to him of how bad children could be but he benevolently, insistently continued to disagree.

Miss Totten, alone among the teachers, was usually immune to visitors, but today she strode restlessly in front of us, and as she pulled down the maps one of them slipped from her hand and snapped back up with a loud, flapping roar. Fumbling for the roll book, she sat down and began to call the roll, something she usually did without looking at the book, favoring each of us with a warning nod instead.

"Arnold Ames?"

"Pres-unt!"

"Mary Bates?"

"Pres-unt!"

"Wanda Becovic?"

"Pres-unt!"

"Sidney Cohen?"

"Pres-unt!"

"L—Lilly Davis?"

It took us a minute to realize that Mooley had not raised her hand. A light impatient groan rippled over the class. But Mooley, her face uplifted in its blank, cataleptic stare, was looking at Miss Totten. Miss Totten's own lips moved. There seemed to be a cord between her lips and Mooley's. Mooley's lips moved, opened.

"Pres-unt!" said Mooley.

The class caught its breath, then righted itself under the sweet, absent smile of the visitors. With flushed, lowered lids but in a rich, full voice, Miss Totten finished calling the roll. Then she rose and came forward with the manila cards. Each time, she held up the name of a State and we answered with its capital city.

Pennsylvania.

"Harrisburg!" said Arnold Ames.
Illinois.
"Springfield!" said Mary Bates.
Arkansas.
"Little Rock!" said Wanda Becovic.
North Dakota.
"Bismarck!" said Sidney Cohen.
Idaho.
We were afraid to turn our heads.
"Buh . . . Boise!" said Mooley Davis.
After this we could hardly wait for the turn to come around to Mooley again. When Miss Totten, using a pointer against the map, indicated that Mooley was to "bound" the State of North Carolina, we focused with such attention that the visitors, grinning at each other, shook their heads at such zest. But Dr. Piatt was looking straight at Miss Totten, his lips parted, his head no longer to one side.
"N-North Cal . . . Callina." Just as the deaf gaze at the speaking, Mooley's eyes never left Miss Totten's. Her voice issued, burred here, choked there, but unmistakably a voice. "Bounded by Virginia on the north . . . Tennessee on the west . . . South Callina on the south . . . and on the east . . . and on the east . . ." She bent her head and gripped her desk with her hands. I gripped my own desk, until I saw that she suffered only from the common failing—she had forgotten. She raised her head.
"And on the east," she said joyously, "and on the east by the Atlannic Ocean."
Later that term Miss Totten died. She had been forty years in the school system, we heard in the eulogy at Assembly. There was no immediate family, and any of us who

cared to might pay our respects at the chapel. After this, Mr. Moloney, who usually chose "Whispering" for the dismissal march, played something slow and thrumming which forced us to drag our feet until we reached the door.
Of course none of us went to the chapel, nor did we bother to wonder whether Mooley went. Probably she did not. For now that the girl withdrawn for so long behind those rigidly empty eyes had stepped forward into them, they flicked about quite normally, as captious as anyone's.
Once or twice in the days that followed we mentioned Miss Totten, but it was really death that we honored, clicking our tongues like our elders. Passing the umbrella stand at home I sometimes thought of Miss Totten, furled forever in her coffin. Then I forgot her too, along with the rest of the class. After all, this was only reasonable in a class which had achieved Miss Steele.
But memory, after a time, dispenses its own emphasis, making a feuilleton of what we once thought most ponderable, laying its wreath on what we never thought to recall. In the country, the children stumble upon the griffin mask of the mangled pheasant and they learn; they come upon the murderous love knot of the mantis and they surmise. But in the city, although no man looms very large against the sky, he is silhouetted all the more sharply against his fellows. And sometimes the children there, who know so little about the natural world, stumble upon that unsolicited good which is perhaps only a dislocation in the insensitive rhythm of the natural world. And if they are lucky, memory holds it in waiting.

For what they have stumbled upon
is their own humanity—their aber-
ration and their glory. That is why I

find myself wanting to say aloud to
someone: "I remember . . . a Miss
Elizabeth Totten."

discussion

Hortense Calisher is probably one of the best short story writers in America
today. She is a careful craftsman always finding the precise word to express
what she wants to say.

As the author observes, in second grade the capacities of the students are
not fully known. Even with good testing procedures, it is known that in the
lower age ranges diagnoses of disabilities are necessarily tentative. When
evidence of deviance is found, as in Lilly Davis' case, the child is assigned to
the ungraded class. The decision to place a child in special education is usually made when the child is eight or nine years of age. The school's assignment may be the first indication to parents that their child is significantly
deviant from other children. The mildly mentally-retarded child with no
physical sign of deviance is a particularly startling discovery for parents.

Because of imprecise testing, it is not unusual to find quite a wide range
of problems among children in the special or ungraded class. Sometimes a
child is placed in a class for the retarded because his learning disability,
which has been undiagnosed, masks the child's intellect. Lilly Davis was
such a case. She probably had a cleft palate as David Hecker, the doctor's
son, mentions.

The disposition of the class to the basement, although not the best
choice, sometimes offers the special child some degree of protection from
name-calling by some children and misunderstanding by some adults. An
optimal environment is one in which the faculty of the special class articu-
lates well with the teaching staff of the school in which they are housed. In
this way the needs and problems of the special student can be interpreted.
In some activities such as auditorium programs and sports programs, the
special classes can be included. It is found that the normal child learns just
as much from his association with children with some problems as the latter
learn from him.

Miss Totten, without benefit of today's special consultation or training,
instinctively knows what to do to help Lilly. She devises methods for her to
respond, such as providing her with a slate so she can write answers which
she cannot say. In addition to providing aids for Lilly, Miss Totten under-
takes to help improve her speech. The bond that grows between Lilly and
Miss Totten is akin to the bond between a mother and her special child.

The differences in philosophy which lead to argument over whether to
educate handicapped students in separate or integrated classes has waxed
and waned over the years. It is not surprising that Lilly shows up in a regular class in the fourth grade. Probably a financial crisis has precipitated the
sudden change to integrated special education. Unfortunately, finances
sometimes dictate policy. Special classes are very expensive. They require
special teachers, a smaller pupil-to-teacher ratio, special supplies, and administrative and consultant time. Integrated programs are also expensive.

When the special student is mainstreamed into the regular classroom, unless paraprofessionals are available to aid the teacher, the educational process often breaks down for both normal and special students. Leadership, resource personnel, and sufficient funding are basics for adequately educating the physically handicapped child.

springboards for inquiry

1. Find out what procedures a teacher should follow when she discovers that she has a student with a handicap who seems to need additional help.

2. Discuss whether you think it would have been possible for Miss Totten to help Lilly Davis in social relationships with her classmates.

3. What do the other children in the class learn from Miss Totten as they observe her treatment of Lilly?

4. Interview a teacher in special education. How do the joys and hardships of her teaching position compare with those of a teacher in the regular classroom?

the gifted

In the 1950s interest in gifted children stemmed from the military and scientific challenge of Sputnik. In response to the Russian display of technical superiority, much criticism was heaped upon the schools for not identifying and nurturing talent, particularly scientific talent. As a result programs for the gifted began to proliferate. As with any new fad, interest in this aspect of education soon lost popular support.

Once again the federal government is renewing efforts to provide special opportunities for the gifted and the talented. In 1972 Sidney P. Marland, United States Commissioner of Education, set up a special office of Gifted and Talented Education in the Bureau of Education for the Handicapped.[1] Marland expressed concern that only 80,000 gifted children out of approximately 2,000,000 were receiving appropriate education. Noting the expedient nature of the gifted programs following Sputnik, he emphasized that the new interest in the gifted was "more soundly based."

Special instructional programs and opportunities for the gifted pose the problem of identifying these children. It is known that giftedness is to be found in all parts of society, among the disadvantaged and minorities as well as the affluent.[2] Yet the same testing instruments cannot be used for differentiating gifted students in all segments of society. A highly verbal, standardized, individually administered I.Q. test such as the Stanford-Binet, which is favored in identifying gifted middle and upper socioeconomic level Caucasian students, is not suitable for assessing disadvantaged students or those who are culturally different. Passow suggests that it is crucial that identification procedures for minority students stress a search for talent rather than be used as a basis for screening out and barring participation in programs for the gifted.[3] Acknowledging the problems in identification procedures, Magary and Freehill support the argument "a) for flexible and impermanent classification; and b) for research on identification procedures that will develop evaluation tools genuinely usable in working with and measuring the less privileged."[4]

Although the myth persists in society that intellectually superior individuals are fragile, neurotic eggheads, Terman found that the gifted are superior in varying degrees not only in intelligence but also in height,

[1]Sidney P. Marland, Jr., "Our Gifted and Talented Children—A Priceless National Resource," *Intellect* 101 (October 1972): 16–19.

[2]Maynard C. Reynolds, "Draft Policy Statement on Education for the Gifted: A Call for Response," *Exceptional Children* 39 (October 1972): 167–69.

[3]A. Harry Passow, "The Gifted and the Disadvantaged," *The National Elementary Principal* 51, no. 5 (February 1972): 24–26.

[4]James F. Margary, and Maurice F. Freehill, "Critical Questions and Answers Relating to School and Society in the Education of the Gifted," *The Gifted Child Quarterly* (Autumn 1972): pp. 185–94.

weight, strength, health, energy, and neuromuscular agility.[5] Some of the characteristics which distinguish them from other children and sometimes set them apart from their age-mates are their ability to conceptualize, the diversity and intensity of their interests, their ability to do independent learning, their critical thinking, and their intellectual curiosity.[6] Not all gifted children possess all these characteristics. There is much diversity among individual children within the gifted category. The general qualities which differentiate them from most other children, however, call for more than simple "enrichment" within the regular classroom. Specialized instruction in small groupings or individual independent work is needed to accommodate their individuality.

As with the handicapped, programming may include special self-contained classes, special grouping within the school day, or the use of a resource center for specialized instruction and exposure to talented and skilled resource personnel. Special schools for the gifted have also been tried. On the high school level, specialized public schools for the talented and gifted such as the High School of Music and Art and the Bronx High School of Science, both in New York City, have been very successful.

Among the continuing responsibilities of those interested in special education for the gifted and talented are the commitment (a) to furnish regional demonstration units to field test and assess model programs; (b) to develop better screening procedures, particularly for identifying the gifted and talented among minority groups and the disadvantaged; (c) to develop leadership and training programs for teachers who wish to specialize in the education of the gifted; (d) to develop a clearing house on education of the gifted and talented.[7]

Robert Rossner

**A hero like me:
a hero like you**

Reprinted from A Hero Like Me: A Hero Like You *by Robert Rossner, by permission of Saturday Review Press. Copyright © 1972 by Robert Rossner.*

So the word ILLUSION goes up on the blackboard in large block letters. Then a list of the illusions they know: rabbits out of hats, parallel lines that seem headed for collision, puppy love, and Santa Claus.

Exactly what is it that takes place inside a classroom? I wish I knew. After twelve years of teaching high-school English, I should be able to

[5]Lewis Madison Terman, B. T. Bladwin, and E. Bronson, "Mental and Physical Traits of a Thousand Gifted Children, *Genetic Studies of Genius* vol. 1, (Stanford, Ca.: Stanford University Press, 1926.)

[6]James J. Gallagher, *The Gifted Child in the Elementary School* (Washington, D.C.: National Education Association, 1969).

[7]*Education of the Gifted and Talented*, Report to the Congress of the U.S. by the U.S. Commissioner of Education (Washington, D.C.: National School Public Relations Association, 1971).

put it down on paper. But after twelve years I still keep finding surprises.

Example: A bright morning in November, with a hard blue sky beyond the windows and just enough breeze to rattle the shade against the glass. We are discussing *Jude the Obscure,* trying to tie up the loose ends of three weeks' worth of talk. What was Hardy trying to say through poor Jude Frawley? We talk about Jude's vision of Christminster, and we get onto the subject of Illusions. A favorite topic of mine—favorite because these kids need this particular lesson so badly and because (why deny it?) it's a lesson that works so well. So the word ILLUSION goes up on the blackboard in large block letters. Then a list of the illusions they know: rabbits out of hats, parallel lines that seem headed for collision, puppy love, and Santa Claus.

"All right," I say, cutting it off. "Now everyone knows what *illusion* means." I swing my legs down from the windowsill, where I've been perched throughout the discussion, and walk to the blackboard. Sixty eyes follow me. "Now, then . . . " I pick up a piece of chalk and print DIS in front of the word on the board. "What does *that* mean?"

"Separated from," Susie Winslow murmurs throatily. Her eyes blink twice and she twists a strand of coppery hair around her thumb. Susie will enter Radcliffe in February, an early-admission winner of a full scholarship.

"That's right, Susie." I circle the DIS for emphasis.

So *disillusion* means to separate from illusion. If you are separated from an illusion, I ask, then what are you left with?

Silence. The wind chitters the shade. Thirty watches tick. Finally Eric Marino half raises a hand. "Reality?"

"Sure," I agree. The class breathes again, grateful to Eric for getting them off the (imagined) spot. "Now," I continue, "which do you think is better for a person—illusion or reality?"

"Reality," Susie says.

"No—illusion," Mary Diamond says, nearly blushing. "Because illusions are nicer," she goes on, staring ferociously at me through harlequin glasses. "That's why they get invented in the first place. I mean, if reality were bearable, who'd need illusions?"

"Mary," I say solemnly, "there . . . is . . . no . . . Santa Claus. Can you bear that?"

General laughter. Mary *does* blush now, but sticks to her guns. "Okay," she says. "But maybe I couldn't have bore—borne?"

"Borne," I say.

"Borne it when I was four years old," she finishes in a rush. And pulls herself into a knot behind her desk.

"Adults are different," someone says.

"Some adults," I say. Slowly Mary is unknotting.

"All right," Eric sighs, his shaggy head resting on his hand. "So kids need them. But when you, like, grow up, you can take reality. It's a sign of, you know, being grown up. Right?"

Suddenly Alex Margolies, a hand in the air. "Mr. Harris?"

The classroom shrinks with sudden tension. A few kids turn their heads. Some ostentatiously refuse to look at him. I brace myself. "Yes, Alex?"

Short, blond, wedge-faced, black-rimmed glasses framing light blue eyes, skinny arms folded. "Has there ever been a true democracy?" *What's he up to now?* I wonder. "No, Alex. Not to my knowledge." "Athens," says Pete Borden, round chin jutting. "Sure," drawls Ames Grover. "If you forget about the slaves." "And the metics," I say. From behind the African mask Ames peers out at me in scorn as I explain. "Foreigners. In Athens only the native-born were citizens." "How about the children of the slaves?" Ames asks. "Did they get full citizenship?" Pause. "In Athens, I mean." For a sixteen-year-old, Ames is pretty subtle. "You'll have to ask your social-studies teacher," I say, and swing back to Alex. "What's your point, Alex?" "There's never been a true democracy," he says. "But there have been fascist states? True fascist states?" We smile at each other. It's a duel, and the class follows it in uneasy silence. They've probably lost track of the original discussion. "That's right, Alex." "Then wouldn't you say," he purrs, "that democracy is an illusion? But that fascism is reality?" Susie's face registers dismay. Unconsciously she stops tugging at her hair, lets her thumb caress the button she wears on her flat chest: MAKE LOVE NOT WAR. Alex, awaiting my answer, wears a button on the lapel of his blue blazer: DROP IT. The others are hushed. Will I avenge them? Or will this be a defeat for the Good Guys? "Fascism, Alex," I say slowly, thinking rapidly, "is based on an illusion—the illusion that a man who has muscles is necessarily smarter than a man without muscles. Democracy is based on reality—the reality that all men are born and all men will die."

The class melts into reverence. A tiny muscle twitches in Alex's jaw. I think to myself, *Harris, you're such a facile bastard. The Socrates of the acne set.* From the corner of my eye I can see Ronald Weiss scribbling furiously into his notebook, and I say, "Don't copy it down, Ronald. It won't be on the final."

Everyone laughs; everyone but Alex. A few minutes later the bell rings. Notebooks, slammed shut, are carried away. In twos and threes, kids break for the classroom door. Alex travels alone. I stuff books into my briefcase, ready for md-morning coffee. Pete Borden chases after me in the hallway.

"Mr. Harris," he says, "you're wrong."

"That's often true, Peter." But I slow down to accommodate him. "What am I wrong about this time?"

"You're trying to teach wisdom. That's wrong."

I bite down on the smile. "What's wrong with it?"

"You can't *teach* wisdom," he insists. "You can't *make* people wise."

"You can try," I say, only half-joking.

"Nope," he says firmly. "All you're doing is making the class think the way you do."

"It's better than nothing," I say.

He grins widely. "Have a nice weekend," he says—his farewell line every day but Friday—and lopes off to his next class. I smile to myself and go on toward the teachers' cafeteria. But for the rest of the morning I find myself remembering Pete

Borden's accusation and wondering if he's right on any or all counts:

Am I trying to teach wisdom?
Is it impossible to teach?
Am I making the kids think the way I do?
Is it better than nothing?

This is how teachers go crazy. Some teachers. That is a beautiful example, if I must say so. Nothing else that happened that day could top it. I led a nice little group of sophomores through the intricacies of adverbial clauses and somehow ended up talking of the value of nonacademic activities; I put in my daily period as teacher in charge of the medical room, distributing four bandages, three cough drops, and a dozen diatribes against hypochondria; and I ate lunch, which involved an encounter with Henry Griffin. As I knew it would on such a day.

"Ah, Mr. Harris," was his greeting, as he settled across from me at the table. "How are you this morning?"

"Fine," I said, and stirred coffee as though my life depended on it.

Henry Griffin removed plates and cutlery from his tray, arranged them symmetrically before him, pushed the empty tray to the end of the table so that its long and short edges were perfectly equidistant from the sides of the table, and rubbed his hands together. He was wearing his blue suit, which meant that his black one was at the cleaners. His scalp shone pinkly through snow-white hair, which probably proved that there was blood flowing in there somewhere. I bit into my sandwich and awaited the inevitable.

At last, after sampling a spoonful of his chicken broth, Henry shook his head at me. "Very interesting story in this morning's *Times*, Mr. Harris. I should think you've read it?"

"About the pornography auction?" I asked, deadpan. "No, I didn't get past the headline."

"That isn't the story I meant." His tone was reproving, as though to remind me that there were twenty-five years between us. "I was referring to the account of last night's tragic incident in Brooklyn."

"Oh, that." I nodded. "You mean the cop who got hit with the brick."

"Yes." He disposed of another spoonful of broth without bending his back an inch. "Now, it seems to me—of course, I may be wrong— that these people primarily do not *want* any police protection. Doesn't it seem that way to you?"

discussion

This selection from a novel views the gifted from the teacher's point of view. Mr. Harris' class is a mixture of advanced and gifted students. He seems to choose an assignment that is adequately challenging.

Mr. Harris' method of teaching is entirely teacher-centered. The students look to him not only as a resource person but also as the final word on what they should think. When confronted by Alex Margolies, Harris is uncomfortable. He sees the confrontation as a duel between himself and the student, and Mr. Harris has a vested interest in winning. Pete Borden, a student who truly understands democracy and freedom of thought, can tolerate a point of view which may be repugnant better than the teacher. Harris is sensitive enough to take Pete's criticism seriously. Unless Harris considers alternatives to his present style, we wonder if he is the best teacher for gifted students.

The teacher is the key to an effective program for the gifted. More important than the teacher's absolute knowledge of a particular field are his behavior and personal characteristics. Mr. Harris has some questionable attributes. He makes fun of Ronald to gain a laugh, but he also humiliates an overzealous student. Surely he can teach Ronald to be less test-conscious in a more appropriate way.

The report on educating the gifted states:

> In general, the successful teachers are highly intelligent, are interested in scholarly and artistic pursuits, have wide interests, are mature and unthreatened, possess a sense of humor, are more student-centered than their colleagues, and are enthusiastic about both teaching and advanced study for themselves.[1]

springboards for inquiry

1. Given the characteristics stated in *The Report to the Congress on the Gifted and Talented* how do you think Mr. Harris rates as a teacher of the gifted?

2. Would you enjoy teaching the gifted? State your reasons.

3. If you were assigned to a gifted class, could you think of some topics and/or ways you would teach gifted children?[2]

[1]Committee on Labor and Public Welfare and Subcommittee on Education, *Education of the Gifted and Talented,* Report to the Congress of the United States by the U.S. Commissioner of Education and Background Papers Submitted to the U.S. Office of Education, 1972 (Washington, D.C.: Government Printing Office, 1972), p. 43.

[2]For some ideas see Alex F. Osborn, *Applied Imagination* (New York: Scribner's, 1965.)

References

ADKINS, PATRICIA G. "A Call for Early Learning Centers." *Academic Therapy* 7 (Summer 1972): 447–50.

BARSCH, RAY H. *The Parent of the Handicapped Child.* Springfield, Ill.: Charles C. Thomas, 1968.

BIRCH, HERBERT G., ed. *Brain Damage in Children.* Baltimore: Williams and Wilkins, 1964.

CRUICKSHANK, WILLIAM M. "The Physically Handicapped Child." *Education of Exceptional Children and Youth.* Ed. Cruickshank, William M., and Johnson, G. Orville, Englewood Cliffs, N.J.: Prentice-Hall, 1967.

DUNN, L. M., ed. *Exceptional Children in the Schools.* New York: Holt, Rinehart and Winston, 1963.

Education of the Gifted and Talented. Report to the Congress of the U.S. Commissioner of Education. Washington, D.C., 1971.

GALLAGHER, JAMES J. *The Gifted Child in the Elementary School.* Washington, D.C.: National Education Association, 1969.

HEWETT, FRANK. "A Hierarchy of Educational Tasks in Children with Learning Disorders." *Exceptional Children* 31 (1964): 207–14.

KIRK, SAMUEL A. "The Illinois Test of Psycholinguistic Abilities: Its Origin and Implications." *Learning Disorders* 3. Ed. Hellmuth, Jerome. Seattle: Special Child Publications, 1968.

LOWELL, EDGAR. "Psycho-Educational Management of the Young Deaf Child." *Deafness in Childhood.* Ed. McConnell, Freeman, and Ward, Paul H. Nashville: Vanderbilt University Press, 1967.

MARGARY, JAMES F., and FREEHILL, MAURICE F. "Critical Questions and Answers Relating to School and Society in the Education of the Gifted." *The Gifted Child Quarterly* (Autumn 1972): 185–94.

MARLAND, SIDNEY P., JR. "Our Gifted and Talented Children—A Priceless National Resource." *Intellect* 101 (October 1972):16–19.

"Minimal Brain Dysfunction." *Medical World News,* May 22, 1970, pp. 30–36.

PASSOW, A. HARRY. "The Gifted and The Disadvantaged." *The National Elementary Principal* 51, no. 5 (February 1972): 24–28.

REYNOLDS, MAYNARD C. "Draft Policy Statement on Education for the Gifted: A Call for Response." *Exceptional Children* 39 (October 1972):167–69.

Rockefeller Brothers Fund. *The Pursuit of Excellence: Education and the Future of America.* New York: Doubleday, 1958.

SOLDWEDEL, B., and TERRILL, I. "Sociometric Aspects of Physically Handicapped and Non-Handicapped Children in the Same Elementary School." *Journal of Exceptional Children* 23 (1957):371–83.

SOLOWAY, MICHAEL, and TAYLOR, FRANK D. "The Madison Plan." *Instructor* 82 (November 1972):94–95.

SPOGEN, DAVID. "Take the Label Off the Handicapped Child." *Education Digest,* September 1972, pp. 44–46.

"Symposium No. 8." *Journal of Special Education* 6, no. 4 (Winter 1972):335–89.

TAICHERT, LOUISE C. *Childhood Learning, Behavior and the Family.* New York: Behavioral Publications, 1973.

TARNAPOL, LESTER, ed. *Learning Disabilities.* Springfield, Ill.: Merrill, 1969.

TERMAN, L. N.; BALDWIN, B. T.; and BRONSON, E. *Mental and Physical Traits of a Thousand Gifted Children.* Palo Alto, Ca.: Stanford University Press, 1926.

VALETT, ROBERT E. *Programming Learning Disabilities.* Belmont, Ca.: Fearon, 1969.

The School As Culture

One of the songs in the musical "Guys and Dolls" is "Sit Down, Sit Down, You're Rockin' the Boat," and the lyrics of this song epitomize the present cultural state of the American school. With somewhat more erudition, Herriott and Hodgkins say, "as an open system, however, [the school's] guiding consideration will be to maintain itself in a viable state—to maintain homeostasis."[1]

Biologists talk of the relationship of living things to one another in a specific environment as an ecosystem. As a sociocultural system, the school has much less control of the organization than one might find in a tropical fish tank. That is, the children in a school culture feed in and out each day and return to environments which may counteract the central purpose of the school.[2] Nonetheless the school is liable to cultural definition.

One need not be a Paul Goodman or Ivan Illich to attest to the fact that schools and individual classrooms exhibit their peculiar cultural attributes in definable ways. Professionals in the field of education like to say that they can "smell" a great school or classroom. Urged to give an operational definition of "smell" they resort either to jargon—"the interactional patterns are two-way"; or to slang—"it was zippy"; or to pedantry—"the support for the ego-structure of each child was deliberate, indeed obvious." Yet no matter how they choose to define it, it may be observed that they rarely say that they cannot identify it. It is entirely possible to approach the definition in a negative way. Paul Goodman's last chapter in *Compulsory Miseducation*[3] has an interesting definition of those kinds of college classrooms which are nonproductive. There is no shortage of books which attack the schools (this volume lists at least 20 of them). Few books eulogize educational institutions. In fact, were one to do a content analysis of the extent to which literary selections either eulogize or condemn the culture of the school, he would likely discover that the bizarre and unusual rather than solid, humdrum insights more often become the subject for the artist.

When a great scientist was asked what he needed to continue his scientific progress he allegedly quipped, "only stand out of my light." Most of the literature which has scientifically studied what happens in the lives of children in classrooms seems to clearly say that not only are schools and teachers not "staying out of the light" but they are *the* light in the classroom.[4] Silberman cites the bulletin board sign in a high school which

[1]Robert G. Herriott and Benjamin J. Hodgkins, *The Environment of Schooling: Formal Education as an Open System* (Englewood Cliffs, N.J.: Prentice-Hall, 1973), p. 90.

[2]With the exception of the fish tank analogy, this idea emanates from ibid., p. 89.

[3]Paul Goodman, *Compulsory Miseducation* (New York: Horizon Press, 1964).

[4]Philip Jackson, Marie Hughes, Herbert Kliebard, Arno Bellack, and others have all zeroed in on the fact that most classrooms are very teacher-dominated. For example, Jackson found that in the most teacher-dominated room, 80 percent of the conversation was teacher-initiated.

read: "FREE. Every Monday through Friday. Knowledge. Bring your own containers."[5] His implication is that the culture in that particular classroom says that there is a dispenser of knowledge, indeed 30 classrooms of them and they are all spelled T-E-A-C-H-E-R.

George Dennison says, "to give freedom means to stand out of the way of the formative powers possessed by others."[6] It takes no special perspicacity to conclude from the vast literature about and against the schools that the pivotal complaint is that the school culture infantalizes the learner. Infantilism is a condition that exists in children whose parents (and particularly their mothers), for whatever reasons, literally refuse to let their children mature. The children remain emotional pygmies.[7] We know of no volume critical of schools where the diminution of the individual within the school culture is not the taproot of the criticism. At a regional conference of the International Reading Association, Herbert Kohl was heard to say that the schools were stifling the young and perhaps playing a mother-role they were ill-suited to assume.[8] In a subsequent discussion others who had heard the remark stoutly defended the school culture as the place where what some termed *infantilism* was, in fact, a necessary state of affairs until the learner was mature enough to explore for himself. It might further be argued that what is called *infantilization* is really the result of the school's having to deal essentially with groups of children rather than with individuals and their inimitability. There are school cultures which, deploring the need for groups, have sought to individualize by putting even kindergarten children into direct, long-term contact with programmed materials which further remove the child from meaningful, human contact even though that contact is primarily in groups. In doing this they have substituted cold text and accompanying "exercises" for many of the benefits of the group culture of the classroom. Greer and Rubinstein, quoting Redl's *What We Learn from Children*, seem to agree that in schools a great many people share the same milieu, and for better or worse this precludes, or at least restricts individualization.[9]

Since B. F. Skinner's *Beyond Freedom and Dignity*[10] the battle over the kind of culture which should suffuse the schools has never ceased. Much of what a teacher does in a classroom constitutes its culture. Thus, if a token

[5]Charles E. Silberman, *Crisis in the Classroom* (New York: Random House, 1970), p. 148.

[6]George Dennison, *The Lives of Children* (New York: Random House, 1969).

[7]It is interesting to note the number of novels that have used the dwarf as symbols of folks in some way stunted who yet retain the urge to grow, to become, to expand their influence (even unrighteously) upon the cruel world that has produced them. Read Lagerkvist's *The Dwarf*, Grass' *The Tin Drum*. In both folk and fairy tale, too, the dwarf, elf, or other diminutive person seems to be a fountain of wisdom out of proportion to physical stature. Nor is it unusual for very small people to persevere and gain knowledge and "stature" out of proportion to their numbers in the population. Even in the entertainment world we have the figures of Sammy Davis, Jr., Edward G. Robinson, and others who personified little people becoming giant-like.

[8]October 11–13, 1973, in Boise, Idaho.

[9]Mary Greer and Bonnie Rubinstein, *Will the Real Teacher Please Stand Up?* (Pacific Palisades, Ca.: Goodyear, 1972), p. 121.

[10]B. F. Skinner, *Beyond Freedom and Dignity* (New York: Knopf, 1971).

economy[11] prevails, the culture of that classroom might seem to rest upon the notion that there is no point in relying upon the child's drive (autonomy) to excel; it must be assumed that he has little or none. Instead, the student is encouraged to display good academic (and social) behavior, for such behavior is reinforced by rewarding him with money, candy or playtime. When students are allowed to be self-motivated, a classroom culture in which there is freedom to choose what one wishes to learn pervades the atmosphere. There will be no evidence of rewards that are observable. The child's "inner drive" and the teacher's creation of a stimulating environment are the basic elements of such a classroom setting.

Evan Keislor cites the example of a fourth grade teacher who in September, in her progressive classroom, set up a variety of Mexican musical instruments, costumes, and handicrafts. Each display was done with imagination and a flair for the spectacular. Beautiful pictures of life in Mexico were everywhere. After fifteen minutes of allowing the children to browse and absorb the beautiful display, she called them together and asked what they would like to study as the new school year began.[12] You may conclude that the vote was unanimous. Who really made the decision to study Mexico? Obviously it was a shared decision. The children could have rejected the study of Mexico. By the time they reach the fourth grade, however, they have learned that when a teacher sets up the environment, he is pointing to the fact that he wants the class to "go along" with his planning. It is barely conceivable that they would reject these efforts of the teacher. Have they acted autonomously? Surely they had more choice than students whose teacher, instead of constructing an exciting atmosphere around Mexican regalia, simply asked, "well kids shall we study Mexico or Canada first this year?"

Suppose you were told that a group of children to be placed in your class in the upcoming academic year were tested and it was found that they were expected to really "spurt" ahead. Would your behavior differ qualitatively had you been told that the children you were going to teach next year were the least likely to succeed? An experiment matching teacher attitudes toward their students with preconceptions they had been given about those students is described in Rosenthal and Jacobsen's, *Pygmalion in the Classroom*. Their preface reads:

". . . it is enough to say that 20 percent of the children in a certain elementary school were reported to their teachers as showing unusual potential for intellectual growth. The names of these 20 percent of the children were drawn by means of a table of random numbers. . . . The names were drawn out of a hat. Eight months later the unusual or "magic" children showed significantly greater gains in I.Q. than did the remaining children who had not been singled out for

[11] A system whereby tangible rewards are given to children for schoolwork done.

[12] Evan Keislor, "The Instructional Environment and the Young Autonomous Learner," in *Changing Education*, ed. M. C. Wittrock (Englewood Cliffs, N.J.: Prentice-Hall, 1973), pp. 124–49. The reader might wish, after reading Skinner's *Beyond Freedom and Dignity*, to go to the various reviews of *Beyond Freedom and Dignity* in dozens of journals and finally read Scriven's "Freedom Beyond 'Beyond Freedom,'" in the volume cited in this footnote.

the teachers' attention. The change in the teachers' expectations . . . led to an actual change in the intellectual performance of these randomly selected children."[13]

The cultures of those classrooms had been materially changed because of an illusion that the teachers were encouraged to sustain—that some children were going to show dramatic intellectual growth while other children were doomed to have little success. The tangible behavioral and attitudinal change on the part of the teacher toward the 20 percent who would "spurt" accounted for the greater gains in I.Q. at the end of eight months. This experiment is a good example of self-fulfilling prophecy. That is, teachers tend to think that if what they expect (their prophecy) is fulfilled, then they have been successful. However, the teachers' biases, based on knowledge, art, morals, customs, etc., combine to define their expectations. Thus, every classroom is a unique culture resulting from the union or friction of the teacher's expectations and the class's desire or ability to meet those expectations.

The rules, regulations, and routines established in the classrooms are part of the culture fabricated by the teacher. Where these rules are benevolent and adapted to the child's developmental level, the culture of the classroom enhances the life in that room. Where there is participation, not merely mute acquiescence, the classroom culture encourages growth and fulfillment. When it is obvious that the teachers' messages to the students are sincere, are not inconsistent and contradictory, then it is more likely that the learning experience will be satisfactory.

Daniel Offer's important work with normal adolescent boys in a high school environment identified school life and school studies as the adolescent boys' most important areas of conflict.[14] Offer was surprised that very few students reported relations with their parents or sexual feelings as being major sources of their problems. Offer implies that the school culture should be as healthy as possible. However, Offer found that school cultures are often destructive when, for example, teachers' goals for students correlated highly with the youngster's social class. In one instance Offer indicates that two C+ students were counseled differently about the future because one came from a prestigious family, the other from a family where the father was a janitor. Despite the desire of the latter student to go to college and study history, he was told to become a construction worker and "makes lots of money."

It is especially disappointing to learn from Offer what has previously been reported by Edgar Friedenberg in *Coming of Age in America*.[15] Both report that the teachers most respected by faculty and students alike were the coaches and the leaders in sports activities. The students report over and over again that "the only teachers in the high school environment who

---

[13]Robert Rosenthal and Lenore Jacobson, *Pygmalion in the Classroom* (New York: Holt, Rinehart & Winston, 1968), pp. vii–viii.

[14]Daniel Offer, *The Psychological World of the Teen-ager* (New York: Basic Books, 1969).

[15]Edgar Friedenberg, *Coming of Age in America* (New York: Random House, 1965).

treat them as individuals" are athletic coaches.[16] Both authors report that coaches often serve as confidants and that they seem to be able to help students overcome emotional problems. While in general, the school environment is tense for both teachers and students, the students' relationships with their coaches is harmonious.[17] Quite probably this good feeling is related to the lower demands and expectations coaches require because they are often nonacademically oriented. Whatever the reason, the give and take relationships between the "jocks" and their adolescent students deserves further study since it may have real implications for the type of teacher personality needed for adolescents.

The world of the school is in many ways a distinct culture. It is a temporary one to be sure. It functions with commuter inhabitants who come and return to a familial and peer culture daily. The extent of its real influence is still not known. Offer and others report that students generally look back at their high school culture with nostalgia. The majority of adolescents report that they enjoyed their high school years even though they find it difficult to name any one teacher who helped them more than others. Whether the school culture is merely a sheep-dip or not may not be readily ascertainable. That it is, during the school years a very potent influence seems to be fairly evident.

[16]Offer, *Psychological World of the Teen-ager*, p. 42.

[17]Apparently there are widespread feelings that the Offer and Friedenberg allegations are off base. Indeed, quite the opposite feeling seems to be prevalent among those we have consulted. A recent conversation with Dean O.N. Hunter of the College of Health, Physical Education, and Recreation of the University of Utah relative to the topic suggested that indeed the data are more true than untrue. Despite some hard-headed tactics of P.E. teachers, there is incontrovertible evidence that they enjoy a closer rapport with students than the average run-of-the-mill teacher of academics.

the curriculum

Like the witches in *Macbeth* who are keeping watch over their boiling cauldrons the teacher in America is charged with tending the frothing curriculum pot. The pot is bubbling because (1) there is a wide chasm between student interest and community expectations, (2) there are countless materials available in a wide range of areas, (3) there is a strong push for individualizing instruction, and (4) the public has not clarified all of its own values in regard to the importance of creative versus cognitive learning—while accountability is one shibboleth, flexibility is another.

In faculty lounges across the country the exchange among teachers reflects their concern for providing a curriculum that is meaningful for the students yet not too far removed from community standards. Many parents cannot understand that the curriculum which was appropriate for them is not suitable for their children. They would like a no-nonsense 3-R curriculum to be pervasive. However, today's children between the ages of six and sixteen watch more hours of TV than they spend in school. They are immersed in a passive medium which dispenses instant gratification. These children obviously need a curriculum different from that which sufficed in the past. Today's curriculum must be more varied, visual and stimulating.

The educational press and media corporations have responded with a deluge of offerings. A visit to any county or university curriculum center will attest to the amazing variety of printed and visual materials now available for all grade levels and subject areas. Harnack in his book on curriculum emphasizes the teacher's dilemma as decision maker in selecting from this array of available materials.[1] It follows that teachers need training in order to approach critically the selection of materials. Teachers must be knowledgeable about the range of curriculum offering as well as discriminating in the selection of those materials which will meet the individual needs of the students in their classroom.

Individualization of instruction is the current focus in education. Responding to this imperative is one of the most absorbing tasks the teacher faces. For example, lesson plans for the teaching of reading must now take into account 25 to 30 abilities; no longer do plans for high, middle, and low reading groups suffice. The curriculum guide published by state and county, which covers a single grade level or department and previously was the major guide for curriculum decision making, is now merely a reference for today's teacher.

The community asks for accountability. By *accountability* is meant some proof of success. The public wants its money's worth. Accountability requires that teachers be able to diagnose the individual student's learning strengths and weaknesses and translate this information into meaningful instructional objectives. Therefore, while the classroom teacher is working

[1]Robert S. Harnack, *The Teacher: Decision Maker and Curriculum Planner* (Scranton, Penn.: International Textbook, 1968).

228

very hard to select and provide vital curriculum materials which are tailored to the individual needs of students, he must also be aware of his students' performance on standardized tests. Data regarding pupil achievement is often published in local papers. The community reacts to these scores by applying pressure on the school board, who in turn pressures the superintendent of schools, who in his turn cajoles the principals of the schools within his jurisdiction for better performance. In the end the buck stops at the classroom teacher's desk. An instance of this unremitting pressure is exemplified by a survey of a consortium of business and community leaders in Chicago who said that the Chicago public schools "appeared to be ineffective in preparing a large proportion of students for business careers."[2]

Curriculum innovation is characteristically the response to the continuing call from the public for school achievement. Ironically some of these "new" curricular options are adoptions of earlier philosophies of education. As an example, the Montessori method is flourishing in programs from preschool through the grades.[3] The attraction of the Montessori method is its emphasis on letting children learn through the five senses in a prepared environment. The Montessori apparatus is self-correcting and offers an opportunity to learn concepts through the use of concrete materials in a step by step progression.

Curriculum changes also reflect recent research in children's thought processes and abilities to comprehend information. Bruner's work on learning has influenced math and science programs at elementary and high school levels.[4] These new courses emphasize concept learning over rote learning of facts that become obsolete with new technology.

School districts, aware of the importance of the issues in curriculum innovation, provide curriculum in-service education as well as curriculum consultants to work with teachers. Thus, the teachers tending the frothing curriculum pot are surrounded by both adversaries and sympathizers.

[2]Herbert J. Walberg and Jeanne Sigler, "Business Views Education in Chicago," *Phi Delta Kappan* (May 1975), p. 610–12.

[3]R.C. Orem, *Montessori Today* (New York: Capricorn Books, 1971).

[4]Jerome Bruner, *The Process of Education* (Cambridge, Mass.: Harvard University Press, 1968).

John Erskine

**Modern ode
to the modern school**

> Just after the Board had brought the schools up to date
> To prepare you for your Life Work
> Without teaching you one superfluous thing,
> Jim Reilly presented himself to be educated.
> He wanted to be a bricklayer.
> They taught him to be a perfect bricklayer.
> And nothing more.
>
> He knew so much about bricklaying
> That the contractor made him a foreman.
> But he knew nothing about being a foreman.
> He spoke to the School Board about it,
> And they put in a night course
> On how to be a foreman
> And nothing more.
>
> He became so excellent a foreman
> That the contractor made him a partner.
> But he knew nothing about figuring costs
> Nor about bookkeeping
> Nor about real estate,
> And he was too proud to go back to night school.
> So he hired a tutor
> Who taught him these things
> And nothing more.
>
> Prospering at last
> And meeting other men as prosperous,
> Whenever the conversation started, he'd say to himself
> "Just wait till it comes my way—
> Then I'll show them!"
> But they never mentioned bricklaying
> Nor the art of being a foreman
> Nor the whole duty of contractors,
> Nor even real estate,
> So Jim never said anything.

"Modern Ode to the Modern School" from
Sonata and Other Poems *by John Erskine
reprinted by permission of Helen Worden
Cranmer.*

Muriel Spark

The prime of Miss Jean Brodie

"If anyone comes along," said Miss Brodie, "in the course of the following lesson, remember that it is the hour for English grammar. Meantime I will tell you a little of my life when I was younger than I am now, though six years older than the man himself."

The boys, as they talked to the girls from Marcia Blaine School, stood on the far side of their bicycles holding the handlebars, which established a protective fence of bicycle between the sexes, and the impression that at any moment the boys were likely to be away.

The girls could not take off their panama hats because this was not far from the school gates and hatlessness was an offense. Certain departures from the proper set of the hat on the head were overlooked in the case of fourth-form girls and upwards so long as nobody wore their hat at an angle. But there were other subtle variants from the ordinary rule of wearing the brim turned up at the back and down at the front. The five girls, standing very close to each other because of the boys, wore their hats each with a definite difference.

These girls formed the Brodie set. That was what they had been called even before the headmistress had given them the name, in scorn, when they had moved from the Junior to the Senior school at the age of twelve. At that time they had been immediately recognizable as Miss Brodie's pupils, being vastly informed on a lot of subjects irrele-

vant to the authorized curriculum, as the headmistress said, and useless to the school as a school. These girls were discovered to have heard of the Buchmanites and Mussolini, the Italian Renaissance painters, the advantages to the skin of cleansing cream and witch-hazel over honest soap and water, and the word "menarche"; the interior decoration of the London House of the author of *Winnie the Pooh* had been described to them, as had the love lives of Charlotte Brontë and of Miss Brodie herself. They were aware of the existence of Einstein and the arguments of those who considered the Bible to be untrue. They knew the rudiments of astrology but not the date of the Battle of Flodden or the capital of Finland. All of the Brodie set, save one, counted on its fingers, as had Miss Brodie, with accurate results more or less.

By the time they were sixteen, and had reached the fourth form, and loitered beyond the gates after school, and had adapted themselves to the orthodox regime, they remained unmistakably Brodie, and were all famous in the school, which is to say they were held in suspicion and not much liking. They had no team spirit and very little in common with each other outside their continuing friendship with Jean Brodie. She still taught in the Junior department. She was held in great suspicion.

Marcia Blaine School for Girls was a day school which had been

From The Prime of Miss Jean Brodie *by Muriel Spark. Copyright © 1961 by Muriel Spark. Reprinted by permission of J. B. Lippincott Company and Harold Ober Associates Incorporated.*

partially endowed in the middle of
the nineteenth century by the
wealthy widow of an Edinburgh
book-binder. She had been an admirer of Garibaldi before she died.
Her manly portrait hung in the
great hall, and was honored every
Founder's Day by a bunch of hard-
wearing flowers such as chrysan-
themums or dahlias. These were
placed in a vase beneath the portrait, upon a lectern which also held
an open Bible with the text underlined in red ink, "Oh where shall I
find a virtuous woman, for her price
is above rubies."

The girls who loitered beneath
the tree, shoulder to shoulder, very
close to each other because of the
boys, were all famous for something. Now, at sixteen, Monica
Douglas was a prefect, famous
mostly for mathematics which she
could do in her brain, and for her
anger which, when it was lively
enough, drove her to slap out to
right and left. She had a very red
nose, winter and summer, long dark
plaits, and fat, peg-like legs. Since
she had turned sixteen, Monica
wore her panama hat rather higher
on her head than normal, perched
as if it were too small and as if she
knew she looked grotesque in any
case.

Rose Stanley was famous for sex.
Her hat was placed quite unobtrusively on her blonde short hair, but
she dented in the crown on either
side.

Eunice Gardiner, small, neat and
famous for her spritely gymnastics
and glamorous swimming, had the
brim of her hat turned up at the
front and down at the back.

Sandy Stranger wore it turned up
all round and as far back on her
head as it could possibly go; to assist
this, she had attached to her hat a

strip of elastic which went under the
chin. Sometimes Sandy chewed this
elastic and when it was chewed
down she sewed on a new piece. She
was merely notorious for her small,
almost nonexistent eyes, but she was
famous for her vowel sounds which,
long ago in the long past, in the Junior school, had enraptured Miss
Brodie. "Well, come and recite for
us, please, because it has been a tir-
ing day."

She left the web, she left the loom,
She made three paces thro' the
    room,
She saw the water-lily bloom,
She saw the helmet and the plume,
    She look'd down to Camelot.

"It lifts one up," Miss Brodie usually said, passing her hand outward
from her breast towards the class of
ten-year-old girls who were listening for the bell which would release
them. "Where there is no vision,"
Miss Brodie had assured them, "the
people perish. Eunice, come and do
a somersault in order that we may
have comic relief."

But now, the boys with their bicycles were cheerfully insulting Jenny
Gray about her way of speech which
she had got from her elocution
classes. She was going to be an actress. She was Sandy's best friend.
She wore her hat with the front
brim bent sharply downward; she
was the prettiest and most graceful
girl of the set, and this was her
fame. "Don't be a lout, Andrew,"
she said with her uppish tone.
There were three Andrews among
the five boys, and these three Andrews now started mimicking Jenny: "Don't be a lout, Andrew," while
the girls laughed beneath their bob-
bing panamas.

Along came Mary Macgregor,

the last member of the set, whose fame rested on her being a silent lump, a nobody whom everybody could blame. With her was an outsider, Joyce Emily Hammond, the very rich girl, their delinquent, who had been recently sent to Blaine as a last hope, because no other school, no governess, could manage her. She still wore the green uniform of her old school. The others wore deep violet. The most she had done, so far, was to throw paper pellets sometimes at the singing master. She insisted on the use of her two names, Joyce Emily. This Joyce Emily was trying very hard to get into the famous set, and thought the two names might establish her as a something, but there was no chance of it and she could not see why.

Joyce Emily said, "There's a teacher coming out," and nodded towards the gates.

Two of the Andrews wheeled their bicycles out on to the road and departed. The other three boys remained defiantly, but looking the other way as if they might have stopped to admire the clouds on the Pentland Hills. The girls crowded round each other as if in discussion.

"Good afternoon," said Miss Brodie when she approached the group. "I haven't seen you for some days. I think we won't detain these young men and their bicycles. Good afternoon, boys." The famous set moved off with her, and Joyce, the new delinquent, followed. "I think I haven't met this new girl," said Miss Brodie, looking closely at Joyce. And when they were introduced she said: "Well, we must be on our way, my dear."

Sandy looked back as Joyce Emily walked, and then skipped, leggy and uncontrolled for her age, in the opposite direction, and the Brodie set was left to their secret life as it had been six years ago in their childhood.

"I am putting old heads on your young shoulders," Miss Brodie had told them at that time, "and all my pupils are the crème de la crème."

Sandy looked with her little screwed-up eyes at Monica's very red nose and remembered this saying as she followed the set in the wake of Miss Brodie.

"I should like you girls to come to supper tomorrow night," Miss Brodie said. "Make sure you are free."

"The Dramatic Society . . ." murmured Jenny.

"Send an excuse," said Miss Brodie. "I have to consult you about a new plot which is afoot to force me to resign. Needless to say, I shall not resign." She spoke calmly as she always did in spite of her forceful words.

Miss Brodie never discussed her affairs with the other members of the staff, but only with those former pupils whom she had trained up in her confidence. There had been previous plots to remove her from Blaine, which had been foiled.

"It has been suggested again that I should apply for a post at one of the progressive schools, where my methods would be more suited to the system than they are at Blaine. But I shall not apply for a post at a crank school. I shall remain at this education factory. There needs must be a leaven in the lump. Give me a girl at an impressionable age, and she is mine for life."

The Brodie set smiled in understanding of various kinds.

Miss Brodie forced her brown eyes to a flash as a meaningful accompaniment to her quiet voice. She looked a mighty woman with her dark Roman profile in the sun.

The Brodie set did not for a moment doubt that she would prevail. As soon expect Julius Caesar to apply for a job at a crank school as Miss Brodie. She would never resign. If the authorities wanted to get rid of her she would have to be assassinated.

"Who are the gang, this time?" said Rose, who was famous for sex-appeal.

"We shall discuss tomorrow night the persons who oppose me," said Miss Brodie. "But rest assured they shall not succeed."

"No," said everyone. "No, of course they won't."

"Not while I am in my prime," she said. "These years are still the years of my prime. It is important to recognize the years of one's prime, always remember that. Here is my tram car. I daresay I'll not get a seat. This is nineteen-thirty-six. The age of chivalry is past."

Six years previously, Miss Brodie had led her new class into the garden for a history lesson underneath the big elm. On the way through the school corridors they passed the headmistress's study. The door was wide open, the room was empty.

"Little girls," said Miss Brodie, "come and observe this."

They clustered round the open door while she pointed to a large poster pinned with drawing-pins on the opposite wall within the room. It depicted a man's big face. Underneath were the words "Safety First."

"This is Stanley Baldwin who got in as Prime Minister and got out again ere long," said Miss Brodie. "Miss Mackay retains him on the wall because she believes in the slogan 'Safety First.' But Safety does not come first. Goodness, Truth and Beauty come first. Follow me."

This was the first intimation, to the girls, of an odds between Miss Brodie and the rest of the teaching staff. Indeed, to some of them, it was the first time they had realized it was possible for people glued together in grown-up authority to differ at all. Taking inward more of this, and with the exhilarating feeling of being in on the faint smell of row, without being endangered by it, they followed dangerous Miss Brodie into the secure shade of the elm.

Often, that sunny autumn, when the weather permitted, the small girls took their lessons seated on three benches arranged about the elm.

"Hold up your books," said Miss Brodie quite often that autumn, "prop them up in your hands, in case of intruders. If there are any intruders, we are doing our history lesson . . . our poetry . . . English grammar."

The small girls held up their books with their eyes not on them, but on Miss Brodie.

"Meantime I will tell you about my last summer holiday in Egypt . . . I will tell you about care of the skin, and of the hands . . . about the Frenchman I met in the train to Biarritz . . . and I must tell you about the Italian painting I saw. Who is the greatest Italian painter?"

"Leonardo da Vinci, Miss Brodie."

"That is incorrect. The answer is Giotto, he is my favorite."

Some days it seemed to Sandy that Miss Brodie's chest was flat, no bulges at all, but straight as her back. On other days her chest was breast-shaped and large, very noticeable, something for Sandy to sit and peer at through her tiny eyes while Miss Brodie on a day of lessons indoors stood erect, with her brown head held high, staring out of the window like Joan of Arc as she spoke.

"I have frequently told you, and the holidays just past have convinced me, that my prime has truly begun. One's prime is elusive. You little girls, when you grow up, must be on the alert to recognize your prime at whatever time of your life it may occur. You must then live it to the full. Mary, what have you got under your desk, what are you looking at?"

Mary sat lump-like and too stupid to invent something. She was too stupid ever to tell a lie, she didn't know how to cover up.

"A comic, Miss Brodie," she said.

"Do you mean a comedian, a droll?"

Everyone tittered.

"A comic paper," said Mary.

"A comic paper, forsooth. How old are you?"

"Ten, ma'am."

"You are too old for comic papers at ten. Give it to me."

Miss Brodie looked at the coloured sheets. "*Tiger Tim's* forsooth," she said, and threw it into the wastepaper basket. Perceiving all eyes upon it she lifted it out of the basket, tore it up beyond redemption and put it back again.

"Attend to me, girls. One's prime is the moment one was born for. Now that my prime has begun—Sandy, your attention is wandering. What have I been talking about?"

"Your prime, Miss Brodie."

"If anyone comes along," said Miss Brodie, "in the course of the following lesson, remember that it is the hour for English grammar.

Meantime I will tell you a little of my life when I was younger than I am now, though six years older than the man himself."

She leaned against the elm. It was one of the last autumn days when the leaves were falling in little gusts. They fell on the children who were thankful for this excuse to wriggle and for the allowable movements in brushing the leaves from their hair and laps.

"Season of mists and mellow fruitfulness. I was engaged to a young man at the beginning of the war but he fell on Flanders Field," said Miss Brodie. "Are you thinking, Sandy, of doing a day's washing?"

"No, Miss Brodie."

"Because you have got your sleeves rolled up. I won't have to do with girls who roll up the sleeves of their blouses, however fine the weather. Roll them down at once, we are civilized beings. He fell the week before Armistice was declared. He fell like an autumn leaf, although he was only twenty-two years of age. When we go indoors we shall look on the map at Flanders, and the spot where my lover was laid before you were born. He was poor. He came from Ayrshire, a countryman, but a hard-working and clever scholar. He said, when he asked me to marry him, 'We shall have to drink water and walk slow.' That was Hugh's country way of expressing that we would live quietly. We shall drink water and walk slow. What does the saying signify, Rose?"

"That you would live quietly, Miss Brodie," said Rose Stanley who six years later had a great reputation for sex.

The story of Miss Brodie's felled

fiancé was well on its way when the headmistress, Miss Mackay, was seen to approach across the lawn. Tears had already started to drop from Sandy's little pig-like eyes and Sandy's tears now affected her friend Jenny, later famous in the school for her beauty, who gave a sob and groped up the leg of her knickers for her handkerchief. "Hugh was killed," said Miss Brodie, "a week before the Armistice. After that there was a general election and people were saying, 'Hang the Kaiser!' Hugh was one of the Flowers of the Forest, lying in his grave." Rose Stanley had now begun to weep. Sandy slid her wet eyes sideways, watching the advance of Miss Mackay, head and shoulders forward, across the lawn.

"I am come to see you and I have to be off," she said. "What are you little girls crying for?"

"They are moved by a story I have been telling them. We are having a history lesson," said Miss Brodie, catching a falling leaf neatly in her hand as she spoke.

"Crying over a story at ten years of age!" said Miss Mackay to the girls who had stragglingly risen from the benches, still dazed with Hugh the warrior. "I am only come to see you and I must be off. Well, girls, the new term has begun. I hope you all had a splendid summer holiday and I look forward to seeing your splendid essays on how you spent them. You shouldn't be crying over history at the age of ten. My word!"

"You did well," said Miss Brodie to the class, when Miss Mackay had gone, "not to answer the question put to you. It is well, when in difficulties, to say never a word, neither black nor white. Speech is silver but silence is golden. Mary, are you listening? What was I saying?"

Mary Macgregor, lumpy, with merely two eyes, a nose and a mouth like a snowman, who was later famous for being stupid and always to blame and who, at the age of twenty-three, lost her life in a hotel fire, ventured, "Golden."

"What did I say was golden?"

Mary cast her eyes around her and up above. Sandy whispered, "The falling leaves."

"The falling leaves," said Mary.

"Plainly," said Miss Brodie, "you were not listening to me. If only you small girls would listen to me I would make you the crème de la crème."

discussion

In an age of innovative education and open questioning of traditional curriculum, Miss Brodie might seem the prototype of the modern school teacher. She is independent, comfortable in disagreeing with the headmistress's personal philosophy of education, and flexible about rules and regulations. Miss Brodie conducts classes on the lawn. She sets aside curriculum to tell personal experiences. Miss Brodie brings to her young listeners the outside world of art and literature, although her presentation is quite biased.

In a school like Marcia Blaine, where the gap between teacher and student is bridgeless, a teacher like Miss Brodie is particularly attractive to impressionable and sentimental pubescent girls. She fills the void created by the impersonal and highly structured school setting. One can see her as the answer to many a young girl's yearning for closeness and a peek into the world of adulthood. Yet there are aspects of her style which are self serving, and she does not deliver to the girls what they crave or need.

The story is dramatically intriguing as we watch the charismatic Miss Brodie enmesh the girls in her own mystique. As the story enfolds, however, "the Brodie set" does not prosper, because Miss Brodie has used her students to keep alive her personal dreams of fulfillment.

From a professional point of view the story is instructive. It helps us to see that what may appear to be a unique and intimate teaching style can ultimately be damaging if the communication with the students is not open and honest. The story of Miss Brodie reinforces the importance of the teacher's personal integrity. Dispensing curriculum in a novel way can be an empty frill when the needs of the students are ignored.

springboards for inquiry

1. Do you think teachers should depart from the curriculum and share personal experiences with their students? Why?

2. As you prepare to teach, which is foremost in your mind—what you will teach, how you will teach, or whom you will teach?

3. How would you feel about someone like Miss Brodie as a co-worker on a school faculty?

4. This book presents many stories of teachers at work in their classrooms. Which teacher would you most want to emulate? Which teacher reveals a teaching style you would definitely avoid?

Wally Cox

Mr. Peepers

Mrs. Gurney smiled at him, "Bless you." She held up the batch of poems. "I have here last week's poems, and I must say you did a splendid job—splendid. Most of them are extraordin—extrord—They're splendid!"

She took the top one and set the rest down. "Suppose we read a few of them." She picked up her lor-

Copyright © 1955, by Peepers Co. & W. M. C. Enterprises. Reprinted by permission of Simon and Schuster, Inc.

"I have here last week's poems, and I must say you did a splendid job—splendid. Most of them are extraordin—extrord—They're splendid!"

gnette and readied herself for reading. "Mmmm," she said, "this is a lovely one. 'My Brown Dog,' by Harold Golden. Ahem!

'My dog is brown
We live in town
Don't ever frown
A king wears a crown
My dog is brown.'"

Mrs. Gurney paused and stared at Harold. "Very nice," she said warmly. "The rhyming is very consistent. However, Harold, the meter leaves just a little to be desired. And perhaps the rhyming was a little *too* consistent. Nevertheless, a good try. Your effort was extraordin—splendid!"

Mrs. Gurney picked up the next poem. "Now, here's Marilee Dagny's. And very spirited, too. It's called 'Yahoo, Yahay!'

'Yahoo, Yahay!
It's Spring today!
Let's go and play
With all our friends
From the corner drugstore.
They're swell kids.
Yahoo, Yahoo, Yahay!' "

Mrs. Gurney frowned. "Very nice, Marilee," she said, "Very . . . You sort of gave up in the middle, didn't you, dear? Well . . . good effort, good effort."

Mrs. Gurney saw Mr. Peepers standing in the doorway. She waved at him brightly. "Now, class," she said, "here's one by Walter Murdock. At first glance it seems rather familiar. The title is different, I'll admit, but it does seem familiar." Mrs. Gurney cleared her throat. "'Things That Grow,'" she said, "by Walter Murdock. Ahem!

'I think that I shall never see
A poem as lovely as a tree
A tree that may in summer
wear . . .' "

Mrs. Gurney paused and looked at Walter. "Are you sure you wrote this, Walter?" she asked. Walter nodded. "You did," Mrs. Gurney said flatly. "I'd like to see you after school. Now, then . . . here's Leonard Gorf's." She smiled at Leonard. "I might have known there'd be a military motif, Leonard," she said warmly. "Bless you! Ahem . . . it's called 'The Big Guns Boom' . . ."

The school bell bonged. Mrs. Gurney started. Then she lowered her lorgnette. "That will be all, class," she said.

The children filed from the classroom, jostling, whispering and making jokes about each others' poems.

discussion

In the 1940s and 50s Wally Cox portrayed a meek school teacher on a television series called "Mr. Peepers." He has put some of these school room sequences into a book. Mrs. Gurney was one of the teachers on the faculty with Mr. Peepers. Like so many English teachers she has assigned poetry writing to the class. There are no alternate choices. All of the students must write poetry. This is a difficult medium which, unlike prose, requires an exceptional command and economical use of words to express an idea. Most people have a great deal of difficulty understanding poetry and would certainly not be able to write a poem that is more than a bit of rhyming doggerel. Yet Mrs. Gurney, who probably had been reading some poetry with her class, felt that the natural extension of a poetry lesson was an assignment to write a poem. Most junior high students are still insensitive to good poetry and certainly are sustaining illusions to believe they could write an honest poem. The assignment serves to embarrass them and either to reinforce their misconceptions of what poetry is or to make them feel incompetent if the teacher exposes them. Therefore the results are bound to be extremely poor. The students who have not developed the ear and experience with words to write meaningful poetry are forced to hand in foolish rhymes. Teachers need to reexamine whether they are rigidly adhering to curricula and assignments which are one-dimensional. Children derive meanings on many levels in any lesson, and the individual learning level and style should help guide the teacher in making assignments.

springboards for inquiry

1. What guidelines should Mrs. Gurney follow to formulate an assignment which would take into consideration the different needs and abilities of her high school freshmen?

2. Recall an assignment from your own school days which you found instructive and worthwhile. Analyze why you found the assignment interesting at the time. In what way would your thinking about the assignment be different now?

3. What is meant by the intrinsic and extrinsic values of assignments? Give an example of the intrinsic and extrinsic values of a particular assignment in your field of interest.

4. Read about creativity in the classroom and state some principles a teacher would follow to make assignments more creative.[1]

---

[1]Suggested readings are Harold H. Anderson, *Creativity and Its Cultivation* New York: Harper & Row, 1959); and Ellis Torrance, *Guiding Creative Talent* (Englewood Cliffs, N.J.: Prentice-Hall, 1962).

affective
environment

In May 1968, there was a student revolt at the Sorbonne in Paris. The rallying cry was "long live the passionate revolution of creative intelligence!" The students who uttered this cry were the intellectuals, the academic elite who, although they were demanding more student rights and less regimentation, were the very students who could cope with the status quo. Ironically, innovations in education are being sought for those least able to verbalize their needs—the "turned-off" students, the non-academic inner-city child. The struggle of educators to find a curriculum suitable for millions of non-academically oriented children demands a different kind of revolution. And almost universally teachers are now trying to create learning experiences appropriate for these types of learners. The humanistic or affective function of instruction is to complement the cognitive curriculum, and although it plays a larger role in teaching the so-called "turned-off" students, all students benefit by a strong affective environment. Sterling M. McMurrin expressed/defined the cognitive and affective (humanistic) functions of the teacher as follows:

> The cognitive function of instruction is directed to the achievement and communication of knowledge, both the factual knowledge of the sciences and the formal relationships of logic and mathematics—knowledge as both specific data and generalized structure. It is discipline in the ways of knowing, involving perception, the inductive, deductive, and intuitive processes, and the techniques of analysis and generalization. It involves both the immediate grasp of sensory objects and the abstractive processes by which the intellect constructs its ideas and fashions its ideals.
>
> The affective function of instruction pertains to the practical life—to the emotions, the passions, the dispositions, the motives, the moral and esthetic sensibilities, the capacity for feeling, concern, attachment or detachment, sympathy, empathy, and appreciation.[1]

The affective environment makes contact with the learner. Weinstein and Fantini list some situations which imply nonconcern for humanistic education:

1. Failure to match teaching procedures to children's learning styles.

Cognitive curriculums stress the verbal, abstract, deductive and ethereal types of learning models. Current literature on lower class children indicates they thrive on the nonverbal, concrete, inductive, and kinesthetic situations. The humanistic curriculum lays stress on concerns, wants, interests, fears, anxieties, joys, and other emotions which motivate. Too often digressions by children are viewed as veering away from content.

[1]Sterling M. McMurrin, "What Tasks for the Schools?" *Saturday Review* (January 14, 1967): p. 41.

2. The use of material that is outside or poorly related to the learner's *knowledge* of his physical realm of experience.

Until very recently, inner-city children were taught from the same stories about little white houses on lovely green lawns surrounded by picket fences which enclosed large spreading chestnut trees and bouncy, pretty puppies frolicking in piles of autumn leaves. Anyone visiting New York City or any of the other large cities of the United States would be horrified by the irrelevance of such approaches to learning.

3. The use of teaching materials and methods that ignore the learner's *feelings.*

A unit of study on our friend the policeman may be a travesty of educational subject matter and relevance when attempting to teach children whose life experiences have taught them to "off the pigs." Feelings are facts and need to be dealt with as such.

4. The use of teaching content that ignores the *concerns* of the learners.

The student's concerns are his immediate needs, his persistent struggle to find his identity and his relationship to the world. Until these concerns are recognized and until the teacher acknowledges his recognition of these concerns to his student, the student cannot learn even those skills that are urgently needed for survival in this sophisticated society.[2]

The affective environment first tends to the business of answering the student's question, "what does it have to do with me?" and then goes on from there to the more cognition-centered tasks of the school.

Marion Hurd McNeely

The Horse

Two months of the fall term of school had passed when Martha Edgewood of Sageville enrolled in the Dubuque High School. Martha was fifteen, and looked as though

Martha shrank within herself at the words. How could she ever dare to face that audience of older boys and girls, all so unconscious of themselves, so intelligent, so sophisticated. Could she offer anything to them?

she had been drawn for the colored supplement before the pigments were added. Eyes, hair, skin, and clothes were all of pale tan, her face was very plain, her gait awkward.

"It is unfortunate that you did not enroll at the beginning of the semester," said the principal, as he helped her fill out her card of admission.

"Sir?" said Martha.

"Too bad you couldn't have start-

[2]Gerald Weinstein and Mario D. Fantini, eds., *Toward Humanistic Education* (New York: Praeger, 1970).

ed two months ago," said Mr. Edwards. "You've lost a big part of the term."

"Yes, sir," the girl looked very scared. "I wanted to, but I couldn't. I had to wait till after corn shucking. I don't know if my father'll leave me come now, but I'm making out to try it. He thinks I've got schooling enough."

"I think you've had enough to start your Freshman year," said Mr. Edwards, kindly. "Latin and algebra will be hard for the first few weeks, but we can help you make up lost work. You're sure you want the Latin course, not the commercial?" And he explained the difference.

"I want to have what'll help me to teach," said the girl. "If I can get a school quick, maybe my father'll be more willing to have me go to High School. But I've got to learn fast, for I'm so far back. I got to learn how to talk right while I'm studying other things. But I can. I learn quick. An' I like to work."

A faint flush mounted the girl's face, and she looked a little less plain.

"The report cards you brought from the Sageville school show that," said Mr. Edwards. "Where are you going to live, in town? Have you found a room?"

"Oh, I ain't goin' to live in Dubuque. I'm goin' home every night, but not noons, of course. I'll carry my noon lunch from home."

"Will they send for you every night?"

"No, sir. I'll walk it."

"But it's four miles."

"Yes, sir."

Mr. Edwards laid her enrollment card on his desk. "Well, good luck to you. I'm sure you'll make good. The teachers will give you a start, and

you'll make friends soon. I hope you won't be lonely."

But being lonely had not entered the girl's thoughts. Companionship was a secondary thing to the miracle that opened before her—the chance of learning. Perhaps it was for that reason, perhaps because she was confused, bewildered and lost in the throngs of strange young people, that she did not notice the looks of amusement on the sea of faces in the study hall, as she went into Latin class.

"Oh, mother, what is that?" quoted David Conroy to his desk neighbor, Naomi Hiltman.

"Something got loose on the farm," whispered back Naomi.

"She must have broken her halter. She looks exactly like a horse, doesn't she?" said David.

And she did. Long narrow face, flat nose, and patient eyes with half-drooped lids. The name was perfect, and it stuck. After that she was always "The Horse" to the girls and boys.

The road to Sageville was dusky and frozen into icy ruts, and the wind from the north slapped Martha's face as she made her way home after her first day at school. But it was neither cold nor fear of the dark road that quickened her steps. It was the thought of the chores and her brother Ben. Ben was two years younger, and cared for books and school as much as Martha. It was his pledge to do Martha's chores, as well as his own, that had wrung from their father the grudging consent that Martha should go in to Dubuque High School. "A turrible waste of money," old Ben had growled. "The more ye know, the more ye got to know." But he had finally given in to the pleadings of both children. Martha's joy had been tempered by the regret that young Ben was not to share in the schooling, but her brother had quickly put an end to expressions of sorrow. "My turn'll come later," he said stoutly, "an' the quicker you get to going, the easier it'll be for me."

Ben was waiting where the lane attached itself to the Sageville road, and Martha knew he had driven the cows home that way in order to meet her. She also knew that the casual "H'are ye?" meant a hundred questions from her reticent brother. And these unasked questions she answered all the way up to the barn—about the school, the lessons, the teachers and her course of study.

"How about the other kids? Did you like any of them?" inquired Ben.

"I didn't meet any of them."

"Didn't any of them come up and speak to you?"

"No." Nobody had, though she hadn't thought of the fact before.

"I think that was queer of them," commented Ben. "We wouldn't let a new kid go all day alone at the Sageville School."

"I suppose they're all too busy," excused Martha.

"Maybe they expected you to speak first."

But Martha, remembering David Conroy's expression when she had made her first recitation, and the amused look on Naomi's pretty face when she had filed into the wrong class-room, shook her head.

"I guess they're different from us at the Sageville School," she said. She hurried into the house, and changed her school costume for farm clothes, before she came back to the barn to milk with Ben.

In the days that came after, Martha often remembered her own words. The school children *were* different. They didn't seem like children, at all, but young men and women—all so sophisticated, so well-dressed, so good-looking, so well-informed. Except upon the subject of lessons. It was curious how little their intelligence seemed to count in their studies. Outside of the class-room, Martha envied them their ease, their grace, their familiarity with the things of life, but at the recitations she wondered at their lack of interest, and was surprised at their stupidity. Martha had a good brain, quick perception, and a wonderful power of concentration. She absorbed her Latin, drank in her history, and devoured her English work. She was soon taking the second class work in algebra, carrying two classes of Latin, and leading the students of the Freshman year.

"There's no beating that horse-girl," said David Conroy, who had always stood at the head of his class before.

Her power of concentration saved the Horse from many a hurt. Youth is the cruelest thing in the world, and there was little effort to hide the sneer, the laugh, the uplifted brow from the victim. If Martha had not been buried so deep in her school work she must have noticed. But the teachers were kindly and appreciative, her work was engrossing, and she had little time to think of being lonely. Besides, the dream of her heart was being realized. Two years, besides this, would give her her diploma, and a chance to teach the Sageville School. Then Ben could have his opportunity, and she could begin to save for college. What was *loneliness?* Besides, they didn't mean to be unkind. They were different—that was all.

Naomi Hiltman and Martha were alone in the school library one morning, along about the first of May. Martha was looking up the word *Pali,* and as she put the encyclopaedia back upon the shelf and left the room, Naomi took down the same volume. A sheet of paper fluttered to the floor. She picked it up, recognized Martha's curious, cramped handwriting, and read:

To My Alma Mater

To thee, who made my youthful
   days
So bright, I offer thee my praise,
And in a hundred different ways
Endeavor to be worthy.

And where thy stately towers rise
So gold and gray against the skies,
The days of happiness I prize
No power can deter me.

Thou made'st my life a happy one,
On my dark chambers turned the
   sun,
And life itself began to run
So I could see it.

Give me a chance myself to prove
A daughter worthy of thy love;
Beneath thy spires that shine above
I swear I'll be it.

—Martha Edgewood

"The Horse a poet!" said Naomi to herself. The paper in her hand shook with her laughter. "What a find, what a find! just the kind of poetry she *would* write. Oh, won't the girls enjoy this!"

At recess she showed it to David. "Gee, that's a gem. Has anyone else seen it?"

"I showed it to some of the girls. They almost laughed their heads off."

"I don't wonder. Say, let's ask her to read it before the Lit."

"She won't do it. She's too bashful."

"It won't do any harm to ask her. She's a member, and she's got to take part on the program before long. This would be a barrel of fun. Can't you see how she'd look—*reading poetry!*"

"I surely can't imagine her reading any worse poetry than this."

"Well, ask her then. You're on the program committee. It will be the best entertainment we've had this semester."

So Naomi had asked Martha. She returned the lost poem to her, told her where she had found it, and invited her to read it at the next meeting of the Literary Society. To her surprise Martha agreed. She blushed a dull, painful red that showed even through her thick tan skin, but she accepted.

"As if it were an honor," Naomi said to Ruth Bradford later.

"I don't think it's a kind thing to do," said Ruth with a decided ring in her usually gentle voice.

"Why not? She'll never know that we're making fun of her."

"But *you'll* know it, and because she doesn't is just why it's mean. I'm sorry for the poor girl. She seems so forlorn."

"Why don't you adopt her, then?"

"I do talk to her when I get a chance, but she is about the schoolhouse so little that I seldom see her. When I do talk to her she seems pleased, even if she does act scared of me. It's just wicked that we don't *make* girls like that come out of their shells."

"She'll walk out of here all right when she reads that ode. It's full of spires, and prayers, and vows, and heights. She'll have to undress her soul to read it."

"I think it's mean," said Ruth again.

"Why, if she doesn't know it?"

"Perhaps she will," said Ruth. "She's no fool."

Martha's rough shoes flew over the dandelion-bordered Sageville road that afternoon. The long walks to and from school were a pleasure these sunshiny spring days. The term was almost over, and Martha meant to make up an extra class at home between canning and cooking, that summer. The year had been a lovely one. She didn't mind the summer of work with the thought of the fall that was ahead. And even her father seemed reconciled to the thought of her going back, and interested in the school reports she brought home. She had not made friends, and she did miss companionship. But perhaps it was just as well that the girls didn't notice her loneliness; she would have nothing to offer them if they did come. The education was what she went for and that, in itself, was enough. She wouldn't let herself wish for anything more.

But surely it was all right for her to be glad of this first bit of human attention, to be flattered by Naomi's invitation, and by her appreciation of the poem. The prettiest and best dressed girl in the school had asked her to read it—it was pleasant to have it so.

Her lonely heart sang.

"What's the matter with *you?*" asked her brother, as they met in the chicken yard in the early twilight.

"Oh, Ben, I've been asked to read before the Literary Society next week." She couldn't tell him what she was to read. Not even Ben knew that she wrote poetry.

Her brother eyed her heightened color curiously. Girls were queer to *care* so much for a thing of that kind.

"Glad of it. Know you'll do fine," he said encouragingly.

After the milking was finished, the dishes washed, and the milk pans scalded, Martha climbed the little ladder that led to the attic loft. She pulled a big box in front of the one tiny window, and carefully laid out, one by one, a pile of old clothes. Down at the bottom of the chest was the dress that had been her mother's best. It was a bright green, selected by old Ben, and worn only because there was no money to substitute a less trying color. It had lain there the two years since her mother's death, no occasion seeming to warrant its making over. But the time for it seemed at last to have come.

She put the other things soberly back into the box, pushed it under the eaves, and went down stairs. A brand new 35-cent paper pattern lay on the bed in her room, the first new pattern she had ever owned. She had bought it for a dozen eggs of her own lame hen.

Ripping the dress took two good hours of work; it took another hour to plan how to cut the pattern from the limited material; still another hour to piece together scraps enough to eke out the gown. But when she went to bed, at midnight, the dress was cut out, pinned together and ready to start.

Three days of that week were devoted to preparations for the coming program. She revised her poem, and committed it to memory as she went back and forth from country to town and town to country. A new light was in her face and a new confidence in her manner. She had been noticed at last. They *had* cared, in spite of that coolness. That had been just the city way. The High School pupils were her friends, they had *asked* her for this. It was only a beginning, but where might it not end?

After nightfall came she was less confident and happy, for it was then she worked upon the gown she was to wear. The green cloth was very garish, and Martha had misgivings about its becomingness. She knew nothing about dress-making, and her rough hands held the needle clumsily. The sleeves certainly had a peculiar look, and though Ben good-naturedly tried to "hang" the skirt for her, the hem was as uneven as her father's temper. Still, she had done her best, material and making were the best she could command, and fortunately there was no mirror at the Sageville house large enough to tell her how it looked. She asked her father for enough money to buy lace for the collar and cuffs, sewed it in with neat, painstaking stitches, and wore the dress to school on the morning of the great day. At noon she spread her handkerchief daintily over the vivid green that not a crumb might drop thereon.

The Literary Society was the largest school organization, and even the august seniors were members. David Conroy, as chairman of the meeting, announced the program to the audience in the large assembly room.

"To My Alma Mater. An original poem by Miss Martha Edgewood."

Martha shrank within herself at the words. How could she ever dare to face that audience of older boys and girls, all so unconscious of themselves, so intelligent, so sophisticated. Could she offer anything to them? She had never thought much of that poem—it was merely the overflow from a grateful heart, put into rhyming form because the words had happened to come that way. Yet Naomi had said it was fine—Naomi the popular and beautiful—and she must know. Moreover, Naomi had asked her, as a personal favor, to do this. It was a symbol of friendship. She must not fail her. And the green dress was new. She mounted the stage. There was a dead hush over the room—almost a gasp, as the awfulness of that green dress burst upon her audience. A dress that never was before, on land or sea—a misguided dress, a dress that was cobbled, not sewed. The skirt rippled like waves above her skin to leather, the old-fashioned shell pin held the fullness in exactly the wrong place.

She began the verses timidly, with a tone of apology for each line. She was right, it *was* too poor to offer such an audience. How had she dared? But as she went on she warmed to her subject, and forgot the sea of faces before her.

"And life itself began to run
So I could see it."

Poor poetry, but the words were true. School had done that for her. Her voice lost its fear:

"Give me a chance myself to prove
A daughter worthy of thy love;
Beneath thy spires that shine above
I swear I'll be it."

There was a wild burst of applause. The room shook. At the chairman's desk she saw David Conroy pounding his hands together, and all the pupils—those who had never noticed her in the months of school life, were applauding enthusiastically. Some of the boys were even stamping their feet. She knew she could never face the room and its wild approval, and she fled across the stage into the dressing room. She pressed her cold hands upon her hot cheeks, and smiled to herself for the very joy of living.

And then she heard. From the assembly room a burst of laughter that deepened into a roar. The room rocked. There was no mistaking the derision. Oh, Youth *is* cruel.

Martha understood. Her color slowly turned from scarlet back to tan. She did not cry, but something stiffened within her, stiffened and then broke. It was something she never got back again.

The study hall was deserted when Martha crept back to her desk after the meeting was over. She took out her Latin grammar, her algebra, all her textbooks, added her paper, her notebooks and her pencils, and tied them into a neat bundle. One of the Latin teachers passed along the aisle.

"Are you going to do that much studying tonight?"

"No'm. I'm leaving. I can't come back any more."

"Why, that's a shame, when you're doing such fine work," said Miss Rountree, pleasantly. "Your teachers all say you're such a good student. Are you sure you can't come back?"

"No, I can't come back," said Martha, "but my brother Ben will come. He's smarter than I am."

discussion

The affective shock that Martha suffers at Dubuque High School may be similar to that experienced by many teenagers who, because of handicaps or race, feel different from the majority of the student body of large high schools they attend in the suburbs or the cities. In order to soften the feelings of alienation, many of these students cluster together between periods or at lunch time in tight subgroups. It is not unusual to find a kind of segregation in most integrated schools as Chicano or black students seek each other's company outside of class. In this case there is no subgroup with whom Martha can identify. She deludes herself into thinking that her motivation to learn will make up for her isolation. Martha is fortunate to have some well developed outlets for her neglected feelings, i.e. writing poetry and diligent studying, but lonely pursuits are not sufficient solace for the craving to be a part of a social group.

When Martha is asked to read her poem for the literary society, her self-esteem rises markedly, and she is filled with good feelings about herself. She even musters the self-confidence to read before the assembly hall. These are the bonuses of social recognition when they are well meaning.

It is notable that only one student, Ruth, feels some compassion for Martha and argues against the cruel plan to humiliate her. The rest of the students seem to need a scapegoat to provide them with fun and entertainment. Martha comments on how different these students seem to her. Although much more sophisticated than her classmates at the village school, she wonders at their lack of enthusiasm. Martha is aware of a phenomenon that is commented on by observers of the student scene. In *The Learning Child* Cohen writes about the increasing boredom and indifference found among today's young people.[1] Is the indifference engendered by the lack of personal contact in our large institutions? Do students so eagerly seek peer approval because there are so few adult models to emulate since the faculty is remote and preoccupied with their own insecurities and dissatisfactions? If being popular and a desire to be part of the in-group prevails above any other interest there will be little energy left for empathy, social service, or serious study. In fact, studies show that girls at high school level mask their intellectual interests lest they appear dull and uninteresting to the boys.[2]

Teachers who see over one hundred students a day can hardly be responsible for making meaningful contacts with individual students. The Dubuque faculty seem to be typical of the well meaning but uninvolved faculties found in so many schools. No one questions the painful incident Martha has experienced. Miss Rountree does not go out of her way to determine the reason for Martha's hasty leaving of school.

Innovative curriculum and registration procedures are not sufficient to improve the affective environment of the schools. Some ideas are being tried on the classroom level to improve trust and communication.[3] Students and faculty need to face the issues of inclusion versus alienation on large school campuses. Martha had a contribution to make but for lack of guidance and personal concern for her damaged ego her talent and dream of teaching probably remained unfulfilled.

springboards for inquiry

1. Recall the feelings you had toward your high school environment. Was there a teacher who was particularly helpful to you? Did you have a trusting relationship with your friends?

2. Describe how another student or an interested teacher might have made a significant difference in Martha's acceptance at Dubuque.

3. Read some chapters in the two books on communication mentioned in this discussion or read some articles on affective education and comment on whether the task of humanizing large high school campuses is possible.

4. Do you think busing students from their neighborhood causes problems of enculturation?

---

[1]Dorothy H. Cohen, *The Learning Child* (New York: Random House, 1972).

[2]James S. Coleman, *The Adolescent Society* (New York: The Free Press of Glencoe, 1961).

[3]Gene Stanford and Albert E. Roark, *Human Interaction In Education* (Boston: Allyn & Bacon, 1974); and William D. Romey, *Risk-Trust-Love: Learning in a Human Environment* (Columbus: Charles E. Merrill, 1972).

References

BELLACK, ARNO. *The Language of the Classroom.* New York: Teachers College Press, 1966.

BRUNER, JEROME. *The Process of Education.* Cambridge, Mass.: Harvard University Press, 1968.

DENNISON, GEORGE. *The Lives of Children.* New York: Random House, 1969.

FRIEDENBERG, EDGAR. *Coming of Age in America.* New York: Random House, 1965.

GOODMAN, PAUL. *Compulsory Miseducation.* New York: Horizon Press, 1964.

GREER, MARY and RUBINSTEIN, BONNIE. *Will the Real Teacher Please Stand Up?* Pacific Palisades, Ca.: Goodyear, 1972.

HARNACK, ROBERT S. *The Teacher: Decision Maker and Curriculum Planner.* Scranton, Penn.: International Textbook, 1968.

HERRIOTT, ROBERT G. and HODGKINS, BENJAMIN J. *The Environment of Schooling: Formal Education as an Open System.* Englewood Cliffs, N.J.: Prentice-Hall, 1973.

HUGHES, MARIE M., et al. *Excerpts from a Research Report: Development of the Means for the Assessment of the Quality of Teaching in Elementary Schools.* Salt Lake City: University of Utah Press, 1959.

JACKSON, PHILLIP W. "Involvement and Withdrawal in the Classroom." *Life in Classrooms.* Ed. Jackson, Phillip W. New York: Holt, Rinehart and Winston, 1968.

———. "The Prevention of Disturbances." *Life in Classrooms.* New York: Holt, Rinehart and Winston, 1968.

KEISLOR, EVAN. "The Instructional Environment and the Young Autonomous Learner." *Changing Education.* Ed. Wittrock, M. C. Englewood Cliffs, N.J.: Prentice-Hall, 1973.

McMURRIN, STERLING M. "What Tasks for the School?" *Saturday Review,* January 14, 1967, p. 41.

OFFER, DANIEL. *The Psychological World of the Teenager.* New York: Basic Books 1969.

OREM, R. C. *Montessori Today.* New York: Capricorn Books, 1971.

ORTEGA Y GASSET, JOSE. *Man and Crisis.* New York: Norton, 1962.

ROSENTHAL, ROBERT and JACOBSON, LENORE. *Pygmalion in the Classroom.* New York: Holt, Rinehart and Winston, 1968.

SILBERMAN, CHARLES E. *Crisis in the Classroom.* New York: Random House, 1970.

WALBERG, HERBERT J. and SIGLER, JEANNE. "Business Views Education in Chicago." *Phi Delta Kappan,* May 1975.

WEINSTEIN, GERALD, and FANTINI, MARIO D., eds. *Toward Humanistic Education.* New York: Praeger, 1970.

The Power Structure
in the School

An easy though superficial answer to the question, who runs the schools in America, would be: the children. Foreign educators often think so; and not without justification. From 1965 to 1973, there was ample evidence to support such a theory.

A more truthful answer, however, is that everyone and no one runs the schools. Even more accurate may be the analogy of the relay race where a baton is passed from one runner to the next, shifting control of the baton periodically. A cursory review of newspaper articles related to the fall 1973 opening of the schools in the United States is revealing. In the *New York Times* of September 10, a United Press International release said:

> Half a million students stayed home again in Michigan while a county judge tried to decide whether to force the teachers back to work.
>
> In San Francisco, a two-day bus drivers' strike . . . left 20,000 school children stranded. . . .
>
> In Cupertino, near San Jose, schools in California's largest district have been kept open . . . by substitute teachers. . . . Custodial workers walked out Thursday. . . .
>
> In Detroit alone 270,000 school children were shut out of school because of striking teachers. . . .
>
> In Pennsylvania one strike ended, a tentative agreement and a truce were reached in two others and two additional walkouts began, leaving 17 districts still closed. . . .
>
> Some 40,000 students in three Rhode Island communities . . . will not begin classes for the new school year. . . .
>
> In Massachusetts, 85 teachers failed to show up for the third day. . . .
>
> Schools were also closed in Kenosha, Wisconsin and Highland, Indiana. About 60 teachers in Hermantown, Minnesota voted to walk out. . . .

And so bus drivers, custodians, and teachers seem to be running the schools.

It was predicted that the 1973–1974 winter, if severe, would force many schools to shut because of America's energy crisis. Two years previously, if a respectable text on the politics, power, and policies of the schools ever mentioned the boiler room as a possible serious focus of power in school administration, its author(s) would have been laughed out of the community of experts. An NBC-TV Special, a three-hour exploration of the energy crisis in America, presented estimates that until at least 1980 this nation will face an energy crisis which will very directly involve the schools. In a very real sense the natural gas, coal, and oil industries and their priorities may "run" the schools for at least the next half dozen years until oil shale, off-shore exploration, solar and atomic energy sources of power, and heat are harnessed. The traditional power triad, parent, teacher, and school boards, may be eclipsed by the fact that without energy for heat the question of control of the schools, at least in winter, will be purely academic. There would be no sense in talking about control over what is not operating.

Until 1973 parents, while wielding power in the schools through their own organization, the PTA, founded officially in 1924 but built upon the 1897 organization, the National Congress of Mothers, seemed to be relegated to the dubious role of cake baking and minor fund raising. With the rise of the women's liberation movement, coupled with some long pent-up quiet desperation over the idea that the public schools were not giving minority children a fair shake, parents became a force to be reckoned with. In New York City, schools were thoroughly decentralized in the late 1960s, leaving more control with each community or district than it had ever had before. The Community School Board replaced the once all-powerful Board of Education, which for more than half a century virtually dictated the educational policy of that city's public schools. It was a new ball game. Clearly the central headquarters of the monolithic Board of Education is only a figurehead. Real power now lies in the community.

Professionals familiar with the history of the public schools of New York City prior to the '70s would never have dreamed possible that protests could be made by lay groups. However, in 1973, parents made strong protests and determined to make school policy. "No principal, no school," Marion Pedowitz, a parent, said.[1]

In September 1973, headlines like those reprinted here seared the New York City educational establishment:

Parents Occupy P.S. 208 in Protest
Some Teachers Begin New Strikes
    But Others Return
Sit-In at P.S. 208 Ends,
    But Parents Plan Boycott

It seems that a new principal was appointed to Public School 208 replacing the school's acting principal. In June 1973, when the announcement was first made, a group of parents occupied the school for 53 days. On September 10, 1973, school was scheduled to start, but fifty parents occupied the school. Even New York City Councilman Theodore Silverman said, "Norman Desser [the newly appointed principal] may come into 208 on Monday, but he won't have many children to teach." Eight hundred of the school's 900 children would be involved in the boycott and were sent to

[1]*New York Times,* September 2, 1973.

eight "minischools" set up in churches, synagogues, and civic centers in the community. Later in the article one reads of the extent of the parental resolve—at a meeting where 300 parents were told of the progress in the courts, they finally left "carrying with them their sleeping bags, cots, and accumulated supplies of their sit-in."[2]

The excerpts quoted at the beginning of this essay refer mostly to teacher strikes. In the larger cities of the United States, the unionization of teachers is a major new factor in the field of education. The following New York City story best exemplifies this development. In 1968, a handful of union teachers were forced to transfer out of an overwhelmingly black district on orders from an experimental community board. Albert Shanker, head of the U.F.T. (United Federation of Teachers, AFL–CIO) called a strike that "disrupted the city's school system for two months and almost tore the city apart in the process."[3] So powerful is this union that in a city where the starting salary was $4800 prior to 1962, under the current contract, the starting salary is $9600. At the top of the scale, teachers will be earning better than $20,000 annually.

Traditionally teachers have been reticent to affiliate with labor unions. Since school boards have been drawn largely from the professional and proprietary classes and since they control teachers' affairs, the general reluctance of teachers to alienate boards has resulted in teachers joining mostly innocuous organizations such as the National Education Association, the Childhood Education Association, and other similarly nonpolitical nonthreatening organizations. Indeed, many teachers felt that professionals do not affiliate with hardhats. Another factor, not often discussed in print, is that 80 percent of American public school teachers are women who work, in some cases, merely to supplement their husbands' incomes. The urgency of wage reform for school teachers never really surfaced. It is entirely possible that the year 1960 marked the beginning of an era of the consciousness of teachers of their power and of their relatively impoverished state. In that year the New York Teachers' Guild tried to pry money from Mayor Robert F. Wagner. He told them the city had no money. Later in the year a hurricane and heavy snowfall hit New York, and millions of dollars were quickly made available to clear the streets. When Albert Shanker of the United Federation of Teachers (U.F.T.) asked how the city had found money for those unbudgeted items, Mayor Wagner told him, "Al, those were disasters."[4] After that, teacher strikes were not rare phenomena. In 1972–1973, strikes closed schools in the entire state of Hawaii, in all of Chicago, in St. Louis, and in dozens of other communities across the nation.

Since 1968 when the student power movement reached its zenith, the power of students on all levels has been felt in the public and private educational sector. Recently, when a college decided to cut back on its nationally

[2]*New York Times*, September 9, 1973.

[3]A. H. Raskin, "Shanker's Great Leap," *New York Times*, September 9, 1973, pp. 64–83.

[4]Raskin, "Shanker's Great Leap," p. 64.

famous scholarship grant program, the students refused to go to classes. In a high school in a small American town, students, rather than cut their hair, took to the courts to secure the right to dress as they pleased. While in the 1970s there has been a distinct tapering off of student activism on all levels of education, it is apparent that Jerry Farber's "student as nigger"[5] can be no more if indeed he ever was. Extreme both in content and language as Farber is, all fair-minded people see reflections of themselves in his accusations. (By his own testimony he even sees himself!) Educational policy making has always been for the students' welfare. We doubt that any profession has spent more time planning *for* the student. In the area of planning *with* the student we are as remiss as physicians have been when they plan hospital care. *Caveat emptor*—let the buyer beware—is no longer an appropriate philosophy in either the educational or business market place.

Who runs the schools? We suspect that in the last quarter of the 20th century, the fairest answer would be that it is very much a case of shared power. If anything characterizes the mood of America since the Watergate revelations, it is that no one power group can ever rip off whatever it chooses. Participatory democracy is nearing realization. Not the Indians, not the Chicanos, not the teachers—no one will any longer stand for callous disregard of any group's legitimate rights. The day of the notion "what's good for General Motors is good for America" is nearly over. While we may not be ready for Illich's complete deschooling of society,[6] we are also not about to turn America's schools over to the U.F.T. More and more the legitimate interests of all segments of society are being heard in the hallowed halls of academia.

[5]In 1969 Jerry Farber wrote a book, *The Student As Nigger* (North Hollywood: Contact Books, 1969). Here are his first few lines: "Students are niggers. When you get that straight, our schools begin to make sense." This book was once referred to by California State Senator John G. Schmitz as an essay "whose contents and language are so vile that no newspaper in this state could print it." (This exact quote is taken from the Senator's October 20, 1967 "Sacramento Report," his weekly release to newspapers.)

[6]Ivan Illich, *Deschooling Society* (New York: Harper & Row, 1970).

the teachers-
administrators

Teacher to teacher chats reveal a real concern on the part of many teachers that they have so little clout either within their school or in the larger school district. New teachers who come to work in schools for the first time are "turned off" when they make the shocking discovery that in many schools teachers have little or no say in instructional policy. Shared decision making frequently does not exist. Administrators decide who, when, and what will be done within individual schools without consulting the teachers. One of our colleagues used to say that in any school building, teachers should never be considered hired hands. They are officers of the instructional system. Indeed they are referred to in study after study as the indispensible and crucial factor in school success.

> Additional funds, new materials, smaller classes, and supportive services are all supplementary to the work of the classroom teacher. For, in the end, whether compensatory education is truly effective . . . depends upon the quality of the teachers working with the children.[1]

Despite articles about teacher strikes and the power of the U.F.T., despite observation of schools where unionism is very strong, there are indications that teachers do not see themselves as centers of authority. Only in the area of "bread and butter" issues do teachers feel any real power. We have observed time after time entire schools and school systems being told, for example, to use such and such a reading program despite the fact that many teachers were opposed to the materials. The "they tell us what to teach" complaint of teachers is precisely what underlies the teachers' feelings that their rightful power and prestige has been denied them. Even unorganized students on American campuses in the late sixties could shout, "hell no, we won't go" and then not budge. In all too many cases teachers have been forced to abdicate power over their real role—that of determining the nature of the curriculum.

It would perhaps be too radical to suggest that each individual teacher should determine what he is to teach in his own classroom. Yet, the intellectual level of the average teacher is certainly high enough so that teachers should be able to plan curriculum by grade level or departments within given schools. Certainly the schools would not stand to lose much since, at the moment, most curricula are allegedly ineffective. In fact, a good case might be constructed for complete autonomy for teachers in their classrooms. At least for teachers in highly specialized areas, such autonomy would provide a healthy intellectual challenge. Since this volume has quoted rather extensively from the more prominent critics of education—the New Establish-

[1]Wilson C. Riles, "Compensatory Education," in *New Models for American Education*, ed. J. W. Guthrie and E. Wynne (Englewood Cliffs, N.J.: Prentice-Hall, 1971), p. 63.

ment, it might be well to note here that respondents to the 1973 Gallup Poll do not see "irrelevant curriculum," "authoritarian teachers," or "joyless classrooms" as major problems. What do you think is the major problem the public identifies?

The September 1973 issue of the *Phi Delta Kappan,* a leading educational journal, contains the results of the Fifth Annual Gallup Poll of Public Attitudes Toward Education. When adults were asked to name the most important problems confronting the public schools, "difficulty in getting 'good' teachers" ranked fourth, while in response to the question "in what ways are the local public schools particularly good?" teachers were rated second just after the curriculum.

It was interesting to note that despite obviously rising teacher militancy, especially in urban areas, no mention was made of this factor by any of the respondents. Though not especially germane to this particular essay, it is interesting to observe that the number one problem identified by those polled was "discipline" which, interpreted behaviorally, means respect for teacher, law, and authority.[2]

It seems quite obvious from a cursory survey of some standard texts on educational administration that teachers are viewed by many administrators as adversaries.[3] Wesley A. Wildman wrote:

> On this interesting subject of [democratic and consultative administration] let me simply observe that to consult with *subordinates* [italics ours] and to encourage them, in the best of faith, to formulate opinions and judgements outside their sphere of ultimate responsibility and control . . . may lead inevitably to a desire to have some actual power over the decision making process. . . . There are indications that where democratic administration is practiced, participation of subordinates is often an uncertain privilege and that unless the right is guaranteed, it tends to be withdrawn; strong desire may exist within homogeneous employee groups to convert privilege to right.[4]

It is insulting to teachers to read about themselves as "subordinates." Would not coordinates be more accurate? It is startling to imagine that even in 1964 there were those who viewed participatory democracy as a privilege which, if not guaranteed, might come back to haunt the school administrator as a "right."

Teachers are a long way from running the schools. Their professional

[2]Should students wish to pursue further the components of the survey just quoted they may write: CFK Ltd., 3333 S. Bannock Street, Englewood, Colorado 80110. Those who wish further to analyze the data might consult the September 15, 1973 issue of the *New Republic* where S. Francis Overlan analyzes the 1973 survey and previous ones.

[3](4th ed.) Roald F. Campbell, Edwin M. Bridges, John E. Corbally, Jr., Raphael O. Nystrand, and John A. Ramseyer, *Introduction to Educational Administration* (Boston: Allyn & Bacon, 1971); Van Miller, George R. Madden, and James B. Kincheloe. *The Public Administration of American School Systems* (2nd ed.) (New York: Macmillan, 1972); and Laurence Iannaccone and Frank W. Lutz, *Politics, Power and Policy: The Governing of Local School Districts* (Columbus: Charles E. Merrill, 1970).

[4]Wesley A. Wildman, "Implications of Teacher Bargaining for School Administration," *Phi Delta Kappan* 46, no. 4 (December 1964): 154.

expertise is not resourcefully tapped. They have, therefore, decided to organize over the "bread and butter" issues. In one school district, all physical education (male) coaches, drama teachers, and journalism advisors negotiated for one extra period of released time. Another teacher group recently held out for a district-paid dental insurance plan. Like the proverbial tooth paste tube sealed at both ends, teachers have erupted over dollars and cents. Despite widespread professional organization, most American school teachers know they have little power. They do not run the schools.

Jerry Weil

The teachers

Corwin leaned forward in his chair and directed hard gray eyes at the principal. "I've heard this stuff about cooperation before. When you cooperate and bear with things, as you say, they just get worse. I know that from experience. The way I figure it, the best thing to do is not to cooperate. I want a classroom now and I will not settle for less."

When the nine o'clock bell rang a shiver went through the frame of C. Ross Denton. The new school year had started. After eight years as principal Ross knew he could expect to devote much of the next ten months to unpleasant matters.

Ross slid out from behind his desk and crossed to the window. He saw Nate Corwin lecturing to his biology class on the lawn below.

"Not a bad idea on a hot day like this," said his secretary.

"Especially if you're assigned to room 104A," said Ross.

The girl looked astonished. "He's assigned to that room?" she asked.

"He is."

"Old Hardhead. He'll never stand for it."

"Unfortunately, you're probably

From The Teachers *by Jerry Weil. Copyright © 1963 by Jerry Weil. Reprinted by arrangement with The New American Library, Inc., New York, New York.*

right," said Ross. "Do you know if he has a class next period?"

"I don't think so."

"Then he'll be coming up here as soon as the bell rings. Try to stop him, will you. Send him away. Tell him I'm not in or something."

"Not me," said the girl. "Not old Hardhead. I'm not going to try to stop him. I won't be here anyway. My coffee break starts when the first period ends."

"How convenient," said Ross.

"I'll get this letter typed right away," said the girl as she left the office.

Ross lit another cigarette and paced the office in thought. The bell ending the first period sounded. Ross went to the window and saw Nate Corwin walking briskly back into the building.

He went back to his desk, sat down, and waited. It was not long. A moment later, there came an angry rapping at his door.

Ross sighed once more and called: "Come in."

The door swung open and Corwin strode defiantly into the office.

"Good morning, Nate. How are you?" Ross asked pleasantly.

Corwin confronted him across the desk with harsh eyes. "You don't care a twig how I am, so why ask?"

"On the contrary, Nate, I'm concerned about the health of every member of the staff."

"One way you can do something about my health is not to bottle me up with twenty-eight students in an orange crate on an eighty-degree day."

"Now Nate, let me explain that—" Ross began.

"I don't want any explanations. I want to be reassigned to another room, a proper classroom with proper space and proper ventilation. I simply will not stay in that broom closet."

"Have a seat, Nate."

"Never mind all that good-morning - how - are - you - have - a - seat stuff. Save that for your school board politicians. I'm a teacher—no more, no less—and I'm demanding a proper place in which to do my work properly."

"You can sit down and demand it as well as you can standing up," said Ross.

Corwin hesitated. "All right." He surrendered with a sulk. "I might just as well sit in one of these hotsy-totsy leather chairs seeing that I helped pay for them like any other taxpayer in this town." He sat down.

"Now Nate, you know as well as anyone how desperately short of space we are right now," said Ross. "Our student body keeps going up, and our bond issues keep going down. You know we've been trying for two years now to get the school

board to agree on a bond issue and without any success at all. Have you seen this morning's paper?" he asked. He held up his copy of the Green Water *Gazette* so that Corwin could see the front page headline.

It read: High School Opens Today. Biggest Budget in History. Below this large headline was a small one that announced: Six More Teachers on Staff.

"Look at that," said Denton. "Biggest budget. Six more teachers. It sounds as if we're rolling in tax money. And not until the very last paragraph of the article, a paragraph buried on page ten underneath an advertisement for dry cleaning, is anything said about the fact that all these increases are not nearly sufficient to cope with the terrific increase in students. Despite the new teachers, we have a higher ratio of students to teachers than ever before."

"You don't have to tell me that," said Corwin.

"Of course, as long as people read stuff like this they'll think everything is just hunky-dory here at Green Water High. We'll never get a bond issue through, and we'll never be able to build the extra space we need so badly. Do you know that we're thinking of converting the storage room on the second floor into a classroom just like 104A? Do you know we're planning to construct four cubicles in the basement behind the furnace for still more space? And frankly, I don't even know where the money is coming from to pay for even these inadequate measures."

"You've got your troubles, I've got mine," said Corwin.

"All I'm asking you to do," said Ross, "is to cooperate and bear with things until we can improve them.

After all, we're all on the same team, aren't we?"

Corwin leaned forward in his chair and directed hard gray eyes at the principal. "I've heard this stuff about cooperation before. When you cooperate and bear with things, as you say, they just get worse. I know that from experience. The way I figure it, the best thing to do is not to cooperate. I want a classroom now and I will not settle for less."

"Nate, you were assigned that room because your class is the smallest one in the first period. If I assign you to another classroom, it will mean that another teacher with a larger class than yours will go into that room."

"Don't appeal to my sentimentalities," Corwin replied, unaffected by this prospect. "If some other fool teacher is willing to go into that room, that's his or her business. The best thing that could happen is that every teacher simply refuse to work in that room. I hope you can't make the switch. And I warn you, if you can't make it, I'll continue to conduct my class out there on the lawn just the way I did today. And I won't care if the thermometer falls to twenty below, I'll still be outside on the lawn. Maybe that, at least, will get into the newspaper and do your bond issue more good than all the namby-pamby cooperation and town politicking will ever do."

Ross could appreciate the picture Corwin had just painted: a biology class freezing on the school lawn for lack of proper classroom space. There was no denying that such an incident would call attention to the plight of the school with a startling impact. It was tempting—but it was not Ross Denton's way.

He was not a revolutionary. He could only seriously address himself to due process, to convincing the school board and then, in turn, the electorate. To manage anything by freezing twenty-eight students would be punishing children for what their parents had neglected to do. Ross had no taste for that. Besides, he reasoned, even if such a stunt got results, it would make for ill feeling in the town.

He looked across the desk at Corwin and saw by the set of his jaw and the hardness in his eyes that there was no point in continuing their discussion. Corwin would get his classroom.

"You really are old Hardhead, aren't you?" said Ross, smiling.

But Corwin did not smile. "Damn right," he said.

"All right, you win. I'll try to manage a switch. But I can't guarantee that I'll find anyone willing to do it."

Nate's face had relaxed in victory. He stood up. "You'll find someone," he told Ross confidently. "You'll give some teacher a bit of sweet talk about cooperation, and there is no shortage of fools in the world and certainly not here at Green Water High. I almost wish you couldn't find anyone. That would renew my faith in people."

Ross smiled. "Nothing will renew your faith in people," he said. "Will you give me a week to arrange it?"

Corwin hesitated. "O.K.," he agreed slowly. "But one week—no more than that. I'll be outside on the lawn until that week is over."

"I hope it doesn't rain," said Ross.

"I hope it does," said Corwin, and with that he was gone.

His secretary rang. "How did it go?" she asked.

"I'd like you to check over the classroom schedule for the first period and pick out the smallest

classes so I can see which are the
likely ones to switch rooms with Corwin." He waited for her to say some
thing, but there was only silence.

"No comment?" he asked.
"No comment." She laughed
shortly.

discussion

The essays on teacher power, student power, and parent power indicate that in the last five years, effective changes in education have often been the result of group efforts. Nevertheless, this selection from *The Teachers* indicates that the individual teacher acting alone can also wield considerable power. Nate Corwin does not make concessions. He has been in the system long enough to know that one concession leads to another. The room he is assigned is unsuitable, and he refuses to teach in a room without proper ventilation. Many people think that when a principal makes a decision, the teacher follows through despite the fact that he may disagree strongly. Although traditionally the teacher obeyed orders from his superiors, today he is more inclined to articulate his feelings. The social climate of the 60s and 70s has condoned individuality and independence on the school campus. Corwin points out to Ross that he feels there is a division of responsibility in the schools. Finding space in a crowded facility is the principal's problem, not Corwin's. Corwin will not participate or cooperate in its solution. That is why he is called "hardhead." Corwin knows Ross will find another teacher who will manage for one period a day in the undesirable room.

springboards for inquiry

1. What would you have done if you were asked to teach in a small windowless room?

2. Can you suggest better ways for school decision-making about controversial issues such as assignments to undesirable rooms?

3. Discuss school situations you have known or read about which illustrate school issues on which it is important for teachers to take a stand—even one unpopular with the administration.

the students

Not since *Uncle Tom's Cabin* exposed the institution of slavery, have there been so many exposés of any other American institution. A cursory look at a half dozen recent titles suggests that students have been just as insidiously enslaved as black Americans were. Listen to them—*Educational Wastelands, The Diminished Mind, Quackery in the Public Schools, Growing Up Absurd, Our Children Are Dying, Compulsory Mis-education, Death at an Early Age, Crisis in the Classroom, Slums and Suburbs.* All of these books concern themselves primarily with the public elementary and high schools where students have been virtually powerless.

While such provocative titles are less common in the critical literature on higher education, there is considerable literature on the confrontations between students and their colleges, where, unlike in the primary and secondary schools, student power has made itself felt. One need only thumb through such volumes as Lipset and Altbach, *Students in Revolt,*[1] Feuer, *The Conflict of Generations,*[2] and Erlich and Erlich, *Student Power, Participation and Revolution*[3] to realize that student dissatisfaction on the higher education level has resulted in everything from open revolt to guerilla tactics in anthropology classes.[4]

In 1969, Julius Lester, a black author and social commentator on station WBAI in New York, interviewed three seniors from William Howard Taft High School in New York City. The interview closely followed the massive U.F.T. (United Federation of Teachers) strike in New York which was precipitated by a confrontation between neighborhood school boards (largely black and Puerto Rican) and the union (largely white and Jewish) over who would control the schools. The atmosphere in the schools between white teachers and black students had by then grown very tense. Black students had set up their own classes while the teachers were on strike. The students had demanded a black library. They had objected to the fact that the works of Leroi Jones were left out of the school library because of their profanity while there were thirty-two copies of Salinger's *Catcher in the Rye.*

The following dialogue from Lester's interview illustrates the sense of student power in this particular clash.

Karen: The incidents after the strike went on and on. We'd like to talk about one important one which led to the expulsion of one of our brothers, Ron Dix. Ac-

[1]Seymour Martin Lipset and Philip B. Altbach, *Students in Revolt* (Boston: Houghton Mifflin, 1969).

[2]Lewis S. Feuer, *The Conflict of Generations* (New York: Basic Books, 1969).

[3]John Erlich and Susan Erlich, *Student Power, Participation and Revolution* (New York: Association Press, 1970).

[4]In the *New Left Notes* of May 15, 1967 Eric Prokosch instructs anthropology students on how to harass their instructors through questions designed to force the instructor to quit forcing students to "memorize dull details."

cording to the administration, it was for distributing "unauthorized literature." But it is like being a slave, going to the owner and saying, "will you authorize this leaflet calling for a rebellion tomorrow night?"

Naomi: There were three students involved . . . they were specifically trying to promote black awareness with their literature. . . . Before Ron Dix was expelled and before the three brothers resorted to printing their own literature, we held three meetings with the faculty and the principal to resolve the problem of "unauthorized literature." The administration claims that literature unsigned by any teacher in the school is "unauthorized." Yet you can walk down the halls any day and have someone shove something into your hand about a new discotheque, a dance, a track meet, about anything at all . . . as soon as the word *black* appears—boom—"unauthorized literature."[5]

The student activism on university campuses in the 60s is now legendary. Commencing with the SDS (Students for a Democratic Society) 1962 Port Huron Statement, now called the contemporary Declaration of Independence for student activists, and the eight years that followed which culminated in the Kent State horror, college students (and to a lesser degree high school students) confronted the adults who ran the schools and made their demands known. College activism ended with the bombing of the science building on the campus of the University of Wisconsin which killed an innocent graduate student.

As indicated earlier, prior to the high school years there has been little evidence of the emergence of student power. The closest we can come to any display of power in the junior high school was the few places where 12- and 13-year-olds wore black armbands during the Viet Nam moratorium days and were hassled by administrators. In November 1970, the *Harvard Educational Review* printed an article entitled, "Another Look at Student Rights and the Function of Schooling" written by the parents and students of the Elizabeth Cleaners Street School. Here students 12–17 joined their parents to write a statement. A bit of that statement will serve to focus on their view of the scope of student power:

> Students have no say whatsoever in how the schools are governed, for example, in the hiring and firing of teachers. In short, control of the schools has been placed in the hands of those whom school does not affect—bureaucratic administrators.[6]

An interview conducted by Ellen Solomon and Gregg Thomson of the *Harvard Educational Review* with seven students of the Cleaners Street School at a summer camp in western Connecticut sheds some very interest-

---

[5]"We're Not Grinning Anymore," in Erlich and Erlich, *Participation and Revolution*, p. 134.

[6]Reprinted in Ray C. Rist, *Restructuring American Education* (New Brunswick: Transaction Books, 1972), p. 187.

ing light upon the maturity of the students interviewed and the character of their parents. This observation seems pertinent—student activists tend to be bred by parent activists. Under the age of 17, children do not protest unless they feel the firm support of their parents. This exchange between the interviewer and three children aged 13, 15, and 12 lends support to the notion that the relationship between parents and children, at least at this age, is very close indeed:

> *THEN MOST OF THE KIDS YOU KNOW ARE WORKING IT OUT WITH THEIR PARENTS IN SOME WAY? AS FAR AS YOU'RE CON-CERNED, THEN, IS THE WHOLE "GENERATION GAP" JUST BLOWN UP?*

Lisa: (15) It was invented by the media. The generation gap was invented by an idiot. I'm sure it exists very little.

Cathy: (12) I don't think it is a generation gap. It's an individual gap between parent and child, and parent and parent, or child and child. It's not a generation gap—that's such a DISGUSTING way of putting it . . . but I think the majority of kids in this school are a lot more radical than their parents are. I don't think the parents realize it either.

Vashti: (13) It's like with Women's Liberation—my mother's into Women's Liberation and she turned to me the other day and she said, "you know, there's one thing wrong with Women's Liberation—you don't have weddings."

> *BUT DO YOU FEEL THAT YOUR PARENTS HAVE SUPPORTED THE SCHOOL, HAVE ALLOWED YOU TO DO THIS?*

Lisa: Yes. But we would have done it anyway.

Cathy: But if our parents had felt much differently, we would have a different kind of environment around us. And maybe we wouldn't be so *into* this.[7]

It is not the purpose of this volume to argue any particular issue. However, it is unthinkable that well-educated adults should imagine that children really know better what needs to be taught than do those who teach. And we are equally appalled at some of the developments in education which view students as dumb consumers. Student power can be no more than human power. The schools cannot be restructured so that—as in Ocean Hill-Brownsville where absolute control passed from educators to the community thus substituting one tyranny with another—students dictate school policy. Student freedom and power must conform to what C. Wright Mills suggested:

> Freedom is not merely the chance to do as one pleases; neither is it merely the

---

[7]Ibid, p. 199.

opportunity to choose among set alternatives. Freedom is first of all, the chance to formulate the available choices, to argue over them—and then, the opportunity to choose.[8]

On the collegiate level, we see much opportunity to operate as Mills' suggests. In certain areas of school policy we would encourage it for the public secondary schools. Nevertheless, freedom for both children and adults must never mean unrighteous dominion by either group.

Wally Cox

Mr. Peepers

He escorted the superintendent through the scrubbed-down hallways, the newly inventoried school library, and also demonstrated the lately adopted student filing system, all of which had been supervised by Mr. Peepers during his first week as faculty adviser. The superintendent seemed pleased. Mr. Peepers hoped that the tidiness of everything might placate what he regarded as Mr. Sidfern's prejudice against him. When at last they arrived at the pressroom of the school paper, Mr. Peepers was relieved to see that all activity had ceased and that the students were seated quietly behind their desks waiting for inspection.

"Very efficient-looking operation, Peepers," Mr. Sidfern said. "Yes, indeed, you've done a fine job this week."

"Thank you, sir," Mr. Peepers said.

[8]Quoted in ibid., p. 11.

Mr. Sidfern shook his head. "I think you'd better delete it, Peepers. You know, criticizing the administration and all that sort of thing."

Mr. Sidfern stopped in front of Arabella Simpkins' desk. "What is your name, young lady?"

"Arabella Simpkins, sir."

"And what is your job on the school paper?"

"I write the social column, sir," Arabella said.

Mr. Sidfern looked surprised. "Social column?"

Mr. Peepers decided not to leave the explanation up to Arabella. He envisioned the entire embarrassing incident concerning Walter Murdock's knee being dredged up into another moment of chaos. "Er . . . you know, sir," he said, "who's going with what girl . . . ah . . . entertainment, parties, skinned knees . . . er . . . bicycle clips—things like that."

Mr. Sidfern looked bewildered. "Yes, yes, of course."

Mr. Peepers piloted the superintendent to Homer Jansen's desk. "This is our editor, Homer Jansen," he said. "This is Mr. Sidfern, Homer."

They exchanged how-do-you-do's and Mr. Sidfern made his way to the mimeograph machine. Tommy Sparks was standing beside it, smiling. Mr. Peepers quietly crossed his fingers behind his back as Mr. Sidfern thumbed idly through the foot-high stack of separate sheets.

"That's this week's edition, sir," Tommy Sparks said. "Hot off the press."

Mr. Sidfern nodded, examining the front page with interest. "Hmmmm," he said. "Very well done, too."

"Thank you, sir," Tommy said.

Mr. Sidfern picked up the editorial page. "Well," he said, "editorials, too, eh?"

Mr. Peepers held his breath for a moment. "Oh, yes," he said, "everything's authentic."

Mr. Sidfern was reading the editorial. Mr. Peepers observed his facial expressions very carefully. After a moment of colloidal suspension, he saw Mr. Sidfern's attitude metamorphose from interest to concern. Mr. Sidfern beckoned Mr. Peepers to one side, away from the eager ears of Tommy Sparks and Homer Jansen.

"Peepers," Mr. Sidfern said, "what's this?"

Mr. Peepers assumed a bland expression. "Sir?" he said softly.

Mr. Sidfern tapped at the page with one finger. "This editorial criticizing the rule prohibiting the students from sitting on the grass."

Mr. Peepers tried to look deprecating. "Oh, that's a mere . . ."

Mr. Sidfern shook his head. "I think you'd better delete it, Peepers. You know, criticizing the administration and all that sort of thing."

"But, sir," Mr. Peepers said, "the students have a right . . ."

Mr. Sidfern placed a hand on Mr. Peepers' shoulder. "You've done a good job this week, Peepers," he said warmly. "A fine job—sterling!"

"But, sir . . ." Mr. Peepers said.

"Have this little matter taken care of at once and I'd say everything was top-notch."

"But, sir . . ." Mr. Peepers said.

Mr. Sidfern patted him on the back. "Good boy," he said. "Stout fellow."

"But, sir . . ." Mr. Peepers said. Mr. Sidfern, however, had left the pressroom.

Later, in the science room, Mr. Peepers discussed the problem with Harvey Weskit, who had just returned to the school from his honeymoon. Mr. Peepers was feeding his pet white mouse, whom he called Louis after the famous Dr. Pasteur. Louis, who was often temperamental, snapped and snarled at each morsel Mr. Peepers fed him. The feeding was slow and patient because Mr. Peepers disapproved of Louis' tendency to bolt his food. Wes Weskit jumped slightly as Louis thrust his voracious head through the small bars of his cage. Mr. Peepers, however, was so used to Louis that he hardly noticed. Wes Weskit found it difficult to listen to what Mr. Peepers was saying. He was too entranced by Mr. Peepers' indifference to Louis' snapping and snarling.

"And then," Mr. Peepers was saying, "Mr. Sidfern told me to take the article out of the paper, Wes."

Wes Weskit shook off his hypnosis and concentrated on Mr. Peepers' problem. "Appalling," he said.

Mr. Peepers put another morsel

of mouse food between his thumb and forefinger. Louis snapped avidly at it. "It isn't fair, Wes," Mr. Peepers said. "The students have a right to express themselves, even if they're wrong."

Wes Weskit moved his head slowly from side to side. "It's a pure case of freedom of the press, sport."

"That's what I say," Mr. Peepers said, as Louis made small sounds of chomping and chewing.

Wes Weskit cleared his throat. "Thomas Jefferson," he said gravely, "had something to say along those lines. It went something like this, and I quote: 'No Government ought to be without critics; and, where the press is free, none ever will.' "

Mr. Peepers nodded. "Thomas Jefferson."

Wes Weskit was amazed. "Right! How'd you know?"

Mr. Peepers looked at his friend. "You just—" he began, but Wes interrupted.

"Oh, yes," Wes said, "I just told you. Well, what are the plans, ace? You gonna take it out of the paper or not?"

Mr. Peepers moved his fingers away from Louis' mouth. The greedy mouse had tried to bite them. "I don't know, Wes," he said, offering the morsel to Louis again. "If I did take it out, I'd never feel right about it."

"You're going to lose a finger," Wes said.

Mr. Peepers smiled. "I don't think so, Wes. Louis' little threats are meaningless, really."

Wes Weskit thought for a moment. "Know what I'd do if I were you?"

"What?"

Wes raised his eyebrows pontifically. Then he began nodding. "'Course," he conceded, "the thing is I'm not you."

Mr. Peepers decided to attend to Wes carefully. He brushed the crumbs of mouse food from his fingers. He thought that Louis should go on a diet, anyway. The mouse was getting unconscionably fat. "I know," Mr. Peepers said, "but if you *were* me, what would you do?"

"And I don't want to confuse you," Wes said, "by a hypothetical situation."

Mr. Peepers shook his head. "I'm not confused."

"Right," Wes said. "So, if I were you—"

"Hypothetically," Mr. Peepers said gravely. "Because you're not me."

"Right."

"And," Mr. Peepers added, "conversely, I'm not you."

"Right," Wes said. He started to go on, but stopped abruptly.

"Go ahead," Mr. Peepers said mildly. "I'm not confused."

Wes nodded. "I know, I know. But I've forgotten what I wanted to say." After a moment's reflection, he continued. "Well, that's what I'd do if I were you. And, I think, what Thomas Jefferson would do, too—if he were you, instead of me."

Mr. Peepers frowned slightly. "Well . . ."

"Do you follow me?" Wes asked.

Mr. Peepers was stunned. "Uh-huh."

"Well," Wes said, smiling broadly, "need I say more, sport?"

Mr. Peepers airily returned Wes's smile. "Thanks a lot, Wes."

Wes Weskit leaned over and gripped Mr. Peepers' shoulders

firmly with both hands. "Don't be afraid," he said.

After he left, Mr. Peepers thought for a moment about Wes's advice. It seemed to him that something had been left out somewhere. He removed the now placid Louis from his cage and gently stroked his head. He wondered if it might mollify the superintendent to be presented with a gift of some kind. He looked at Louis. "How would you like to belong to the superintendent of schools?" he queried. Louis snapped savagely at one of his fingers.

Mr. Peepers took a bus to Melton the following afternoon. He wanted to discuss the problem further with Mr. Sidfern. He had decided not to eliminate the students' editorial, no matter how much Mr. Sidfern might hold it against him. Somehow he thought there must be a way to reach Mr. Sidfern, to persuade him. As his Grandmother had so often said: The best defense against prejudice is to be offensive about it. Mr. Peepers pondered the thought for a moment. There were times when his Grandmother's homilies got slightly mixed up in his memory.

He had to wait for Mr. Sidfern quite a long while. The superintendent sent word through his receptionist that some pressing business had detained him. Mr. Peepers was ushered into a conservatively decorated office with several leather chairs, a desk, a couch and an enormous globe of the world. Mr. Peepers passed the time by examining the beautifully painted globe. The world is a very large place, he thought. It occurred to him that perhaps many people were facing

the same sort of problem he was in many different countries. Far worse ones, too. The thought comforted him somehow. He spun the globe gently and smiled.

At that moment he heard Mr. Sidfern's voice. "Sorry I kept you waiting, Peepers," it said.

"That's quite all right, sir."

Mr. Sidfern seated himself behind his desk and beckoned Mr. Peepers to sit down before him. "Now then, what's on your mind?"

"Well, sir," Mr. Peepers said, controlling his anxiety as much as possible, "it's about that article in the school paper. The one about sitting on the lawn."

"Oh, yes," Mr. Sidfern said. "The one you deleted."

Mr. Peepers cleared his throat. The time for valor was upon him. "That's why I'm here, Mr. Sidfern," he said. "We didn't delete it."

Mr. Sidfern nodded proudly. "Good!" he said. "I'm . . ." Suddenly the full import of Mr. Peepers' remark seemed to have struck him. Abruptly his jowls began to quiver and redden. "You didn't delete it?"

"Well, no, sir, I didn't," Mr. Peepers said. "I feel, right or wrong, that the students have a right to express themselves."

Mr. Sidfern's expression hardened. Mr. Peepers had visions of his teaching career winging into the distance like last month's *Thecla titus.*

"Peepers," Mr. Sidfern said, "I won't have students criticizing my administration. That rule was made for a specific purpose."

"I'm sure it was," Mr. Peepers said. He tried desperately to think of some eloquent way to present his case for the students. For a moment nothing occurred to him. Then he remembered his conversation with Wes. "Er . . . Mr. Sidfern, do you know Thomas Jefferson?"

Mr. Sidfern frowned. "Only by reputation."

Mr. Peepers decided to bull his tactic through. "Well," he said quietly, "Thomas Jefferson said something like this: 'No Government ought to be—' "

"I know what he said, Peepers," Mr. Sidfern interrupted, with some choler. Then he softened slightly. "A great man, Peepers. I'm a great admirer of Jefferson, but—"

"He said a lot of things about freedom of the press," Mr. Peepers interjected.

"I know, I know!" Mr. Sidfern said. "I feel the same way. But, Peepers, this is nothing but the scribblings of children—"

Mr. Peepers interrupted, with a new sense of confidence. "Mr. Sidfern," he said carefully, "you will excuse me, but, when you were their age did you consider your own critical writing 'just the scribblings of children'?"

Mr. Sidfern seemed to get the idea. "Well, no," he said, somewhat uncomfortably. "Quite the contrary. But there was a difference, Peepers. The school paper I helped put out presented the facts fairly—*all* the facts, not just one side! In this case, the editorial makes no mention of the fact that it costs the school department three times as much to maintain the lawns if we allow the students to go on the grass. I simply do not have that much money in the maintenance budget."

Mr. Peepers smiled at the superintendent. "The students don't know that, Mr. Sidfern."

Mr. Sidfern had not quite heard him. "We simply cannot afford . . ." he continued vehemently. And then, "What?"

"The students don't know about that," Mr. Peepers said. "About not enough money."

Mr. Sidfern scraped thoughtfully at his jowls with his fingernails. "No," he said quietly, "I suppose they don't, at that."

Mr. Peepers decided to pursue his advantage. "If Tommy Sparks had understood your point of view, perhaps he wouldn't have written the editorial."

Mr. Sidfern thought the problem over for a moment. "Hmmmmm," he said.

"Or," Mr. Peepers added, "he would perhaps have written the editorial explaining to the students *why* they aren't allowed to sit on the lawns."

Mr. Sidfern looked at Mr. Peepers and nodded. "Well, Peepers," he said, "I confess I never looked at it that way."

Mr. Peepers continued earnestly. "Perhaps what the students need, sir, is a closer relationship with the administration."

Mr. Sidfern looked a little forlorn. "True!" he said. "But I can't spend all my time just running around to the schools."

"I realize that, sir," Mr. Peepers said, "so I have a small suggestion to make. Now, suppose once a week . . ."

The following afternoon a "Do Not Disturb" sign was hung on the outside of Mr. Sidfern's office for one hour. Inside, Mr. Peepers and Mr. Sidfern were conferring with Tommy Sparks, Homer Jansen and Arabella Simpkins. Tommy Sparks was taking notes in a small looseleaf notebook.

"Sir," he said respectfully to Mr.

Sidfern, "I've got all the information I need now on the lawn ruling. I'll be glad to change my editorial, if the editor approves."

Homer Jansen nodded. "With you all the way, scoop."

"Now," Tommy added, "if it's all right, we'd like to ask about the monitor system, too."

"Yes," Arabella Simpkins said earnestly. "Why should all the monitors be Seniors? A lot of the Juniors are quite concerned about this."

Mr. Sidfern folded his hands together and leaned forward. "The reason is this: The Seniors are more mature, know the school better, and it gives the Juniors something to look forward to. That way, being a monitor becomes a privilege rather than a task."

Tommy Sparks looked up from the notes he was taking. "Is this for the record, sir?"

Mr. Sidfern nodded. "You may quote me," he said. "Well, any more questions from the press?"

The students shook their heads.

"In that case," he said, getting up from his desk, "suppose we adjourn until our press conference next week at the same time?"

The students stood up and smiled. "Thank you very much, sir," Homer Jansen said. His fellow pupils nodded approvingly.

As Mr. Peepers was making his way out of the office along with the students, Mr. Sidfern beckoned him aside. "Peepers," he said quietly, putting a hand on Mr. Peepers' shoulder, "I feel you handled this problem very adroitly. Very adroitly indeed. I thought I'd like to let you know."

Mr. Peepers could hardly conceal his pleasure. "Thank you, sir. I couldn't have done it without your wonderful co-operation."

"Not at all," Mr. Sidfern said. He looked at Mr. Peepers strangely for a moment. There was a peculiar glint in his eye. "Peepers," he continued, "there's something I'd like to talk to you about sometime in the future. Perhaps at graduation. Would you be at all interested in changing your job for a good deal more money?"

Mr. Peepers swallowed nervously. He hadn't even thought that Mr. Sidfern liked him. To hear him offering a better job struck Mr. Peepers nearly dumb. "Well, sir," he said, "I . . . er . . . wouldn't want to leave the school or Jefferson City. I . . ."

Mr. Sidfern smiled. "Well," he said, "it's a bit premature anyway. I'll see you at graduation. Keep up the good work in the meantime. You have a fine relationship with your students."

"Thank you, Mr. Sidfern," Mr. Peepers said. "Thank you very much."

Outside, as Mr. Peepers and his three pupils boarded the return bus for Jefferson City, Mr. Peepers could not help smiling to himself. Homer Jansen nudged Arabella Simpkins. "Look, Arabella," he said. "Mr. Peepers must be telling himself stories."

Mr. Peepers overheard him but didn't let on. No, Homer, he said to himself happily, not just a story. Not a fantasy or a dream. The real thing.

For almost the first time in his life, Mr. Peepers felt as though he had won a victory.

discussion

The student newspaper is frequently the point of friction between adminis-tration and students. How much freedom of the press can students have, in fact, when the newspaper is supported by the taxpayers' dollars? School ad-ministrators are particularly conscious of possible criticism from the com-munity if students express opinions which conflict with the mores and mo-rality of the community. In the case of the incident in the excerpt, Mr. Sid-fern is concerned with the school budget for upkeep of the school grounds. He also objects to any criticism of the administration as a general policy. He does not respect the judgment of young people. As he says, "this is nothing but the scribbling of children."

Although Mr. Peepers and Mr. Sidfern are intended to be comic charac-ters, they represent the entrenched forces in a typical school district. Teachers who might like to defend the student's point of view do so at peril of their jobs or school assignments.

Attempts to bring administrators and students together as is done in this incident are often looked upon by the students with some suspicion. The school, which is a microcosm of the larger society, views the press confer-ence like its counterpart in the political arena. Students are wary lest the conference turn into a forum for disseminating the views of the adminis-tration. Because the student newspaper generally has a faculty adviser who must answer to the administration for the content of the paper, particularly its editorials, there is a trend toward off campus newspapers in order to give students the freedom of expression they desire.

Mr. Sidfern's promise to Mr. Peepers at the end of this selection is both a promise and a threat. There is implied in Mr. Sidfern's offer an obligation to keep the press conferences at Mr. Sidfern's level of tolerance. Mr. Peep-ers may very well find himself in the untenable position of mediating be-tween further demands for editorial freedom on the part of students and a desire for more restriction on the part of the administration.

springboards for inquiry

1. Defend your position regarding the function of the high school newspaper vis à vis the administration of the school system.

2. Comment upon Mr. Peepers' defense of the editorial.

3. To what extent do you feel it is possible for two generations to interpret one another fairly?

4. In this excerpt there is an unreality about the seemingly total understanding be-tween the students and the central administration once they met weekly. What do you think of the first press conference? What do you think of its chances for lon-gevity and amiability?

M. J. Amft

No boy. I'm a girl!

No boy shall be allowed to wear blue jeans during school hours nor while in the school building. Unobservance of this rule shall meet with immediate suspension.

In the middle of junior year I became a civilian rights agitator. Not civil rights—that's no problem in our town—but civilian rights. School wasn't the army, right? They didn't own us, right? They couldn't put us in uniform. Soldiers had to wear GI clothes and GI haircuts, and polish their buttons and shoes, but this was *civilian* life, a high school in a free country, and they suspended three boys for wearing blue jeans to school. Actually they just sent them home and told them to come back wearing something else, but it was the principle of the thing that mattered to me.

I kept thinking about it all afternoon, getting madder and madder. What if those boys were so poor they didn't have anything else to wear? Are the poor to be punished? Is that Democracy? Is that the Great Society? I happened to know that those particular three boys weren't poor, but what if they had been?

"It's the principle of the thing," I said. I was walking home with Allen Newman the way I always did because (for one) he lived at the end of my block and (for two) I had a hopeless crush on him. Hopeless because girls meant absolutely nothing, nothing in Allen's life. Clothes meant nothing to him either. He wore plain, conservative, utilitarian clothes that his mother ordered

from a catalogue. She took his measurements and sent away for plain white shirts and plain dark wash pants. He had one lightweight windbreaker, one heavy windbreaker (both dark blue), one dark blue suit (which he never wore) and three neckties. When his shoes wore out, he went to Clark's Shoe Shop and asked for "a pair of the same." Brown moccasins. Every second Saturday he went up to the barber and had his hair trimmed, and he refused to wear the cologne his grandmother gave him, the after-shave lotion his aunt gave him, or the Aphrodisia I gave him. He hated perfume for men.

The reason I knew all these intimate things about Allen and the reason I gave him a Christmas present is that his mother and mine are old best-friends who are always on the telephone talking about their children.

My mother was on the phone that day when I got home. "Just be glad you don't have a daughter. Speaking of which, here she is. Good-by, Ruthie. I'll call you tomorrow. Tell Allen I'm very proud he got another A."

"That was Ruthie Newman," she said. "Allen got another A."

"I know. Listen, Mother, there's something terrible going on at our school. Allen doesn't care because he has absolutely no feeling of civic responsibility, but I think it's criminal. I'm sure it's illegal."

"Drugs!" my mother said. "Airplane glue? Or worse?"

"No, no. It's the school authorities. It's the principal, actually, Mr. Hayden. I mean he *is* the school authority. He's the one."

"Mr. Hayden is pushing drugs?!"

"Mother, will you listen? Nobody said anything about drugs. Mr. Hayden is the one saying you can't wear blue jeans to school."

"Why should I wear blue jeans to school? Much as I hate those PTA meetings, when I do go, I wear my good black suit. Where did Mr. Hayden get the idea I wanted to wear blue jeans?"

You see how it is with my mother. She's very emotional, and she jumps to conclusions. I finally managed to explain that by "you" I meant "one," or three: the three boys in the blue jeans. I didn't think any public school or any principal had the right to dictate to any student in regard to personal appearance, and I thought all parents should write a protest letter.

My mother wasn't interested and changed the subject.

"Are you going out with that ugly Roger tomorrow night?" she asked.

When I told her no, that was all over, she was glad; but when Ralph showed up, she dragged me into the kitchen and said, "For months you dated a boy who needed a good dermatologist. Now it's a boy who needs an orthodontist. What's wrong with their parents? Where do you find these boys whose mothers neglect them? Why can't you find a nice boy whose parents take an interest in his welfare, a boy like Allen?"

Why indeed? I was willing. Meantime I didn't want to spend weekends doing chemistry experiments. That's what Allen did. He had all these smelly things in his basement which really bugged his mother. As

Ruthie said, maybe daughters washed their hair so much it clogged up the drains; at least daughters didn't cause terrible smells to come up the hot-air registers. To which, of course, my mother replied that smells in the basement result in A's in chemistry, whereas hair in the drains results in nothing but a plumber's bill.

I didn't think Ralph was anything much, myself—but he was a date, he was a way to get out on Saturday nights, and he agreed with me about the blue jeans.

Monday morning every home room teacher had a mimeographed "Memo from the Principal's Office," which he read aloud and then stuck on the bulletin board:

No boy shall be allowed to wear blue jeans during school hours nor while in the school building. Unobservance of this rule shall meet with immediate suspension.

I don't think Mr. Hayden is literate. Unobservance? Is that a word? And what right had he, what right?

On the way home I fumed about it to Allen, who said there was no reason for me to get excited. Why should I concern myself over what boys couldn't wear as long as I was allowed to wear what I pleased?

"Because if one group's rights are infringed upon, another group's rights are in danger." And then I screamed and hugged him—which I did every now and then, being unable to restrain myself; he never reacted one way or the other—and said, "You've given me a great idea! I'm a girl!"

"I thought you knew that," he said.

I ignored that because I had suddenly realized the right way to protest. Not with letters and petitions, not with marches and sit-ins . . . the way to protest was to take Mr. Hayden's directive word for word, but *only* word for word. The letter killeth. Ah ha! No *boy* it said. I'm a girl.

Of course, I knew my mother wasn't going to let me wear blue jeans to school. As it was, one of her big complaints about me was my clothes. She hates colored stockings, textured stockings, fake fur, vinyl, wild colors, dots, stripes and patterns except "a nice, soft herringbone or a muted plaid." She had a running lecture on what a pretty girl I could be if I would wear a nice tweed skirt, a cashmere sweater, a string of small pearls and nylons. Fashionwise she lives in the past. I'd never get out of my own house in blue jeans. But Ruthie Newman slept late mornings, and Harry, Allen's father, left very early, so Allen was the only one up and around, and I could stuff jeans in my bookbag and change at his house. The trouble was if I told him about my plan, he might say no. So I simply asked him if he would let me use his powder room the next morning.

"I don't want to wake your mother," I said, "so I won't ring the bell. I'll just whistle two bars of *Help!* through the kitchen keyhole. You'll be out there eating your cereal, and you'll hear me and let me in."

Allen eats six bowls of cold cereal every morning. He will not eat "a good, hot breakfast," which is why Ruthie sleeps late. What mother wants to torture herself watching a growing boy eat nothing but bowl after bowl of cold cereal when she would be only too glad to cook him some eggs and bacon?

Allen is shy enough so that he started to say, "Why do you want to use our—" and then gulped and blushed, which was what I was counting on.

The next morning I whistled at the keyhole. Allen let me in, looked embarrassed, and poured out another bowl of Crispy Critters, while I slipped into the powder room and my blue jeans.

As we walked along to school I said, "Don't you notice anything about me?"

Of course he hadn't. Allen never noticed anything about anybody. That was another thing that bugged Ruthie, who said he was only interested in *things,* not people, that there was something abnormal about him because he didn't seem to be aware of other people; he didn't *relate.* To which my mother said, "Be glad. Debbie is aware of other people. Debbie relates. And to whom? Stupid boys and boys with dandruff."

But as soon as I got to home room, wow. Mrs. Saunders gave me a talk on how she was a teacher, hired to teach, not to discipline. I could march right down and present myself to Mr. Hayden as *his* problem. I was really kind of scared. I'd never been sent to the principal's office, but I kept telling myself it was the principle that mattered, so the heck with the principal.

Mr. Hayden exploded. You'd have thought I was wearing a bikini. I just kept looking gee-gosh-bewildered, I'm-just-a-little-girl, and when he finally ran out of steam I said, "Gee, Mr. Hayden, sir, I sure am sorry, but your directive specifically stated 'No *boy.' I'm a girl.*"

I stuck out my chest, which is only 32A but enough to get the idea over. Mr. Hayden closed his eyes and clenched his teeth and fists.

"And you can't send me home," I said, "because there's nobody there and I don't have a key and the temperature is below freezing, twentynine degrees, humidity fifty percent, barometer—"

Mr. Hayden opened everything: eyes, teeth, fists and the door to the outer office.

"Miss Nussbaum!" he screamed. "Take a memo!"

No boy and no girl, no man and no woman shall be allowed to wear blue jeans during school hours nor while in the school building. Unobservance of this rule shall meet with immediate suspension.

The next day I was a big hero with the original three blue jean boys. I hadn't even known them to talk to, but they all stopped me in the hall and told me I was the greatest and they really appreciated what I had done for them. I said I hadn't done it for them. I had done it for all free people, all civilians.

"Yesterday the armed forces, today the schools, tomorrow the world. It's not 1984 yet," I said, "and I'm not through fighting!"

When they asked me if I was going to wear blue jeans anyway and get suspended, I told them about my plan. It made them so happy they all introduced themselves and invited me to have a Coke at the Snackaroo. Paul, Chris and Peter. They were all quite cute, not as cute as Allen but cute enough to impress Mary Jo and Cathy, who were in the Snackaroo and at loose ends. I'm not at all convinced that Mary Jo and Cathy really had civilian rights in their hearts, but they were more than willing to join the protest.

The next morning I whistled two bars of *Help!* into Allen's keyhole. He opened the door and whispered "I didn't know you were going to be coming here every morning."

I looked at him with my Quiet Desperation look, and he said, "Uh, it's right down the hall to your left," and poured out a bowl of Alpha Bits. He still didn't notice anything until we got to school and Mrs. Saunders turned pale purple and sent Paul, Chris, Peter, Mary Jo, Cathy and me down to Mr. Hayden's office. We were all wearing wheat jeans.

"Now let me do the talking," I said, "and remember not to look defiant or sullen."

Paul, Chris and Peter—who had spent years standing in front of the mirror getting those eyebrows right *down* there, man, right in the old eye socket, cool—opened wide and grinned.

"No, no!" I said. "*Not* 'What—me worry?' Look *innocent* and bewildered." It's not easy to learn my gee-gosh look in one hurried lesson on your way to the guillotine, but they tried, and they did keep their mouths shut.

Mr. Hayden opened his, and when he had to inhale after a ten-minute rant, I quickly said, "Gee, Mr. Hayden, sir, the directive plainly says, right there in black and white, *blue.*"

"Young lady," he said, "I don't know what your game is, but you're not going to win."

The new memo had to be altered several times. Its original form was:

No boy and no man (except school janitors and repair men) shall wear jeans or cowboy pants or work pants of any kind or color during school hours nor while in the school building. Furthermore at these same times and in this same place no girl nor woman shall wear any kind of pants.

"Mrs. Saunders," I said, "I do not believe that the mothers of this community want their daughters to go to school without any kind of pants. I believe that if the press obtained the information that a high school principal was forbidding the girls to wear underwear—"

Bedlam, of course. Mrs. Saunders flounced out of the room while everybody cheered and whistled for me except Allen, who was using the free time to work on an extra credit assignment.

Of course, *No girl shall wear any visible pants* was a mistake that even as confused a writer as Mr. Hayden shouldn't have made. After a great deal of hilarity in the halls— But I don't own any *invisible* pants; does that mean visible to the naked eye, sir?—a monitor was dispatched, on Mr. Hayden's orders, to rip down all memos. But he hadn't surrendered.

The following Monday there was a new one. He must have labored on it all weekend:

> In the school and on school grounds or property boys (unless engaged in legitimate and authorized athletics) shall wear at all times trousers or slacks or wash pants (not jeans, cowboy pants or work pants). The slacks or pants or trousers shall not be cut-off nor torn-off nor folded nor rolled up. Boys shall also wear shirts or sweaters. Girls shall wear dresses or skirts and blouses or skirts and sweaters. No other form of clothing will be tolerated. Underwear shall be concealed.

"That about ties it up," Chris said. "Now what are you going to do?"

"I'm going to keep fighting," I said. "Civilian rights shall not perish."

That evening I asked my mother if I could wear that jumper to school, the nice, royal blue one she bought me for Christmas.

"Well, of course!" she said. "Debbie, I'd love it! I shopped all over, and it *hangs* there."

"Can I wear the shirt with the button-down collar?"

"You'll look adorable! Why, a girl with lovely—"

"You'll have to write a note, Mom. And I don't even know if that will work. You may have to get a lot of outside support. Mr. Hayden has absolutely forbidden any girl to wear anything except a dress or a skirt and blouse or sweater."

That did it. My mother leaped to the bait like a starving trout. That lovely jumper, that sweet little shirt. Was Mr. Hayden crazy? First she called Ruthie, then she called everyone else she knew in PTA; eventually, of course, she got Mrs. Franklin, who talks even louder and faster than my mother and therefore got a word in edgewise. Several words. Words like Debbie, blue jeans and wheat jeans.

"An utter untruth!" my mother said. "I am here every morning to see to it that my daughter is properly dressed. Never has she left this house on a school morning in jeans. Kooky things, yes. Green stockings, nouveau art, London look, baby doll, mod, rock, pop, op. I'll admit she's done everything to look like a freak, even though she is really a very pretty girl if she would only take my advice and—"

But it was Mrs. Franklin's turn to tell how her Bonnie was also a lovely girl, who never lied to her mother and certainly was not a troublemaker or talebearer, but who said positively that . . .

When my mother hung up, she looked at me. "It's true, Mom," I said. "I changed in Allen's house."

"*Allen* suggested this to you?"

"No, mom. It wasn't his fault. He just let me use the powder room."

By that time she had Ruthie on

the phone again, and for a while I thought a lifelong friendship was going to end right there. But pretty soon a new, purring note crept into her voice.

"You know, he might be beginning to relate, Ruthie. I mean, he's bound to begin to become aware someday, and remember that terrible girl who kept making eyes at him last year? In the alley when he took out the garbage? What if he relates to somebody like that? A girl like that in your powder room, and Allen could become a changed boy. For the worse. It might even affect his grades, and you know Harry will kill himself if Allen doesn't get into Harvard. Well, I'd be very happy if Debbie and Allen became interested in each other, but I doubt it. Who has that kind of luck? Girls only want to go out with boys who come from terrible families. Be glad you don't have a daughter."

The PTA got in on it then, and so did the student council and the local newspaper. Everybody had conflicting opinions. There were mothers (of daughters) demanding that all boys wear suit jackets to school; dressed like gentlemen they would act like gentlemen. Whereupon a mother screeched that her son grew six inches in six weeks and she was not going to be stuck with a lot of expensive outgrown suit jackets. There was a compromise suggestion that all boys wear ties, but that was voted down when someone explained that it had been tried at another school and the boys wore the ties around their waists or ankles.

All boys wear ties around necks resulted in ties being wound around and around like a choker. *All boys wear ties under collars and tied.* They tied them in the back. One lady got up and said that in this temperature zone there was a problem, but no clothes meant no uniforms! No uniforms meant no war. Her family was from the South, and if there had been no boys in blue or in gray, if all had been dressed only in the skin God gave them, there would have been no war. *All* clothes were unnatural.

The controversy went on for months. When there was a memo *No girl's skirt shall be more than two inches above the kneecap,* I dutifully dragged out my last year's granny dress and shuffled off in sure anticipation of a new memo: *No girl's skirt shall be more than three inches below the kneecap.*

But my heart wasn't in it anymore. I didn't really care at all. All I really cared about was Allen. I didn't just have a crush on him. I really *liked* that Allen. He kept getting bigger and cuter every day. Those cold cereal commercials don't lie. Sugar Dots and Frosty B's were giving him muscles and rosy cheeks. Even though he spent all his time studying or doing homework or down in the basement, while his mother begged him to please, please get a little fresh air, he kept blossoming. And I was going out on Saturday with Randy, whom I hated.

By now it was almost the end of the school year; and Mr. Hayden had washed his hands of the whole thing. His final memo was: *Anybody can wear anything. What do I care?* Mr. Hayden was cracking up, but so was I. Every Saturday night when my mother came up and said, "He's here. He's waiting down there. In that furry vest with his skinny bare arms," I shuddered. For Sonny and

Cher, okay. But I really wished Randy would wear a nice soft herringbone or muted plaid, something that would blend into the background so you wouldn't notice how ugly he was. He also wore a toothpick in the corner of his mouth. He said it kept him from smoking.

I had almost forgotten about the civilian rights fight, and so had everybody else except Mr. Hayden, a sore loser who decided to get back at me. At the last day assembly, right in front of the entire junior class, Mr. Hayden took his last shot.

"To those of you who doubted that there is a correlation between conservative dress and scholastic achievement, I would like to point out that no boys with long hair and pointed shoes made the honor list. And Miss Debbie Markam, the first girl to enter these halls of learning wearing blue jeans, and who has consistently advocated and agitated for extremes in styles, has received a final grade of C minus in advanced algebra, which certainly keeps her out of the upper ten percent. Contrariwise the top student in the class, a boy with straight A's, has managed to maintain his fine school record under the so-called dictatorial militarism of my original directive asking for a degree of prudence and decorum in personal appearance. Allen Newman, please stand up."

And that's when Mr. Hayden lost the fight. The last thing Allen wanted to do was stand up in the assembly hall, but Mrs. Saunders kept poking and hissing at him. Mr. Hayden said, "Look at him. Our top student. And what is he wearing? Clean cut!" Everyone looked at Allen, and Allen looked at the floor. I felt Mr. Hayden had made a mistake there, but I didn't know how big a one.

On the way home Allen said, "Mr. Hayden is a boob! First of all, it was a real achievement for you to get a C minus in advanced algebra. If he knew anything about education, he would have known you have a definite math block, probably developed from incorrect teaching in the formative years. Next, no one has the right to force someone to stand up in the middle of assembly and be stared at just because he's not wearing a furry vest!"

"Well, Allen, he was really asking you to stand up because of the A's."

"That's no excuse. People have the right to be the way they want to be without being pointed out. It's the principle of the thing!"

Allen spent the summer in the country up at his grandmother's. He was killing several birds with that stone. He was growing sunflowers to prove some sort of involved thing about seed pods, number ratio and phototropism. I couldn't understand it, but whatever it was, he proved it. He was making his grandmother deliriously happy because she's crazy about him. He was making his mother happy because he was getting a lot of fresh air and because she had the chance to clean out their basement.

I got rid of Randy and spent a dull summer baby-sitting, lying on the beach, and trying to sit on my hair. It was everybody's ambition: hair so long you could sit on it. I never made it. By the end of August I was so bored with everybody's measuring and measuring that I had the whole works chopped off except for some thick bangs and sideburns. My mother fainted.

As she was conveniently sitting on our down-filled sofa at the time, it wasn't much of a faint, and in about two minutes she was up and on the phone with Ruthie.

"You know how I begged her to get a haircut? This is my payment for opening my mouth. Just be glad you don't have a daughter."

A week before school started, Allen came home. Then Ruthie fainted. She called my mother, and my mother dashed over, and I dashed along with her because I couldn't believe it! Allen?

"Debbie," he said, "I like your haircut. The back of your neck is very sexy-looking."

He asked me to go to a movie with him and said he wanted to go places all week long so he could get used to people staring at him. He wanted to be in full control of his emotions when school started. He kept giving me little hugs right from the start, and by the end of the week, well, Allen was relating.

The first day of school he called for me and we walked off hand in hand. I was wearing a brown skirt and white blouse. He was wearing brown slacks and a white shirt. We both looked nice and neat, our hair clean and shiny. His was about eight inches longer than mine, hanging down around his shoulders. It was the principle of the thing. He had decided that Mr. Hayden had no scientific basis for the assumption that long hair or pointed shoes led to low marks, or that blue jeans were the cause of a continuing math block in the female.

"I intend to prove to Mr. Hayden that I can be an A student without ever getting a haircut. But I'm nervous! Stick by me, Debbie."

I was willing. Mr. Hayden was standing in the main entrance, welcoming the students. When Allen shook his hand and said, "Good morning, sir. Nice to be back," Mr. Hayden's lips started to tremble. He turned pale and his eyes rolled back, but he didn't faint. He just turned slowly away and walked into his office, a defeated man. I almost felt sorry for him except that when it comes to something as important as civilian rights you've got to be strong. After all, we only have a few years to fight before 1984.

discussion

Experience has taught the schools that student power is a reality. During the 1960s most student groups learned methods of active and passive resistance that could not be ignored by the school administrations. Debbie does not choose direct confrontation such as a sit-in or a protest march; she merely carries out Mr. Hayden's directive to the letter. She tries to enlist others in her cause so the administration will be unable to follow through on a punishment program.

Challenging the dress code has frequently been the first "cause célèbre" of high school student activists. At the high school level the whittling away process has been slow but continues, and most high schools are probably more lenient than they dreamed they would be when negotiations for concessions started. Looking back now, some schools probably find certain rules and regulations they adhered to already oldfashioned. Student power led the way to reforms for teachers, too. Today teachers, male and female, come to school dressed quite casually, and on many campuses women wear pants while men wear sport shirts without ties.

In this story, it is a girl who leads the way to student power. Allen's mother observes that he is only interested in things, not people, while Debbie's mother says "Debbie is aware of other people, Debbie relates." The difference in the male and female orientation at this age may account for Debbie's interest in pursuing her defense of the boys in blue jeans. Her intuitive knowledge of people helps her to instruct the culprits how to look and how to reply to Mr. Hayden in order to gain points for their side. In short order all the adults are in turmoil. The parents and the administration cannot agree on the appropriate attire for school, and the battle goes on for months at the adult level. Although Debbie says she carried the torch for civilian rights, it is obvious that the incident was a diversion for her and a way to get Allen's attention. The serious student, like Allen, learns from the tempest that there are inconsistencies in rigid thinking, and attempts to pursue his rational course based on independent judgment. Many student vs. administration battles are carried out on a rational basis, but there seems unquestionably to be a vogue for confrontation for confrontation's sake. It seems appropriate and inevitable that the high school years will be a time of testing the adolescent's ability to defy authority and gain independence. The only differences from generation to generation are the specific issues over which students and administrators can wrangle.

springboards for inquiry

1. What is your opinion of a dress code at school at any level of education?

2. If you were in the administrator's place how would you have dealt with Debbie's protest and the ensuing furor with the parents?

3. What do you think of high school students being permitted to smoke on campus? Do you feel the same way about junior high school students?

4. Do you think it is desirable for students to have restrictions that they can try to change, or would it be better if there were as few restrictions placed on students as possible?

the parents

Recently one of the editors of this volume wrote a heated letter to his city's superintendent of schools. He wrote the letter in the capacity of a parent, and by Monday of the following week the two were having lunch at the invitation of the superintendent. Such is parent power.

In the essay, "Who Runs the Schools?" we described a situation in Brookly, New York where parents occupied a school for two days at the start of school in September 1973 and where these same parents, in June of that year, occupied the school for 53 consecutive days. Such is parent power.

In Orange County, California parents overwhelmed the Board of Education meeting, demanded that sex education courses be banished from the schools, and they were! And that is parent power.

When parent-teacher conferences started nearly 50 years ago, it was a revolution on the educational scene. Who would have believed that parents deserved input about their children's education? Today parents and teachers study how to confer successfully, and classes in many communities are cancelled to allow time for effective parent-teacher conferences. There are even those zealots who believe that it is possible to make parent-teacher conferences creative![1]

The educational level of parents has risen so that in many middleclass communities the teachers and parents hold identical degrees. As parents have become more knowledgeable they have felt more confident about confronting teachers regarding all areas of their children's education. For many teachers this has been a mixed blessing. Prior to World War II teachers invariably were better educated than the parents of the children they taught. There was rarely then the educational equality which exists today for WASP (White Anglo-Saxon Protestant) America. Typically parents were summoned to school, told what was wrong with their children, and intimidated by teachers whose educational level was vastly superior to theirs.

The world has changed—a bit. In many ways the parents control the schools through PTA organizations which are often quite self-directed. Together with the principal and/or his staff, parent conferences are planned, parents are included on school/community relations councils, and parents have even been heavily involved in staff and curricular decisions. Indeed it is not at all unusual both in suburban and ghetto America to find that parents can and do force the transfer/resignation of both teachers and principals.

Callahan, in an old and venerable text says, "The fact that America is a group society has had some important implications for the schools. The primary reason is that many of these groups have attempted at various times to *interfere* [italics, ours] with the operation of the school."[2]

[1]Elliott D. Landau, *Creative Parent-Teacher Conferences* (Salt Lake City: Wheelwright Press, 1968).

[2]Raymond E. Callahan, *An Introduction to Education in American Society* (New York: Knopf, 1956) p. 151.

Whether parent pressure is justifiably seen as "interference" depends on the reader's point of view. Nevertheless, America's propensity for the formation of common-interest groups (this might even be termed our desire for serial nuclear family associations) has resulted in church groups having their children excused from saluting the flag, and families organizing to exclude their children from attending health and hygiene courses. In some communities it is taboo to mention Darwin's theory of evolution, the U.N., and UNESCO programs.

Such educators as Willard Goslin, George Stoddard, and George Ebey, to mention just a few, have been ousted from their positions as superintendents when enough parents have banded together at a Board of Education meeting to force their resignation. In other instances parents have influenced school lunch programs, teacher pay and hours, the participation of girls in intramural programs, and countless other areas heretofore the private domain of the educator. In fact, Ellen Lurie's volume, entitled *How to Change the Schools,* is a primer on how parents can begin to have their influence felt in a large urban school system.[3] This book details explicit instructions on how to fight the administrative hierarchy of a large school system. There is an entire chapter devoted to parents' rights; everything from the courtesy due parents to how to evaluate a good teacher is carefully outlined. Faced with such an informed opposition, few school superintendents could resist change very long.

The recent history of community rebellion against the schools, which has led to some very direct confrontations and even violence between parents and principals particularly in urban school systems, has prompted three school administrators to collaborate on a volume entitled, *Crucial Issues in Education: A Problem-Solving Guide for School Administrators.*[4] Unlike the volume cited above by Lurie, this book is a primer for administrators. It tells them how effectively to use school community relations personnel, how to involve teachers in planning for innovation and, in a particularly relevant chapter, how to respond to militant students and parents. The authors, quoting a guidance counselor's essay say, "Education in the past decade has taken on a new dimension so as to confront people in administrative positions with parental and student pressure never before imagined. Everyone in the school community now claims to have a sincere interest in what is happening. . . . Unfortunately school issues are sometimes used in deplorable ways to gain notoriety for individuals who have less than a child's education at stake."[5]

We found it interesting that in *How to Change the Schools,* Lurie counsels parents to be wary about a principal's motives if the principal immediately surrounds himself with aides. Dwyer says, " . . . [a] wise administrator will

---

[3]Ellen Lurie, *How to Change the Schools* (New York: Random House, 1970).

[4]James J. Lewis, Jr., Robert M. Bookbinder, and Raymond R. Bauer, *Crucial Issues in Education: A Problem-Solving Guide for School Administrators* (Englewood Cliffs, N.J.: Prentice-Hall, 1972).

[5]Ibid., p. 205 in Thomas J. Dwyer, "Responding to Militant Students and Parents."

always call his assistant to be present in circumstances which are likely to take on an ugly dimension.[6]

Only time will tell whether girding one's loins for battle will renew or destroy the schools. The kid gloves are off, for better or worse, and parental interest no longer is at a distance or discreet. It is where the action is and often crude rather than genteel.

Although parents have been aggressive, all of parental power is not characterized by sit-ins, strikes, or front-office confrontations. Thousands of parents have lent support to schools in the roles of volunteer aides, assistants, and para-professionals. Untold numbers of minority group parents have been studying child development in order to contribute to the management of their children in their neighborhood schools. Other thousands are more directly involved in school affairs and are not storming the Bastille. Although parent power makes the news more often when it erupts than when it silently operates as a force in the educational lives of children, certainly parents are working with the schools as well as against them.

Irwin Shaw

Rich man, poor man

"In whatever country you went to school, Mr. Jordache, would it be considered proper for a young boy to draw a picture of his teacher nude, in the classroom?"

The classroom was silent, except for the busy scratching of pens on paper. Miss Lenaut was seated at her desk reading, occasionally raising her head to scan the room. She had set a half-hour composition for her pupils to write, subject, "Franco-American Friendship." As Rudolph bent to his task at his desk toward the rear of the room, he had to admit to himself that Miss Lenaut might be beautiful, and undoubtedly French, but that her imagination left something to be desired.

Half a point would be taken off for a mistake in spelling or a mis-

placed accent, and a full point for any errors in grammar. The composition had to be at least three pages long.

Rudolph filled the required three pages quickly. He was the only student in the class who consistently got marks of over 90 on compositions and dictation, and in the last three tests he had scored 100. He was so good in the language that Miss Lenaut had grown suspicious and had asked him if his parents spoke French. "Jordache," she said. "It is not an American name." The imputation hurt him. He wanted to be different from the people around him in many respects, but not in his American-ness. His father was German, Rudolph told Miss Lenaut, but aside from an occasional

Chapter from Rich Man, Poor Man *by Irwin Shaw. Copyright © 1969, 1970 by Irwin Shaw. Reprinted by permission of Delacorte Press.*

[6]Ibid., p. 207.

word in that language, all Rudolph ever heard at home was English.

"Are you sure your father wasn't born in the Alsace?" Miss Lenaut persisted.

"Cologne," Rudolph said and added that his grandfather had come from Alsace-Lorraine.

"Alors," Miss Lenaut said. "It is as I suspected."

It pained Rudolph that Miss Lenaut, that incarnation of feminine beauty and worldly charm and the object of his feverish devotion, might believe, even for a moment, that he would lie to her or take secret advantage of her. He longed to confess his emotion and had fantasies of returning to the high school some years hence, when he was a suave college man, and waiting outside the school for her and addressing her in French, which would by that time be fluent and perfectly accented, and telling her, with an amused chuckle for the shy child he had been, of his schoolboy passion for her in his junior year. Who knew what then might happen? Literature was full of older women and brilliant young boys, of teachers and precocious pupils . . .

He reread his work for errors, scowling at the banality which the subject had imposed upon him. He changed a word or two, put in an accent he had missed, then looked at his watch. Fifteen minutes to go.

"Hey!" There was a tortured whisper on his right. "What's the past participle of *venir*?"

Rudolph turned his head slightly toward his neighbor, Sammy Kessler, a straight *D* student. Sammy Kessler was hunched in a position of agony over his paper, his eyes flicking desperately over at Rudolph. Rudolph glanced toward the front of the room. Miss Lenaut was engrossed in her book. He didn't like to break the rules in her class, but he couldn't be known by his contemporaries as a coward or a teacher's pet.

"*Venu,*" he whispered.

"With two *o's?*" Kessler whispered.

"A *u*, idiot," Rudolph said.

Sammy Kessler wrote laboriously, sweating, doomed to his *D*.

Rudolph stared at Miss Lenaut. She was particularly attractive today, he thought. She was wearing long earrings and a brown, shiny dress that wrinkled skin-tight across her girdled hips and showed a generous amount of her stiffly armored bosom. Her mouth was a bright-red gash of lipstick. She put lipstick on before every class. Her family ran a small French restaurant in the theatrical district of New York and there was more of Broadway in Miss Lenaut than the Faubourg St. Honoré, but Rudolph was happily unaware of this distinction.

Idly, Rudolph began to sketch on a piece of paper. Miss Lenaut's face took shape under his pen, the easily identifiable two curls that she wore high on her cheeks in front of her ears, the waved, thick hair, with the part in the middle. Rudolph continued drawing. The earrings, the rather thick, beefy throat. For a moment, Rudolph hesitated. The territory he was now entering was dangerous. He glanced once more at Miss Lenaut. She was still reading. There were no problems of discipline in Miss Lenaut's class. She gave out punishments for the slightest infractions with merciless liberality. The full conjugation of the reflexive irregular verb *se taire*, repeated ten times, was the lightest of her sentences. She could sit and read with only an occasional lifting of her eyes to reassure herself that all was well, that there was no whispering, no passing of papers between desk and desk.

Rudolph gave himself to the delights of erotic art. He continued the line down from Miss Lenaut's neck to her right breast, naked. Then he put in her left breast. He was satisfied with the proportions. He drew her standing, three-quarter view, one arm extended, with a piece of chalk in her hand, at the blackboard. Rudolph worked with relish. He was getting better with each opus. The hips were easy. The mons veneris he drew from memory of art books in the library, so it was a bit hazy. The legs, he felt, were satisfactory. He would have liked to draw Miss Lenaut barefooted, but he was bad on feet, so he gave her the high-heeled shoes, with straps above the ankle, that she habitually wore. Since he had her writing on the blackboard, he decided to put some words on the blackboard. *"Je suis folle d'amour,"* he printed in an accurate representation of Miss Lenaut's blackboard script. He started to shade Miss Lenaut's breasts artistically. He decided that the entire work would be more striking if he drew it as though there were a strong light coming from the left. He shaded the inside of Miss Lenaut's thigh. He wished there were someone he knew in school he could show the drawing to who would appreciate it. But he couldn't trust the boys on the track team, who were his best friends, to treat the picture with appropriate sobriety.

He was shading in the straps on the ankles when he became conscious of someone standing beside his desk. He looked up slowly. Miss Lenaut was glaring down at the drawing on his desk. She must have moved down the aisle like a cat, high heels and all.

Rudolph sat motionless. No gesture seemed worthwhile at the moment. There was fury in Miss Lenaut's dark, mascaraed eyes and she was biting the lipstick off her lips. She reached out her hand, silently. Rudolph picked up the piece of paper and gave it to her. Miss Lenaut turned on her heel and walked back to her desk, rolling the paper in her hands so that no one could see what was on it.

Just before the bell rang to end the class, she called out, "Jordache."

"Yes, ma'am," Rudolph said. He was proud of the ordinary tone he managed to use.

"May I see you for a moment after class?"

"Yes, ma'am," he said.

The bell rang. The usual chatter broke out. The students hurried out of the room to rush for their next classes. Rudolph, with great deliberation, put his books into his briefcase. When all the other students had quit the room, he walked up to Miss Lenaut's desk.

She was seated like a judge. Her tone was icy. *"Monsieur l'artiste,"* she said. "You have neglected an important feature of your *chef d'oeuvre.*" She opened the drawer of her desk and took out the sheet of paper with the drawing on it and smoothed it with a rasping noise on the blotter of the desk top. "It is lacking a signature. Works of art are notoriously more valuable when they are signed authentically by the artist. It would be deplorable if there were any doubts as to the origin of a work of such richness." She pushed the drawing across the desk toward Rudolph. "I will be much indebted to you, Monsieur," she said, "if you would have the kindness to affix your name. Legibly."

Rudolph took out his pen and signed his name on the lower right hand corner of the drawing. He did it slowly and deliberately and he made sure that Miss Lenaut saw that he was studying the drawing at the same time. He was not going to act like a frightened kid in front of her. Love has its own requirements. Man enough to draw her naked, he was man enough to stand up to her wrath. He underlined his signature with a little flourish.

Miss Lenaut reached over and snatched the drawing to her side of the desk. She was breathing hard now. "Monsieur," she said shrilly, "you will go get one of your parents immediately after school is over today and you will bring it back for a conversation with me speedily." When she was excited, there were little, queer mistakes in Miss Lenaut's English. "I have some important things to reveal to them about the son they have reared in their house. I will be waiting here. If you are not here with a representative of your family by four o'clock the consequences will be of the gravest. Is it understood?"

"Yes, ma'am. Good afternoon, Miss Lenaut." The "good afternoon" took courage. He went out of the room, neither more quickly nor more slowly than he usually did. He remembered his gliding motion. Miss Lenaut sounded as though she had just run up two flights of stairs.

When he reached home after school was over, he avoided going into the store where his mother was serving some customers and went up to the apartment, hoping to find his father. Whatever happened, he didn't want his mother to see that drawing. His father might whack him, but that was to be preferred to the expression that he was sure would be in his mother's eyes for the rest of her life if she saw that picture.

His father was not in the house. Gretchen was at work and Tom never came home until five minutes before supper. Rudolph washed his hands and face and combed his hair. He was going to meet his fate like a gentleman.

He went downstairs and into the shop. His mother was putting a dozen rolls into a bag for an old woman who smelled like a wet dog. He waited until the old woman had left, then went and kissed his mother.

"How were things at school today?" she asked, touching his hair.

"Okay," he said. "The usual. Pa around anywhere?" "He's probably down at the river. Why?" The "Why?" was suspicious. It was unusual for anyone in the family to seek out her husband unnecessarily.

"No reason," Rudolph said carelessly.

"Isn't there track practice today?" she probed.

"No." Two customers came into the shop, the little bell over the door tingling, and he didn't have to lie any more. He waved and went out as his mother was greeting the customers.

When he was out of sight of the shop he began to walk quickly down toward the river. His father kept his shell in the corner of a ramshackle warehouse on the waterfront and usually spent one or two afternoons a week working on the boat there.

Rudolph prayed that this was one of those afternoons.

When he reached the warehouse he saw his father out in front of it, sandpapering the hull of the one-man shell, which was propped, upside down, on two sawhorses. His father had his sleeves rolled up and was working with great care on the smooth wood. As Rudolph approached, he could see the ropy muscles of his father's forearms hardening and relaxing with his rhythmic movements. It was a warm day, and even with the wind that came off the river his father was sweating.

"Hi, Pa," Rudolph said.

His father looked up and grunted, then went back to his work. He had bought the shell in a half-ruined condition for practically nothing from a boys' school nearby that had gone bankrupt. Some river memory of youth and health from his boyhood on the Rhine was behind the purchase and he had reconstructed the shell and varnished it over and over again. It was spotless and the mechanism of the sliding seat gleamed with its coating of oil. After he had gotten out of the hospital in Germany, with one leg almost useless and his big frame gaunt and weak, Jordache had exercised fanatically to recover his strength. His work on the Lake boats had given him the strength of a giant and the grueling miles he imposed on himself sweeping methodically up and down the river had kept him forbiddingly powerful. With his bad leg he couldn't catch anybody, but he gave the impression of being able to crush a grown man in those hairy arms.

"Pa . . ." Rudolph began, trying to conquer his nervousness. His fa-ther had never hit him, but Rudolph had seen him knock Thomas unconscious with one blow of his fist just last year.

"What's the matter?" Jordache tested the smoothness of the wood, with broad, spatulate fingers. The back of his hands and his fingers were bristling with black hairs.

"It's about school," Rudolph said.

"You in trouble? *You?*" Jordache looked over at his son with genuine surprise.

"Trouble might be too strong a word," Rudolph said. "A situation has come up."

"What kind of situation?"

"Well," Rudolph said, "there's this French woman who teaches French. I'm in her class. She says she wants to see you this afternoon. Now."

"Me?"

"Well," Rudolph admitted, "she said one of my parents."

"What about your mother?" Jordache asked. "You tell her about this?"

"It's something I think it's better she doesn't know about," Rudolph said.

Jordache looked across the hull of the shell at him speculatively. "French," he said. "I thought that was one of your good subjects."

"It is," Rudolph said. "Pa, there's no sense in talking about it, you've got to see her."

Jordache flicked a spot off the wood. Then he wiped his forehead with the back of his hand and began rolling down his sleeves. He swung his windjacket over his shoulder, like a workingman, and picked up his cloth cap and put it on his head, and started walking. Rudolph followed him, not daring to suggest that perhaps it would be a good idea if his father went home and put on a suit before the conversation with Miss Lenaut.

Miss Lenaut was seated at her desk correcting papers when Rudolph led his father into the room. The school building was empty, but there were shouts from the athletic field below the classroom windows. Miss Lenaut had put lipstick on at least three more times since Rudolph's class. For the first time, he realized that she had thin lips and plumped them out artificially. She looked up when they came into the room and her mouth set.

Jordache had put his windjacket on before entering the school and had taken off his cap, but he still looked like a workman.

Miss Lenaut stood up as they approached the desk.

"This is my father, Miss Lenaut," Rudolph said.

"How do you do, sir?" she said, without warmth.

Jordache said nothing. He stood there, in front of the desk, chewing at his moustache, his cap in his hands, proletarian and subdued.

"Has your son told you why I asked you to come this afternoon, Mr. Jordache?"

"No," Jordache said, "I don't remember that he did." That peculiar, uncharacteristic mildness was in his voice, too. Rudolph wondered if his father was afraid of the woman.

"It embarrasses me even to talk about it." Miss Lenaut immediately became shrill again. "In all my years of teaching . . . The indignity . . . From a student who has always seemed ambitious and diligent. He did not say what he had done?"

"No," Jordache said. He stood there patiently, as though he had all day and all night to sort out the matter, whatever it turned out to be.

"Eh, bien," Miss Lenaut said, "the burden devolves upon my shoulders." She bent down and opened the desk drawer and took out the drawing. She did not look at it, but held it down and away from her as she spoke. "In the middle of my classroom, when he was supposed to be writing a composition, do you know what he was doing?"

"No," said Jordache.

"This!" She poked the drawing dramatically in front of Jordache's nose. He took the paper from her and held it up to the light from the windows to get a better look at it. Rudolph peered anxiously at his father's face, searching for signs. He half expected his father to turn and hit him on the spot and wondered if he would have the courage to just stand there and take it without flinching or crying out. Jordache's face told him nothing. He seemed quite interested, but a little puzzled.

Finally, he spoke. "I'm afraid I can't read French," he said.

"That is not the point," Miss Lenaut said excitedly.

"There's something written here in French," Jordache pointed with his big index finger to the phrase, *"Je suis folle d'amour,"* that Rudolph had printed on the drawing of the blackboard in front of which the naked figure was standing.

"I am crazy with love, I am crazy with love." Miss Lenaut was now striding up and down in short trips behind her desk.

"What's that?" Jordache wrinkled his forehead, as though he was trying his best to understand but was out in waters too deep for him.

"That's what's written there." Miss Lenaut pointed a mad finger at the sheet of paper. "It's a translation of what your talented son has written there. 'I am crazy with love, I am crazy with love.'" She was shrieking now.

"Oh, I see," Jordache said, as though a great light had dawned on him. "Is that dirty in French?"

Miss Lenaut gained control of herself with a visible effort, although she was biting her lipstick again. "Mr. Jordache," she said, "have you ever been to school?"

"In another country," Jordache said.

"In whatever country you went to school, Mr. Jordache, would it be considered proper for a young boy to draw a picture of his teacher nude, in the classroom?"

"Oh!" Jordache sounded surprised. "Is this you?"

"Yes, it is," Miss Lenaut said. She glared bitterly at Rudolph.

Jordache studied the drawing more closely. "By God," he said, "I see the resemblance. Do teachers pose nude in high school these days?"

"I will not have you mock of me, Mr. Jordache," Miss Lenaut said with cold dignity. "I see there is no further point to this conversation. If you will be so good as to return the drawing to me . . ." She stretched out her hand. "I will say good day to you and take the matter up elsewhere, where the gravity of the situation will be appreciated. The office of the principal. I had wanted to spare your son the embarrassment of putting his obscenity on the principal's desk, but I see no other course is open to me. Now, if I may have the drawing please, I won't detain you further . . ."

Jordache took a step back, holding onto the drawing. "You say my son did this drawing?"

"I most certainly do," Miss Lenaut said. "His signature is on it."

Jordache glanced at the drawing to confirm this. "You're right," he said. "It's Rudy's signature. It's his drawing, all right. You don't need a lawyer to prove that."

"You may expect a communication from the principal," Miss Lenaut said. "Now, please return the drawing. I'm busy and I've wasted enough time on this disgusting affair."

"I think I'll keep it. You yourself said it's Rudy's," Jordache said placidly. "And it shows a lot of talent. A very good likeness." He shook his head in admiration. "I never guessed Rudy had it in him. I think I'll have it framed and hang it up back home. You'd have to pay a lot of money to get a nude picture as good as this one on the open market."

Miss Lenaut was biting her lips so hard she couldn't get a word out for the moment. Rudolph stared at his father, dumbfounded. He hadn't had any clear idea of how his father was going to react, but this falsely innocent, sly, country-bumpkin performance was beyond any concept that Rudolph might ever have had of how his father would behave.

Miss Lenaut gave tongue. She spoke in a harsh whisper, leaning malevolently over her desk and spitting out the words at Jordache. "Get out of here, you low, dirty, common foreigner, and take your filthy son with you."

"I wouldn't talk like that, Miss," Jordache said, his voice still calm. "This is a taxpayer's school and I'm a taxpayer and I'll get out when I'm good and ready. And if you didn't strut around with your tail wiggling in a tight skirt and half your titties showing like a two dollar whore on a street corner, maybe young boys wouldn't be tempted to draw pictures of you stark-assed naked. And if you ask me, if a man took you out of all your brassieres and girdles, it'd turn out that Rudy was downright complimentary in his art work."

Miss Lenaut's face was congested and her mouth writhed in hatred. "I know about you," she said. *"Sale Boche."*

Jordache reached across the desk and slapped her. The slap resounded like a small firecracker. The voices from the playing field had died down and the room was sickeningly silent. Miss Lenaut remained bent over, leaning on her hands on the desk, for another moment. Then she burst into tears and crumpled onto her chair, holding her hands to her face.

"I don't go for talk like that, you French cunt," Jordache said. "I didn't come all the way here from Europe to listen to talk like that. And if I was French these days, what with running like rabbits the first shot the dirty Boche fired at them, I'd think twice about insulting anybody. If it'll make you feel any better, I'll tell you I killed a Frenchman in 1916 with a bare bayonet and it won't surprise you that I stuck it in his back while he was trying to run home to his Mama."

As his father talked, calmly, as though he were discussing the weather or an order for flour, Rudolph began to shiver. The malice in the words was made intolerable by the conversational, almost friendly, tone in which they were delivered.

Jordache was going on, inexorably. "And if you think you're going to take it out on my boy here, you better think twice about that, too, because I don't live far from here and I don't mind walking. He's been an *A* student in French for two years and I'll be here to ask some questions if he comes back at the end of the term with anything less. Come on, Rudy."

They went out of the room, leaving Miss Lenaut sobbing at her desk.

They walked away from the school without speaking. When they came to a trash basket on a corner, Jordache stopped. He tore the drawing into small pieces, almost absently, and let the pieces float down into the basket. He looked over at Rudolph. "You are a silly bastard, aren't you?" he said.

Rudolph nodded.

They resumed walking in the direction of home.

"You ever been laid?" Jordache said.

"No."

"That the truth?"

"I'd tell you."

"I suppose you would," Jordache said. He walked silently for awhile, with his rolling limp. "What're you waiting for?"

"I'm in no hurry," Rudolph said defensively. Neither his father nor his mother had ever mentioned anything about sex to him and this afternoon was certainly the wrong day to start. He was haunted by the sight of Miss Lenaut, dissolved and ugly, weeping on her desk, and he was ashamed that he had ever thought a silly, shrill woman like that worthy of his passion.

"When you start," Jordache said, "don't get hung up on one. Take 'em by the dozen. Don't ever get to feel that there's only one woman for you and that you got to have her. You can ruin your life."

"Okay," Rudolph said, knowing that his father was wrong, dead wrong.

Another silence as they turned a corner.

"You sorry I hit her?" Jordache said.

"Yes."

"You've lived all your life in this country," Jordache said. "You don't know what real hating is."

"Did you really kill a Frenchman with a bayonet?" He had to know.

"Yeah," Jordache said. "One of ten million. What difference does it make?"

They were nearly home. Rudolph felt depressed and miserable. He should have thanked his father for sticking up for him that way, it was something that very few parents would have done, and he realized that, but he couldn't get the words out.

"It wasn't the only man I killed," Jordache said, as they stopped in front of the bakery. "I killed a man when there was no war on. In Hamburg, Germany, with a knife. In 1921. I just thought you ought to know. It's about time you learned something about your father. See you at supper. I got to go put the shell under cover." He limped off, down the shabby street, his cloth cap squarely on top of his head.

When the final marks were posted for the term, Rudolph had an *A* in French.

discussion

This selection, chapter three from the novel *Rich Man, Poor Man* by Irwin Shaw, reveals a series of poor judgments made by a teacher who knows enough French to pass the teaching examination but is lacking in understanding of adolescents. Miss Lenaut is totally unaware of herself in relation to her students and deceives herself about her own provocative appearance. When a student succumbs to her seductiveness Miss Lenaut is angry and vindictive. She is self-protective and keeps the incident from the school administration, while expecting Rudolph's parents to be ashamed of their son. She anticipates humiliating Rudolph in front of them to satisfy her own need for revenge.

However, Rudolph's father is not intimidated by Miss Lenaut. He is more perceptive than the teacher. He does not see the drawing as an attempt to degrade the teacher but rather, with no vulgar overtones, a reflection of his son's sexual arousal. Despite his foreign background the school cannot intimidate him. He is a man who has shown moral and physical courage in wartime experiences in the past, and the teacher cannot demean him or his son. The teacher's expectation is another example of her poor judgment, and she must back down in face of his anger.

springboards for inquiry

1. How do you account for Mr. Jordache's defense of his son?

2. How might Miss Lenaut have handled this situation differently?

3. Under ordinary circumstances parents usually take the side of the school against their own child. Why?

4. Examine your feelings about parent-teacher interviews. What are some techniques for dealing with angry parents? Do you think you would be uncomfortable talking with parents who are obviously much older than the parents you are used to dealing with? Why? Do you think you would be uncomfortable talking with parents who speak broken English? Why?

the school board
- the community

When all is well in the land, no one hears much about the Board of Education. But let trouble start to brew—length of hair, sex education, closing neighborhood schools, firing a popular teacher, the clamor for local control, bussing, or educational accountability—and suddenly this publicly elected body of men (almost all Boards of Education are elected and men constitute the vast majority on any board) come out of their educational closet and are exposed to the full view of the community. There are now 50 books available on educational administration which describe the Board and its elections, work, relations with the media, and a welter of details about the intricacies of their functioning.

The supposition that in America education and politics exist as separate entities has been exposed in the 1960s and 70s as a myth. Today everyone knows that education is politics. While school board members are not chosen by a political party as a general rule, the decisions they make are not relegated to simply ordering pencils, paper, and straws. Indeed it may fairly be said that "the relationship between those who teach, when they teach, and politics is recognized as probably the single most important question in determining the course, present and future of American education."[1]

Too often teachers uncommitted to the politics of education and only concerned with their school and their classroom do not realize that how and what they teach, who and where they teach is no longer their prerogative. Local associations of teachers (N.E.A., U.F.T., etc.) now know that there is no such place as the "cloistered retreats of Academia" where teachers, pupils, and parents can go trippingly through educational Gardens of Eden oblivious of the fact that thoroughly political Satans are observing their oblivious meanders. Only at the higher education level are academicians still largely unaware of the politics of education. In certain places—California and New York, for example—professors have finally eaten of the fruit of the tree of the knowledge of good and evil and now know full well that they are not merely sand-blind pedants puttering about like proverbial Mr. Chips.

The schools then are not "bipartisan," not "impartial," and not "apolitical." The Board of Education today is a very political animal. Here's why. First, local taxes no longer support the schools so there is a frantic search by the Board to compete for state and federal funds. To get the dollars needed the local Boards have become intimately involved with federal decision making and national power politics. Where once school boards rarely even knew the name of the state senator or assemblyman and barely knew who sat in Congress, such naïveté today would mean educational asphyxiation.

Since 1954 and the Brown v. the Board of Education desegregation deci-

---

[1]Laurence Iannaccone and Frank W. Lutz, *Politics, Power and Policy: The Governing of Local School Districts* (Columbus: Charles E. Merrill, 1970).

sion, education has become a major political issue. The urban-racial crisis literally centers about the schools. The "poverty cycle"—neighborhood violence, unemployment, and local control of the schools—has brought school boards under sharp public scrutiny. The Ocean Hill-Brownsville debacle of 1968 has left New York City and state politics still shaking.

In suburban school districts the clamor for excellence, accountability, and performance along with the search for individualizing education has upped those budgets, thus moving local boards more and more into political arenas.

Finally, should the reader still have dreams of education's being a virgin bride, remember that the American Federation of Teachers has become the sole collective bargaining agent with school boards in New York, Detroit, Boston, Chicago, Cleveland, and Philadelphia. This development throws the teachers and the board into yearly power struggles.[2]

Research efforts in educational administration are today highly sophisticated. The politics of education have created the necessity to study communities systematically in order to determine exactly what has and is happening. A rather spectacular study of a single school district has resulted in a series of statements and hypotheses about school board power which are here summarized.[3] The intention of this case study, which has been validated in many other places, is to give administrators some knowledge of what they can expect to have happen in their district when school board members are defeated. The course of school board power seems to be linked with the relationships between the board, the superintendent, and the district the board represents.

The first two statements indicate that the school board and the school district are social systems which may be placed on a continuum: open–closed. The third and fourth statements describe what happens when the school board is relatively closed and the school district is relatively open. If the school board is not on the same wave length as its constituents in the district, that is, if the board is closed to the inputs of the district, school boards elections will correct the situation. What follows next is a series of hypotheses and predictions that may be generated from the four statements. The first five hypotheses indicate that when the board and the superintendent develop a homogeneity and a "he is our leader" relationship, a certain stability is generated. Hypotheses six through eight prophesy what may happen if gaps between the board and the people of the district widen. These are quoted verbatim:

Hypothesis 6. Under the above conditions, when the school district is relatively open and changing (exchanging inputs and outputs with its environment), the gap between the school board and the school district develops and continues to

---

[2]On Tuesday, October 18, 1973 the Detroit teachers settled with their board after 44 school days of a strike. Over 240,000 children were schoolless. If it isn't politics, it will become so soon.

[3]Iannaccone and Lutz, *Politics, Power and Policy.*

widen, and the board becomes progressively segregated. This situation can develop through the following steps:

a. The community changes through population increase or mobility; thus, there is a shift in the community's socioeconomic class.

b. Meanwhile the school board remains relatively unchanged in composition and values. It becomes progressively segregated from the school district but not from the superintendent.

Hypothesis 7. When the school district (the macrosystem) perceives the progressive segregation of its school board (the central subsystem), it will attempt to prevent further segregation. The district will attempt to reverse the process by initiating messages to the board in the hope that these messages (outputs) will be received (become inputs of the board). Being basically a political system, these messages consist of political action.

Hypothesis 8. When the board becomes progressively segregated from the district, it decreases the linkage between itself and its changing macrosystem. Thus, it decreases the opportunity of processing the necessary inputs for self-correction (the modular effect). School board incumbents will consequently be defeated at election time.

The last four hypotheses foretell what will happen when incumbent board members are not reelected. Though not specifically stated, this cracking of the power of the board will, if the district does not change, result in the superintendent's dismissal.

In New York, Washington, D. C., and Boston we are witnessing community-oriented leadership where old boards, which once never really received or cared about input from the district, are being replaced by governance from neighborhoods. This decentralization strips power from central school boards and local participation of which they never dreamed.

Evaluation of these reforms varies. From some teachers in New York and Washington are heard only vituperation and bitter agony over the community's takeover of power. However, Mario Fantini's "Participation, Decentralization, Community Control and Quality Education" offers hard data which points to solid improvements in rate of suspensions, vandalism, attendance, daily teacher absences and reading scores in Ocean Hill Demonstration District after the community assumed the responsibility for governing the schools in its district.[4]

Finally, there seems to be some evidence that where school boards have ultimate and final power over the schools, the creativity of teachers is seriously inhibited. In Harry L. Gracey's book, *Curriculum or Craftsmanship*, a two-year study of an East Coast school system seems to suggest that a tight, board-controlled power system has a permanent and irreversibly negative effect upon teacher effectiveness. Gracey concluded his study by saying,

---

[4]Mario Fantini, "Participation, Decentralization, Community Control and Quality Education," in *Restructuring American Education*, ed. Ray C. Rist (New Brunswick, N.J.: Transaction Books, 1972), pp. 64–67.

"the bureaucratic social organization of the school seems to rule out implementation of individualistic philosophy and practice of education."[5]

For those contemplating teaching, much of what appears in this brief essay seems to suggest that salary and fringe benefits alone are not sufficient to induce one to work. Some research regarding the Board of Education and its power and support from the people who live in the district is essential if one is to consider investing a year or more in a school system. The degree to which teachers and parents share in the real decision-making powers in a district ought to be considered. For a generation interested in "doing one's own thing," inquiry about the politics of education in a prospective school system might be very important.

Jerry Weil

The teachers

"The Green Water *Gazette* has not and will not editorialize on this matter." "And that is a sin of omission," Denton countered. "To editorialize for the common good is your function." "Don't tell me how to run my newspaper." "Why not? You are telling me how to run my school."

The room was no longer furnished for conferences. Two years before the oval table and leather chairs had been replaced by standard classroom furniture. The luxury of a meeting room yielded to the urgency for classroom space. Walter J. Prescott presided at the teacher's desk in front of the room, while the other four members sat with Ross Denton at the pupils' desks.

Miss Hartwell was well to the front of the room, as near as possible to Prescott, since she acted as secretary of the board, taking the

From The Teachers *by Jerry Weil. Copyright © 1963 by Jerry Weil. Reprinted by arrangement with The New American Library, Inc., New York, New York.*

minutes and managing all other paper work. At Prescott's instruction she began by establishing that all board members were present and that Mr. Denton was also there.

"I am sorry," said Ross Denton . . . "if I've punctured anyone's illusion of Green Water as a place of perfection, but the constant delay by this school board of a desperately needed bond issue is proof enough to me that the school system in this town is not as highly valued as a lot of people say it is. They may say so, but they don't act like it."

Miss Hartwell's head turned sharply as if pulled by the string of Denton's words. "You are not puncturing any illusions, Mr. Denton," she said haughtily. "I'm quite sure

[5]Harry L. Gracey, *Curriculum or Craftsmanship* (Chicago: University of Chicago Press, 1972), p. 193.

that no one in this room believes for a moment that everything is perfect in Green Water. But we have a good community here and a good school system. If there are problems in the high school, I venture to say that some people are under the illusion that exorbitant amounts of money will solve them, which is absurd."

Ross was about to continue this exchange, but Prescott interrupted . . .

"The first item is ninety-five dollars and sixty-two cents needed for a new water pump."

"What's wrong with the old one?" demanded Jennings.

"It isn't working right anymore," Denton explained. "It's ten years old."

"All right now," said Prescott, "let's not have a big discussion about a water pump. Those in favor say 'aye.' "

They all said "aye."

"That's passed," said Prescott impatiently. "Now let's get on to the next one. Seven hundred and fifty dollars for snow tires for the buses."

"How many tires do you need, Ross?" asked Doppel.

"Twenty."

"Well now, I think I can get those for you at cost. That'll cut the expenditure in half, almost."

"Can we rephrase the request to buy the tires from Doppel without mentioning the exact amount?" asked Prescott.

"That's all right with me," said Ross.

"Is anyone opposed to that?" asked Prescott. "All right, that's passed too. Now let's get down to it. We've got to get squared away on the bond issue.

"You have all been given detailed copies of the entire building plan

more than a week ago, and I'm assuming, therefore, that everyone here is acquainted with it. So let's open discussion. Mr. Jennings?"

Slim stretched his long, bony frame out of his seat and into its full height. Keeping one hand on his desk he began to speak with a lazy drawl in a tone indicating a tired, sarcastic, fed-up attitude.

"It's a fine plan, very lovely and architecturally sound. Who could object to it? But the cost makes it out of the question. And may I say that Mr. Denton by submitting it is completely ignoring the facts of life. Now, last year he came in here with a half-million-dollar idea that we trimmed down to $340,000. So now, naturally, he's asking for $700,000. I'm surprised it isn't a million. The whole thing is absurd."

"Mr. Denton," said Prescott.

"What is absurd is that last year's plan never got to the voters," said Ross. "It was bottled up right here in the school board, allowing an already urgent situation to become a desperate one.

"Last year's half-million-dollar plan was what was needed then to cope with the situation. Since this plan got nowhere and this is a year later, we need that much more. Any fool must realize that we need more. We have more students. We have a larger district now too. We are going to have still more students next year and more the year after. We must have the added space and facilities proposed in this plan if only to give these future students the same sort of education that our current students are getting, without any improvement.

"But even more, we want to improve this education in the future. We must. The world moves fast. Every day there is something new to learn. And we simply must plan and build if we are ever going to cope with the increase of students and the increase in what they must be taught.

"If one were to read any other newspaper in the country besides the Green Water *Gazette,* one would realize that there is a crisis today in education, that the plant we have now is not sufficient for today and completely inadequate for tomorrow. It doesn't take a mathematical genius to count the children in elementary schools in the country who will be coming of high-school age over the next eight years. If this plan were to pass the voters tomorrow and we started building the next day, we would still not be in a position to avoid double sessions next year.

"Yes, that's right, we are going to have double sessions next year, whether we pass the plan or not. We can no longer avoid it. We can, however, make it temporary, that is for one year only, by passing this bond issue, getting it to the voters, and starting construction as soon as possible."

"If the shortage is in classroom space," said Miss Hartwell, "I can't understand the necessity for the auditorium in the plan and it seems that there are an awful lot of laboratories."

"This is the nuclear age, Miss Hartwell," said Denton. "Our children are going to live, let's hope, in a world of undreamed marvels, more wondrous by far than the miracles with which we now live. It is the feeling of the school administration that it is important for them to have some understanding of this world they will live in through laboratory instruction in science. How else, under a democratic system, will they be able to make the decisions necessary to keep that world running?

"And as for the auditorium, in view of the expected enrollment over the next decade what we now make do as an auditorium will not be adequate. If we want to graduate our senior class in view of their families, we shall have to do it one fifth at a time. Imagine five days of graduation ceremonies! Imagine double sessions and triple sessions! Imagine the increased burden on the teachers! Imagine the need for more teachers to handle the sessions! Imagine the increased cost of heat, light, and transportation! Imagine the upset in home routine, in the leisure life of the student! Imagine all of that, for those are the alternatives to voting this bond issue and this construction."

"That's all very well, Denton," said Slim Jennings, "but all we are asking is that you be practical enough to realize that the voters will not pass so expensive a plan."

"They will not pass it," Denton answered, "because they don't understand it, and they don't understand it because the only means of mass communication in the county, the Green Water *Gazette,* refuses to educate them to the desperate plight of their high school, but instead chooses to make them believe that everything is just hunky-dory here when the walls are about to fall in on all of us."

"I resent that," said Jennings, leaning forward, an angry freckled tower. "The Green Water *Gazette* has not and will not editorialize on this matter."

"And that is a sin of omission,"

Denton countered. "To editorialize for the common good is your function."

"Don't tell me how to run my newspaper."

"Why not? You are telling me how to run my school."

"Gentlemen, gentlemen, let's have a bit more decorum here," Prescott interrupted.

"Just one thing," said Denton, now holding up a copy of the Green Water *Gazette*. "Here is a copy of the *Gazette* that was published on the opening day of school. As you can see by the headline we have our biggest budget in history and we have six new teachers, and it is not until the last paragraph, which has been buried under a dry-cleaning advertisement on page ten, that the reader is told about the increased school population, which amounts to nothing less than a flood."

"This is a school-board meeting," said Jennings, "and not a symposium being held to criticize my paper."

"Mr. Jennings is right," said Miss Hartwell.

Ross sighed as if to say "What's the use?" Then he sat back and lit a cigarette. It was always the same with those two, the hopeless expression on his face implied.

Mr. Prescott spoke: "My feeling about the plan is that it is really quite modest in view of the information we have about the expected student increase over the years and also in view of the expanded program the high school should and actually must institute. However, in view of the strong objections raised on the part of the two most senior members of the board, I do not feel that I would want to cast my vote today until I could hear some coun-

terproposals on their part. Am I correct, Slim, in assuming that you haven't prepared such proposals yet?"

"That's right, but I will."

"Then I think it best, much as I don't like to, to table the matter until the next meeting. But do let's settle it at that time. As Mr. Denton has told us, time is running out and we have got to put something before the voters so construction can begin."

"Mr. Doppel, what about you? How do you feel about all this?"

"Well I think it is a fine plan and certainly not immodest. It might call for a slight tax increase, but we are going to have that no matter what happens. After all, double sessions are expensive too. The plan for the gym looks great and I am glad about the new stands for the football field. I was hoping we might get a swimming pool in there somewhere, but Ross told me that it would be too expensive, and I'll go along with him. It looks pretty good to me as it is."

"Mr. Firenze?"

"I can't really say right now, Mr. Prescott," said Frank. "I am glad we're not going to decide today. Seven hundred thousand dollars is a terrible amount of money. I was just sitting here trying to imagine what sort of pile it would make in one-dollar bills, but it is simply beyond me. I would not want to make any sort of decision about it until I thought more, a lot more, and maybe studied it a bit."

"Of course," said Prescott, "but perhaps it would be helpful if you would divide the amount of money by the number of people in the school district and see what you think of it then in terms of what each person would then be spending on the school."

"That's a good idea," said Frank. "I object to that sort of thing," said Jennings. "The chairman is prejudicing the new member's vote. Please remind him that every person in the district is not paying for it, but only the owners of land and property."

"If a man pays rent," said Denton, "then be sure he's paying property tax indirectly."

Jennings started to reply, but Prescott stopped him.

"That's enough of this. We'll table the bond issue until next meeting. Now, is there any other business?"

There was none.

"I need a motion to adjourn," said Prescott.

It was made by Doppel and carried easily. Denton had a strong temptation to try to leave the meeting with Firenze, to talk to him, to get to know him better. He felt, after noting Frank's reaction to the book-burning idea, that a rapport would be easily established between them.

But then he hesitated. That sort of ill-concealed politicking might just turn someone like Firenze against him. Ross was almost certain now of Firenze's support for the bond issue, and he decided that it would be best not to press his luck.

He left the meeting and went back to his office for a moment before leaving the building. He could not remember when he had felt so optimistic.

Ross found Stanley Doppel looking for him in the parking lot.

"Looks like a tough road to hoe," said Stanley.

"It depends on Firenze," said Ross. "If he's for the plan, that's it. With you and Prescott that makes three, and then it goes to the voters."

"Yeah, but then the trouble really starts," said Doppel.

"Jennings won't help with the paper, and without that it will be very difficult to convince enough people."

"That's where I want you to help me, Stanley. I want you to arrange for me to speak to the Rotary Club, to the Lions, the Elks, to every group you can line up. You are a member of just about everything around here, aren't you?"

"Sure. Glad to help. But that's really doing it the hard way. If only there were some way we could get to Jennings, why then it would—"

"Don't count on Jennings for anything except opposition," said Ross.

"If only you would handle him a little different," Stanley suggested.

"What difference would that make?" Ross asked. "You and I both know that he's afraid of the taxes, and that's it. It's the same thing with old Miss Hartwell. The two of them feel they'll be paying the whole bill between them."

"That would not be too far from the truth," said Doppel laughing. "But I think you are wrong about both of them thinking only of the taxes. Take Regina now. People like her, who have had money their whole lives, don't worry about it like we do. I don't think Miss Hartwell is against you because of taxes as much as she is simply because she doesn't like you, Ross. And you don't help matters very much by spouting off at her every chance you get."

"I just can't help being funny," said Ross.

"She didn't think it was funny. She wants people to—"

"She wants them to bow down to her. She would like a principal who would go to her for advice every time he wanted to scratch his ear. She thinks she's Queen Regina and owns the whole town."

"Well, let's face it. The Hartwell plant has been drawing big business here for more than twenty years now. It's the base of the whole town's prosperity. Regina is important, Ross, and she likes to feel that everyone knows it. It wouldn't hurt you any to sugar her up a little."

"It's too late to start that now," said Ross. "Anyway, I don't think it will be necessary. You, Prescott, and Firenze constitute a majority. If all goes well, the plan will go to the voters just as it is. And if the voters understand it, I'm certain they'll pass it. I'll just have to get around a lot and talk a lot and make sure that they will understand it, despite Jennings and the *Gazette*."

"Don't be too sure about the voters," Doppel cautioned.

"It's the only thing I am sure about," said Ross.

"Ah, don't look so serious," said Stanley suddenly pounding Ross on the back. "Life has its brighter side. I was talking to the coach yesterday and he said that the team looks great."

"You mean Panzer Pilzer looks great." Ross smiled.

Doppel had taken a cigar from his pocket, and he now lit up.

"All right, then," he chuckled, "Panzer Pilzer looks great. We might just win the state championship this year." Then he added slyly,

"That is, if we can count on Panzer Pilzer.

"Who knows? He might be ineligible. I hear that he's not nearly the student that he is the football player. I sure hope he passes everything, Ross," Doppel winked and poked the principal in the ribs.

"He'll slip by, I suppose. A lot stupider ones do," said Ross.

"That's right," Stanley agreed. "And it doesn't do him any harm to have friends in the principal's office, eh?" Doppel added another poke in Ross' ribs. Ross managed a sick smile.

"Well, I'd better get back to work," said Doppel moving toward his nearby car. "Some of us don't get off at three-thirty." He laughed.

Ross forced himself to join Doppel's mood. He would have liked to call Doppel's attention to the work he carried home each day, to the scores of evenings when he was called upon to attend meetings, athletic contests, dances, plays, and so on. Doppel was just joking. If there were others who gave credence to the three-thirty myth and felt anger and envy because of it, that was no reason to take it out on Doppel. Besides, Stanley represented one-third of the needed majority.

The day of the Drake City game was cold and overcast with gray clouds. Midway in the third period it began to drizzle. By the time the final whistle sounded it was pouring.

Through this drenching rain, huddled against the biting cold, the crowd of spectators went quickly and silently from the field and around the school building to the parking lot. In the midst of the moving crowd was a group of three men, who wore their topcoat collars turned up around their necks and the brims of their hats snapped down over their faces.

One of these men was Stanley Doppel. Another, who like Doppel was large and plump, was Harry Hacker. The third was a short, slim, nervous fellow called Bert, who was president of the Green Water Chamber of Commerce. As they hurried through the wet and chill along with the many other spectators, they spoke to one another, their words muffled by the wool of their coat collars.

"Boy! What a miserable rain!" Bert commented.

"What a miserable day!" Hacker agreed.

"You can say that again," said Doppel sadly. "What was the final score?" he asked.

"I lost count," said Harry Hacker.

"Boy! They just rolled over us," said Bert.

"The whole team fell apart without Panzer," Doppel commented.

"Well, there's always next year," offered Hacker.

"Next year, hell!" snapped Doppel. "This was the year. You don't get talent like Pilzer every year. Maybe you get something like him once in twenty years, and then only if you're lucky."

"He can't play next year, can he?" Bert asked.

Hacker chuckled. "It would be easy enough to keep him in school. That French teacher would just love to leave him back."

"It wouldn't matter," Doppel sadly explained. "He's played three seasons, and that's all state law will allow. It's a pity he didn't have the weight last year. This year he really filled out. This should have been the year."

"It's a shame," said Bert softly as they reached Doppel's car. They scurried into it quickly and then, safe from the rain, they all lit cigars while Doppel waited for the motor to warm up.

"Just think of the business it would have meant to the town to have a state championship game played here," said Bert from behind an acrid cloud of cigar smoke.

"Yeah," said Hacker. "Yeah."

Doppel's voice rose briefly in anger. "Jesus! Who in hell does that woman think she is anyway!"

And Bert supported him. "A perfect stranger coming down here and messing up the whole works."

"A foreigner, too," said Harry Hacker.

"She probably doesn't even understand what she did to this town," Bert conjectured.

"If she don't understand, then she should have kept her nose out of it," Doppel stated, anger still in his voice.

"Goddam women," said Hacker.

"Damn teachers!" Bert concurred.

"Women ought to stay in the kitchen where they belong," Hacker announced.

"Those who can, do. Those who can't, teach," Bert recited.

"Ahh, let's forget about it," Doppel offered as he put the car into gear and backed it out of its parking place. They joined the stream of traffic that filed slowly out of the parking lot and down to the town road.

"I could sure use a little drink right now," said Harry Hacker.

"Good idea," said Bert.

"Let's go down to the Chipakee," Doppel suggested, and the other two agreed with nods and short grunts. . . . Doppel, who had been

the third and deciding vote for Denton's plan, withdrew his vote after Green Water's gridiron defeat. . . .

discussion

The school board is probably the most influential body affecting educational decisions. Most people do not realize the range of areas in which they make decisions nor the extent of their power. This selection from the popular novel, *The Teachers*, written in 1963 is an accurate portrayal of the functioning of one kind of school board. Green Water's school board includes two well-known business persons in the town as well as the editor of the newspaper and two members who are not well-known.

In this case it is a liability to have the editor of the one newspaper in Green Water on the board because he can manipulate the town's opinions on school issues by biased reporting or printing school business on the back page, where it will most likely go unread. Slim Prescott is first and foremost an advocate of maintaining low taxes even though costs for education are rising. Green Water cannot have it both ways—low taxes and first rate schools. There is a cost attached to quality education. With the paper opposed to a building program for the schools, Ross Denton knows there is little chance of its passing. However, he is particularly angry that the board never permitted the proposal for additions to the high school to have reached the voters the previous year. This kind of bottleneck indicates the amount of power the board holds in a school district.

The flurry of words between Ross Denton and Slim Prescott emphasizes that schools, unlike private business, are community controlled. Educators must expect to be told by non-educators how to run their business. This can be very difficult for a principal or superintendent, particularly if he has some hostile board members. At the same time the board is very sensitive to the accusation that they are rubber stamps for the educators. When there is the kind of personal animosity that Stanley Doppel suggests Miss Hartwell feels for Ross, it can be particularly unproductive for the schools.

Usually the superintendent's position is reviewed every four years by the board. Obviously it is important for the school board to be free of factions representing particular interests that may be politically motivated to oust the superintendent. At the same time the electorate passes on the decisions of individual board members at the ballot box every four years. These are built in safeguards for a democratic process to prosper.

springboards for inquiry

1. Find out as much as you can about the school board in your community. Who are the members; what is their attendance record; what topics have they discussed this year that you consider important for the future of education in your community? How did you get your information?

2. If you were a school board member in your community what topics would you like them to discuss?

3. Do you think ethnic and minority groups should be balanced on the board to represent the balance in the community?

4. Should certain people be automatically disqualified from being on the school board such as the editor of the local paper or the president of the local branch of a sociopolitical society like the John Birch Society?

References

CALLAHAN, RAYMOND E. *An Introduction to Education in American Society.* New York: Knopf, 1956.

CAMPBELL, ROALD F.; BRIDGES, EDWIN M.; CORBALLY, JOHN E., JR.; NYSTRAND, RAPHAEL O.; AND RAMSEYER, JOHN A. *Introduction to Educational Administration* 4th ed. Boston: Allyn & Bacon, 1971.

DWYER, THOMAS J. "Responding to Militant Students and Parents." *Crucial Issues in Education: A Problem-Solving Guide for School Administrators.* Ed. Lewis, James J., Jr.; Bookbinder, Robert M.; and Bauer, Raymond R. Englewood Cliffs, N.J.: Prentice-Hall, 1972.

ERLICH, JOHN, and ERLICH, SUSAN. *Student Power, Participation and Revolution.* New York: Association Press, 1970.

FARBER, JERRY. *The Student as Nigger.* North Hollywood: Contact Books, 1969.

FEUER, LEWIS S. *The Conflict of Generations.* New York: Basic Books, 1969.

"FIFTH ANNUAL GALLUP POLL RESULTS." *Phi Delta Kappan,* September 1973.

GRACEY, HARRY L. *Curriculum or Craftsmanship.* Chicago: University of Chicago Press, 1972.

IANNOCCONE, LAURENCE, and LUTZ, FRANK W. *Politics, Power and Policy: The Governing of Local School Districts.* Columbus: Merrill, 1970.

ILLICH, IVAN. *Deschooling Society.* New York: Harper & Row, 1970.

LANDAU, ELLIOTT D. *Creative Parent-Teacher Conferences.* Salt Lake City: Wheelwright Press, 1968.

LEWIS, JAMES J., Jr.; BOOKBINDER, ROBERT M.; and BAUER, RAYMOND R. *Crucial Issues in Education: A Problem-Solving Guide for School Administrators.* Englewood Cliffs, N.J.: Prentice-Hall, 1972.

LIPSET, SEYMOUR MARTIN, and ALTBACH, PHILLIP B. *Students in Revolt.* Boston: Houghton Mifflin, 1969.

LURIE, ELLEN. *How to Change the Schools.* New York: Random House, 1970.

MILLER, VAN; MADDEN, GEORGE R.; and KINCHELOE, JAMES B. *The Public Administration of American School Systems.* 2nd ed. New York: Macmillan, 1972.

New York Times, September 2, 1973.

RASKIN, ABRAHAM H. "Shanker's Great Leap." *New York Times,* September 9, 1973, pp. 64–83.

RILES, WILSON C. "Compensatory Education." Guthrie, James W., and Wynne, Edward. *New Models for American Education.* Englewood Cliffs, N.J.: Prentice-Hall, 1971.

RIST, RAY C. *Restructuring American Education.* New Brunswick, N.J.: Transaction Books, 1972.

WILDMAN, WESLEY A. "Implications of Teacher Bargaining for School Administration." *Phi Delta Kappan* 46 (1964):154.

The Future–
Alternative School

An apocryphal story is told of two first graders who stood in the schoolyard just before school started. A sharp crack split the air, and off in the distance two Phantom jets clawed at the air. One child remarked, "Golly, look at the vapor trails!" The other wondered aloud if swept back wings would affect their cracking the sound barrier. The school bell rang.

"Well, let's get inside and start stringing those damn beads," one sighed as they trudged into the front door.

Since schools started in the American colonies, things have not changed too much. They caned children then; they still do.[1] They had "blab" schools then—all eight and often twelve grades in one building, mostly in the same room. We have returned to that "nongrading" concept today. There was one teacher in every room then. At least 85 percent of American schools are still that way. There was homework and grading then, and there is today. And so it goes. . . .

The year 1976, according to Professor J. R. Platt, Director of the Mental Health Research Institute at the University of Michigan, would really be World Year 031. Since World Year Zero (1945) to the present there has really been the most startling technological advancements in the history of man.[2] It is possible then, that from 1976 to the beginning of the next century, we may see not minor changes on the educational scene but major leaps which will leave the colonial days faint memories in time, valuable only because they are history. On the other hand, it is entirely plausible to expect a culture gap to persist. While man may no longer need oil or electricity or never know death from disease, it is entirely possible that in 1999 he will still be keeping school the way it was in the pre-technological era, 1609–1945.

Alvin Toffler, in his book *Future Shock*,[3] however, presents a school which will be decentralized, portable, computer assisted, use outside faculty and in general adhere to the following admonition: "Schools of the future, if they wish to facilitate adaptation later in life, will have to experiment with

---

[1] The entire September, 1973 issue of *The Journal of Clinical Child Psychology* was devoted to child abuse in homes and schools. The recitation of events in one school system makes the caning of children in the 1700s somewhat pale. For a detailed study of caning in modern times read Joseph A. Mercurio, *Caning: Educational Rite and Tradition* (Syracuse: Syracuse University Press, 1972).

[2] We are indebted to Robert Stein, graduate student in the Department of Educational Administration, University of Utah, for this data which is part of his paper in Dean Steven Hencley's "Change Strategies" class.

[3] Alvin Toffler, *Future Shock* (New York: Random House, 1970).

far more varied arrangements. Classes with several teachers and single students; classes with several teachers and a group of students; students organized into temporary task forces and project teams. . . ."[4]

Harold Shane and Owen Nelson list the following nine changes which appear to them to be inevitable for the school of the future:

a) the use of multi-media partially to replace texts

b) student tutors[5]

c) the development of a new English alphabet

d) the greater utilization of the expressive arts

e) the inclusion of controversial issues in Social Studies curricula

f) the twelve months school

g) early childhood education (down to age 2–3)

h) some rethinking of compulsory education

i) the psychiatric treatment of children at no cost to the child's family

j) massive adult education

k) improving the measurement and use of the I.Q.[6]

Theodore W. Hipple feels that the crucial issue in education is the battle between cognitive and affective education. He says,

> A . . . group of goals is the affective, or attitudinal purposes. These have to do with values, attitudes and opinions students possess and, of course, are the more important kinds of objectives if behavioral change is the desired outcome of formal schooling . . . divided on the amount and kind of tampering a school ought to engage in with respect to a student's values, . . . most (educators) agree on two points: that, whether they try or not, teachers . . . exert an enormous influence on the values their students hold and that in it is an arguable proposition that the schools ought deliberately to encourage its students to examine their own goals, this latter a derivative, perhaps, of the Socratic dictum: "The unexamined life is not worth living."[7]

The literature on the future school seems primarily to be tinkering with the carburetor of education. Perhaps this is really all that could or even should occur. The emphasis on affective education, compulsory education, adult education, and early childhood education seems, if affected, to be those innovations which would most likely give a new shape to the entire educational establishment.

[4]For further insight on this topic read, *Computers in the Classroom,* ed. Joseph B. Margolin and Marion R. Misch (New York: Spartan Books, 1970).

[5]The only complete text we are aware of in this area is Peter S. Rosenbaum, *Peer-Mediated Instruction* (New York: Teachers College Press, 1973).

[6]Harold Shane and Owen Nelson, "What Will the Schools Become?" *Phi Delta Kappan* (June 1971), 596–98.

[7]Theodore W. Hipple, "Education for the Space Age—Cognitive or Affective," in Theodore W. Hipple, *Crucial Issues in Contemporary Education* (Pacific Palisades, Ca.: Goodyear, 1973), p. 316.

Both of our volumes[8] were conceived because of our belief that the only true education affects ideals, attitudes, and values. We have said before that what we know may not change what we do until we feel what we know.[9] Thus, attention to one's self, one's values and goals results in the examined life. Lest we educate scientific cretins, education in the future needs to deal explicitly (albeit not exclusively) with the affective domain. The feelings of humans ought not to be a byproduct of education but a prime product. Perhaps man has not learned from history because he has only memorized it in school. He has been exposed to time lines, crucial periods and the problem-solving approach. He goes back to war eon after eon. He goes back to barbarism time and again—yet he only "knows" the lessons of history. Does he "feel" the bite of history?

During the height of immigration in North America and during its earliest founding days, it became urgent to make education compulsory. What would happen tomorrow morning if education were to be made purely voluntary is anyone's guess. Whether elitism would again return or whether the gates would be stormed by those who had previously found arbitrariness something to revolt against would be hard to say.

There is much concern over the fact that too many high school students in search of their identity drop out, work, and often discover too late that getting back into school is not easy.[10] Many advocate a swinging door approach to secondary education, i.e., allowing students to drop out at any time, and then drop in, again, too. Today's youth are not the "greenhorns" who came here at the turn of the twentieth century, not speaking English, not being familiar with the culture, and not knowing what the future held. Mass media have made today's students far more sophisticated. They sense what kind of education is valuable for them. But for each person the time when he can best benefit from academic or vocational instruction may vary. Education does not begin and end in a particular three or four year period of time. To push every adolescent into the same mold at the same time will not yield optimum results. If the schools can be more flexible, the students may eventually profit tremendously in the development of their ultimate intellectual capacity and work skills.

The schools of the future may change the present age limits of six to 18 for the beginning and ending of grades one to twelve. Children will enter school as they are ready to learn more formally. Some will enter at four or even earlier, more at five, most still at age six. School may not be "over" at graduation from high school. Even for the students not going on to college all school districts may provide ongoing education—day and evening classes for anyone interested in continuing his education.

Think madly for a moment. We know a man of 23 who, when he was 14,

---

[8]The present one and *Child Development Through Literature* (Englewood Cliffs, N.J.: Prentice-Hall, 1972).

[9]See the introduction to *Child Development Through Literature*.

[10]Claude Buxton's study of adolescent attitudes toward school complements Offer, *The Psychological World of the Teen-ager*. Buxton's title is *Adolescents in School* (New Haven: Yale University Press, 1973).

walked out of junior high school one day and down to the nearby university. He said he was bored in junior high so he was admitted to the summer session at the "U." He liked it; it liked him. He never returned to his local secondary school. He graduated from college at 17, entered medical school at 18 and at 23 became a senior resident in psychiatry. He skipped the usual secondary education route and accepted the very routine path of higher education. But a psychiatrist needs more than school. He needs wisdom and maturity, and one doesn't get that at 23 no matter how bright he is. Perhaps in the future our precocious lad could have stopped his medical education to grow up a bit. The penalty now for dropping out of graduate school is onerous. Education in the future may not penalize for respites of growth. Indeed, we see no valid reason why qualified senior citizens should be discouraged from studying careers in fields heretofore unfamiliar to them. Our society is too preoccupied with age.

For years we have been collecting informal and personal as well as technical data about schools. We have done very little about what we feel and know. The schools of the future must finally incorporate new knowledge lest we "get used to the chains we wear, and . . . through custom . . . finally embrace what first wore a hideous mien."[11]

There have already been devised alternatives that actually add to the list of Shane and Nelson. Perhaps the most radical alternative school since World War II was A. S. Neill's Summerhill School described in his volume *Summerhill: A Radical Approach to Child Rearing*.[12] Unfortunately, Neill's apostles misinterpreted his innovation, and hundreds of eager educationists went into slums and suburbs to establish their idiosyncratic versions of Summerhill. The havoc wreaked by these souls bent upon freeing the children from the shackles of school slavery resulted in Neill's next volume entitled, *Freedom—Not License!*[13] In it he explains that, in fact, "freedom, overextended, turns into license."[14] He continues that freedom is give and take—there is freedom for children, freedom for teachers, and freedom for parents. Unfortunately, too often the freedom granted to children in America's alternative schools is license—license to be vulgar, loud, and unresponsive to adult authority. Neill says, "In my book *Summerhill*, I pointed out that it is this distinction between freedom and license that many parents cannot grasp. In the disciplined home, the children have NO rights. In the spoiled home, they have ALL the rights. The proper home is one in which children and adults have EQUAL rights."[15]

Neill brought his school to England from Austria in 1924. Then as now freedom in the schools was not a new idea. (It would not be at all surprising to discover a polemic about the schools on some Sumerian tablet.) Neill was therefore amazed at how badly he was understood.

Despite distortion of A. S. Neill's ideas and the failure of many educational ventures based on these distortions, A. S. Neill had a profound effect

[11]Quoted from John Dewey, *The Child and the Curriculum*, as cited in Charles Silberman, *Crisis in the Classroom*, p. 363.

[12]Alexander S. Neill, *Summerhill: A Radical Approach to Child Rearing* (New York: Hart, 1960).

[13]A. S. Neill, *Freedom—Not License!* (New York: Hart, 1966).

[14]Ibid., p. 7.

[15]Ibid., p. 9.

upon American education.[16] Over 200,000 copies of *Summerhill* were sold in the U.S. and Summerhill became a household word. Widespread interest in A. S. Neill's philosophy increased people's awareness of possible alternatives to traditional education. The effect of this kind of thinking was to shift emphasis from the cognitive domain, which had preoccupied American education since Sputnick, to an interest in the humanistic component of education. Trouble in the overburdened urban schools and the rising drop-out rate in suburbia helped to give a sense of urgency to the need for alternatives in educational style. It was plain that not everyone could accomodate to a pattern of conformity in curriculum, grading, and discipline which most schools demanded. The way opened for a great deal of experimentation in curriculum, student and parent input, and school organization.

A new development which will have far-reaching effects on the diversification of educational alternatives is the Alum Rock voucher experiment.[17] In 1972 the parents in the Alum Rock, California school district were given a voucher equal to the cost of one year's schooling which they were able to turn over to any public school of their choice within the school district. This permitted the consumer (the parent and child) to choose among educational alternatives. No longer did the school around the corner have a monopoly on education in the community. Parents were able to choose a school in the district from among various alternatives—one offered a traditional approach to learning, another offered an "open classroom," and another school provided outlet for special interests (i.e., for children especially interested in art, music, writing and so forth).

Educators like Christopher Jencks of Harvard University view the voucher system as a way to give parents of poor and minority chidren the kind of options in choosing schools for their children which previously had been a privilege only of the affluent. Jencks supports an economically regulated voucher plan which has built-in incentives for schools to accept disadvantaged children. In this way schools would compete to educate the poor and culturally different students and would also provide incentive for upgrading local school quality. The voucher system is certain to engender controversy among educators and taxpayers, for wherever it is implemented there will undoubtedly be greater diversity in the range of educational philosophies available to the community.

Alternatives In Education by Allan A. Glatthorn[18] provides a practical guide for students of education who want to know about the many innovations in curricula, staffing, and facilities which have been tried with varying degrees of success across the country. Glatthorn advocates an eclectic design for education. He speaks of "disciplined knowing" for those courses which he feels cannot be taught without structure, such as advanced mathematics, foreign languages, and biology. He also advocates individualized instruction based on specialized diagnostic tests in reading, math, and writing to ensure that these basic skills are learned. However, at the same time,

[16]William E. Broderick, "A Tribute to A. S. Neill," *Phi Delta Kappan* 4, no. 10 (June 1964): 685–87.

[17]James A. Mecklenburger and Richard W. Hostrop, eds., *Education Vouchers: From Theory to Alum Rock* (Homewood, Ill.: ETC Publications, 1972).

[18]Allan A. Glatthorn, *Alternatives in Education,* (New York: Dodd, Mead, 1975).

he encourages experiential learning in volunteer work or on-the-job training. He supports the concept of personal growth seminars in which small groups of students meet with a counselor two to three hours a week during which role playing, improvisation, and discussion would be encouraged in order to help the student become more aware of his personal values and to help him explore his relationship with others.

Today the major types of alternative school environments are: the Storefront School, the Minischool, Drop-Out and Drop-In Schools, Free Schools, and Tutorial Community Schools. All of these schools are departures from the traditional public and parochial schools.

The storefront school

In many urban communities the neighborhood school standing on the street represents a symbol of "the enemy." Usually, even in ghetto communities the staff is Caucasian. If not, the tower of bricks often represents hostile territory. The great numbers of bodies packed inside may be frightening to many. Its very size necessitates rules that appear to be oppressive. For too many the walk from home to the school is "the last mile" repeated daily. In many of these communities there are innumerable vacant stores. These stores are ground level, small, and easily accessible from the street. There is no physical gap between the streets and the store. And so stores have become places where schools have been formed to meet the needs of those who cannot bear the thought of hassling the usual school building.

The storefront school usually develops a very close relationship with the student and is usually staffed with people who more nearly represent the ethnic composition of the neighborhood. Rules, regulations, systems, large numbers of teachers, and students are absent. So, too, are the facilities such as gyms and labs. The storefront is a very simple operation and offers only the barest rudiments of a planned curriculum. It is, in reality, a holding operation—an intermediate or transition point. The storefront school follows the success of other storefront operations.[19]

The mini-school

The mini-school concept is predicated on the theory that especially in the elementary school years (six through eleven) children need close and intimate surroundings so that learning will be more natural. Presently most elementary schools house at least 400 children, and some approach the 1000 mark. This crowd is not a convenient number with which to develop positive human relationships. Paul Goodman in 1967 proposed to the borough president of Manhattan mini-schools of no more than 28 children,

[19]Odyssey House, a residential drug-free community, uses the storefront concept to "lure" the addict into out-patient treatment and later perhaps (transition) into the therapeutic community itself. In one city the storefront is located in the heart of the red-light/addict district. Many who would otherwise never seek help in a big hospital (there is the fear of bureaucracy, the shame of being addicted, etc.,) will amble into a storefront just to "rap" and join regular outpatient group therapy sessions. The storefront, tucked away from the middle class surveillance, has an accessibility which beats elevators and escalators and subway trips to hospitals. The storefront is home turf.

four adults (a master teacher, a graduate student in education, a literate mother, and a literate high school graduate).[20] This ratio of seven to one would be ideal. He asked for rooms (three to four) to be set aside in housing projects, church buildings, large storefronts. He spoke of no principals, secretaries, assistants, custodians, or attendance clerks. In the mini-school, children would be halftime on the streets, visiting museums, businesses, and other neighborhoods. Catching the most current, passionate interest of each child might be possible under these circumstances. Goodman also proposed that the school could dispense with professional teachers in favor of people drawn from the streets surrounding the mini-school. He finally recommended that there be a moratorium on new construction of school buildings while the city adopted the mini-school plan. As of 1975, his idea has not been met with much enthusiasm.

Drop-out and drop-in schools

Although it has been quipped that most of the dropouts are still sitting in schools, there is some movement which provides storefront-type schooling to those who have either dropped out or who are about to. In one city the school for dropouts (called there an academy) has 100 percent attendance. The entire curriculum is geared to what the dropout said he didn't find in the local high school. It should also be noted that every teacher in the academy asked to be placed there for the specific purpose of helping dropouts. In another school district one part of a school building is manned by college volunteers and one sympathetic college professor. Their clientele are any and all students who have so infuriated their regular teachers that they have been temporarily or permanently assigned to report to the professor and her "staff" of university students. One would assume that whatever the students get out of attendance in these classes would be superior to expulsion from school to roam the streets.

In October 1973, the *National Observer* devoted part of its front page to a discussion of the high school as an "aging vat." It questioned the concept of compulsory attendance. One of the writer's recommendations was the concept of the drop-in school. By this he meant that the sometime-attenders would not be penalized by absences but taught whenever they appeared. The necessary attendance records and their accompanying red tape in the traditional school are often so discouraging to the perpetually truant students that an alternative drop-in school offering a less hassling, more open and convenient method of returning to school might encourage certain types of students to drop in more often. It would certainly encourage students whose only motive in cutting in the first place was to defy authority.

Free schools

Parents of children with severe learning and emotional disabilities often end up sending these children to free schools such as the First Street School

---

[20]Paul Goodman has written *Compulsory Mis-Education* (New York: Horizon Press, 1964); *Growing Up Absurd* (New York: Rand, 1960); and *The Community of Scholars* (New York: Random House, 1962).

run by George Dennison.[21] The Fifteenth Street School run by Orson Bean, the Berkeley Free School of Herbert Kohl, and the First Street School are three schools that are committed to the idea of relationships "between children and adults, adults and adults, children and other children."[22] Free schools don't subscribe to the notion made often by John Dewey that school is preparation. It is their profound belief that school deals with the present lives of children. Free schools abolish the conventions of the usual public and parochial school. Military discipline, schedules, punishments, rewards, and standardization are forbidden. School is based upon certain truths of the human condition such as the ideas that feelings are facts, that there is no such thing as knowledge unrelated to the world, and that an "active moral life cannot be evolved except where people are free to express their feelings and act upon the insights of conscience."[23]

Although Dennison refers to his school as "the first of the minischools,"[24] he has developed the free school after Neill and Tolstoy. When children are in deep trouble, the last thing they need is the strict routine of traditionalism. Though they do need limits, the free school is a clear alternative to the usual public/parochial school. In a very real sense children with deep-seated emotional/learning problems are the *Hibakusha*[25] of our society. That they are most often cast out of the public schools is true. It is almost as if their only way to get attention in the learning/living process is to become exceptional.

The tutorial community concept

In Guthrie and Wynne's *New Models for American Education,* the authors comment about critics of traditional education: "While critics such as George Leonard may broadcast prescriptions in works such as *Education and Ecstasy,* the task of bringing human values into large institutions will not be solved by preaching."[26] In the Guthrie and Wynne text, Melaragno and Newmark describe the "Tutorial Community Concept."[27] These researchers, unlike Neill, Kohl, and Dennison, do not propose to move or close the traditional schools but to utilize a hitherto largely untapped source for individualizing teaching—the use of elementary school students to assist each other in learning. Their purpose is to "develop a 'tutorial community' involving an entire elementary school."[28] Thus, while not requiring the relocation of buildings to house alternative schools, they have designed a school which utilizes everyone, students, teachers, and com-

[21]George Dennison, *The Lives of Children* (New York: Random House, 1969).

[22]Ibid., p. 7.

[23]Ibid., p. 9.

[24]Ibid., p. 29.

[25]The Japanese survivors of Hiroshima were so named because they were the "explosion-affected persons." The children at First Street School were affected by the explosions of their family and neighborhood milieux.

[26]James W. Guthrie and Edward Wynne, *New Models for American Education* (Englewood Cliffs, N.J.: Prentice-Hall, 1971), p. 98.

[27]Ralph J. Melaragno and Gerald Newmark, "Tutorial Community Concept," in Ibid.

[28]Ibid., p. 101.

munity, in an atmosphere of openness. Using fifth grade students in the same school to tutor kindergarten children was very successful. More kindergarten students began reading in pre-primers than ever before. Almost all of the kindergarteners were ready for formal reading instruction in first grade where previously first grade teachers spent two to four months in reading readiness activities.

All of the alternatives discussed (except the tutorial concept) were programs which were separate from the regular schools. All of these school options seem to be possible even in the most traditional of school districts if the board of trustees is willing to experiment. The Fifth Annual Gallup Poll of Public Attitudes Toward Education reflects that the major concern of the public in regard to education is discipline.[29] However, discipline in a democratic society must work within a framework of options and alternatives. The future is bound to see an increasing number of alternative educational programs in the public schools.

Sylvia Ashton-Warner

Spearpoint

"What about picking up your blocks, Henry?"
"I dowanna."

One day in the autumn, I go straight from the plane into a foreign school of a culture I thought I knew. I'm agog with confidence in my own work, knowing it like ABC, but not knowing that I, from the tail end of civilization, have descended upon the spearpoint. True I have lived in other countries at varying stages of civilization, so that I know what civilization is and what a stage of civilization is, but here, in no time, the days are a matter of survival and my work is XYZ. There's no time space or mind space to remember romantic conceptions of life about being a wandering exile or to dream about the stars. My

comfortable principle of life . . . "Ask of no man but give to all" . . . fails in the face of survival. My new watchword, clumsily assembled, becomes . . . "Adapt and survive."

The school has been born but one week only, and is making grunts like primitive man. Teachers have barely arrived and don't know the children, children themselves are newcomers and don't know the teachers, and teachers don't know each other, like a crew hired the night before. Nor is there known any common philosophy, none of us having had time to talk, other than the idea of an open school. I myself could have done with a year's preparation, but Fate doesn't like preparation and looks round for a crisis like this and for me when he finds himself bored.

[29]For a complete tabulation see the September 1973 issue of *Phi Delta Kappan.*

There is no headmaster, director or commander of the spaceship, since all are equal . . . this much of a philosophy is established early . . . and parents take turns for the day in the office, which to me, prepared or not, appears successful. They're competent, kind, purposeful people who'll do anything for you. Very early in the chaos, I learn to like this and turn to them for everything except teaching techniques. For teaching techniques we'll turn to each other, the staff being a composite headmaster. In theory excellent, but in practice there's no time. Too many problems crowd by the hour like fragments of shattered glass in a lunar module damaging pressure suits . . . with no Mission Control to solve it.

My part is to implant a new kind of learning in this new kind of school, the organic style in the infant room. Except that no one has told me so. "Why don't you give us a lead?" asks Carl.

"Who, me? Why me? Aren't we all equal?"

"You're the director of this end."

"Me? Am I?"

"Yes, you. We're all hanging round waiting for you to give us a lead."

"Interesting. I didn't know."

So I'm the director of the infant room but must not direct, as all are equal. Irrespective of how much one has learnt and thought, how long one has lived, how much experience one has clocked up, I'm told that no teacher likes any other teacher to be above him and no child likes any teacher to be above him, from which I read that equality means that none can be above the least and laziest. Authority turns out to be a very dirty multi-letter word

indeed, though all very sweetly implied in the kindliest and sincerest voices and which I learn at once. Direct, please, but don't direct. "What about picking up your blocks, Henry?"

"I dowanna."

"You used them. Come on, I'll help you." Kneel and start.

"I said I dowanna and I don have to."

Where do you go from here? "Well, who else is to pick them up?"

Long legs planted firmly apart, he looks me contemptuously in the eye: "Not me, you dum-dum!" and sticks out his tongue for emphasis. So he wins, for we are equal. Equality on board appears to mean inverted authority. There's authority here but not from me.

Instead of easing into the school happily and confidently as I'd expected, I find myself engaged on all fronts, alarmed: exploring a new culture with no compass, colonizing new lands of thought and action without equipment, climbing new mountains of education without ropes and pickaxes, warily rounding new heights; my only nutriment the charm of the teachers and parents, my only fuel an alien's survival. How do you direct yet not direct? Even the words "coax," "advise," or "suggest" are *persona non grata* in the vocabulary of the spaceship; even the word "request." To a young volunteer teacher, "Would you please bring in the children?"

She clicks her heels to attention and salutes.

I go and call the children myself. The only acknowledged difference between me, teachers and children is that I have the misfortune to be older, having committed carelessly the indefensible offense of aging. Generation gap is all over the place, yet not, as the young suppose, between the youth of the holy present and the old of the unholy past but, which they don't know, between the youth of the present and the future, for I am the future in disguise. This generation gap is not a matter of a few decades between the Now and the Then but a matter of several hundred years between the Now and an era hence. For this is where the thoughts of a young French poet of the nineteenth century and of mine abide . . . in the palpitating silences of clusters of stars interweaving their rounds. Not grounded in the hackneyed present.

The only way I see to direct and yet not direct is to teach by example and hope for the best, so that I return to the daily round I'd completed thirty years ago when I was young, when I was strong, intent and lured by a dream. Down I get on the floor with the children, from half past eight till three. Not that I mind being on the floor with our children; I'd rather be there for the present and forever, for you don't get bored among children, never knowing what they're going to say or do; and besides this is my level anyway, being a child myself, though professionally I'm surprised at the sudden demotion.

My word, there is something I forgot to ask for: a place for teachers to go for a retreat from this freedom. A place where one can make the tea and sit a moment in peace; at least a place to make the tea, if not a place to sit. I'm impressed indeed by what they call freedom among the incoming children, but less impressed by the freedom for teachers. Impressed even less than that

by the concern for teachers as people. Wait a minute . . . are we people? Do we have feet that tire, throats that dry or senses with a human limit? Perhaps we don't. Something else to learn. I'm already learning that children are the lords of creation whose desires and whims are law. Well . . . it's something to have some kind of law. Quite something to know where you are.

Oh, the size of the dream, the dimensions, the multiplying accumulating bulk of it! With the weight of twenty atmospheres.

"What we really need," I say to Carl, cross-legged on the carpet, "is a systems of jobs for which each is responsible. One for the pencils, one for the papers, another for the chalk and so on." From the children all over him, Carl smiles up at me. His eyes behind the glasses smile, his beard smiles and his whole long folded body is a long folded smile, from spare ears to bare feet. "You can't do that, Mrs. H.," he says. "Each owns his things. Each looks after his own."

"I can't say I've noticed it, Carl."

"That's what we do."

"Owning is one thing, looking after it another. Who's to know which-pencil-is-which sort of thing?"

He should be able to answer, "They keep them in their desks," but there are no desks. Not only because there is no room for tables but also because "desk" is a four-letter word from the public system.

"They're all exactly the same," I continued. "And who has used what. And these children are only five, mostly, and I don't see their servants with them. What about the things we all use: blocks, books, paints, and soon there'll be sand, water and clay and blackboards and . . . It goes like this: each one needs to be responsible for some one thing. Responsibility comes into this, to the equipment. We really need this list of jobs."

"They won't like it" is all he says.

"But these mine-yours sequences go on all day."

"That is capitalism."

"Oh? But the concern of possession oversteps the substance."

"Capitalism," gravely.

"Capitalism takes time."

"So do jobs."

"Good answer."

A little girl is wrapped round his neck like a scarf, possibly short of a father. "Well, leave me out of it, Mrs. H."

"Oh, I'll do it."

"But that will be to assume collective ownership."

"Does that hurt children?"

There's much more to say, but this is not the time. The time was before school started, for at least the length of the summer, but teachers met each other only on the day school started. Opened, I mean, not started. Only the engines have started, and the countdown. "Rocky, please pick up those pencils."

"They're not mine."

"Gelo, will you pick them up, then?"

"I didn't use them." Finish.

All the teachers are on the floor with the children, since there are no chairs and because it looks more equal, but I stand at the BB, having a job to do. "So," after explaining it to those who are listening, "who will be the pencil girl?"

Odile says, "Me," with a smile too. Her proportions are straight from

Fairyland and all that's missing is wings.

"Pencils," I print on the BB and beside it "Odile." And look at it. Fancy someone agreeing to do something! "And you need to count them each day, Odile, to see if you've got them all. Who will be the book people? Two."

"Me," from Peter, dark eyes glowing. Very dark eyes and a dimple, and snuggling between the knees of an American teacher. Other children nestle up to the teachers on the floor, though there are better attitudes of attention. If I were other than a groping alien, I'd see to this attitude of attention. Rapport between teacher and children has priority in learning, but listening is not unknown. There's a time and place for snuggling and nestling and a time and place for listening, but I have much more to learn myself before making the distinction; all I have really learnt so far is that everyone is equal. Not the nature of equality itself, which is different in this country.

I'm sitting in silence over a solo meal in the big yellow house: a castle with six bedrooms and three bathrooms and a reception room nearly as large as my own at home, housing a grand piano better than mine at home. All for just little me. Lent for me at no rent for a few months, all of which itself is a statement of some kind; what? An act of faith in a new kind of school by one under no obligation. There's no boom of a furnace, no trash cans, no crowds and no high frantic freeway through the room, and I find my own thoughts again. Fragmented thoughts, fragmented vision, but my own at least.

Why think, anyway? Why teach at all? Why try to preserve the third dimension of a young personality? Who will want a rounded and full personality out there among the stars; on some distant planet at some distant time, stabbed by the spearpoint of civilization? Because it protects a man's originality so that he stays as interesting as he was when he was born? Not wholly. Because it's natural for him to think and say and do what he wants to? Not necessarily. It's because . . . - since feeling is alive . . . the pressure of it makes him act. If its passage outward is blocked in some way, his native desires denied too much, frustration could breed hatred.

The love he is born with could change to hatred, the pictures in his mind become images of hatred, his thoughts words and actions become captions of it . . . could. The imagery of love could be replaced by the imagery of hostility, pressed into his throat and over his tongue to be communicated to others. He would still have feeling to make him go, but it might be the way of hatred, which does not build but destroys.

Not that I find any hatred here in our new kind of school, not a sign of it. I find quarrelsomeness, discontent, unwillingness and rudeness to a degree I've never encountered before, but I do not sense hatred. I've known far more naked hatred in small children in other parts of the world. But I don't sense love here, either. What's happened to the dynamo of feeling; where is the third dimension? Why don't they think and do things, rather than loll on the floor between the knees of teachers; why don't they *want* to do

things, why can't they grow, why don't they *go*?

It's time to get going on the Key Vocabulary to find out things for myself, in the teeth of trash cans, freeways, indisciplines, opposition and the reigning wannadowanna. Somehow I'll work my way through it . . . circumvent the ruling ogres striding from one end of the ship to the other: Authority and Equality. Fancy wasting energy and thought on these damned obsessions. Let's forget them, for crissake, and find education . . .

I can't stand closed doors where children are segmenting the family fluidity, and when I see the door of the math room shut I take the liberty of opening it. I'm not one to intrude or invade if I can help it but, "That's no way for big boys to behave." Six and seven they are.

"We'll do what we like!" Crash the Cuisenaire rods on the floor.

"Standing on a table hurling things on the floor. That's like babies, not boys."

"We have every right to do what we like!" Bang, whiz, spin . . .

"Not like six and seven," I say. "You're both like little babies standing up there throwing valuable material that other children need. Babies."

"When you say something about someone," he shouts, "it sticks on yourself. It's you like the baby. You, you!" Crack, skid. "It's you that's the baby."

It's true. They're far cleverer than me. This is a modern open school and I've got to be that too. No pride or anything like that. No hurt. All being equal, he can say what he likes. And do what he likes too. I'm learning that reciprocal respect is not necessary to equality.

On the other hand, am I respecting their right to release their imagery; who am I to criticize?

"It's you that's the baby," he repeats.

"Could be too. Me the baby. But in any case you bore me."

"And you bore us."

A jolly good answer. I'm floored again. Like the Cuisenaire rods. I try another way: "What makes you two think you're so clever?"

Flings more rods but he's thinking. "Because" . . . bash! . . . "we *are* clever."

"I agree. But does that make you interesting too?"

No answer from either.

"Why don't you answer?"

The bombs still pound the target but still there is no answer, so I walk toward the door, ashamed of victory.

"Yes, go," they say, "and shut the door. We want to be by ourselves."

I obey and shut the door. I'm getting the hang of equality and the evils of authority.

I stand in the tunnel-corridor while children run, collide and wrestle. What would the American teachers have done? I think I know. Without any debate, they might have got down on the floor, collected some rods as they landed and set about making a math pattern illustrating and honoring the function of the rods, so that in time the two might have joined them. But only might have. The rapport between American and American at work. But what did I do? Attacked.

I still stand while the children gambol. The corridor is lit by nylon lighting, the air by my standards overbreathed, overhot, reverberating from some tom-tom beat pulsing from a stereo. Too enclosing the architecture, built for thoughtful men rather than exploding children. Whose life am I living, mine or someone else's? Can't I stop the ship and get off?

I like children's voices, high, wild or low, solo or in unison, but the beat and the boom of stereo and the hitting of the suffering piano in the foyer . . . what is this thing, freedom, supplied to the children in overspilling glassfuls, in tankards, in brimming kegs? Must glorious freedom mean all this? Is this, indeed, freedom? If it is, what good is it? How long is the equipment going to last which they need for learning; the piano, the guitar, the Cuisenaire rods? And, as equipment, how long will I last? Astonishingly the Americans don't notice the noise; you can tell by their faces. They can talk and think along with it. Think and talk *better* along with it . . . with all the dire discords. Maybe they've made a mistake in summoning me, inviting an alien to them. Alien. There's the word. I should reel from it but I don't. I don't dislike being an alien. An artist must be an alien in life. Art must walk alone, a pariah of the human family.

But can't I get off? Where's a window? It's wide outside, the plain, within the cradling mountains. And still. What I need is a moment of seclusion or two to regroup my faculties. Adapt and survive . . . remember it.

discussion

Sylvia Ashton-Warner is a New Zealander by birth. She has written several novels, but her best known work is probably *Teacher*. Her writing style is distinctive, making prose sound like poetry. A good word to describe the style of her newest book, *Spearpoint*, is *organic*; it is a natural expression coming from deep within her, conveyed by the natural starts and stops of thinking.

This selection from *Spearpoint* describes Miss Ashton-Warner's experience in a newly formed experimental school in the Rocky Mountains of Colorado. She is asked to join the faculty because of her expertise as a teacher of the infant school. (In England the first two years of school are called the infant school.) There are many schools throughout England which have adopted an organic curriculum for the beginning years at school.[1] The organic curriculum means that the material used for learning comes directly from the children, e.g., the words the children learn to read and write are culled from the children's vocabulary as they pursue their interests. Subjects are not compartmentalized, and there is no set time for a particular subject. The amount of time a child spends in each pursuit, whether drawing, building, or writing, flows from the child's interest. Miss Ashton-Warner is a great believer in the cultural influence on education. She says in *Spearpoint*, "A style of teaching suiting one nation does not necessarily suit another. A look into schools, Asian and Western, is to see the subtle differences in children and the not always subtle differences."[2] As a foreign visitor to America she is struck by the fact that we live at the spearpoint of civilization. As a swiftly evolving society we sometimes do not even have the terminology for our ideas and conditions. She observes that education lags behind cultural change by three or four decades. No wonder there is a rising interest in establishing alternative schools in America.

Miss Ashton-Warner finds her experience in this school enlightening and painful. She cannot get used to the overwhelming fear of authority which immobilizes action at times. She is troubled by, yet respects, the tyrannical emphasis on equality. Although asked to provide direction for the infant room she can provide none in an environment which by insisting upon equality negates direction.

The author is concerned about the disregard for an attitude of attention. She can only assume that the children, snuggling and nestling on the floor entwined in the arms and legs of teachers, are listening, for one activity is never curtailed for the other.

Miss Ashton-Warner comments on the lack of hatred she encounters in American children, an emotion she has observed among very young chil-

[1]For more information about the British infant school see Lillian Weber, *The English Infant School and Informal Education* (Englewood Cliffs, N.J.: Prentice-Hall, 1971); and Joseph Featherstone, *Schools Where Children Learn* (New York: Avon, 1971).

[2]Sylvia Ashton-Warner, *Spearpoint*, p. 172.

320 *The Future—Alternative School*

dren in other cultures. She does find rudeness, indifference, and an unwillingness to pursue self-directed activity which she has never encountered before. In an environment which has promised children unequivocal freedom and equality the author attempts to "adapt and survive."

springboards for inquiry

1. Would you like to work in an alternative school like the one described in this book? Explain.
2. How would you have handled the incident in this selection in which the children are standing on the table throwing Cuisenaire rods?
3. What kind of alternative schools do you think we need?
4. Describe the school of your fantasy.

Isaac Asimov

The fun they had

Margie even wrote about it that night in her dairy. On the page headed May 17, 2155, she wrote, "Today Tommy found a real book!"

It was a very old book. Margie's grandfather once said that when he was a little boy *his* grandfather told him that there was a time when all stories were printed on paper.

They turned the pages, which were yellow and crinkly, and it was awfully funny to read words that stood still instead of moving the way they were supposed to—on a screen, you know. And then, when they turned back to the page before,

"The Fun They Had" by Isaac Asimov reprinted by the kind permission of the author. Copyright © 1951, by NEA Service, Inc.

The part she hated most was the slot where she had to put homework and test papers. She always had to write them out in a punch code they made her learn when she was six years old, and the mechanical teacher calculated the mark in no time.

it had the same words on it that it had had when they read it the first time.

"Gee," said Tommy, "what a waste. When you're through with the book, you just throw it away, I guess. Our television screen must have had a million books on it and it's good for plenty more. I wouldn't throw *it* away."

"Same with mine," said Margie. She was eleven and hadn't seen as many telebooks as Tommy had. He was thirteen.

She said, "Where did you find it?"

"In my house." He pointed without looking, because he was busy reading. "In the attic."

"What's it about?"

"School."

Margie was scornful. "School? What's there to write about school? I hate school." Margie always hated school, but now she hated it more than ever. The mechanical teacher had been giving her test after test in geography and she had been doing worse and worse until her mother had shaken her head sorrowfully and sent for the County Inspector.

He was a round little man with a red face and a whole box of tools with dials and wires. He smiled at her and gave her an apple, then took the teacher apart. Margie had hoped he wouldn't know how to put it together again, but he knew how all right and, after an hour or so, there it was again, large and black and ugly with a big screen on which all the lessons were shown and the questions were asked. That wasn't so bad. The part she hated most was the slot where she had to put homework and test papers. She always had to write them out in a punch code they made her learn when she was six years old, and the mechanical teacher calculated the mark in no time.

The inspector had smiled after he was finished and patted her head. He said to her mother, "It's not the little girl's fault, Mrs. Jones. I think the geography sector was geared a little too quick. Those things happen sometimes. I've slowed it up to an average ten-year level. Actually, the over-all pattern of her progress is quite satisfactory." And he patted Margie's head again.

Margie was disappointed. She had been hoping they would take the teacher away altogether. They had once taken Tommy's teacher away for nearly a month because the history sector had blanked out completely.

So she said to Tommy, "Why would anyone write about school?"

Tommy looked at her with very superior eyes. "Because it's not our kind of school, stupid. This is the old kind of school that they had hundreds and hundreds of years ago." He added loftily, pronouncing the word carefully, "*Centuries* ago."

Margie was hurt. "Well, I don't know what kind of school they had all that time ago." She read the book over his shoulder for a while, then said, "Anyway, they had a teacher."

"Sure they had a teacher, but it wasn't a *regular* teacher. It was a man."

"A man? How could a man be a teacher?"

"Well, he just told the boys and girls things and gave them homework and asked them questions."

"A man isn't smart enough."

"Sure he is. My father knows as much as my teacher."

"He can't. A man can't know as much as a teacher."

"He knows almost as much I betcha."

Margie wasn't prepared to dispute that. She said, "I wouldn't want a strange man in my house to teach me."

Tommy screamed with laughter, "You don't know much, Margie. The teachers didn't live in the house. They had a special building and all the kids went there."

"And all the kids learned the same thing?"

"Sure, if they were the same age."

"But my mother says a teacher

has to be adjusted to fit the mind of each boy and girl it teaches and that each kid has to be taught differently."

"Just the same, they didn't do it that way then. If you don't like it, you don't have to read the book."

"I didn't say I didn't like it," Margie said quickly. She wanted to read about those funny schools.

They weren't even half finished when Margie's mother called, "Margie! School!"

Margie looked up. "Not yet, mamma."

"Now," said Mrs. Jones. "And it's probably time for Tommy, too."

Margie said to Tommy, "Can I read the book some more with you after school?"

"Maybe," he said, nonchalantly. He walked away whistling, the dusty old book tucked beneath his arm.

Margie went into the schoolroom. It was right next to her bedroom, and the mechanical teacher was on and waiting for her. It was always on at the same time every day except Saturday and Sunday, because her mother said little girls learned better if they learned at regular hours.

The screen was lit up, and it said: "Today's arithmetic lesson is on the addition of proper fractions. Please insert yesterday's homework in the proper slot."

Margie did so with a sigh. She was thinking about the old schools they had when her grandfather's grandfather was a little boy. All the kids from the whole neighborhood came, laughing and shouting in the schoolyard, sitting together in the schoolroom, going home together at the end of the day. They learned the same things so they could help one another on the homework and talk about it.

And the teachers were people . . .

The mechanical teacher was flashing on the screen: "When we add the fractions ½ and ¼ . . ."

Margie was thinking about how the kids must have loved it in the old days. She was thinking about the fun they had.

discussion

Isaac Asmiov is a professor of biochemistry as well as a prolific writer. He is known for his science fiction and for his many popular books on scientific subjects. In the world of academic scholarship he is the author of books and articles for scientific journals.

This short story on education in the world beyond the printed page is written for children. The future education Asimov describes is probably technically possible today. The story confirms that what may be technologically advanced may not be best for people. Healthy children thrive on interaction with their peers. Tommy and Margie are enchanted with the idea of many children laughing, playing, and going to school together.

The individualization accomplished in one hour by the County Inspector who mechanically adjusts the machine for Margie is also not a futuristic fiction. Programs of instruction are available today, but their cost and desirability are factors which have not been worked out. Most teachers today would probably welcome a certain amount of computer assisted instruction adjusted to each child's learning rate.

It is hard to believe that in this story of the future Mother is still the disciplinarian pushing the child to pay attention, to watch the screen, and to keep his mind on the mechanical instructor. We seem doomed to create educational systems for which parents must nag and children resist. In the future society the children hope the computer will break down much like today's children who hope the school will burn down. The children in the story think that education is vastly different for them than it was in the age of the printed words and books. Curiously, despite the change in method and physical arrangement for schooling, there is little change in the attitude toward learning.

springboards for inquiry

1. What do you think are the most serious deficiencies that would exist in total home computer education?

2. Learn which schools if any in your community are using mechanical devices for learning, i.e., The Talking Page, Word-Master, computers. If you have an opportunity to observe them, write about your impressions.

3. Explain your reasons for preferring a listening center for hearing stories in your classroom to a teacher reading to the class. Or do you prefer the teacher as reader? Is the "listening center" as capable of "turning the student on" as a teacher-reader?

4. Read about education in *Walden Two*,[1] the modern utopia described by B. F. Skinner. Explain whether you would want this kind of education for your own children.

---

[1]Burris F. Skinner, *Walden Two*. (New York: Macmillan, 1948).

References

BUXTON, CLAUDE. *Adolescents in School.* New Haven: Yale University Press, 1973.

DENNISON, GEORGE. *The Lives of Children.* New York: Random House, 1969.

"Fifth Annual Gallup Poll of Public Attitudes Toward Education." *Phi Delta Kappan,* September 1973.

GOODMAN, PAUL. *Compulsory Mis-Education.* New York: Horizon Press, 1964.

———. *Growing Up Absurd.* New York: Random House, 1960.

———. *The Community of Scholars.* New York: Random House, 1972.

GUTHRIE, JAMES W., and WYNNE, EDWARD. *New Models for American Education.* Englewood Cliffs, N.J.: Prentice-Hall, 1971.

HIPPLE, THEODORE W. *Crucial Issues in Contemporary Education.* Pacific Palisades, Ca.: Goodyear, 1973.

LANDAU, ELLIOT D.; EPSTEIN, SHERRIE L.; and STONE, ANN P. *Child Development Through Literature.* Englewood Cliffs, N.J.: Prentice-Hall, 1972.

LEONARD, GEORGE B. *Education and Ecstasy.* New York: Delacorte, 1968.

MARGOLIN, JOSEPH B., and MISCH, MARION R., eds. *Computers in the Classroom.* New York: Spartan Books, 1970.

MELARAGNO, RALPH J., and NEWMARK, GERALD. "Tutorial Community Concept," as quoted in Guthrie, James W., and Wynne, Edward. *New Models for American Education.* Englewood Cliffs, N.J.: Prentice-Hall, 1971.

MERCURIO, JOSEPH A. *Caning: Educational Rite and Tradition.* Syracuse: Syracuse University Press, 1972.

NEILL, ALEXANDER S. *Freedom—Not License!* New York: Hart, 1966.

———. *Summerhill: A Radical Approach to Child Rearing.* New York: Hart, 1960.

OFFER, DANIEL. *The Psychological World of the Teen-ager.* New York: Basic Books, 1969.

ROSENBAUM, PETER S. *Peer-Mediated Instruction.* New York: Teachers College Press, 1973.

SHANE, HAROLD, and NELSON, OWEN. "What Will the Schools Become?" *Phi Delta Kappan,* June 1971.

SILBERMAN, CHARLES E. *Crisis in the Classroom.* New York: Random House, 1970.

TOFFLER, ALVIN, *Future Shock.* New York: Random House, 1970.

index

self-concept and achievement in, 119
Reality therapy, 107
Reasoning
developing a student's ability for, 140
inductive and deductive, 134
during pre-operational stage of development, 95
Regimentation on first day of school, 97
Regrouping to help the isolate, 119
Reinforcement
in behavior modification, 29
and motivation, 143
of positive behavior, 107
of school attendance as treatment for school phobia, 178
Rejection
a cause of psychopathology, 69
by peers, 60-61, 119
of student by teacher, 68
Relevance
and humanistic education, 241
learners choose to ignore what they think has no, 92
of subject matter, 38
Resentment in teachers' personalities, 2
Respect, treating children with, 38
Response to learning environment affected by heredity, 132
Responsibility, building a sense of, in students, 140
Rewards
forbidden in free schools, 312
token economy, 224-25
"Rich Man, Poor Man" (Shaw), 282-90
Rights, 308
Rives, Fern, "Friday, Thank God!" 62-66
Rogers, Carl
on the fully functioning personality, 3
non-directive teaching model, 28
on the school's responsibility to build a child's self-image, 139-40
Rosaire, Forrest, "The Pod of a Weed," 194-202
Rosenthal, Robert, on teacher expectations and student performance, 95, 225-26
Rossner, Robert, "A Hero Like Me: A Hero Like You," 216-19
Rote learning, 229
Routines in the classroom, 226
Rules
in the classroom, 226
inflexible imposition of, 73

Salary, 295
Salisbury, Lee H., on Eskimo culture, 154-55
Santa Monica Madison School Plan, 190
Sarason, Seymour B.
on motivation to learn and cultural background, 141
underachievement and self-perception, 118-19
Sarcasm, 73
Saroyan, William, "The First Day of School," 100-2
Schedules, forbidden in free schools, 312
Scheduling
arena, 60
flexible, 60
Scholar, teacher as, 2
School board. *See* Board of education
School district
relationship of school board to, 293
responsibility for meeting needs of the learning disabled child, 203
School lunch programs parental influence, 281
School phobia, 177-85
behavioral approach for curing, 184-85
intensive treatment for difficult cases, 179
and separation anxiety, 178
treatment for, 178
Schools
community control of, 302
control of, 251
as culture, 223-49
drop-out and drop-in, 311
experimental, 219
free, 1, 311-12
inadequate programs for exceptional children, 189
mini-school, 310-11
open, 1
power structure in, 251-304
pressure on, from common-interest groups, 281
responsibility for psychologically damaged students, 139-40
storefront, 310
Search for identity in adolescence, 69
Security, trust and autonomy give feeling of, 93
Seeking for explanations and interpretations of the world, 91
Segregation in integrated schools, 247
Selective brain injury, 192

Van Tassell, Donna, "Home Thoughts," 137-39
Verbal learning model, 240
Violence
  neighborhood, 293
  between parents and principals, 281
  seeds of, rooted in low self-esteem and peer rejection, 119
  student, 106
Vision impairment, 193, 204-5
Vocational aspirations, counselor's role, 60
Voice disorders, children with, and early speech training, 204

Walsh, Ann M., relationship of underachievement to self-perception, 118-19
Wattenberg, William W., on self-concept and reading achievement, 119

Wechsler Intelligence Scale for Children, 193
Weil, Jerry, "The Teachers," 257-60, 295-302
Weil, Marsha, on models of teaching, 27
Weinstein, Gerald, on humanistic education, 240-41
Wepman Test of Auditory Discrimination, 193
"Who is Virgil T. Fry?" (Michener), 39-43
Wildman, Wesley A., on teacher bargaining and school administration, 256
Wolpe, Joseph, behavioral approach for curing phobias, 184
"Wreath for Miss Totten, A" (Calisher), 205-13
Wright, Herbert Fletcher, older children and family environment, 117
Writing retardation, 192
Wynne, Edward, on critics of traditional education, 312